Screen Enemies
of the American Way

ALSO BY FRASER A. SHERMAN

Cyborgs, Santa Claus and Satan:
Science Fiction, Fantasy and Horror Films Made for Television
(McFarland, 2000; paperback 2009)

The Wizard of Oz Catalog: L. Frank Baum's Novel, Its Sequels and
Their Adaptations for Stage, Television, Movies, Radio, Music Videos,
Comic Books, Commercials and More (McFarland, 2005)

Screen Enemies of the American Way

Political Paranoia About Nazis, Communists, Saboteurs, Terrorists and Body Snatching Aliens in Film and Television

Fraser A. Sherman

McFarland & Company, Inc., Publishers
Jefferson, North Carolina, and London

Acknowledgments: This book would have been harder to write and poorer in final quality without the help of my friend and fellow movie buff Ross Bagby, who suggested a lot of movies, taped more than a few, and helped me figure out which *X-Files* episodes were absolutely essential.

It would also have been a lot harder without the many writers referenced in the bibliography, whose work was invaluable in making sense of the movies and their times.

And a special thanks to my fiancée, LeAnn Spradling, for her support and patience while I was working on this.

LIBRARY OF CONGRESS CATALOGUING-IN-PUBLICATION DATA

Sherman, Fraser A.
Screen enemies of the American way : political paranoia about Nazis, Communists, saboteurs, terrorists and body snatching aliens in film and television / Fraser A. Sherman.
p.   cm.
Includes bibliographical references and index.
Includes filmography.

ISBN 978-0-7864-4648-3
softcover : 50# alkaline paper ∞

1. Motion pictures — political aspects — United States. 2. Motion pictures — Social aspects — United States. 3. Television and politics — United States — History. 4. Television — Social aspects — United States. 5. Paranoia in motion pictures. 6. Motion pictures — United States — History. I. Title.
PN1995.9.P6S54   2011   791.43'658 — dc22   2010048313

British Library cataloguing data are available

©2011 Fraser A. Sherman. All rights reserved

No part of this book may be reproduced or transmitted in any form or by any means, electronic or mechanical, including photocopying or recording, or by any information storage and retrieval system, without permission in writing from the publisher.

On the cover: Jeff Bridges in the 1999 film
Arlington Road (Rogue Pictures/Photofest)

Manufactured in the United States of America

McFarland & Company, Inc., Publishers
Box 611, Jefferson, North Carolina 28640
www.mcfarlandpub.com

Table of Contents

Introduction   1

1. German Fifth Columns: The Hun, the Third Reich and the Rise of the Fourth Reich   7
2. The Yellow Peril and the Fear of Japan   27
3. The Red Menace: Bolsheviks, Commies and Atheists in America   44
4. Red Scare: Fifth Column Anticommunist Films from 1949 to 1960   55
5. Communist Fifth Columnists After 1960   73
6. Muslim Fifth Columns in America   89
7. Invasion of the Body Snatchers   97
8. Brain Eaters, Human Duplicators and Other Science Fictional Fifth Columns   111
9. Invaders, X-Files and Dynamators: Alien Fifth Columns on Television   134
10. Sexual Politics and the War Between Men and Women   146
11. The Master Race   153
12. Satanic and Supernatural Infiltration in Film and Television   157
13. Miscellanea: Corporate Takeovers, Secret Societies and the JFK Assassination   163

Appendix 1: Film Credits   181
Appendix 2: Television Series Credits and Synopses   209
Bibliography   213
Index   215

To my family: Dad, Mum, Craig, Tracy, Marianne and Paige.
To Cindy and Dori, who are as close as family.
And to LeAnn, who changed my life so much for the better —
I could have done it without you, my love,
but it wouldn't have been half as much fun.

Introduction

From the beginning, Americans have worried about the enemies within.

Evil, un-American adversaries, who have betrayed the founding principles of the United States. Enemies who want to subvert the nation and destroy its free, democratic, independent character.

There were Jacobins, admirers of the French Revolution intent on spreading its tactics and its mob rule to North America. There were the Freemasons, who drank the blood of their enemies; their secret pacts to each other trumped their loyalty to the U.S.A. And, of course, Catholics, who'd stop at nothing to bring this bastion of Protestantism under the Catholic yoke.

In 1835, telegraph inventor Samuel Morse warned that Austria plotted to install one of its royal family members as emperor of the United States with the help of Jesuit missionaries and "the minds and the funds of despotic Europe." Chinese coolies and later Japanese farmers were seen as imperial agents hoping to claim the Pacific Coast for their respective emperors. In the early twentieth century, German spies plotted all manner of devilry, and the Elders of Zion schemed to take over America and the world.

After World War I, Bolshevik immigrants threatened to stir up the workers and wreck the American economy. Nazi fifth columnists sought to cripple America before World War II, as did Japan's Black Dragon Society. After World War II, the American Communist Party, under direct orders from Moscow, committed murder and sabotage until the heroic agents of the FBI and the House Un-American Activities Committee brought the traitors down. And at the end of the century, we learned that entire towns were infiltrated with Satanists who tortured pets, murdered witnesses and molested children.

In the 21st century we have some Americans convinced that Hispanic immigrants are agents of "reconquista," plotting to seize the Southwest back from the U.S.A. And that all American Muslims are allied with radical Islam to destroy the West. That George W. Bush authorized the 9/11 attacks and Barack Obama is a Muslim sleeper agent.

Every one of these paranoid fantasies has had fervent believers, not only among fringe extremists and oddballs, but in the mainstream and the corridors of power. Henry Ford believed in the Protocols of the Elders of Zion; the American government had hundreds of thousands of Japanese-Americans interned as a threat in World War II; fear of communism was as widespread and mainstream in the 1950s as the fear of Muslims is today.

With these fears of infiltration so widespread, it's no surprise that fears of a fifth column have been a recurrent feature in American movies.

Introduction

Nazi fifth columnists plotted mass destruction in *All Through the Night. Little Tokyo USA*, *Across the Pacific* and *Betrayal From the East* showed that even American-born Japanese were more loyal to their emperor than to America. *Big Jim McLain* branded communists as worse than lepers and charged that all American communists were guilty of high treason. TV's *24* shows Islamic terrorists hiding among us like ordinary people; *Arlington Road* showed the same was true of terrorists on the radical right.

The same fear has been translated into science fiction and horror films: *Invasion of the Body Snatchers* had emotionless pod people living among us, scheming to replace the rest of us. In *Rosemary's Baby*, Mia Farrow discovers that everyone around her, even her husband, is part of a Satanic conspiracy. In *The Stepford Wives*, Katharine Ross realizes that the women around her have all been transformed into something inhuman and she worries she'll be next.

This book is about political paranoia and the fear of the fifth column, as it's been captured in film and television. Since films in this vein aren't a clear-cut genre the way "western" or "mystery" is, I'll start by defining my terms.

The fifth column. Spain's General Emilio de Mola, who fought on the Nationalist side in the Spanish Civil War, is credited with coining the term in 1936. De Mola announced that in addition to four columns converging on Madrid, a "fifth column" of Nationalist supporters was waiting inside the city to rise up and strike. "Fifth column" entered the language as a term for infiltrators, agents living among us, pretending to be one of us but secretly working against us (whoever "us" might be) on behalf of some outside master.

Political paranoia. As Richard Hofstadter puts it in *The Paranoid Style in American Politics*, political paranoia is different from the clinically defined mental illness. Clinical paranoids fear they've been personally targeted; political paranoids see their entire country under the gun. Clinical paranoids worry someone's poisoned their coffee; political paranoids believe communists are poisoning America by putting fluoride in the water.

The Game is a gripping story of paranoia as businessman Michael Douglas finds himself caught in a web of danger, unable to figure out what the rules are, who's behind it or who is on his side—but it's a personal threat, not targeting anyone else. Likewise, Sean Gullette in *Pi* appears to be surrounded by conspiracies; they're focused on him, not America.

In some of the films in this book, on the other hand, the target of the conspiracy is the entire country. Even when the protagonists are at personal risk, it's only part of the overall threat: Kurt Russell in *The Thing* knows one of his friends is an alien shapeshifter plotting to kill him, but the long-range goal is world conquest. In the original *The Stepford Wives*, the men of Stepford are plotting to replace Katharine Ross with a robot duplicate, but they're doing the same to every woman in her town.

Political paranoia has little to do with any real threat; as Hofstadter put it, if fluoridation turned out to be harmful, it still wouldn't make it a communist plot. When there is a real threat, political paranoia blows it all out of proportion: Japan did have spies in America, but interning all Japanese as traitors was politically paranoid. All the convicted

Introduction

Japanese spies were Caucasian. The Soviet Union had an espionage operation too, but contrary to *I Led Three Lives* and *I Was a Communist for the FBI*, the Communist Party of the United States of America (CPUSA) wasn't composed entirely of Soviet agents, and didn't murder people who opposed it.

The book is about the American movies in which America has been infiltrated by the enemy, whether that enemy is Japanese, German, Muslim, Soviet or extraterrestrial. The people around you aren't what they seem; even your friends and family may not be who you think they are; and the reality behind the facade is a threat to your way of life, your country, and possibly your entire world.

That kind of political paranoia has been a constant in America, and the movies mirror that. Hollywood hasn't covered all the forms of political paranoia — the movies don't have a history of anti–Freemason, anti–Semitic or anti–Catholic stories — but it has reflected many of our fears as America has moved through World War I, World War II, the Cold War and the War on Terror.

While the different waves of paranoia might seem to be separate phenomena, they have a lot in common. As Susan Sontag said of science fiction films, the "imagination of disaster" is the same in every age: The fifth column may differ in details, but all that really matters is that they hate our freedoms (or our capitalism, or our democracy, or for aliens, our emotions) and want to destroy them.

Or as my friend and fellow film buff Ross Bagby has put it, fifth columnists and enemy spies are "bogeymen"—generic, interchangeable adversaries. Soviet villains, for example, are never motivated by love or patriotism for their own country, but only by hate for America. The USSR itself has no character in most movies other than to be "the enemy"; it has no history, no scenic beauty, no literature or music, nothing that might inspire affection from its citizens. Movies such as *Jet Pilot* and *Silk Stockings* show that exposure to good American food or jazz is enough to convince some Russians to switch sides. Bogeymen aren't defined by who they are or where they come from as much as by not being American.

As a result, the different strains of bogeymen blur together. RKO's *The Whip Hand* assumes that a Nazi scientist will be just as happy working to destroy America for the Reds; *Strange Holiday*, an anti–Nazi short released in 1945, was rereleased in the 1950s as an anticommunist short, just by replacing the swastikas with a made-up symbol.

Or consider 1999's *Arlington Road*. Tim Robbins and Joan Cusack play right-wing terrorists but since nothing is said about their agenda other than their hatred for "godless society," they could just as easily be post–9/11 Islamic terrorists — or for that matter sixties radicals or agents of SPECTRE The villainous South African diplomats in *Lethal Weapon 2* (1989) could just as easily have been villainous Soviets if the Cold War hadn't been coming to an end; instead, South Africa, with its apartheid government, served equally well in the role of an evil nation we don't like, and whose representatives can therefore be assumed to be plotting evil.

Likewise, the *Rambo* cartoon of the late eighties showed us that ninjas, Nazis, Arab terrorists and street punks with Mohawks can all work together in a common cause, as

Introduction

long as that cause is evil and anti–American. The original Broadway production of *It's a Bird ... It's a Plane ... It's Superman* featured Chinese communist spies among the villains but they became mobsters in the TV version and then Arab terrorists in later touring shows. Even in the original production, the Chinese villains were there only because the director wanted to incorporate a Chinese acrobatic troupe into the show.

Why do the movies go for political paranoid themes? In *Voodoo Histories*, David Aaronovitch concludes that in the real world, conspiracy theories are a way to make random acts of violence a little less random. If John F. Kennedy's assassination was the work of a disturbed lone gunman, it's something that could happen again, to any leader, any time; if it's the work of a conspiracy with an agenda, as suggested in *Executive Action* and *JFK*, then it's less likely — and if the villains can be exposed, defeated and punished, then some kind of balance for the tragedy has been achieved.

As Hofstadter points out, paranoid thinking is also a way to deal with unacceptable defeats and setbacks. After Mao defeated the Nationalists in China, communist subversion in America was one way to explain how we "lost" China to the enemy. Sen. Joe McCarthy argued that "the laws of probability" were against our leaders being that inept, so "how can we account for our present situation unless we believe that men high in our government are concerting to deliver us to disaster?"

Similarly, some Christian fundamentalists have blamed a "secular humanist" conspiracy for the end of mandatory prayer in schools and the teaching of evolution in science class. World War I has been blamed on munitions dealers provoking war to improve sales; the oil crisis of the 1970s prompted speculation that oil companies were rigging the market or holding back inventions that would let cars run on less oil.

Peter Knight, in *Conspiracy Culture*, suggests another reason: It's fashionable to be cynical, and conspiracy theories, the belief that everything going on around us is a lie, are very cynical. Trust our leaders? Trust big business? Yeah, right. That they're up to *something* is a given; it's only a matter of figuring out *what*. Even if a given conspiracy turns out to be no such thing, only stupid sheep who believe what they're spoon-fed would assume that invalidates conspiracy-thinking in general.

In the movies, there are added reasons for telling tales of political paranoia. For one thing, stories of Nazi spies, communist spies or Muslim terrorists plug into what are or were topical real-world concerns. Taking a politically paranoid approach to the threat — regardless of whether the filmmakers share the paranoia or not — raises the stakes and adds to the excitement. Why take on one communist spy or lone wolf terrorist when you can portray a vast coast-to-coast conspiracy with limitless resources and matchless ambition?

If you want a dark ending, the hero can smash part of the conspiracy while knowing the others are out there (*Betrayed*). For a more upbeat ending, the entire conspiracy can be destroyed and their evil plan thwarted (*Betrayal from the East*). While journalist David Neiwert has argued that lone wolf terrorists are a bigger threat — no cells to smash, no organization, no weak link you can turn — Hollywood tends to favor the conspiracy, even suggesting that a Timothy McVeigh counterpart in *Arlington Road* was framed by the conspiracy that was really behind it.

Introduction

Fifth column bogeymen movies can also be used to spread political messages. Besides the obvious message that communism is bad, anticommunist films of the fifties, for example, taught us that real Americans never go on strike (labor strife is caused by Reds infiltrating the unions to cripple our economy) and "civil rights" was just a ploy by communists to turn Americans against each other. In *My Son John*, director Leo McCarey warned college students that if they start questioning what their parents or their church taught them, those questions are by definition wrong, evil and subversive. On the left-wing side, Oliver Stone's *JFK* tells us the military-industrial complex is so corrupt, it had Kennedy killed in order to keep reaping fat profits from military contracting in Vietnam.

This book will recount the bogeymen stories of movies and TV in all their forms: Prussian, communist, Nazi, Japanese, German, Islamic, right-wing, corporate, Satanic and extraterrestrial. Each chapter will tackle one branch of American political paranoia, looking at both the real-world background that fed it (science fiction excepted, of course) and the movies and television inspired by it.

Many movies with American traitors or spies posing as Americans could technically qualify as fifth-column films, but this book will focus on politically paranoid fifth columns rather than realistic ones. *Breach*, a fact-based story about American traitor Robert Hansson, doesn't qualify; neither do most movies with just one or two enemy agents such as *Eye of the Needle* or *Keep 'Em Flying*. *All Through the Night*, where a Nazi fifth column includes hundreds of agents in major cities, capable of massive acts of sabotage, goes in the book.

Likewise, a single alien passing as human in *Not of This Earth* doesn't qualify as a fifth column the way the pod people in *Invasion of the Body-Snatchers* do. The lone Horla controlling Vincent Price in *Diary of a Madman* isn't included, but the mind-controlling slug army of *The Brain Eaters* is. Films about assassinating or removing a president (*The Sentinel*, *Shadow Conspiracy*) to effect a policy change don't make the cut; but removing the president as part of a total takeover (*Seven Days in May*, *The Manchurian Candidate*) qualifies. I've also included films dealing with the JFK assassination, since that has become such a font of political paranoia and conspiracy thinking.

I've included some films that fall slightly outside these parameters. Films about the actual invasion of the United States contain enough political paranoia to be worth including, even though the fifth column aspect may be slight. Films which deal with the replacement of humanity itself (by androids or genetically engineered super-humans), or with fifth columns of a sexual nature such as *The Stepford Wives* or *Invasion of the Bee Girls*, are also in here.

Even so, the dividing line between plausibility and paranoia is somewhat subjective, so the selection may not suit everyone. Some readers may think the spy films I've passed over show more political paranoia than I found in them. Other readers may disagree with my position that the Communist Party of the United States of America wasn't a Soviet spy network, and that Japanese and Muslim Americans shouldn't be assumed to be traitors without actual evidence. In those cases, we'll have to agree to disagree.

Now prepare yourself: The enemy is among us and as you're about to learn, nothing less than the survival of America is at stake.

1

German Fifth Columns

*The Hun, the Third Reich
and the Rise of the Fourth Reich*

Few foes have proven such durable fodder for American film (and TV and print fiction) as the National Socialist Party of Germany. In the 65 years since the end of World War II, Nazis (and more recently neo–Nazis) have been a recurrent fictional threat, whether plotting to rebuild the Fourth Reich, cozying up to communists or trying to clone or resurrect Hitler.

While Nazis dominate the image of the German villain today, Germans were playing bad guys in American movies well before Hitler rose to power, and fueling paranoid fantasies as well.

Germany's triumph in the Franco-Prussian war seems to have marked the point at which Europe began to perceive Germany not as a collection of postage-stamp kingdoms but as a potential military powerhouse, courtesy of Prussian Chancellor Otto von Bismarck's work wielding the Germans into a solid, efficient military machine. England, which had regarded France for years as the great continental threat, reacted to the war with fantasies of German invasion such as 1871's *The Battle of Dorking*, generally considered the forerunner of all "future war" thrillers (a tradition carried on today by such writers as Tom Clancy, Harold Coyle and Dale Brown).

Then came the Great War, as it was known at the time, and with it fears of German spying and infiltration, even on the American side of the Atlantic. It was a valid fear, as Germany did carry out a variety of spy operations in the United States. Author Francis MacDonnell says that between 1915 and 1917, 47 firebombs were found aboard American vessels headed for Allied nations; Mexico was invited to ally with Germany, with the return of Texas as Mexico's reward; and German sabotage was suspected in multiple explosions at ammunition dumps and defense factories between 1914 and 1916.

In two cases it went beyond suspicion. In 1916, a fire on Black Tom Island — a powder and munitions depot where war goods for the Allies were picked up by barge for merchant vessels — spread to nearby railroad cars and barges carrying munitions, resulting in a $20 million explosion that destroyed trains, boats, warehouses and munitions. In January of the following year, German agents who had infiltrated the workforce at the Canadian Car and Foundry Company started a fire that destroyed the New Jersey factory (along with munitions, fuses, cartridge cases and detonators), for a total of $17 million in damage. A final decision on reparations in both cases was reached in 1939, but Hitler rejected demands for payment and Germany didn't make reparations until 1954.

In another case, the Secret Service acquired papers from a German military attaché that showed Germany planning to legally buy up media to print pro–German propaganda, and to divert American manpower and factory output from war work. German Undersecretary Arthur Zimmerman warned the American ambassador to Germany that thousands of German-born American citizens would rise up and fight for the Fatherland, a possibility our government took seriously.

The German sabotage campaign did more harm to their cause than good, by convincing many Americans that we were already at war with Germany. It also prompted a wave of political paranoia about a German fifth column even more viciously destructive than the real one. As the war continued in Europe, America buzzed with rumors of Germans putting glass in food shipments for the Allies, German submarine captains infected with influenza and mingling with crowds to spread it, and German bands giving coded messages to spies in their music.

In 1915, President Woodrow Wilson told Congress that some American citizens "have poured the poison of disloyalty into national life"; in 1917, he warned that Germany had "filled our unsuspecting communities with spies and conspirators." The government's Committee on Public Information made similar claims that German agents were widely operating throughout the country.

The result was a wave of hostility for all things German. The push to rename sauerkraut "liberty cabbage" is well known, but there were less amusing incidents in which mobs assaulted German-Americans who showed signs of disloyalty—which included speaking German in public, or not giving enough to bond drives. The victims were tarred and feathered, beaten or forced to kiss the American flag. The worst incident was the 1918 lynching of German immigrant coal miner Richard Prager.

As a socialist, Prager was already unpopular with the other local miners; after he made some comments deemed disloyal to the president, he was attacked. Prager escaped, and police placed him in jail for his own safety. A mob broke into the jail and dragged Prager out of town. The mob accused Prager of spying, and of stockpiling gunpowder to blow up a nearby mine. Prager denied the charges, but the mob hung him anyway.

Small wonder that in that atmosphere, German spies abounded in the silent films of the Great War, and afterwards. A 1919 *Vanity Fair* article joked that "the villain has to be a German spy—the audience wouldn't feel at home if they were confronted with a villain of any other variety.... [W]hat a frightful lot the former Kaiser has to answer for." Movies during the war portrayed America as a hotbed of espionage where German spies lurked around every corner. Most of these movies are now lost, which makes assessing their level of political paranoia difficult, but several sound like they might qualify.

Fair Pretender (1915) Stenographer Madge Kennedy poses as a socialite to prove to her theater-producer boss that she can act. At a high-society party, she discovers a nest of German spies.

Her Country First (1915) Vivian Martin, the daughter of a munitions maker, becomes

1. German Fifth Columns

convinced her butler is a foreign spy. It turns out he's in the Secret Service, but everyone else on the staff is a spy.

The Prussian Cur (1918) Prussian schemer Count von Eidel (William W. Black) runs a spy ring in America which arranges labor strikes (blaming labor troubles on outside agitators would be a running theme in later anticommunist films), explosions and transportation disasters. When the spy ring is exposed, von Eidel is arrested. German sympathizers try to free him, but a lynch mob storms the jail, shoots von Eidel and locks up his would-be liberators.

The Highest Trump (1919) German spies running an aircraft company plot to sell the Allied forces defective planes.

Other lost films appear to have a much higher level of political paranoia. *The Battle Cry of Peace* (1915), for instance, has American pacifist Emanon (L. Rogers Lytton) manipulated by foreign spies to cut Washington's military buildup and promote talk of peace. While one peace meeting is in progress, the enemy fleet begins its bombardment of New York. Washington and New York (and from most comments on the film, the country) fall to the enemy, Emanon pro-military friend Harrison (Charles Richman) dies on a bayonet and Harrison's future mother-in-law shoots his fiancée and her sister to save them from being raped. The foreign power is never identified by name — America was two years from entering the war — but as one contemporary review put it, "they are certainly not Portuguese."

Film historians credit *Battle Cry* with prompting more anti–German films. That must have suited J. Stuart Blackton of Vitagraph, who created and wrote the film to boost support for intervention in Europe and showed it to military encampments and government figures before it went into general release. The military liked it enough to provide a regiment of extras and Gen. Leonard Wood, Admiral Dewey and Secretary Garrison all made cameo appearances. Some sources say Frederick Delano Roosevelt, Teddy Roosevelt and even Leon Trotsky also appeared (Trotsky as an unbilled extra). Despite those credentials, censors worried after America entered the war that the pacifist arguments were too persuasive and required a number of cuts.

Henry Ford, who opposed intervention, sued Vitagraph over the film, arguing that it was propaganda designed to bring America into the war and enrich munitions makers (it was based on a story by machine-gun manufacturer Hiram Maxim). Ford lost, but suspicions that corporate power leads to warmongering would be a common fear throughout the century (check out *The President Vanishes*, *JFK* and *Loose Change* in later chapters).

The Fall of a Nation (1916) In this drama, multimillionaire banker and newspaper publisher Charles Waldron (Arthur Shirley), backs the disarmament crusade of Virginia Holland (Lorraine Huling), proud feminist. Waldron uses the crusade to build his own power, guided by instructions from an unspecified European power (but like *Battle Cry of Peace*, it's unlikely to be Portugal). Eventually Waldron proclaims himself governor general of North America and oversees an attack on New York, only to die in the attempt. No longer pacifist, Holland now leads the resistance movement.

Fall of a Nation's Waldron may have been modeled on newspaper magnate William

Randolph Hearst, who was known to be pro–Germany and pro–American neutrality in the war. Hearst's film *Patria* (1916) will be covered in the next chapter.

The Kaiser's Finish (1918) foreshadows *The Boys from Brazil* in its premise that Kaiser Wilhelm, years before the war, fathered a number of illegitimate children whom he scattered around the world to be raised by his agents, with no knowledge of their true parentage. Robert Busch (Earl Schenck) grows up believing himself the son of a wealthy German-American and when World War I breaks out, is eager to enlist. Then his minder, Von Strumpf (Fred G. Hearn), reveals Robert's true heritage, assuming he will then agree to serve the Fatherland (presumably as some sort of sleeper agent, though it's unclear from the synopses I've read).

Robert, however, offers his services to the U.S. government, travels to Germany, kills the crown prince and the Kaiser and sacrifices himself to blow up the Kaiser's palace, ending the war and ensuring the triumph of democracy.

Like *The Fall of a Nation*, the never-released — possibly never finished — film *Enemies Within* (1919), based on a play of the same name, may have been influenced by Hearst's image as a German propagandist. The film concerned two well-connected businessmen

President Monroe expounds the Monroe Doctrine in the prologue to 1916's *The Fall of a Nation*. The actors in this scene from the lost film are unknown.

1. German Fifth Columns

working as spies and propagandists for Germany, even though they're not German themselves; in fact, it assures viewers that it's a well known fact that "the most effective enemy agents operating in America today are not of German birth and rarely of German descent."

Movies featuring German World War I espionage would continue through the silent era and on into the talkies, such as the 1935 film *Rendezvous*. The movies also portrayed plenty of other enemy infiltrators during that period: Russian, Japanese and Mexican spies all appeared in films (Mexico was placed on the threat list after Pancho Villa raided across the border into New Mexico in 1916). Fritz Lang's *Spies* (1928) presented a SPECTRE-style international conspiracy detached from any nationality.

As the thirties drew to a close, however, the rise of the Nazis would give American films a new fifth column to worry about.

Nazis Come to the Movies

The threat of Nazi Germany played little role in the movies or most other popular culture for most of the 1930s, for multiple reasons:

- Joe Breen was the head of the Hays Office — more formally the Production Code Administration, which approved films for release. (The system was voluntary, but a studio film wouldn't be shown without Hays Office approval.) Breen saw anti–Nazi films as warmongering Jewish propaganda. Proposed films that seemed pro-intervention or anti–Nazi were shot down, sometimes on the grounds they were unfair to Germany, since the Code forbade films from disparaging races or nationalities.

  The idea that intervening in Europe would mean fighting in a "Jewish war" was a common one at the time, and Breen didn't like Jews much to start with: Steven J. Ross quotes him as saying that the problems in Hollywood were the fault of "lousy Jews ... eastern Jews, the scum of the Earth," and that the studio heads were "simply a rotten bunch of vile people with no respect for anything beyond the making of money."
- Although many of the studio heads were Jewish, they didn't see a need to deal with the Nazis in film. MGM executive Irving Thalberg said that while a lot of Jews would die under the Nazis, "Hitler and Hitlerism will pass; the Jews will still be there."
- Movies didn't usually tackle such weighty political issues, and nobody in Hollywood could be sure whether it would sell with American audiences.. As late as 1939, Adolph Zukor told a reporter that current events were the job of the newsreels, not the movies.
- Germany and Italy were both good markets for Hollywood films.

Combined, these elements guaranteed rough going for anti-fascist films. In 1935, the Hays Office vetoed a proposal to adapt Sinclair Lewis' antifascist novel *It Can't Happen*

Here; *Idiot's Delight* (1939) based on a play set on the borders of Italy, was gutted of political content to the point the country was unidentifiable and the language foreigners spoke in the film was Esperanto.

Breen worked to soften *Blockade* (1938), an anti-fascist film set in Spain, so that it wouldn't appear to be taking sides (groups such as the Knights of Columbus still condemned it as left-wing propaganda), and *The Nation* accused Production Office head Will Hays of leading a covert campaign to sink the film at the box office. Breen later talked producer Walter Wanger out of adapting Vincent Sheehan's anti-fascist memoir *Personal History*, even though he conceded it met the provisions of the code. (Wanger would later make it stripped of controversial material as *Foreign Correspondent*.)

That didn't stop the studios from making spy films, but they often avoided taking sides: In *Mr. Moto's Last Warning* (1939), for example, the agents plotting to sink a French fleet at the mouth of the Suez Canal never identify the nation they work for. Nor are the spies plotting to steal a new Navy bombsight in 1941's *Meet Boston Blackie* given a nationality.

Even before Pearl Harbor, however, the tide was turning. For one thing, Germany cut the number of American films that could be shown there and restricted how much of the profits could be sent back to the U.S.A. As the decade progressed, the British Empire became a much larger market.

For another, Warner Bros. was ready and willing to "call a swastika a swastika," in the words of one ad for *Confessions of a Nazi Spy*. The Warners had closed their German offices in 1934 after the Reich placed restrictions on Jewish businesses, and refused to do business with the Nazi regime. When war broke out, they favored American intervention, and in contrast to Zukor's views, they believed in tackling topical issues: organized crime in gangster movies, labor struggles in *Black Fury* (1935) and homegrown fascism in *Black Legion* (1937). When the FBI announced it had uncovered a Nazi spy ring, the Warners saw their opportunity: A movie based on the facts of the case could hardly be accused of unfairly defaming Germans, could it?

Confessions of a Nazi Spy (1939) Leon G. Turrou, the agent who broke the spy ring, serialized his account in the *New York Post*; it became the book *Nazi Spies in America* (over the objections of J. Edgar Hoover, who didn't approve of his agents becoming famous in their own right). The case was the FBI's first crack at international espionage and the bureau's own website admits that it didn't cover itself with glory.

Acting on a tip from British Intelligence, the government captured an Austria-born U.S. citizen, Guenther Rumrich, who was attempting to obtain blank U.S. passports by posing as the secretary of state. Rumrich offered to cut a deal and name his cohorts. After much debate which agency should take point, the FBI got the job, although Hoover was concerned the involvement of multiple agencies had already compromised the case. Turrou was assigned to the investigation.

According to the FBI, Turrou botched the interrogation by telling the spies they'd be called before the grand jury to answer questions; once warned, most of them fled the country. Other sources, however, blame Hoover for going public with the investigation

1. German Fifth Columns

FBI agents (actors unidentified) confront Schneider (Francis Lederer, center) about his espionage work for the Nazis. A few scenes later, Schneider makes the *Confessions of a Nazi Spy* (1939).

before everyone involved was in custody. Either way, 14 agents, including the ringleader, Dr. Ignatz Griebl, escaped, leaving only four to stand trial.

Confessions of a Nazi Spy opens with the narrator promising a story "revealing the existence of a vast spy ring operating against the naval, military and air forces of the United States." We shift to America, where Dr. Karl Kassel (Paul Lukas) tells an enthusiastic American Nazi Party meeting that he loves America because it was "founded on German blood and culture," and that German-Americans must unite to fight for America's "German destiny" and "save America from the chaos that lies in democracy and racial equality." Nazi fanatic Kurt Schneider (Francis Lederer), based on Rumrich, later asserts that wherever Germans are, the Fatherland is.

Schneider studies the history of German World War I espionage and offers his services to the Reich as a spy. The film tracks his activities — helped by his Army buddy Werner Renz (Joe Sawyer) — interweaving them with scenes of Kassel's work as a Nazi propagandist. Storm troopers silence protesters at Kassel's speeches; an anti–Nazi German immigrant is seized by Gestapo agents and shanghaied back to Germany; Kassel's superiors tell him, "National Socialism must wrap itself in the American flag," pushing pro–German propaganda while weakening America by fanning race, religious and class hatred (a plot element that turns up repeatedly in both anti–Nazi and anticommunist films). Nazi doctrine will become the hammer and "America will be the iron we beat into another swastika."

When British Intelligence exposes a link in the network, they notify the Americans, who call in federal agent Renard (Edward G. Robinson). Renard tells the investigators that Germany is already at war with the United States and will strike once the fifth column has done its work. The G-men hunt and find Schneider, who's ultimately busted, like Rumrich, trying to obtain fake passports. Pegging Schneider as an egomaniac, Renard flatters him into bragging about his work; the spy ring collapses and Kassel is forced to rat out his cohorts. Germany contrives to have Kassel released and deported home, where he's told to renounce his confession as obtained under torture.

As in real life, only four of the defendants come to trial. The prosecutor brands them as part of a "worldwide spy network whose efficiency leaps all oceans and boundaries," which is driven home for the audience by shots of Europe and a warning that the Germans took Czechoslovakia by "stirring up racial prejudices and national prejudices, fomenting riots and disorder," then seizing power on the pretense of restoring law and order. The prosecutor tells the jury that fifth column tactics have given Europe to Germany and "God alone knows what peace-loving nation will be next."

After the jury delivers its guilty verdict, Renard and the prosecutor go out for a drink and hear nearby diners loudly condemn the Nazis. "The voice of the people," the prosecutor says. Renard: "Thank God for such a people."

Although based on a true case, *Confessions of a Nazi Spy* uses many the elements that would recur in fictional fifth column films:

- The enemy is trying to set Americans against each other. This point would be made in other anti–Nazi films and would also be used in the fifties to label the civil rights movement as a communist front.
- The enemy can't beat us in a fair fight. If we're united against them, they lose; they can only win by subversion and sabotage.
- Our government makes no mistakes. In contrast to the FBI's real-world performance, Renard cracks Schneider smoothly, and Kassell's escape is due to German political influence, not any error on our part. Later anticommunist movies would testify to the flawless efficiency of the FBI and the House Un-American Activities Committee, and assured viewers that criticism of them all came from the subversives they were hunting. Only enemies of America would criticize those institutions.
- The enemy has a huge spy network, seemingly composed of law-abiding American citizens but in reality blindly loyal to its evil foreign masters.

Contemporary attacks on the movie singled this out as proof that *Confessions of a Nazi Spy* was an exercise in political paranoia. While the movie depicts some German immigrants as loyal Americans, the German-American Bund is shown as not only supporting Hitler (which it did), but a sleeper organization willing to turn on America in favor of Germany.

1. German Fifth Columns

German-American Bund leader Fritz Kuhn filed a $5 million libel suit against Warner Bros. and requested a temporary injunction against showing the movie; he lost both times. The German government filed official objections and one Nazi propaganda organ described *Confessions* as attacking Christianity in the interests of "Jewish Bolshevism and all other subversive internationalism." The Hays Office raised the argument that all nations spy on each other, so there were no grounds for making an issue out of the Rumrich case, let alone implying Germany wanted to conquer the United States. Even some Americans condemned it as Jewish propaganda. What now looks like a tame, matter-of-fact account of the case was sensationalistic by 1939 standards.

The Warners argued that sensationalism was necessary to alert people to the Nazi threat, and they weren't alone in that view. An editorial in the *South Bend Tribune*, for instance, suggested that every loyal American should see *Confessions* to "awaken these wishy-washy Americans to the fact that their national sentiments need rejuvenation." Warner Bros. promoted the film with what the FBI called "startling methods," such as creating an "Americanism week" in schools; giving out cards with swastikas on them; producing fake Nazi handbills warning of reprisals against people who saw the film; and movie posters asking "What do you know about the man next door?"

Despite the promotional stunts and the angry rhetoric, the film did poorly at the box office; even rereleasing it with European war footage spliced in didn't help. However, the publicity about the film, and the spy case itself, marked a clear break from earlier years and fueled the growth of American fears about fifth columnists

In the years between *Confessions* and Pearl Harbor, that paranoia grew. *Time* reported that in Michigan, one man almost killed a neighbor he thought was a fifth columnist; a group of matrons in Manhattan took up rifle practice with an eye to picking off parachuting troops; Anderson, South Carolina, staged a mock attack on the town by fifth columnists. By 1940, according to one poll, 48 percent of Americans thought their communities had been infiltrated by the enemy

Germany's victories in Europe intensified American concerns about the possibility of Nazi infiltration. MacDonnell says German triumphs in Poland, Czechoslovakia and Austria had indeed been partly due to fifth column work, but it was the fall of nations further west — France, Belgium, Holland, Norway — that America blamed on subversive tactics.

In *Watch on the Rhine* (1943) one character asserts, "It is German practice to send men into such countries to — prepare the way." In *Once Upon a Honeymoon* (1942), chorus girl Ginger Rogers thinks she's landed in clover when she marries a wealthy German aristocrat (Walter Slezak), having convinced him she's from a wealthy family back home. They begin a long honeymoon traveling across Europe, and curiously, wherever they visit, violence and destruction occur, followed by the Nazi takeover.

The narrator of *The Nazis Strike*, a 1943 entry in the *Why We Fight* documentary series, quotes Hitler saying that Nazis would "demoralize the enemy from within by surprise, terror, sabotage, assassination. That is the war of the future." The film identifies fascist political parties in western Europe as subversive agents of the Reich, and the narrator accuses the German-American Bund of engaging in the same tactics (although emphasizing that most German-Americans are loyal). In the *Divide and Conquer* entry, the falls of Norway and France are both blamed on the fifth column; in France's case, the words "sabotage" and "riot" appear on the screen as the narrator tells us that "Hitler's political termites gnawed away at the binding of national unity."

In point of fact, MacDonnell says, fifth column activity was largely ineffective in Western Europe; nevertheless, fears of an American fifth column reached a fever pitch after the fall of France in 1940. President Roosevelt further fanned the flames by suggesting that his political adversaries were, so to speak, objectively pro–Nazi.

In real life, the Nazis' espionage success in the United States was limited. After federal agents busted the Duquesne spy ring in 1941, the Nazis had no large-scale spy rings operating in America, and even the Duquesne ring was smashed before it could carry out its sabotage plans, thanks to a German immigrant who infiltrated them for the FBI. In the movies, however, fifth columnists were omnipresent and much more formidable.

Saboteur (1942) Many of Alfred Hitchcock's films play with personal paranoia; *Saboteur* goes for the political kind. When a fire breaks out at an aircraft factory, Nazi saboteur Frank Fry (Norman Lloyd) hands factory worker Barry Kane (Robert Cummings) a fire extinguisher filled with gasoline; Barry hands it to his best friend, who dies when the fire blazes out of control. When Barry realizes he's the prime suspect, he takes off to find Fry.

Barry and Pat Martin (Priscilla Lane) — a young woman who initially tries to capture Barry, then winds up helping and falling in love with him — discover a sizable spy network capable of tremendous acts of sabotage. It has bases in an abandoned mining town, wealthy Charles Tobin's (Otto Kruger) country ranch house and Mrs. Van Souter's (Alma Kruger) society parties, where guests unwittingly mingle with the Nazis who show up to plot in her study. Anyone from a newsreel photographer to a factory worker can be an enemy agent.

Like many of the fifth columnists who would follow him, Tobin can't resist speechifying on the inferiority of Americans and the American way, dismissing loyal Americans who "plod along without asking questions — I hate to use the word 'stupid' but it's the only one applies.... A few of us are clever enough to see there's much more to be done than live small complacent lives. A few of us in America who desire a more profitable government. The competence of totalitarian nations is much higher than ours." Despite Tobin's supposed competence, Barry and Pat block his plan to destroy a newly launched battleship, then capture the spies and clear Barry's name.

All Through the Night (1942) At the insistence of his mother, shady gambler "Gloves" Donahue (Humphrey Bogart) reluctantly agrees to investigate the disappearance of her neighborhood baker. He doesn't know that sneering Nazi killer Pepe (Peter Lorre) killed the baker, a German immigrant, when the man refused to spy for the Reich and threatened to report Pepe instead.

Digging into the mystery, Donahue and his Runyonesque crew discover a spy ring that includes Pepe, sexy Hamilton (Kaaren Verne) and Epping (Conrad Veidt), a Nazi spymaster who has hundreds of agents in New York and in every major city in America.

1. German Fifth Columns

Gangster Gloves Donahue (Humphrey Bogart) uncovers the Nazis' latest victim in *All Through the Night* (1942). To him, the Reich is the deadliest mob the world has ever seen.

Much like Tobin, Epping plans to strike a blow at America's spirit by blowing up a battleship leaving Brooklyn Navy Yard that night.

As in *Confessions of a Nazi Spy*, Epping also plans to weaken America from within by stirring up racial and religious hatred to set Americans against each other. At the climax, when Donahue's underworld cronies break into Nazi HQ, Hamilton — who's only working for Epping because her father is imprisoned in Dachau — sneers that he's being beaten by "the people that you despise so much, that you said you'd split into angry little groups!"

The Nazis are so vile, even the underworld despises them: When Epping tells Donahue that they're alike — taking what they want, scorning democracy — Gloves replies, "I've been a registered Democrat ever since I could vote. I may not be a model citizen but I pay my taxes, stop at traffic lights and buy 24 tickets regular to the policeman's ball." Later in the movie, Gloves awakes the mob to the Nazi threat by portraying them as an even bigger, more ruthless mob. The ideas that America's enemies were no better than criminals, and that real criminals had more patriotism than fifth columnists, would crop up several times in later films.

Screen Enemies of the American Way

They Got Me Covered (1943) Kit Kittridge (Bob Hope) is an inept foreign correspondent who guaranteed in print that Germany would not attack Russia (this makes the movie's setting a few months before Pearl Harbor). He lost his job and now needs a big scoop to restart his career. When a tipster offers him the exclusive story on an Axis spy ring operating in Washington, D.C., Kittridge sets out to get proof. While his encounters with the spy ring are typical Hope bumbling, we learn at the climax of the film that the Nazi plot is vast: A series of bombings throughout Washington (fire stations, waterworks, and other official buildings) timed to create maximum terror, followed by similar bombing campaigns in other cities. Kittridge and his girlfriend Chris (Dorothy Lamour) successfully bring them to justice.

Mission to Moscow (1943) This USSR–set film from Warner Bros. is based on the same-name memoir by Joseph E. Davies, about his experiences as ambassador to Moscow in the thirties. Warners made the film with the government's blessing to boost support for our alliance with Russia; Jack Warner claimed President Roosevelt himself asked them to make the movie, but Davies said he's the one who originated it.

In the film, Davies (Walter Huston) and his wife (Ann Harding) arrive in Moscow in the 1930s and are stunned to discover how modern, sophisticated and just like Americans Russians are. This was a standard theme in World War II morale-builders: *The Good Earth* (1937) and *Mrs. Miniver* (1942) did their best to show that Chinese peasants and upper-class Brits (respectively) were no different from Americans at heart. In *Mission to Moscow*, Stalin (Manart Kippen) is an enlightened leader, devoted to his people but surrounded by enemies out to subvert the revolution. When Davies discovers his embassy is bugged, he assures his aide that it's a sensible precaution for Stalin to take.

In 1937, Stalin purges the military of political opponents with a series of show trials. The movie embraces the official Soviet view that the accused were a fifth column, plotting with the Axis to seize power; in return for Axis support, they would cede part of the Ukraine to Germany and Russia's eastern coast to Japan. The trial exposes the plot for the world to see, but Stalin tells Davies afterwards that he still needs to sign a Non-Aggression Pact with Germany: The west isn't ready to fight the Nazis, and Stalin needs to buy time to build up his forces against the inevitable war. (Davies tries to change that, but America refuses to budge until Pearl Harbor.)

Davies endorsed the trials in his book and insisted the confessions the state secured were 100 percent true. He wasn't alone in that view (even some people who were neither Stalinists nor communists agreed, as David Aaronovich details in *Voodoo Histories*). But history has thoroughly refuted the idea of an Axis-backed takeover plot. Similarly, the idea that Stalin was a prescient anti-fascist is nonsense; in reality, he trusted in Hitler's offer of a peace treaty (a startling contrast to his usual paranoia) and was blindsided by the 1941 German attack on the USSR. That, however, would have made U.S. support a much harder sell; it's no surprise that the *Why We Fight* segment *The Nazis Strike* makes the same buying-time argument.

Ministry of Fear (1944) In this film (based on an Eric Ambler novel), Stephen Neale (Ray Milland) is released from an asylum where he's spent two years after mercy-killing

Many viewers found this ad's enthusiastic recommendation for *Mission to Moscow* (1943) with its whitewashed account of Stalin's political purges somewhat over-generous.

his terminally ill wife. Heading to London, he stops off at a charity fête run by the Mothers of the Free Nations, enters a contest and wins a homemade cake (a big deal, given wartime rationing). As he leaves, the women running the booth suddenly rush up and tell him they made a mistake in awarding him the cake; it turns out, however, that Stephen made two bids and one of them is still closer than the supposed winner.

Leaving town by train, Stephen shares his cake with a blind man in his compartment. When the train stops during a German bombing raid, the man, fully sighted, clobbers Stephen and steals the cake, only to be destroyed by a bomb as he runs away from the train. A baffled Stephen begins to investigate the charity, and meets Mrs. Bellane (Hillary Brooke), the fortune-teller who urged him to compete for the cake. This glamourous beauty is not the same woman as at the fête, but she invites Stephen and Willi Hilfe (Carl Esmond), one of the charity organizers, to participate in a séance. In the dark, Stephen hears whispers about his wife and breaks the circle. One of the others winds up dead; Stephen recognizes him as the man who delivered the cake to the fête.

With the help of Willi's sister Carla (Marjorie Reynolds), Steve goes on the run from the police; Carla checks the charity files and discovers several staffers could be Nazi spies. After a bomb almost kills Steve, he awakens in police custody for the murder at the séance. He convinces the police to search the site where the blind man died and they discover a roll of microfilm holding the plans for Britain's channel defenses. The government realizes that Forrester (Alan Napier), a prominent consultant on the psychology of Nazism, was present when the documents were brought from the vault, and that a tailor recommended by Forrester visited the building recently. Stephen discovers that the tailor plans to smuggle out another copy of the film sewn into a suit, and successfully thwarts the plan.

The noirish atmosphere of this effective film, directed by the great Fritz Lang, adds greatly to the sense of paranoia and menace.

The Master Race (1944) As Germany's defenses crumble, Nazi officers scatter throughout Europe to prepare for the Fourth Reich by destabilizing government and setting people against each other. Col. Von Beck (George Coulouris) is assigned to a small Belgian town, shooting himself in the leg to pose as a wounded resistance fighter. After American Major Carson (Stanley Ridges) takes over the newly liberated town and helps it rebuild, Von Beck works to undercut him, hinting to the local miller, Katry (Paul Guilfoyle), that the Americans are exploiting him, seducing a young townswoman whose father was a Nazi collaborator and warning the major about non-existent schemes among the residents. Eventually, Von Beck is exposed; he warns the town that Germany will rise from the ashes, but that doesn't stop him from dying in front of a firing squad.

Similarly, the Nazi villain Jarnac (Luther Adler) in *Cornered* (1945) informs Lawrence Gerard (Dick Powell) that in the aftermath of the war, Nazis will slip into the population, exploiting men's dissatisfaction and suffering to turn them against legitimate governments: "Wherever men do not have enough to eat, we'll be there."

Strange Holiday (1945) This film opens with John Stevenson (Claude Rains) sitting in a prison cell, struggling to make sense of what's happened to him. We flash back to a recent weeks-long camping trip, which he took with a friend in the belief "they can win

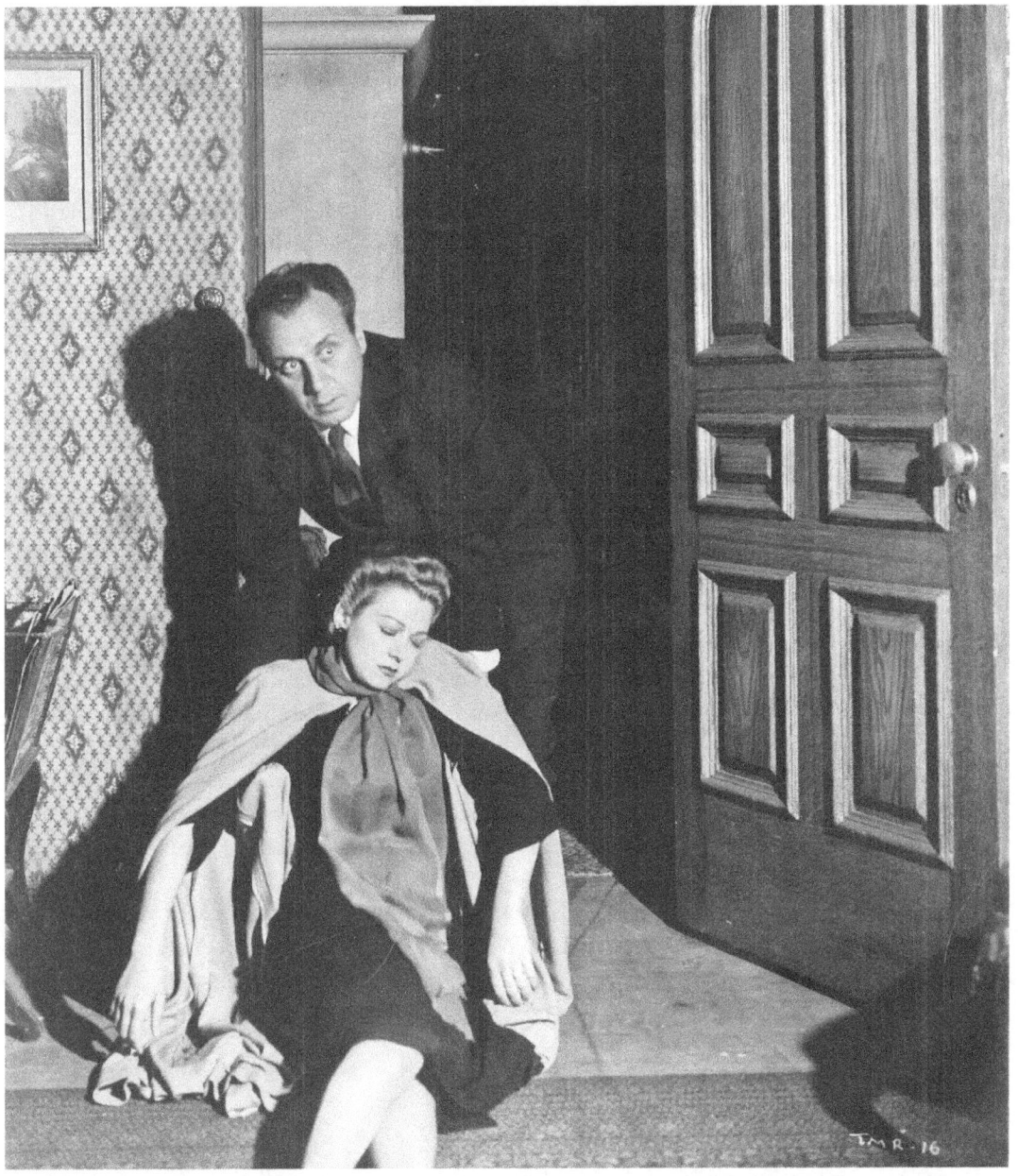

The war may be over but the Nazi threat lives on. Von Beck (George Coulouris) drags away his latest victim (Helen Beverly) so that he can continue his postwar treachery in *The Master Race* (1944).

this war without me breaking my neck." When he realized it was his anniversary, however, he insisted on his friend flying them back to town.

When the plane crashes in a field, John hitches a ride with a truck driver who is oddly evasive about the absence of any other vehicles on the road. In town, the sales clerks are afraid to sell him anything, his office has been ransacked and his family has vanished. Two cops enter his house and kayo him when he asks for a warrant. When John wakes up in jail, his black cellmate tells him "they" have thrown out the Bill of Rights. A foreign-accented interrogator demands to know what John's really been up to the past few weeks. John pleads innocence, so the cops start beating answers out of him.

In between beatings, the interrogator tells John how the fifth column "hid behind many faces as we spoke, as we whispered" and we hear the voices of people blaming Catholics, blaming Protestants, crying that the government has failed, democracy has failed and the nation needs to start over. After the system dissolves into chaos and civil war, "they" emerged and gave the citizens the order they were desperate for. Back in his cell, John realizes he was a fool to think freedom came easily or automatically, and vows that "we're fighting and we're going to go on fighting." At this point he wakes and realizes that it was all a dream — which doesn't stop him from rushing back to the city, fueled by his new-found commitment.

This film had its roots in *Precious Freedom*, an award-winning 1940 radio play written and directed by Arch Oboler, one of the biggest names in radio drama. The difference from *Strange Holiday* was at the end, as the protagonist realizes he not only undermined America by apathy, but by arguments such as "Don't antagonize them! We'll have to do business with them! Let them talk! Mind our own business!"

Writing about *Strange Holiday* and *Precious Freedom*, Matthew Rovner states that General Motors hired Oboler to turn the play into a short film that could be shown to its employees as a reminder not to strike during the war. GM never did show the film but Oboler and Rains bought back the rights, expanded the film to a short feature and released it in 1945. It was rereleased as an anticommunist film in the 1950s by covering the swastikas in the montage of the takeover with made-up symbols. Since the Nazis are never named, this worked fine, in best "bogeyman" style.

Red Nightmare (1962) used a similar dream-warning format to make the same points. The 1968 TV movie *Shadow on the Land*, about a near-future totalitarian America, invoked a similar explanation in the opening (Americans grew complacent, took their freedom for granted, etc.), though the conquest isn't attached to any particular movement.

After the War

As anyone who's watched a movie knows, the Nazi threat in fiction didn't end when World War II did.

Aging Nazis continued to pop up as villains, sometimes plotting to raise the Reich from the ashes, sometimes going around and doing bad things because, well, they're Nazis and that's all the reason they need. Most Nazi villains, even those plotting a new Reich, don't qualify for this book; in *The Stranger* (1946), for example, former Nazi Orson Welles has reinvented himself as a New England history professor, but assures a former comrade that he's only biding his time, like others, until the Reich rises again. The movie, however, is a straight murder mystery that does nothing further with the infiltration angle.

1. German Fifth Columns

Some movies looked back at the war. In *The Argyle Secrets* (1948), columnist Allen Pierce (George Anderson) is working on an exposé of prominent Americans who collaborated with the Nazis during the war. After going into the hospital, Pierce entrusts reporter Harry Mitchell (William Gargan) with a photocopy of the cover of the Argyle Album, the document naming the fifth columnists. Shortly afterwards, Pierce winds up dead with a steel scalpel in his chest. The cops suspect Harry, who goes on the run, hunting the album in the hope it will enable him to clear himself.

Harry's not the only one hunting it. A woman named Marla (Marjorie Lord) has Harry beaten to try and force him to give her the album. She tells him that her boss, Winter (John Banner), plans to use the information to blackmail the traitors. As Harry weaves his way through the factions angling to exploit the album, Police Lt. Samson (Ralph Byrd) tells him that Pierce was dead before the scalpel went in, courtesy of a drug overdose. It turns out Winter was one of the traitors named in the album and paid Pierce's doctor to kill him. Harry ultimately outwits Winter and the other schemers and arranges to have Pierce's exposé published post-mortem.

Other movies tackled the supposedly continuing Nazi threat in the present.

The Quiller Memorandum (1966) After two British agents investigating the German neo–Nazi movement are murdered, Quiller (George Segal), is dragged from vacation to replace them. His handler, Pol (Alec Guinness), tells him that unlike the old days of cheering crowds shouting sieg heil, "Nobody wears a brownshirt now ... consequently they're difficult to recognize. They look like everybody else." The neo–Nazis exist in many walks of life, spreading the doctrine of National Socialism, but under their everyday facade, they're hardcore believers and deadly dangerous. Quiller's target is a spy ring led by Oktober (Max Von Sydow) that backs up the movement's velvet glove with the iron fist of direct action.

Quiller's only lead is the case of a schoolteacher who committed suicide after being outed as a neo–Nazi. Arriving at the man's Berlin school, Quiller meets Inge (Senta Berger), an attractive teacher who tells him she rejects the old ways in favor of "the new Germany." Shortly afterwards, Oktober's men capture Quiller. Even drugged, he refuses to give away Pol's Berlin base. Oktober implants the idea that he's in love with Inge and she's eager to return his feelings.

This tactic pays off after Quiller is released: When he finds Oktober's base again, he discovers they're holding Inge hostage and he has until dawn to save her by giving up the information they want. With Nazi agents shadowing him, Quiller can't contact his superiors; finally, he gives the Nazis the slip and reaches his headquarters. Dawn is already breaking, however. When a joint British-German raid rounds up Oktober and his cell, they report to Quiller that there was no woman there.

It's therefore something of a shock to Quiller to run into Inge at her school the next day. She tells him that Oktober simply let her go, without explanation; he realizes it's more likely that she was one of them and he'd been duped all along. With no proof that Inge's ideal of a "new Germany" is a Nazi one, Quiller walks away, leaving Inge spreading her influence among Germany's children.

The Odessa File (1974) The movie opens in 1963, as an Israeli officer tells Mossad that Egypt's President Nasser is ready to erase Israel from the map with missiles bearing bacteriological and radioactive warheads. All he needs is for something called "Odessa" to provide the missile guidance systems.

In Germany, freelance journalist Peter Miller (Jon Voight) stumbles across the diary of a Holocaust survivor. Reading his account of SS commander Roschman (Maximilian Schell) and his crimes — including his murder of a Nazi officer who locked horns with him — Miller begins digging, discovers that Roschman is still alive and becomes obsessed with finding him. (We eventually learn that the murdered officer was Miller's father.) Someone is bothered by this enough to try to kill Miller.

Nazi hunter Simon Wiesenthal (Schmuel Rodensky) tells Miller that Roschman is part of Odessa, a secret network set up at the end of the war, financed by the gold and art that Germany stole from the rest of Europe. Odessa helped hundreds of SS members escape capture by the Allies and created new identities for them; the resultant spider-web stretches from Germany to Paraguay, Spain and Argentina (all fascist or sympathetic to fascists at the time). Odessa members have infiltrated big business, the judicial system,

A veterans' reunion isn't a happy occasion when the vets are ex–Nazis still mourning the premature end of the Thousand Year Reich in *The Odessa File* (1974).

1. German Fifth Columns

local government and the police; Wiesenthal shows Miller photos of five cops he knows, then reveals that the photos come from their SS identity cards.

With Mossad assistance, Miller infiltrates Odessa and confronts Roschman. Roschman insists he's not a Nazi, then tries to kill Miller, only to die himself. Miller gathers enough information to smash Odessa, and for Mossad to destroy the guidance systems and the factory making them.

This is unusual for a post-war Nazi thriller, inasmuch as the Nazis aren't looking to build a Fourth Reich or take over the world, only to live well and protect themselves from war crimes trials. Even helping Nasser attack Israel seems to be more a business deal than any continued interest in the Final Solution.

Hitler's Daughter (1990) In the opening scene, a woman gives birth in 1945, after which her German companions murder the doctor and nurse involved

In the present, we meet Ted Scott (Patrick Cassidy), press secretary to presidential contender Elliott Benedict (George R. Robertson). Ted is puzzled when his old friend Baumann (Donald Davis), now a Nazi hunter, shows up after a campaign debate, insisting that Ted summoned him and provided him with a security pass. Even odder, he claims a Nazi conspiracy named Phoenix has built more power in America than the Nazis had in Germany sixty years earlier, and that he needs Ted's help exposing the woman leading it. Before Ted can sort this out, a security guard murders Baumann, frames Ted and knocks him cold; Ted wakes up in a car in the woods with Baumann's evidence file in his hand and escapes seconds before the car explodes. (The fact that the Nazis didn't burn the file immediately makes them, and this movie, idiotic.)

Ted, his girlfriend Jill (Carolyn Dunn) and FBI agent Jim (Lindsay Merrithew) soon discover that Baumann was onto something: The file holds copies of documents proving the baby born in the opening scene was Hitler's illegitimate daughter, hidden in America by Phoenix. However the copies are too damaged to prove this to anyone else and Jim can't convince his bosses that Ted is innocent.

During all this, we learn the campaign is rife with backstage scheming involving three women: Benedict's wife Patricia (Veronica Cartwright), who wants her husband to appoint her secretary of state; his lover Sharon (Melody Anderson), who's eager to become the president's mistress; and Sen. Gordon (Kay Lenz), vice-presidential candidate to Benedict's opponent Averil Rutledge.

Ted and Jill stay ahead of the FBI long enough to contact Trautmann (Cec Linder), the one surviving witness to the mother being shipped out of Germany. Trautmann tells Ted that the leader of Phoenix is definitely one of the three women.

As the heroes continue digging, Jill winds up dead and the guys realize that Mrs. Benedict is the Phoenix (at various points, it seems to be both her code name and the organization's). Jim's boss immediately warns someone; Jim returns home and discovers Mrs. Benedict dead, then is murdered himself by his fellow FBI agents. The official story released by the FBI is that Patricia Benedict was involved in some dirty tricks to revive the campaign after Ted was labeled a murderer when Jim tried blackmailing her, she shot him and then herself.

The Benedict campaign collapses, but Gordon tells the public that America remains strong despite the tragedy: "Like the Phoenix who rose from the ashes of sorrow, we will rise from the ashes united." Realizing the true enemy at last, Ted tries to kill her, but dies in the attempt. Rutledge becomes president, only to die soon afterwards of a heart attack, leaving Hitler's daughter as the new leader of the free world.

Before his death, Ted mailed Benedict's advisor Edward Holland (Gary Reineke) a package containing the evidence. After examining its contents, Holland calls the secretary of state...

And so ends the story of the most recent neo–Nazi fifth column to threaten America. Given the Nazis' durability as villains, it's a safe bet it won't be the last.

2

The Yellow Peril and the Fear of Japan

The fear of Japanese infiltration is different from most of the others recounted in this book: Unlike Russian spies, pod people, Stepford Wives and Nazi agents, a Japanese-American cannot pass for "one of us" if "us" is defined as white (or for that matter, black) Americans.

Nevertheless, political paranoia about the Japanese has a lot in common with paranoia directed at Jews and Catholics: They might live here, they might call themselves Americans, but their real loyalty is to their own kind, so they could never be true Americans. In the case of the Japanese, this produced much uglier results: 110,000 Japanese-American citizens, many of them American by birth, were forced into internment camps in the Midwest, away from the Pacific Coast where their supposed imperial Japanese masters were using them to subvert America's defenses. None of them were tried before being imprisoned, and there was no evidence of any fifth-column activity.

The Yellow Peril

American hostility to Asians living in America began with 19th-century Chinese immigrants who came to the West Coast, took jobs for lower wages than whites would accept, and worked hard. It was intensified after the Society of the Harmonious Fists— the Boxers—rose up against Western and Christian power in China, an act of (from a Western standpoint) unreasoning hostility that further marked the "yellow race" as a threat. Fears of white women miscegenating with Asian-Americans also became a factor as the numbers grew. (This also became a popular theme in silent films, where handsome Japanese men offered a fantasy—never consummated—of forbidden desire.)

In fiction the threat was often personified as the "sinister Oriental" villain, cunning, subtle and steeped in a cruel, callous disregard for human life (supposedly a typical Oriental trait). Sax Rohmer defined the image with his creation of Chinese mastermind Dr. Fu Manchu, "the yellow peril incarnate in a single man." Sinister Orientals of the 20th century would all owe a debt to Rohmer.

In the world of political paranoia, however, it was Japan, not China, that loomed as a menace in the early 20th century. Japan's victory in the Russo-Japanese War shocked the many Americans who thought the "yellow race" was inherently inferior to whites. As

Japan's Pacific power grew, Americans began to see Japanese immigrants as a threat; one rumor after the war said that the Japanese were planning to set up a naval base at Magdalena Bay in Baja. In 1907, William Randolph Hearst's *San Francisco Examiner* coined a phrase when it discussed the possibility of Japan ruling the Pacific and concluded that "the yellow peril is here."

Years before Pearl Harbor, Homer Lea's 1909 novel *Valor of Ignorance* predicted a future war between the United States and Japan. California's Asiatic Exclusion League (formed in 1905) pushed to extend the ban on Chinese immigration to Japanese and Koreans, asserting that the "unlimited Asiatic coolie invasion" meant "there would be no more California." (Similar fears would be expressed decades later about Hispanic immigration.) San Francisco Mayor James Phelan described Japanese immigrants as an "enemy within our gates."

As journalist David Neiwert puts it, in the 20th century the Yellow Peril fear became "a conspiracy theory which posited that the Japanese emperor intended to invade the Pacific Coast, and that he was sending these immigrants to American shores as shock troops to prepare the way for just such a military action, and lay the groundwork for acts of sabotage and espionage when the signal was given."

In 1912, Hearst's newspapers spread the rumor that the Japanese were establishing a colony in Magdalena Bay, then that they had 75,000 soldiers stationed in Baja (they didn't). In 1915, the Japanese ship *Asama*, on a mission against German ships in the Pacific, ran aground in Turtle Bay. It was pulled free 98 days later, but by that point, the rumors included the Japanese mining Turtle Bay, establishing a radio station, landing 4,000 Japanese troops and even crossing the border from Mexico to invade.

The premise of the 15-chapter serial *Patria* (1917) now sounds slightly comical—a joint Japanese-Mexican invasion from south of the border—but it wouldn't have seemed so at the time. The movie involves Patria (Irene Castle), an heiress who survives plane crashes, auto chases, train wrecks and an exploding munitions warehouse, then inherits $100 million which she uses to reorganize the army and beat back the combined Japanese and Mexican forces. Her boyfriend Dan, a Secret Service agent, is on hand, but she usually saves the day without him.

According to *Hearst Over Hollywood*, the story was probably the brainchild of Edward Lyell Fox, an American reporter covering the war in Germany, and also working as an editorial chief in the pay of the German Information Service. Fox told the service that Germany could benefit from a campaign to paint Japan (an ally of England in the war) as America's enemy and that he would contact Hiram Moe Greene, a playwright, screenwriter and Hearst magazine editor, to propose the idea to the pro–German Hearst. After the movie became controversial, Greene and Fox both denied any responsibility. The film's foreword credits Irene Castle for proposing a film about "preparedness."

The movie did its best to whip up hostility against the Japanese, even inserting footage to blame the Black Tom explosion on Japan. That didn't suit President Wilson, who condemned the film for attacking Japan "when in a sense Japan is our ally." He sought to have the film banned, only to be told there was no legal ground for doing so.

2. The Yellow Peril and the Fear of Japan

Pathé did compromise by eliminating references to Japan in the script and identifying enemy mastermind Warner Oland as Mexican, but the visuals worked against them: Japanese troops were still looting and pillaging, Oland wore a kimono, his interior decorations were Japanese-style and he commits hara-kiri when cornered. (Some of these elements were eliminated by further cuts.)

Patria's foes were hardly the only Japanese working against America in the silent movies (a few films, such as 1919's *Bonds of Honor* did show a good Japanese, but they were the exception). One film, *The Pride of Palomar* (1922), springs from political paranoia about the Japanese buying American land: Mike Farrell (Forrest Stanley), son of a Spanish don, returns from Army service in Siberia during the Great War to discover his father is dead and his ranch, Palomar, has been taken over by John Parker (Alfred Allen) who plans to turn it over to Okada (Warner Oland), a Japanese potato baron who wants the land for a colonization scheme.

Post–World War I Americans believed land purchases were one of the ways Japan was waging economic war against us, a fear that would resurface during Japan's economic boom in the 1980s. Publisher Miller Freeman, for example, sketched out a worst-case scenario based on the inaccurate premise that Washington state's Japanese owned most of Seattle's hotels and leased so much farmland — legally, they couldn't buy it — that they could shut Great War veterans out of the labor market. Whites, he argued, would become jobless and have to move back east, passing control of the West Coast to the Japanese, and thereby to Japan, since "Japan retains control of her people everywhere."

Opposition to Japanese-American fishermen working on the West Coast ran much in the same vein: economic rivalry (they outperformed the competition) coupled with accusations they were part of a vast spy network and still, at heart, residents of Japan.

The latter point was a recurring theme in the political paranoia of the time: The Japanese could never become true Americans because even after a couple of generations here, they remained true Japanese in manner, outlook and especially loyalty. Whatever their emperor commanded, they would do. The 1943 *Batman* serial takes this view in describing Little Tokyo as "foreign land transplanted bodily to America."

Nevertheless, the threat of a European war loomed much larger in Hollywood eyes in the thirties than the menace of a battle with Japan and so did the threat of espionage. When Hollywood began dipping its toe into pro-war movies in the thirties, the focus was almost entirely on the Nazi threat. Even as late as 1941, *Secret Agent of Japan*, despite the title, foresaw war with Germany, not Japan (a *Leading Comics* story from November 1941 likewise predicted Germany attacking Pearl Harbor, though only as a diversion from a Nazi attack on the mainland). Even after Pearl Harbor, there were suspicions that Germany had been the real mastermind behind it.

One noteworthy exception, *Across the Pacific*, began filming in late 1941 as a dramatization of Robert Garson's magazine serial "Aloha Means Goodbye," about a Japanese sneak attack on Pearl Harbor. When the December 7 attack took place, it was reworked into a thriller about a follow-up attack on the Panama Canal.

When Pearl Harbor did come, it shocked Hollywood along with everyone else, and

Hollywood reacted with the same anger as everyone else. The fact that Japan had been in peace negotiations up until the attack only enhanced the sense that Japan had stabbed America in the back. Although the diplomat, Saburo Kurusu, insisted he knew nothing of the military's plans, the Kurusu mission would be held up in several movies as proof of Asian perfidy and ruthlessness.

The conviction that Japan couldn't have taken Pearl Harbor through sheer military skill added to suspicions about America's Japanese population, whether first-generation immigrants (Issei) or American-born citizens (Nisei, the children of Issei, and Sansei, the children of Nisei). These suspicions were fueled by the conviction that the Japanese military couldn't have pulled off the Pearl Harbor attack unaided. It was easier to believe that Japanese fifth columnists had done the real work, and that Japanese "tourists" who'd been seen taking photographs of Pearl Harbor were spies. Secretary of the Navy Frank Knox asserted a week after the attack that "the most effective fifth column work of the entire war was done at Pearl Harbor, with the possible exception of Norway."

Even after concerns about Japanese disloyalty faded, the idea that Japan outfought us was hard to swallow. A 2009 *Naval History* article points out that histories of Pearl Harbor even years later tend to focus on how the U.S. screwed up and let it happen rather than how well executed the attack was.

The end result of this racist political paranoia was the internment.

Japanese Spying and Internment

Japanese spymasters knew perfectly well that America's eyes were on the West Coast Japanese and concentrated much more on recruiting African-Americans and whites. MacDonnell recounts several Japanese spy cases between 1936 and Pearl Harbor, most of which involved white Americans acting as Japanese agents. Although there is evidence that FDR considered internment camps as early as 1936, by 1941, MacDonnell says, the government viewed Japanese-Americans as trustworthy (though the general public and some individuals in government were less sanguine) and believed that by rounding up 2,000 suspected spies, mostly Issei, the threat had been smashed.

After Pearl Harbor, however, West Coast rumors of Japanese espionage — contaminating food and water, sabotaging defense plants, laying the groundwork for an invasion, lighting flaming arrows to direct bombers toward their targets — ran rife. (Steven Spielberg's *1941* [1979] parodies this without acknowledging how seriously the fears were taken at the time.) Army Lt. General John DeWitt claimed, inaccurately, that the military had picked up short-wave broadcasts from spies targeting American shipping for Japanese subs; his 1942 final report stated that "the very fact that no sabotage has taken place to date is a disturbing and confirming indication that such action will be taken."

Newspaper columnists, West Coast politicians and those who stood to gain financially — white farmers and fishermen, for instance — demanded the Japanese be locked away. In a *Saturday Evening Post* column typical of this mix of racism and self-interest,

Bogart doesn't actually make it *Across the Pacific* (1942) because December 7, 1941, made a movie about Bogie thwarting an attack on Pearl Harbor a moot point. The Panama Canal became the target instead.

Screen Enemies of the American Way

Frank Taylor wrote in 1942, "We're charged with wanting to get rid of the Japs for selfish reasons. We might as well be honest about it. We do. It's a question of whether the white man lives on the Pacific coast or the brown man. They came into this valley to work, and they stayed to take over.... If all the Japs were removed tomorrow, we'd never miss them in two weeks, because the white farmers can take over and produce everything the Jap grows. And we don't want them back when the war ends either."

Likewise Alan Hynd's 1943 book *Betrayal from the East* asserts that Nisei are overwhelmingly disloyal — look how many of the Japanese we interned say they feel no love for this country!— and that America's biggest mistake was not locking them up sooner. In Hynd's world, Japanese-owned hotels are hotbeds of espionage, and all positioned next to power lines in order to take down the electrical grid. American companies that did business with Japanese-Americans — tuna canneries, for instance — were selling out America for the almighty buck.

Hollywood Goes to War describes how the studios tried to balance out wartime portrayals of Germany by showing good Germans alongside the Nazis. *Why We Fight* emphasizes that despite Hitler's claim on the loyalty of all Germans everywhere, most German-Americans are 100 percent American, and many serve in the armed forces.

Portrayals of the Japanese were almost uniformly negative (there were rare exceptions, such as 1943's *Behind the Rising Sun*) and even American citizens were assumed to be treacherous rats. In *Across the Pacific*, one Nisei college student has an American accent and spouts slang, but he turns out to be a spy and a stone-cold killer (several other films show Nisei college students as villainous).

It was a given that Japanese-Americans were "blind worshippers of their emperor," in the words of *Little Tokyo, USA*, and that internment had neutralized a deadly threat. *Batman* sums up the prevailing view: "A wise government rounded up the shifty-eyed Japs."

Little Tokyo USA, (1942) The prologue asserts that "for more than a decade, Japanese mass espionage was carried on in the United States and her territorial outposts while a complacent America literally slept at the switch." The movie opens on November 1, 1941, as the spies of the Black Dragon Society initiate Issei businessman Ito Takimura (Harold Huber) as a member. Takimura agrees to use his importing business as a front to gather information about West Coast industry and American defense plans. Back in Los Angeles' Little Tokyo district, he recruits Kingoro (George E. Stone), Satsuma (Abner Biberman) and the German-American Marsten (Charles Tannen) into a spy network. Hendricks (Don Douglas), a German-American radio station manager, lets the cell use his station to relay signals to Japanese ships (which as noted above, was one of the rumors after Pearl Harbor).

Takimura tells his cell that Japan is about to strike at its greatest enemy, the USA: "We have planned long and thoroughly. The first bomb will fall on Pearl Harbor exactly on schedule." (It's a commonplace in the movies that knowledge of the Pearl Harbor attack was widespread among Japanese in America.) The only fly in the ointment is the possibility the government might intern the Japanese, which would cripple the emperor's spy operations.

2. The Yellow Peril and the Fear of Japan

Two-fisted police detective Michael Steele (Preston Foster) suspects there's a spy network in Little Tokyo, but Takimura insists otherwise and Mike's girlfriend Maris (Brenda Joyce), a radio commentator working for Hendricks, believes that Mike is unreasonably biased against the Japanese. By today's standards Maris is spot on: Mike's fears include Japanese farmers spraying poison on their vegetables, Japanese engineers sabotaging the power and water supply, and Japanese farms next to airfields, factories and dams. By the politically paranoid standards of 1942, however, Mike is the sensible one and Maris is a naive ninny — as witness she cites the Kurusu mission as proof that Japan's intentions are peaceful.

Mike's suspicions are confirmed when Satsuma's son brags about his dad talking to Tokyo every night on the radio. Mike asks his buddy Oshima (Richard Loo) to investigate. When Mike and Maris later drop by Oshima's apartment, they find the Okono family living there, claiming no knowledge of Oshima and insisting on their Fourth Amendment rights. Mrs. Okono also shows her un–Americanness by wearing a kimono and speaking broken English. Mike then busts into Satsuma's house — asserting his badge is the only warrant he needs — but can't find a radio. Oshima turns up dead in the morgue, decapitated Black Dragon–style, and to top it all off, the Japanese business community pressures the LAPD into transferring Mike to another precinct.

The LAPD's Det. Michael Steele (Preston Foster) gets to know treacherous Japanese beauty Teru (June Duprez) in *Little Tokyo, USA* (1942). Teru's lover will soon murder her to frame Steele.

Mike refuses to quit spy-hunting, so Takimura uses Hendricks' mistress Teru (June Duprez) to lure Mike to Satsuma's house where he's drugged, Teru is killed and Mike is framed for the deed. The next day, Mike hears about Pearl Harbor while sitting in jail; hero that he is, he escapes, tracks down the spies and finally tricks them into exposing themselves to the cops. The Japanese are interned; the movie used newsreel footage of the event and we see Little Tokyo turned into a ghost-town. (It really was a ghost town, which is why much of the film had to be shot in Chinatown.) Maris, no longer naive, tells her listeners that while some Japanese may be innocent, "in time of war, the loyal must suffer inconvenience with the disloyal."

The film condemned the Japanese so strongly — though it was in line with the prevailing public views — that the Office of War Information, which worked with Hollywood to shape movies for the war effort, put in an objection. The OWI worried that portraying all Japanese as traitors would pose major race-relations problems when they returned home, and that Mike's disregard for the Bill of Rights would hurt the image of the Allies as the side of justice and the rule of law. The War Relocation Office worried that the movie would trigger protests in the Midwest against building relocation camps there. Fox PR man Jason Joy told the government that the movie would be willing to make some changes, but the guts of the film would remain as they were, since the movie only promoted hostility toward traitors.

The Black Dragon Society (Korukoryai in Japanese) that Takimura joins was the successor to the Black Ocean Society, an ultra-nationalist group formed during the Russo-Japanese War to help drive Russia out of Manchuria. The Black Ocean became tainted with criminal activity, so the Black Dragons arose to replace it. After the war ended, Black Dragon activities expanded to include supporting Japan's espionage network, pushing a militaristic foreign policy and attacking Japanese liberals and democracy advocates.

In fiction, perhaps because the name sounded so sinister to Western ears, the Black Dragons were a creation of pure political paranoia, a powerful spy network that would battle American heroes in multiple movies (as you'll see) and even a few comic books. In the 1986 *Rambo* cartoon, the ninja member of the terrorist network S.A.V.A.G.E. is named Black Dragon (with a heroic brother named White Dragon) though I'm not aware of any formal ties between him and the Korukoryai.

Across the Pacific (1942) This film is best known for reuniting director John Huston with three of the stars of *The Maltese Falcon* (1941), Humphrey Bogart, Mary Astor and Sydney Greenstreet. It deserves to be at least as well-known for almost being the first Pearl Harbor film (substituting a Panamanian setting means the characters never actually leave the Atlantic). The hero is Rick Leland (Bogart), ostensibly an embezzler dishonorably discharged from the Army but in reality an agent for military intelligence out to penetrate a Japanese espionage ring.

Taking a Japanese tramp steamer out of New York, he befriends his fellow passengers: sexy Alberta (Astor); Dr. Lorenz (Greenstreet), a Japanophile American living in the Philippines who sees Japanese dominance there as inevitable; and Joe Totsuikio (Victor Sen Yung), a geeky Japanese-American college student who hates that his father is sending

2. The Yellow Peril and the Fear of Japan

him to Japan to study. A Filipino tries to kill Lorenz during a stop, but Rick saves him and the crew kills the assassin.

The ship docks in Panama on December 6, and Lorenz offers $1,500 if Rick can bring him the airplane patrol schedule for the nearest lock by the end of the day. Rick tells his intelligence contact that it would be too easy for Lorenz to check a fake schedule, so it would be better to give him a real one; after all, with Kurusu negotiating in Washington, the Japanese can't be planning an immediate attack.

Of course, that's exactly what they're planning, and not just on Pearl Harbor: Joe knocks Rick cold to steal the information, and the spy ring murders Rick's handler to prevent him changing the schedule. Rick tracks Lorenz to a plantation owned by Alberta's alcoholic father, whose drunkenness has enabled the spy ring to replace his staff with Japanese spies. (In Pearl Harbor, of course, Japanese plantation workers would be unremarkable.) The Japanese have smuggled in a plane and aerial torpedo, piece by piece, to destroy the nearest lock, rendering the canal unusable.

Fortunately, Alberta's father redeems himself by tackling Joe. It costs the old man his life, but Rick is able to kill Joe and escape, then use a guard's machine-gun to destroy the plane. Rick captures Lorenz, who tries to commit seppuku, but doesn't have the guts.

The movie hits on the standard anti–Japanese themes: the treachery of the Kurusu diplomatic mission; Joe, the all–American college kid, still totally loyal to Japan; and the portrayal of the Japanese in Hawaii (under the original concept) as a fifth column just waiting to happen (the attack we have to fear here is sabotage from within, not a military attack).

Black Dragons (1942) The film opens with a banner headline screaming about Pearl Harbor and the Kurusu mission, then we shift to a cocktail party where several wealthy businessmen listen attentively as their colleagues discuss which shipyards are busiest, and where the new ammunition dumps have been built. Unsurprisingly, the next headline announces "Fifth column activity prominent in treacherous attack on U.S." and we see ships sinking, factories burning, bridges exploding, etc.

The traitors celebrate at fellow spy Dr. Saunders' (George Pembroke) house, their glee dimmed when Colomb (Bela Lugosi), a vaguely familiar figure, shows up and claims he needs to see the doctor urgently. A few minutes after meeting Colomb, the doctor screams in horror. When the other men rush in, he insists everything is fine, but he's going to be busy with Colomb.

Kearney (Max Hoffman, Jr.) takes a taxi home from the party, but finds Colomb waiting in the cab; Colomb addresses him by a Japanese name. When the cab reaches its destination, the two men have vanished. Kearney's body shows up outside the Japanese embassy, with a Japanese dagger in his hand.

More murders by the "Jap dagger killer" follow, and the surviving fifth columnists start receiving business cards in the mail from a plastic surgeon, which causes them to shudder. Saunders' niece Alice (Joan Barclay) and detective Dick Martin (Clayton Moore) investigate, but the bodies keep piling up. Finally, with his collaborators dead, Saunders tells all: Colomb is really a Nazi surgeon who transformed a half-dozen Black Dragons into exact doubles of kidnapped American businessmen. The society locked the doctor away to ensure secrecy, but he escaped by impersonating the real Colomb, a soon-to-be-released prisoner. "Colomb" coerced Saunders' cooperation by injecting a drug that causes massive deformities.

The movie ends with a flag flying in front of the Capitol building and a headline announcing "Jap Spy Ring Smashed!"

Let's Get Tough! (1942) Caught up in the post–Pearl Harbor patriotic fever, the young toughs known as the East Side Kids decide to enlist but get turned down because of their youth. (In real life, stars Huntz Hall and Leo Gorcey were in their twenties and looked it, but they'd keep playing kids on into the 1950s.) The boys decide to contribute, instead, by hunting fifth columnists in their neighborhood.

"All men are in danger of dying," Colomb (Bela Lugosi) warns a victim in *Black Dragons* (1942). "The only question is—when." Here, he strikes a publicity pose.

When they see an Asian store owner, Kino (name not listed in the credits), driving respectable Heinbach (Gabriel Dell) out of his store, they pelt the shop front with vegetables. Kino drives them off with a sword cane, which convinces them of his perfidy. The kids sneak back into the store after dark and find Kino dead.

The police take the kids in, but don't have enough evidence to charge them. The police captain points out that the same Bill of Rights that protects them also protected Kino, so they were wrong to harass him without proof—especially since he was Chinese (and as we later learn, a spy for his government), not Japanese.

We then see the real spy, Joe Matsui (Philip Ahn), receiving propaganda broadcasts about the destruction of multiple American cities (which he grumbles don't get any time in the biased American media) and working on sabotage with Phil (Tom Brown), a dishonorably discharged naval officer. When the East Side Kids see Joe sneak into Heinbach Sr.'s (Sam Bernard) pawn shop, they become suspicious, more so when they spot Joe stealing something from Kino's store. The guys pick his pocket and discover the item contains a message in Japanese.

Muggs (Leo Gorcey) takes the message to Joe's father (Moy Ming), a tea-room owner who reads it, then commits hara-kiri. When Muggs brings the cops to the store, Joe has disguised himself as his father and denies everything. (He explains to Phil later that his honorable father committed suicide for fear his son would be exposed as a spy.) Phil's girlfriend Nora (Florence Rice) takes the message to her old college friend Joe, who has her kidnapped as a threat (we never learn what the message says, only that it's enough to bust the ring).

2. The Yellow Peril and the Fear of Japan

After the East Side Kids discover a stockpile of magnesium (usable for flares or explosives) in the pawn shop, they start watching the store and that night see dozens of people sneaking in. Following them inside, they find the visitors donning hoods for a big meeting, swipe some spare hoods and join them. Heinbach and a Japanese envoy announce the beginning of a devastating wave of sabotage that will destroy democracy, then introduce Phil as their star agent. Fortunately, Phil is actually a double agent and by the time the police arrive, he and the boys have the spies knocked cold.

This forgettable film does capture the time-honored message of political paranoia that anyone in your neighborhood could be an enemy spy (apparently the risk was so great, China even thought it worthwhile stationing Kino there).

G-Men vs. the Black Dragon (1943) This 15-chapter serial starred Rod Cameron, Roland Got and Constance Worth (respectively American agent Rex Bennett, Chinese agent Chang and Brit Vivian Marsh), pitting them against Haruchi (Nino Pipitone), a Fu Manchu–style villain in charge of the Black Dragon's American espionage ring. In Rex's words to the sinister mastermind, "Anyone who knows of your treachery before Pearl Harbor and in the Philippines knows your face."

After taking a suspended animation drug so that his agents can smuggle him into America inside a mummy case, Haruchi launches a wide variety of sinister schemes: stealing a camera that can detect any surprise attack; stealing an experimental submarine detector; buying a paint company in order to coat U.S. troop ships with an incendiary chemical; and blowing up electrical towers throughout the Los Angeles area in order to destroy the power grid. The battle runs 15 yellow peril-filled episodes before Haruchi, fleeing by speedboat, crashes into a waiting Japanese submarine while trying to outrace Rex's pursuit.

The Black Dragon Society itself is described as "organized in Japan for the purposes of terrorism, sabotage and espionage." They have an undercover organization in America and "behind it are all the cunning and treachery of the keenest Oriental minds." The Dragons have been preparing for war well in advance; for example, the bombs that tear up the power grid were planted three years earlier by white engineers working for the Black Dragons.

When some of the Japanese agents are caught in the chapter "Celestial Murder," Haruchi gloats that they can count on America's own court system to protect them; Vivian later ponders, "Odd, isn't it, that America grants such privileges to men who are trying to destroy it." Despite Haruchi's impressive batting average in destroying things, it's emphasized that the Black Dragons have been crippled by the internment; in one chapter, they have to break a top agent out of the Manzanar camp to accomplish a mission.

We've Never Been Licked (1943) Brad Craig (Richard Quine) attends Texas A&M in the 1930s; he befriends Japanese students Matsui (Roland Got) and Kubo (Allen Jung), remaining friends with them despite the flak he gets from his white buddies — until he learns about Japan's brutal occupation of China.

When Brad discovers that his friends are spies (the movie establishes that they knew about Pearl Harbor before it happened), he begins working against them, supposedly

A lobby card captures one scheme of Japanese saboteur Haruchi (Nino Pipitone) — using incendiary paint to destroy American ships — in the serial *G-Men vs. the Black Dragon* (1943). Fifteen chapters of "yellow peril" would follow.

2. The Yellow Peril and the Fear of Japan

helping them steal an explosive formula but actually securing a fake. After Pearl Harbor, Matsui and Kubo return to Japan, and Brad goes with them. He alerts the Navy to the Japanese location, assuring a victory, then crashes his plane into a Japanese aircraft carrier.

Headin' for God's Country (1943) Enigmatic Michael Banyan (William Lundigan) arrives in Sunivak, Alaska, in September 1941, dead broke and not giving any hints why he's there. Despite the town's suspicions, Banyan makes friends with meteorologist Laurie (Virginia Dale) and printer Clem (Harry Davenport). When Banyan gets into trouble fighting Hugo (Eddie Acuff), the local bully, Laurie hides him in her weather station. When the radio is sabotaged, cutting Sunivak's only link to the outside, Laurie questions her judgment.

Banyan uses Clem's press to print a fake Seattle newspaper showing that America has joined World War II. When Hugo's father (J. Frank Hamilton) sees it, he offers to buy Laurie's abandoned mercury mine, knowing the metal will be valuable for munitions manufacturing. All the townspeople (unaware of the real Pearl Harbor attack) prepare to defend themselves except for Ness (Harry Shannon), a collaborator who destroyed the radio to facilitate a Japanese submarine's attack on Sunivak.

When Banyan discovers Ness welcoming a Japanese landing party, he tries to warn the town, but they've figured out his prank and refuse to believe it. A wounded townie confirms the attack, though, and the townspeople's defense training enables them to hold off the invaders until Laurie can repair the radio and get a message to the Air Force, directing them to the sub so they can destroy it.

Betrayal from the East (1945) The book *Betrayal from the East* by Alan Hynd is subtitled "the inside story of Japanese spies in America" and includes in its pages accounts of, among others, the Miyazaki case (a Japanese spy who recruited a Navy veteran to gather naval information for him) and the Tachibana spy ring (which was smashed shortly before Pearl Harbor). Hynd's racism makes it hard to trust his account, since he takes it as a given that any Japanese business is a potential spy base, that almost all Japanese are disloyal and that internment was necessary. Foreshadowing the arguments over Guantanamo Bay in the 21st century, he also charges that the government is releasing prisoners without conclusive proof they are loyal Americans.

The movie version opens with columnist Drew Pearson informing us that this is a true story and that "nobody could have made it up," though in point of fact it mingles two separate espionage cases and makes up quite a lot. The spymaster is named Miyazaki (Richard Loo), but the plot hews to the Tachibana spy case. Where Miyazaki's American recruit did indeed deliver military information, Al Blake — an entertainer the Tachibana ring recruited as a spy — went to work as a double agent to undermine the cell. Nevertheless, Pearson assures the audience that he knows from personal involvement (although he doesn't appear in the story) that "it happened in America right here — it must never happen again!" And any similarity to persons living or dead is quite intentional.

The story proper opens in pre-war Japan where reporter Jack Marsden (Louis Jean Heydt) tells his editor he has conclusive proof that the Kurusu mission is a smokescreen;

worse, a spy ring including several powerful men on America's West Coast will destroy the coast's defenses. Marsden memorizes a list of spies and ships for home. But when G-2 (military intelligence) agents show up to meet the boat, the smug captain and his steward Tanni — an American college student who speaks flawless English — tell them that Marsden fell overboard drunk and drowned.

Tanni — actually Lt. Commander Miyazaki of the Japanese Navy — leaves the ship, smirking at a newspaper article on Marsden's editor's "accidental" death. He tells his top agents, Kato (Philip Ahn) and Yamato (Abner Biberman), that Japan's propaganda machine will call for peace and "our diplomats will delude the Americans" but all the while Japan and its agents will be preparing to strike. The spies reply that they still haven't found a way to destroy the Panama Canal — a key part of the plan — but Kato knows an ex–GI, Eddie Carter (Lee Tracy) who's desperate for money and willing to help find a turncoat in the Canal Zone who'll give them the needed information.

Eddie agrees to work for Miyazaki, but secretly contacts G-2 and becomes a double agent. He doesn't get to see Miyazaki's face when they meet, though he does spot a college pin on his jacket. The spy ring takes care of Eddie's money problems and he picks up a new girlfriend, Peggy (Nancy Kelly), then discovers she's another G-2 agent. Yamato learns Peggy's a spy and tells Eddie to bring her to them; Peggy tries to convince Eddie she needs to be sacrificed for the greater good, but she's killed in a car accident first.

In Panama, Eddie meets with Jimmy Scott (Regis Toomey), a soldier picked by G-2 to provide him with outdated plans. Scott warns Eddie to hang onto the plans until G-2 can help him escape, otherwise Miyazaki will have him killed as soon as Eddie delivers the information. Eddie also finds Peggy in Panama, posing as the girlfriend of a Nazi spy; it turns out that G-2 faked her death to get her away from Yamato.

G-2 arranges a fake family emergency to give Eddie an excuse to leave Panama. His Japanese contact, Araki (Hugh Hoo), tells Eddie to take the plane to L.A., secretly plotting to kill him on the way to the airport. Peggy gets Eddie to the plane safely, but refuses to go with him. Unfortunately, the Nazis are on to her, and boil her to death in a steam bath when she refuses to talk.

Eddie delivers the plans to Tanni on the boat, and recognizes from his college pin as the spymaster. Searching the boat, Eddie finds the Japanese sabotage plan, but Miyazaki catches him. Miyazaki gloats that Eddie will die just like his girlfriend, for "the Japanese do not regard war as a game — war is not a sport contest." Miyazaki kicks Eddie's butt with his martial-arts skills, but then Eddie's good American fists start to take their toll. Miyazaki finally resorts to gunplay, but Eddie grabs the gun and shoots him, only to be shot himself by Miyazaki's men. Fortunately, G-2 arrives, captures the surviving spies and the target list; America is saved.

Pearson wraps up the film by telling us that Eddie was a soldier in an undeclared war that would have been fought in Texas and California if not for heroes like Eddie. The war will end "when the price of complacency has been paid.... The war against underground enemies never begins and never ends. We must not relax again. It can't happen here again!"

2. The Yellow Peril and the Fear of Japan

After the War

In the post-war world, China's conversion to communism and Japan's turning from war meant that China became the Asian menace once again — the threat behind *The Manchurian Candidate*, *Goldfinger* and countless other movie spy schemes. (Anything relevant will be included in the next chapter on the Red menace.)

Despite the hostility toward Japan during the war, the Japanese never became a staple of post-war villainy the way leftover Nazis did. Japan was the setting for a number of films such as *Back at the Front* (1952) and *Stopover Tokyo* (1957) but the villains were Red spies or American schemers rather than leftover imperialists. *Tokyo File 412* (1951) has a Japanese communist spy ring, but even though one spy, Tako, is a former kamikaze pilot, nothing in the movie suggests that non-communist Japanese are hostile to America. Tako is mentally unbalanced because he failed to die honorably (the war ended too soon) but once he regains his wits, he dies fighting for the good guys.

Even movies set back in the war were softer on the Japanese. *Jungle Heat* (1957) opens in Kaui, Hawaii, in November 1941 as hardnosed labor negotiator Roger McRae (Glenn Langan) arrives with his wife Ann (Mari Blanchard) to settle labor problems on local sugar plantations. Unfortunately, his idea of negotiation is to crush the laborers with an iron fist, and he refuses to listen to Dr. Jim Ransom's (Lex Barker) warnings that the sabotage and murder happening around them are the work of Japanese fifth columnists. Mathews (James Westerfield), a white planter working for Japan, tries to exploit McRae's racist contempt for labor radical Felix Agung (Glenn Dixon) to promote dissension and further the sabotage plot.

In the end, Agung kills Mathews, and McRae dies stepping on one of the land mines Mathews planted around his home. Ann and Jim have fallen in love, and as the film ends, Jim assures her that with the spy ring smashed, Japan will give up on invading Hawaii. Today, December 7, begins an exciting new life for both of them.

This hits several familiar themes — Hawaii is rife with Japanese saboteurs, and labor strife is all caused by outside agitators (as was true in fifties anticommunist films). But it also shows a Japanese-American intermarriage among the supporting cast and the wife doesn't turn out to be one of the spies.

Rising Sun (1993) Fresh fears of Japan surfaced in the 1980s, as Japanese cars and home electronics became increasingly popular in America. Just as Arab investment in America was seen as a threat during the 1970s (see chapter five), there were likewise theories that Japan was "attacking" our economy or even that their economic success was revenge for their defeat in World War II.

That was the message of Michael Crichton's 1992 novel *Rising Sun*, in which LAPD Detectives Web Smith and John Connor are assigned to investigate the murder of an American party girl in the boardroom of the Nakamoto Corporation during a major corporate event. Although Connor is a Japanophile who spent years in that country, he's completely pragmatic about the Japanese intentions: Business is war to them, and they'll do whatever it takes to gain economic dominance, including lying through their teeth, which is perfectly ethical by their way of thinking.

It's 1941 and Japanese spies are everywhere in Hawaii, according to *Jungle Heat* (1957). The movie perpetuated the myth that Pearl Harbor was a hotbed of fifth columnists before World War II.

Throughout the book, Connor, helped by some of the other characters, provides readers with a checklist of Japanese schemes: buying up American land (yep, same worry as fifty years earlier), buying up cutting-edge businesses and gaining control of entire technologies by selling below cost in America while keeping American products out of Japan. Nakamato is frighteningly formidable: It has pull with the cops and influence with politicians, and when Smith and Connor go to a university video-technology lab to study a security tape, Nakamoto has the lab closed overnight (they donate a *lot* to the college). Connor admits that France and the United Kingdom are also buying up land and investing in American companies, but insists that's totally different because it's just business, free of any ulterior motives.

The 1993 movie adaptation of *Rising Sun* tones down the racism and political paranoia by eliminating most of Connor's (Sean Connery) lectures on how the Japanese are systematically taking us over, and how their approach to business is totally different from that of westerners. An off-hand comment that "business is war, war is never over ... all's fair in love and war ... and we're in the war zone" is as close as we get.

General economic warfare is also toned down as a plot element. The book centered on control of MicroCon, a cutting edge computer company that would increase Japan's

2. The Yellow Peril and the Fear of Japan

clout in that field if Nakamoto bought it up. In the film, MicroCon is a defense contractor, and the danger is that control of MicroCon would give Japan some sort of control over U.S. weapons (the explanation is a little fuzzy). In best "boogeyman" fashion, the plot hardly changes at all (though the killer in the movie is now an American character, rather than the Japanese murderer in the book); generic corporate skullduggery works just as well as innate Japanese treachery to explain things.

With Japan's economy no longer the wonder of the world and multiple other foreign threats overshadowing it, paranoia directed at Japan seems to have faded. But who knows what the 21st century may bring us?

3

The Red Menace
*Bolsheviks, Commies and
Atheists in America*

The fear of Communism and related "unAmerican" ideologies has with us a long while. In the 19th century, Americans worried about anarchists; before World War I they feared socialists and Bolsheviks; even in the 21st century, charges that President Barack Obama is a socialist or communist are taken seriously by some Americans

America's first serious "Red scare" took place in 1919 and 1920. In his book on the panic, Robert Murray lists several reasons why communism became a hot issue at the time, starting with the Bolshevik overthrow of the Russian government and Russia subsequently making peace with Germany in World War I. That, in itself, branded communism or Bolshevism (and the number of Americans who could distinguish Trotskyites, Bolsheviks, Mensheviks and other strains of communist thought was small) as an enemy of "100 percent Americanism."

Labor radicalism and the opposition of American socialists to World War I, coupled with wartime America's general intolerance of dissent (speaking out against the war or the draft became illegal under the Espionage and Sedition Acts), also fueled anticommunist paranoia. Critics of organized labor portrayed several prominent strikes — including a general strike in Seattle in support of a shipyard walkout, and a police strike in Boston — as the work of communist subversives whose goal was not better wages but the destruction of the American system.

The mood of America worsened when radicals carried out multiple terrorist bombings. Then anti–Bolsheviks attempted to storm a union hall in Centralia, only to be met by gunfire. The shooters were arrested and a mob dragged one from his cell and lynched him. Newspapers and groups such as the Ku Klux Klan milked the events for all they were worth, whipping up hysteria against the Red menace. All of this ultimately erupted into a general war on communists and radicals. Attorney General Mitchell Palmer, whose house had been destroyed by one of the bombs, rounded up foreigners in the so-called Palmer Raids and deported hundreds of immigrants for their radical beliefs, using administrative procedures to avoid court trials.

Many states passed laws against sedition or against membership in radical groups. In January 1920, the New York legislature expelled five socialists from their seats, solely because of their beliefs, despite the fact that they hadn't been charged or even accused of

3. The Red Menace

any crimes. (An earlier case, involving a Wisconsin national representative, had at least invoked the Espionage and Sedition Acts.) When the special election to replace them put them back in office, three of them were once again expelled.

For many Americans this marked a turning point: Denying the people their right to have their elected representative seated was a blow to everyone's concept of democracy. It didn't hurt that with the war behind them, the public was ready to embrace peace and peacetime concerns and the hysteria drained away. When a bomb went off on Wall Street on September 20, 1920, Palmer, who had presidential ambitions, once again uttered dire warnings of an ominous conspiracy and a national threat. But despite the 29 people killed by the bomb, there was no repeat of the Red scare.

Even so, Murray argues that the panic left its mark on America, spurring the growth of Americanist groups such as the KKK and the American Legion, which was founded in 1919 to support "100 percent Americanism." The scare also gave America a continuing hostility to labor organizing and a lingering suspicion that there was no peace to be had with the Soviet Union . The U.S.A. didn't recognize the USSR until 1933, making it the last nation to do so.

During the silent era, several films portrayed the subversive threat of communism on labor. In *Dangerous Hours* (1920), John King (Lloyd Hughes) is seduced by Bolshevik agitator Sophia Guerni (Claire DuBrey) and joins her in a campaign of labor agitation, even when it targets the shipyard run by his childhood sweetheart May (Barbara Castleton), who supports John's poverty-stricken father. When Sophia and her ally Blotchi (Jack Richardson) try to extort protection from May, John's father is wounded trying to protect her. The agitators attack and bomb the plant, but John drives them off and renounces Bolshevism.

The idea that labor unrest was all the work of commie agitators would be a recurrent movie theme during the 1950s. Films showed that sensible, anticommunist labor leaders are always able to negotiate a deal with their bosses; only radicals push for strikes and they never do it to improve wages or working conditions, but only to paralyze American industry or cripple American's war machine.

In the thirties, the fear of American communism remained strong, but movies tended to portray it more for laughs than anything else: In *Public Deb. No. 1* (1940), embracing communism is just one of those silly things that madcap heiress Penny Cooper (Brenda Joyce) does, and eventually gets beaten out of her. *Soak the Rich* (1936) likewise portrays Communism as a crackpot notion that kids get when they're young.

The same attitude is present in *Fighting Youth* (1935), a fifth-column college comedy (and how often does anyone get to say that?). Wealthy campus radical Carol Arlingon (Ann Sheridan) accepts an assignment from "the Central Committee" (of what, the movie doesn't say, though it's unlikely the viewers had any problem figuring it out) to whip up the student body against college football. Her handler, Markoff (Alden Chase), explains that student movements aren't strong enough to take on the system, but destroying State College's football program will whet their appetite for revolution, making it easy to turn them against "the existing social order."

Screen Enemies of the American Way

Charles Farrell and June Martel embrace in this publicity pose for *Fighting Youth* (1935), the movie in which communists scheme to destroy college football to give their dupes practice at smashing American institutions.

Carol flirts with Larry (Charles Farrell)—All-American quarterback, ROTC student and devoted swain to his girlfriend Betty (June Martel)—and makes radical accusations that football is actually a money-machine for colleges, exploiting students and putting them at risk of injury. ("You get a licking, they get the money.") Reformers did in fact make these arguments in the 1930s (particularly after several fatalities in college football), though they had little traction with the public. Invoking them in *Fighting Youth* may have been a way to imply they were un–American ideas, or that commies were crackpots for believing such things.

When Larry sides with Carol's views during a meeting of the radical League of Freedom, Betty accuses Carol of manipulating Larry, knowing he's too dumb to catch on. This infuriates Larry, who's also shaken by the controversy. At the next big game, his fumble costs the team a win, and rumors start flying that he threw the game. The coach schedules a brutal practice session, during which Larry injures his best friend. Convinced that Carol was right, Larry quits.

The cops are on to Markoff's shady activities by now, searching his room for his contact list for the Central Committee and frisking him whenever he leaves. Tony (Edward

3. The Red Menace

Nugent), a League of Freedom member, helps out by asking Betty to pick up the code book, then steals it from her when she does. In the dean's office, Tony reveals he's one of a hundred federal agents infiltrating colleges "to help uncover enemy agents who are taking definite steps to destroy the American form of government." He identifies Markoff as a foreign spy and arrests him, then tells the dean that "where you give them intellectual freedom, we must give them protection from enemy agitators." Larry returns to the team and reunites with Betty. The college expels Carol, who gets a spanking from the police before leaving for home.

This lightweight comedy foreshadows several themes that would be used in fifties anticommunist films: Activists and radicals are either enemy agents or Red dupes; leftwing issues are only a tool for attaining power; and when the feds spy on us, it's always for the greater good.

The 1950s Red Scare

After Pearl Harbor, and Germany's declaration of war on the U.S., the Soviets became our allies and criticism of them in the movies ceased; instead, we got *Mission to Moscow* and similar starry-eyed views of the USSR, such as 1943's *Song of Russia* and *The North Star*. It was the post–World War II period when the fear of communism blossomed into a major political force that would influence American politics until the collapse of the Soviet Union.

One reason was that the end of World War II had left the Soviets solidly in control of Eastern Europe, and the U.S.A. was in no position to do much about it. Under Stalin's control, the repression was brutal, totalitarian and ruthless, horrifying the rest of the world.

Then China's corrupt, nominally democratic government fell to Mao's revolutionaries — which many Americans saw as us "losing" China rather than an internal power struggle. Since it was assumed that communism was a monolithic block with all communist nations united and marching in lockstep (much the same way some Americans assume all 21st century Muslim leaders and movement at odds with the United States are working together), that meant the greater part of Eurasia was under the control of an international conspiracy. Years of effort by American missionaries to Christianize and Americanize China (as David Halberstam recounts in *The Coldest Winter*) made the loss all the more shocking.

The combination of all these setbacks, as Halberstam says, made it easier to believe that communist agents within the American government had undermined our fight against Russia; for many people, that made more sense than believing Chiang's government was incompetent, that the luck of the draw in postwar Europe had favored the USSR or that America had screwed up. Other events intensified this belief:

- The Alger Hiss trial, which exposed Hiss, a State Department official, as a communist spy. The fact that he'd served in a minor function at Yalta was cited as proof that America's post-war policies had been shaped by subversives.

- The USSR permanently changed the balance of power by detonating Joe One, its first atom bomb. As Air Force General Curtis LeMay said, using our nukes to wipe them off the map was no longer an option. More alarming still, it turned out the Soviets had gained the technology through espionage with the help of Manhattan Project physicist Klaus Fuchs and spies Julius and Ethel Rosenberg.

And then, of course, came Sen. Joe McCarthy. Speaking in Wisconsin in 1950, McCarthy claimed 205 people in the U.S. State Department were communists or communist fellow travelers (i.e., sympathetic, but not Party members). Even though McCarthy couldn't keep the number consistent from one speech to the next, the press seized on his charges and propelled him to national fame. Other anticommunist activists were even more extreme: Robert Welch, founder of the John Birch Society, claimed that both Eisenhower and Truman were communist puppets.

A big difference between this panic and the fears of Nazi infiltration is that where Nazi agents were passing themselves off as ordinary Americans, the Communist Party of the United States of America was easily identifiable as the public face of the supposed Soviet conspiracy against us. To be a member of the Communist Party was by definition to be against America.

The House Un-American Activities Committee (HUAC) grilled communists in the movie industry; the movie and television industries aggressively pink-slipped communists, alleged communists, and people who'd done something left-wing that might be construed as communist; the FBI aggressively hounded and harassed party members, and used double agents to infiltrate the party (informant Herb Philbrick said he was recruited in 1939).

Under Truman, communists were driven out of the government. Starting in 1949, party leaders were put on trial under the Smith Act, which made it a crime to advocate the overthrow of any federal, state or local American government by force. As Victor Navsky notes in *Naming Names*, even when the accused hadn't advocated anything of the sort, there were plenty of "expert" witnesses to testify that communists talked in code and violent overthrow was what their innocuous statements really meant.

One of the first major anticommunist films, *Walk a Crooked Mile* (1948) portrays the combined efforts of British and American agents to derail a communist plot to steal A-bomb secrets by using a spy with a photographic memory. The movie assures us that our government will always be ready to protect us from the enemies who "walk a crooked mile." Done in quasi-documentary style and patterned after *The House on 92nd Street* (1945)—which dramatized the capture of the Nazi Duquesne spy ring—the movie isn't politically paranoid, focusing more on Red spies than CPUSA members. Realism about Soviet spy efforts would disappear, however, in the next decade as McCarthyism took hold of Hollywood.

Time and again, the movies would dive into a pool of paranoia and emerge with the same themes:

- The Communist Party is directly controlled by Moscow, is dedicated to the destruction of America and spies, kills and spreads propaganda for the USSR.

3. The Red Menace

It's certainly true that the American Communist Party followed dutifully along with whatever political winds blew out of Moscow. When Russia and Germany had a non-aggression pact, the party condemned Lillian Hellman's play *Watch on the Rhine* for its anti-fascist themes; when the movie version came out in 1943, after the two nations were at war, it was hailed for its anti-fascist themes.

In movies, however, it goes further: Every last American communist is a Soviet spy or a "useful idiot" who doesn't see the truth. American communists are constantly getting orders and directions from Soviet emissaries, spymasters and couriers.

- Fighting the communists in America is no different from fighting the Korean War.

  In *Big Jim McLain* (1952), American communists in Hawaii are plotting to disrupt America's supply lines to Korea. Mal (Jim Arness), a Korea veteran turned HUAC investigator, sees American Reds as no different from the North Korean armed forces. In *My Son John* (1952), a federal agent tells Helen Hayes that just as her sons are fighting for America in Korea, Americans must support the troops by fighting communists at home.

- The Communist Party actively engages in murder and espionage, and many members are trained for that purpose. In the *I Led Three Lives* episode "Newsreel," a

Driving away from *The Red Menace* (1949), Bill (Robert Rockwell, right) and Nina (Hanne Axman) wonder if they'll survive the party's murderous revenge on turncoats (other two actors unidentified).

communist-controlled newsreel company makes training films for party members to learn about explosives and sabotage. In *The Red Menace* (1949), *The Woman on Pier 13* (1950) and *I Was a Communist for the FBI* (1951), people who leave the party or try to name names get murdered.

- The integrity of our government isn't in question. The FBI and HUAC are above reproach.

HUAC's hunt for communists in Hollywood never turned up any spies, but the movies present the committee as a formidable threat to the Red espionage agenda, much as they portrayed Japanese internment as a success. Like *I Was a Communist...*, *Big Jim McLain* presents HUAC as heroes fighting to save us from communism, "undaunted by the campaign of slander waged against them." In *My Son John*, Stedman (Van Heflin) asserts that the FBI's methods are only questioned by those it hunts.

The same is true of the informants in television's *I Was a Communist for the FBI* and *I Led Three Lives*. Screen informants were heroes, exposing a terrible threat to America at great personal risk. As the FBI tells Matt Cvetic (Frank Lovejoy) in *I Was a Communist for the FBI*, the bureau can't reveal that it's infiltrating the party, so if informers are publicly identified as Reds, their careers and lives will be ruined.

In reality, many informers and repentant communists went on to highly successful careers as "professional witnesses," giving lectures, serving as consultants, writing books or becoming the subject of flattering movies; Pittsburgh proclaimed a Matt Cvetic Day. Critics have charged that despite the witnesses' professions of patriotism, some of them, such as Cvetic, were on the FBI payroll. Some of them also lied: Informant Manning Johnson told a court that labor leader Harry Bridges had attended a 1936 communist convention, only to have Bridges prove conclusively he'd been elsewhere. Manning later said that he'd willingly lie "if the interests of my government are at stake ... I will do it a thousand times." In another case, Johnson said perjury was justified if it was necessary to hide FBI intelligence-gathering methods. (He later recanted both statements.)

The movie Cvetic, however, is all patriot, soldiering on even when his own son despises him for being a Red. And that's despite the fact that the party will have him killed in an instant if they realize which side he's really on. In *I Led Three Lives*, Philbrick (Richard Carlson) constantly reminds us of the incredible risk if he's exposed as a spy; in the memoir on which the series is based, by contrast, the most danger Philbrick can offer is to hint that one suicide he heard about might have been murder, maybe.

- Communists are horrible human beings.

There are two kinds of communists in the movies of this period: The dupes who believe in the ideals the party spouts, and the real communists, who don't believe in anything but power. Cvetic's cohort Blandon (James Millican) is a complete hypocrite who makes rabble-rousing civil rights speeches, then laughs at the

3. The Red Menace

"niggers" who believe him, and mocks Matt for actually caring about the working class. In *Big Jim McLain*, a Red spy likewise grumbles about how annoying the genuine idealists are. In *Conspirator* (1950), Robert Taylor doesn't say much about Marxism but one of the first warning signs he's not a good guy is when he's completely unmoved by the sight of a rabbit injured in a steel trap.

This, of course, simplifies the problems of anticommunist heroes turning against their friends in the party: They don't have any. They might have grown fond of some of the well-meaning dupes, but those characters either renounce communism and leave or renounce communism and die; by the time the hero calls in the cops, there's nobody to arrest but seriously evil people. In 1987's *Pack of Lies*, Ellen Burstyn is wracked with guilt over helping the government spy on her best friend; anticommunist heroes of the forties and fifties have no such qualms. In the nine years Philbrick spent as a Red, he apparently never met anyone he liked, judging from his book.

In fifties films, even love of family crumbles when communism is involved. *Big Jim McLain* and *My Son John* both tell viewers that if their children become Reds, the ethical thing to do is report them immediately. In the latter movie, Dan (Dean Jagger) tells John (Robert Walker) he would kill him if he were a Red, and tells John's mother (Helen Hayes) that "that's communism's specialty — splitting up families." In *Conspirator*, Taylor is told that his marriage is against the will of the party and is later ordered to murder his wife after she learns about his spying.

- Commies are atheists.

Movies and propaganda repeatedly held up communism's atheism as proof and explanation of their evil: As one communist's father tells Jim McLain (John Wayne), it's impossible to reason with "heartless men who've turned their back on God!"

In an informational short, *What Is Communism?*, Herb Philbrick claims that "atheist" is the most frightening word he can use to describe commies because it means they have no moral compass, hate religion and that "any wrong they do is right." (The same argument, of course, is still routinely made against atheists who aren't communists.)

In *My Son John*, John tells a group of students that questioning Catholic teaching was his first step to becoming an enemy of America; when he swears on the Bible that he's not a communist, Dan tells Lucille that such an oath is meaningless to a Red. In *Red Nightmare*, the hero discovers Reds have turned his local church into a museum exhibiting the accomplishments of Soviet science, such as the Russian invention of the telephone.

- The civil rights movement is a communist plot.

In the real world, the Communist Party took a stand in favor of civil rights at a time when Republicans and Democrats found it politically convenient to keep quiet. In the movies, this is a sham, and minorities are just one more tool for destroying America. The heroes themselves aren't bigots—Matt Cvetic objects to Blandon's use of the word "nigger"—but they understand that Americans must stand united against the Red Menace, and the party is stirring up racial hatred to undermine that.

The films' handling of the civil rights movement dovetails with real-world accusations that "outside agitators" were whipping up African Americans who would otherwise be perfectly happy under segregation. It also carries over from anti–Nazi films, where we were repeatedly warned that dissension and disunion were the fifth column's greatest weapons.

In *My Son John*, John's concern for minorities is one of the signs that he's no longer thinking like a real American. Philbrick's book says one of the first things that troubled him about the pacifist Red-front group he joined in the thirties was when they started pushing civil rights. In one episode of the *I Led Three Lives* series, the party plots to spread propaganda that minorities in America suffer from racial discrimination.

In *The Red Menace*, a black writer on a communist paper quits after his father tells him that America ended slavery, whereas thousands of people behind the Iron Curtain are enslaved by the communists. In 1955's *Trial*, heroic attorney Glenn Ford is clearly sympathetic to his client—a Hispanic boy whose real crime is falling for a white girl—but there's no hint that a legitimate civil rights movement exists. The only organized support is a phony fund-raising group created by commie attorney Arthur Kennedy, who plans to give the cash to the party, then turn the boy into a martyr to American racism.

The link between civil rights and communism still exists for some conservatives. In 1996, pundit Robert Stacy McCain asserted that communists were promoting affirmative action and interracial dating in the hopes that whites, who have "an altogether natural revulsion" to interracial relationships, will respond by trying to reassert white supremacy in America, resulting in the country tearing itself apart. *I Was a Communist*'s Blandon would be proud.

- Labor unrest is all the work of commies.

    In contrast to the portrayal of the Civil Rights movement, anticommunist films never suggest that unions and labor rights are bad, and we run into plenty of "good" labor leaders who hate communists.

    Strikes, however? As noted earlier, those are invariably portrayed as the work of communist agitators overriding the good, honest laborers. This fits the concept of communists turning us against each other—and, of course, Hollywood studio heads were notoriously anti-union.

- Communists can exert influence way out of potential to their numbers.

    The movies make this point over and over again: Sure, there aren't many communists in America, but with their skills at subversion, it doesn't take many to seize control of a labor union, or a nation. In *The Woman on Pier 13*, Christine (Janis Carter) asserts that one Party member can indoctrinate a thousand more;

In *I Married a Communist* aka *The Woman on Pier 13* (1950), Nan Collins (Laraine Day) makes the mistake of marrying Brad (Robert Ryan) after a one-week relationship. His communist past will destroy their marriage and get her brother killed.

Jim (Richard Rober), an honest union leader, says that while the union only has a few Party members, "every one is an active Party agent" who manipulates "well-meaning liberals, the underprivileged, the unemployed."

This was a belief taken seriously in the real world. In 1936, the American Legion announced that "there are more Communists in the United States today than there were in Russia when the government was overthrown."

- At the same time, communists are everywhere.

Philbrick warns us in his book that respectable businessmen, teachers, artists and laborers can all be Party members, which is to say, Soviet agents. Eve in *I Was a Communist ...* is one of dozens of teachers corrupting the minds of youth, while Cvetic and his cohorts infiltrate the unions. A prominent anticommunist in *Big Jim McLain* is a Red agent. In *The Fearmakers* (1958), seemingly nonpartisan political messages are being shaped by a Red-controlled PR firm to promote a "peace at any price" outlook in America.

The next chapter shows how these themes play out in individual films of the late forties and 1950s

4

Red Scare

Fifth Column Anticommunist Films from 1949 to 1960

The Woman on Pier 13 (1949) An excellent example of the "bogeyman" principle, this film — also known by the more memorable title *I Married a Communist*— amounts to a gangster movie with "communist" penciled over "crime syndicate." It fits perfectly with Herb Philbrick's claim that "the communist mind is a criminal mind."

As the movie opens, things look great for Brad Collins (Robert Ryan): He's risen from dockworker to middle management, representing a shipping firm in upcoming labor negotiations. He's also newly married to Nan (Laraine Day) after a whirlwind weeklong courtship, winning her away from his best friend Jim (Richard Rober), a union leader.

Then the sinister Vanning (Thomas Gomez) shows up with proof that Brad is really Frank Johnson, a communist enforcer and labor agitator during his "angry young man" days in the Depression. Brad tells Vanning that he's rejected communism and nobody will hold it against him now — but Vanning also has proof that Frank killed a strikebreaker during a brawl. Vanning summons Brad to his headquarters in an abandoned waterfront warehouse, where Brad watches a Red hitman, Bailey (William Talman), throw a squealer off the dock in concrete shoes.

Vanning orders Brad to wreck the negotiations, setting management and labor at each other's throats and shutting down the waterfront. His return to the party also reconnects him with his former lover Christine (Janis Carter). When Brad makes it clear he's going to stay faithful to Nan, Christine spitefully seduces Nan's brother Don (John Agar). Her friends soon have Don indoctrinated, turning him into a firebrand agitator spouting radical ideas and poisoning the negotiations further. He and Christine fall in love for real; when Don realizes she's a communist, he rejects her. Knowing he idolizes Brad, Christine reveals Brad's membership to prove Reds can be decent people.

Big mistake: Vanning doesn't want Brad outed, so he has Don killed, then arranges Christine's "suicide." Christine, however, has already told Nan about Brad in hopes of hurting her. Nan, suspecting the deaths were murder, flirts with Bailey to get the goods on Vanning, but winds up a prisoner at the warehouse. Brad arrives and saves her, but gets fatally wounded in a shootout. As he dies, he tells her to go back to Jim.

In contrast to most other anticommunist films of this era, *The Woman on Pier 13* does very little explaining of communist doctrine and focuses far more on their criminal

Robert Ryan (left) gives advice to love-smitten brother-in-law John Agar in *The Woman on Pier 13* (1950) — a waste of time since neither one will make it to the end of the movie alive.

deeds. It's also unusual for having Brad wind up dead, rather than turning on the party and redeeming himself as Bill (Robert Rockwell) does in *The Red Menace*. The 2004 alternate-history documentary *C.S.A. — Confederate States of America* parodied this as *I Married an Abolitionist*.

The Red Menace (1949) After the opening credits roll — imposed on the image of an octopus encircling the world — we see Bill (Robert Rockwell) and Nina (Hanne Axman) driving desperately through the night. Both are so afraid "they" will find them that when a gas station attendant asks a question, Nina flinches.

"What is this fear that has sent them racing along a lonely Arizona road?" the narrator, Los Angeles City Council member Lloyd Davies, asks. "Is it the FBI? Immigration? ... They could be running for something far more terrifying."

We flash back a few months and learn that Bill, a veteran, lost his last cent buying a home in a crooked housing project, and is outraged that the government can't get his money back. Jack Tyler (William J. Lally) convinces Bill that when the system screws people over, it's the Communist Party that fights for them; Tyler introduces Bill to flirty

4. Red Scare

Molly (Barbra Fuller), idealistic poet Henry (Shepard Menken), and Yvonne (Betty Lou Gerson), an East European femme fatale who is displeased that Molly moves in on Bill first. (It's clear, though unstated, that Molly takes Bill to bed.) Partridge (Lester Luther), who publishes the Red newspaper *The Toilers*, tells Tyler that once Bill joins the party, he won't be able to leave.

Molly, a typical dupe, doesn't understand the ideology or big words the party higher-ups use, but tells Bill the party is anti-fascist, pro-labor and pro-civil rights. Having seen her non-union father screwed over by his employer, she's pleased that communists are "trying to end the exploitation of humanity... We're for people, not privileges or property." Her mother, however, believes that any system that let Molly's father support his family is a good one, and refuses to accept any of the support money Molly makes working for *The Toilers*.

After Bill becomes a member, he meets Nina, an East European and lifelong communist in charge of bringing veterans, students and professors to the protest over the crooked housing deal. Narrator Davies tells us that Bill "has fallen under the spell of Marxian hatred and revenge, unaware that he is only the tool of men who would destroy his country. The [protest] signs didn't tell of the worldwide Marxist racket intent on spreading dissension and treason." Sure enough, Yvonne urges the protesters to turn the event into a riot.

Later, when Nina invites Bill to her Philosophy of Communism class, Davies explains that whatever communists claim to believe, the real message is that "there are no positive values, no eternal principles of right and wrong — it's the old doctrine of atheism, sugar-coated with highbrow terms. It says men are not responsible to anyone except the totalitarian state." And since Stalin embraces ruling through force, that proves that all American communists think the same.

To prove Davies' point, when Reachi (Norman Budd) asks how dictatorship of the proletariat can be better than any other dictatorship, Yvonne tells the "dago" that "we'll have our way if it means bloodshed and terror, if we have to liquidate a million milksops like you." Commie goons fatally beat Reachi; *The Toilers* blames his death on anticommunist thugs. When Nina is visibly upset by these recent events, Yvonne begins to suspect her as a possible turncoat.

Nina's not the only doubter. Molly's family priest (Leo Cleary) shakes her and Henry's faith by telling them that in contrast to great American principles such as In God We Trust, "atheistic systems are always based on hatred — race hatred in fascism, class hatred in communism." Then Partridge condemns Henry for writing a poem that states (accurately) that Marx built on the work of previous thinkers. Henry suddenly realizes that the party doesn't accept freedom of speech and can't be compatible with American democracy.

Henry tells Partridge and Yvonne that true communists are "sociopathic misfits" spreading dissension and hate, and he tears up his membership card. It isn't that easy, however: Partridge keeps getting him fired by tipping off his employers about his party membership, and his Red friends are forbidden to speak with him. Molly remains loyal to him, but Henry realizes that Partridge might give her the same treatment. To avoid that, he kills himself, after convincing Molly to leave the party. The priest consoles her with the thought that "the best way for us to defeat communism is for us to live Christianity and American democracy every day of our lives."

Sam (Duke Williams), a black writer on *The Toilers*, is the next to leave, after his father (Napoleon Simpson) compares America, which ended slavery, to communism, which keeps millions in chains. Before quitting the paper, Sam, who was reluctantly working on an obit smearing Henry, rewrites it to show the poet as a proud patriot.

Next it's Nina's turn. She tells Bill — they've fallen in love — that America is the utopia communism pretends it will bring about. Nevertheless, it would only require a small group of disciplined communist fanatics to take over America, the same way they've enslaved so many other countries. When Bill learns that Nina is at risk for deportation (she lied about her party membership to Immigration), they take off into the night, unaware that Yvonne has been arrested for Reachi's murder. When the police identify her as an East German spy, Yvonne conveniently goes insane, hallucinating that Red troops are already invading and not only confessing to the murder but implicating Partridge and Tyler in another killing.

Bill finally convinces Nina they need to go to the police. In the next town they come to, they pull over and visit with the folksy sheriff, who laughs that they've been living in a world of deceit so long, they've forgotten how good and decent America is. As they've renounced communism and haven't committed any crimes — except the immigration lie, which will certainly be forgiven — they should stop worrying and get married. Heartened, they leave the sheriff's office, then realize they never learned his name. A kid playing nearby tells them that everyone calls the sheriff by his nickname — Uncle Sam.

Having Uncle Sam show up, sort of, is typical of the American symbols that anticommunist films like to invoke. In *The Fearmakers*, a fistfight between the hero and villain resolves the movie on the steps of the Lincoln Memorial, which is also where John (in *My Son John*) dies when he turns against the party (after his mother has a key discussion at the Jefferson Memorial). *Red Nightmare* ends with a string of images, from the Capitol building to Fourth of July picnics.

The movie touches on the idea that communist women used sex to seduce men into joining or collaborating with the party, something supposedly made easier because as atheists, they had no moral standards. Bill accuses Molly of coming on to him to manipulate him; Matt Cvetic makes a similar suggestion to one woman in *I Was a Communist for the FBI*.

I Was a Communist for the FBI (1951). East Germany's Gerhard Eisler (Konstantin Shayne) — "Communist agent, spy, convicted perjurer" — arrives in Pittsburgh, which steelworker and FBI informant Matt Cvetic (Frank Lovejoy) describes in voice-over as "the strong heart of American might — but commies have planted themselves to throw that heart off-beat." As a rising star in the Pittsburgh Communist Party, Matt — after an awkward visit with his family, who think of him as a "slimy Red" — is summoned to meet Eisler.*

At Eisler's suite, Matt and the local party leaders enjoy a sumptuous meal, which one Red assures Matt will be the norm once they take over. When Matt asks if workers

---

*In the real world, according to Ellen Schrecker in *Many Are the Crimes*, Eisler had been a representative of Moscow's Comintern in the thirties but had lost his clout by the end of the forties, and wanted nothing more than to leave America and go home.

4. Red Scare

will eat this well, fellow commie Blandon (James Millican) sneers that "the workers will still be the workers." While mocking Matt's idealism, Blandon commends him to Eisler for finding party members jobs in the steel industry while keeping loyal Americans out. Eisler promotes Matt to local party organizer, telling him that to derail America's economy, the party "must incite riots, discontent, open warfare."

Blandon, a Moscow-trained orator, starts (in Cvetic's words) "cooking up a hellbrew of hate from a recipe written in the Kremlin"—that is, he delivers a civil rights speech to the city's black community. We don't hear the specifics, but Cvetic assures us it's "the same old line they'd used for years on all racial minorities to create unrest and confusion.... [W]hat he's doing is as dangerous as blowing up defense plants—it's the old rule of divide and conquer." Blandon admits later that he hopes to incite the "niggers" to riots or assault, after which the party will raise money for a defense fund, then funnel the cash into its own operating funds. Matt's FBI contact Crowley (Richard Webb) tells Matt that these same tactics have triggered riots elsewhere, and gotten blacks killed.

Matt's personal life takes another hit when his son Dick (Ron Hagerthy) learns he's a communist. Dick reminds his pop he's almost old enough to be drafted and sent to

Matt Cvetic (Frank Lovejoy) stands symbolically alone, cut off from the good guys to his left by his Communist Party membership, and from the commies on his right by his counterspy work for the FBI. A publicity shot for *I Was a Communist for the FBI* (1951).

fight commies and adds that he'd sooner die than follow in Matt's footsteps. Unable to tell Dick the truth, Matt writes a letter explaining everything and asks the family priest to give it to Dick if he (Matt) dies.

Dick's teacher Eve (Dorothy Hart) flirts with Matt, then reveals herself to be a communist who admires Matt's heartfelt speeches. Eve admits that her party membership breaks her loyalty oath as a teacher, but the chance to spread communism to Pittsburgh's youth justifies her lying (ditto the thirty other Red teachers in the schools). Matt suggests she's also using sex to spread communism, but Eve makes it clear she isn't. She is, however, spying on Matt for Blandon, but even after finding the letter, she tells Blandon that Matt is a loyal party member.

Increasingly frustrated with the estrangement from his family, Matt tells Crowley he wants "the Red stain" washed off. Crowley tells Matt that the FBI can't identify its spies, so even after his work is done, his name will remain tarnished. Matt decides that he values American freedom too much to stop fighting for it.

At the next union meeting, Red agents pack the hall and outlast the real Americans, who are exhausted from the hard day's work. By 3 A.M., enough men have gone home that the party has the votes to force a strike. When it begins, the commies spread further dissension by having thugs assault strikers with lead pipes wrapped in Jewish newspapers. When Eve objects, one woman tells her that in Moscow she'd be executed; Eve points out that they're in Pittsburgh. The brutal incident makes Eve realize that communism's real goal "is to gain complete control of every human mind in the world!" She tells Blandon she's going to "out" every Red teacher, then goes to Matt and thanks him for showing her the truth. Matt realizes Blandon will have Eve killed and helps her escape, killing a party assassin who tries to stop her (the gunmen do manage to knock off a G-man watching over Eve).

At the next party gathering, another envoy from the party leaders tells Matt and Blandon that HUAC is badly damaging the Red spy network so "all communists are to spread the word that the members of the Un-American Committee are a bunch of fat-headed politicians whose only interest is to crash the headlines." The party will also help the communists in Korea by criticizing the military, "spreading doubt, fear, defeatism.... [W]hen Comrade Stalin calls the play, the panic of the American people will mean power and glory for us all."

Matt asks why the Party isn't raising money to defend its leaders in the Smith Act trials. Blandon tells him the party has created a fake fascist movement and will follow it up by creating an antifascist front group that will divert any funds it raises to the Smith Act legal costs.

Matt is thrilled when he's called to New York to testify in the trial and redeem his reputation — but the FBI decides the case is a slam-dunk, and he's still too valuable as a double agent to waste. Apparently his value plummets after that because a few days later, the FBI authorizes him to testify before HUAC. Matt happily tells the committee that the CPUSA's "political activities are nothing more than a front. It is a vast spy system founded in this country by the Soviet. It is composed of American traitors whose only purpose is to deliver the Untied States into the hands of Russia as a slave colony."

4. Red Scare

In the aftermath, Blandon assaults Matt only to learn the hard way that he's no match for a 100 percent American. Dick, now drafted into the Navy, rushes up and embraces Matt, who tells Dick that "even when you hated me, I loved you for it."

In addition to the movie, *I Was a Communist for the FBI* became a radio series from 1952 to 1954.

The Whip Hand (1951) RKO's *The Whip Hand* began life as *The Man He Found*, in which a reporter discovers that Nazis have covertly taken over a small town and that Hitler himself is holed up on a nearby estate, plotting his return to power. This didn't suit the studio boss, Howard Hughes, who reworked it into a fifth column thriller about a communist outpost plotting germ warfare.

The film begins "behind the walls of the Kremlin" where Soviets are studying a map of the United States and singling out the town of Winnoga as if it were as vital as New York.

Cut to Matt Corben (Elliott Reid), a reporter on a fishing vacation who heads to Winnoga after injuring himself out in the wilderness. After a wrong turn that takes Matt to a heavily guarded estate, he reaches town and Dr. Keller (Edgar Barrier) and his sister Janet (Carla Balenda) patch him up. Matt learns that Winnoga's famous trout lakes had a massive fish kill a couple of years back, ending the tourist trade, yet a man named Loomis (Raymond Burr) arrived and bought the local hotel right after that happened.

We learn the townies are constantly watched and that there's plotting afoot at the estate. Matt learns that Keller is a bacteriologist and suspects the trout die-off was man-made. Matt photographs a laboratory on the estate and although the guards destroy his photos, he gets a message to his editor about a man he saw there. The editor identifies him as Buchholtz (Otto Waldis), a Nazi scientist now working for the USSR, and alerts the FBI, who suspect that Buchholtz is working with American communists.

Keller is ordered to kill his sister, but Matt saves her. Matt and Janet sneak onto the estate and discover that Buchholtz is using Soviet traitors as guinea pigs for a bubonic plague bio-weapon. The Reds capture them, but they escape and hitch a ride with an old woman — who's a spy and returns them to Buchholtz. Matt escapes again, while Keller dies to save his sister from becoming a guinea pig.

Matt leads the FBI back to the state to confront Buchholtz. One agent asks Buchholtz how a legendary humanitarian — a description that comes completely out of left field — can become a mass murderer; Buchholtz replies that by wiping out the enemies of communism, he's serving humanity (no explanation how his Nazi work fits with his humanitarian vision). Buchholtz plots to blow up the lab from inside, sacrificing his own life to spread the plague, but Matt makes it inside, saves the day and, of course, gets the girl.

The idea that Nazis would naturally go to work for communists was a popular one in spy thrillers of the period — after all, both were evil forces that wanted to destroy democracy — and it's true that a number of Nazis did. However, the argument ignores that a great many Nazis were just as happy to work for us.

Invasion USA (1952) There's only a little fifth-column activity in this film, but the paranoia level is pretty high. We open in a New York bar where the patrons direct the bartender to mute the TV, which is running some silly story about mystery planes flying over Alaska. Potter (Gerald Mohr), a reporter, grills the others on the merits of the government forcing factories to switch to armament-making and instituting a draft for factory labor.

Nobody's enthused. Mulfory (Erik Blythe), a rancher, grumbles about taxes and over-regulation; glamour girl Carla (Peggie Castle) says she quit volunteering in World War II because factory work spoiled her hands; Sylvester (Robert Bice), a San Francisco tractor-maker, has already turned down requests to switch to tanks; and Congressman Harroway (Wade Crosby) says his constituents want communism crushed, but without having to fight or make sacrifices themselves. Mr. Ohman (Dan O'Herlihy) suggests that if they want the Cold War ended magically, they should just elect Merlin president, then gives the barflies a hypnotic stare and leaves.

Suddenly, the television news reports that the Alaskan planes have begun bombing runs, and we see footage of a merchant vessel dropping its American flag and bringing out hidden munitions. Airfields and ports fall to the enemy forces; the aggressors are

Love in a time of war: Gerald Mohr and Peggie Castle embrace in *Invasion USA* (1952), only to die a few scenes later as communist forces storm New York.

never identified but once again, they're definitely not Portuguese. The enemy then moves south to hook up with their Pacific fleet, taking over the West Coast with the strategic use of A-bombs and atomic torpedoes. The barflies soon pay the price for their apathy: Sylvester, after learning ten more tanks could have saved San Francisco, dies fighting after the enemy takes over his factory (his window washer reveals himself as a fifth columnist); Mulfory drowns when Boulder Dam is obliterated; Harroway dies during the invasion of D.C. Potter and Carla, who have fallen in love, survive the bombing of New York, but the enemy kills Potter for refusing to broadcast propaganda, and Carla chooses suicide to escape rape. At this point, everyone wakes in the bar from their trance and Ohman tells them this is what will happen if they don't realize that eternal vigilance is the price of peace.

This movie is not only a striking piece of political paranoia, it's authoritarian even by the standards of fifties anticommunist films. The idea of forcing factory workers and manufacturers into the war effort — regardless of the fact nobody was attacking us — is presented as the kind of sacrifice real Americans should be willing to make. When Sylvester tells a military officer that switching to tanks would be a financial blow to the tractor dealers he supplies, the officer replies that if they're loyal Americans, they should be happy to pay that price.

Walk East on Beacon (1952) Producer Louis de Rochemont made this film in a similar style to his *The House on 92nd Street* (1945), a based-on-truth film about the capture of the Duquesne spy ring. This later film, however, veers considerably further into political paranoia territory in showing how the FBI thwarted Soviet spies plotting to steal Project Falcon, a super-MacGuffin that can improve ballistics and radar as well as putting Americans into space.

Based on a magazine story written (at least his name was on it) by J. Edgar Hoover, the movie is a battle between the FBI — professional, ever-vigilant and equipped with top-of-the-line spy gadgets (such as cameras disguised as car headlights) — and "a worldwide conspiracy that seeks to destroy organized government everywhere." The movie repeatedly emphasizes that Soviet spies are all around us, and that unless citizens do their duty and alert the government to anyone who looks suspicious, the FBI can't do its job.

A woman contacts the FBI and says her husband is being forced by a man named Robert Martin (Ernest Graves) to spy for a Soviet ring. The G-men investigate and identify the other agents in the network, helped by tips from loyal Americans about suspects' looks, clothes and body language. This profiling work leads to the memorable line, "Police already knew many suspected communists with shoulder bags, and some of them had peculiar walks."

At one point, after Inspector Belden (George Murphy) is told that neither Martin's wife or his neighbors saw him as a threat, Belden replies, "In other words, he's a perfect sleeper." Not perfect enough for the commies, it turns out: The ruthless spymaster Lazchenkov (Karel Stepanek) informs Martin that he's being sent back to Moscow for his failures. When Martin protests, "You can't make me go — I'm an American citizen!" Lazchenkov's sneering reply is, "Don't insult me."

The spy ring tells Kafer (Finlay Currie), one of the Falcon researchers, that they might be able to free his son from East Germany if he plays ball with them; instead, he works with the FBI to feed them false information in hopes of trapping the ring. The title of the film refers to his instructions for making contact with the spies: Walk east on Beacon Street and when someone asks him about directions to Trinity Church, reply, "I live in Nantucket."

Another Red agent successfully records Kafer's official presentation on Falcon, but the FBI captures him. Lazchenkov captures Kafer, but the FBI rescues him and busts the ring; we learn that Kafer's son has also been freed by military intelligence. According to the concluding voice-over, this "was but a brief chapter in the long history of the FBI's continuing war against the enemies of the nation," but "there are others in secret alliance with communism" so it's up to us to warn the FBI when we see anyone who looks suspicious.

What constituted suspicious behavior? According to one 1954 survey, Americans said signs of communism included not attending church; "not like us"; and "I just knew."

My Son John (1952) Dan and Lucille Jefferson (Dean Jagger, Helen Hayes) are giving their sons Chuck and Ben (Richard Jaeckel, James Young) a last family dinner at the start of the movie before they head off to Korea. Much to Lucille's disappointment and Dan's displeasure, big brother John (Robert Walker), a Washington official "with more degrees than a thermometer," blows off the dinner.

When John shows up a week later, he condescends and winces at his folks' homespun values, flaunts "two-dollar words," laughs at the patriotic song his father sings at American Legion meetings (with good reason — it's really awful) and snarks to the parish priest about how many free meals his position nets him. When the family doctor (Minor Watson) drops by with medicine for Lucille, John talks about his respect for science and is quite put out when the doctor replies that religion is a higher priority: Science may discover many things, but didn't God put them there for us to find?

More damning incidents and conversations follow, showing us that John's just not right:

- Dan and Lucille learn he's giving a commencement address at his old school and didn't invite them; Lucille thinks that's because they're too lowbrow.
- John dismisses talk of romance and girlfriends as "sentimentalizing over the biological urge."
- John edits a speech Dan is making at the American Legion, cutting out sentiments such as "if the state gives us freedom it has the power to take it away" and "When the state denies God-given rights and defines itself as the source of liberty, freedom is doomed." Dan later tells John that he sounds like one of the guys America "ought to be alert about" and if that were so, he'd personally execute his son.
- John tells Lucille that Dan's views are out of date and that John's generation values helping the downtrodden and aiding minorities. Lucille tells him this is something St. Paul would approve of, but John says his father would consider it subversive.

4. *Red Scare*

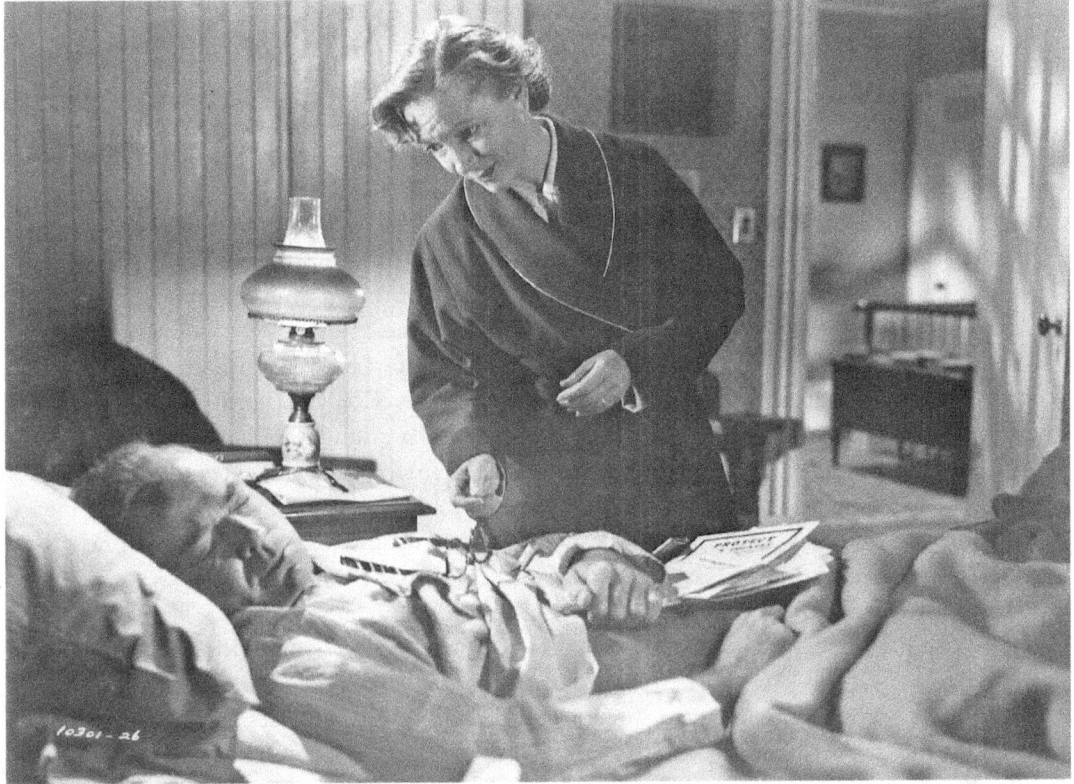

In *My Son John* (1952) Lucille and Dan Jefferson (Helen Hayes, Dean Jagger) learn "it's a commie specialty ... breaking up homes."

> To prove otherwise, he swears on the Bible that he's not a communist. Dan, however, points out that the Bible means nothing to commie atheists and makes it clear that John's politics are just plain wrong.
> - A chance meeting between the parents and Stedman (Van Heflin) turns out to be not so random: After visiting Lucille again, he tells her he's an FBI agent investigating John.

As a result, when John insists on Lucille recovering a pair of old trousers she gave to the church rummage sale, she checks the trousers carefully and finds a key. Suspecting the worst, she gives John the trousers and, when he asks about a key, says she didn't find one. Stedman meets Lucille in Washington, points out all the patriotic monuments around, and tells her they have to fight for Chuck and Ben on the home front just as Chuck and Ben are fighting for them in Korea.

Stedman suggests that John is tied to a communist courier the FBI just busted and, sure enough, Lucille learns the key fits the door of the courier's apartment. Shaken and weak, she returns home and tells Dan, "You've got more wisdom than all of us because you listen to your heart ... clear and honest and clean."

Lucille tells John that she won't let him poison the minds of the grads at commencement, even if it means turning him in to Stedman. John threatens to have her declared insane, but Lucille won't budge. In a long rambling conversation, she blames his moral failings on his never having played football and on her constant assurances that intellectual achievements was just as good. She tells him to "carry the ball" for God's side "before the clock runs out."

All this hits John with a crisis of conscience, so instead of fleeing the country, he records his commencement address and calls Stedman for a meeting. The party's killers riddle his taxi with bullets and it crashes on the steps of the Lincoln Memorial, where he dies telling Stedman to play the tape as a warning to the student body. (This was a desperate last-minute rewrite when Walker died before shooting was finished.)

In his taped speech, John tells the students how the Reds seduced him by hooking him intellectually the way a pusher hooks addicts, first stimulating him with new ideas and flattering him as an intellectual, then addicting him to defying the views of his parents and his faith and finally corrupting his American love of justice "until somewhere along the line our brain has been numbed so that we have substituted faith in man for faith in God." In this fashion, he became a traitor and a spy — and even now, Red spies are watching the students, scheming to hook a new generation.

Unusually for the period, the film has nothing to say about communist methods, goals or doctrines; we never even learn what John did as a spy. As far as director-screenwriter Leo McCarey is concerned, all we need to know is that commies "break up families" and disrespect the Catholic Church. And they're intellectuals, which the film makes clear is a bad thing.

At one point, Dan, who teaches at "the little red school house," condemns parents who are more interested in their kids' grades than the marks he gives them for character. Being illiterate, he tells Lucille, isn't as bad as a lack of morals ("Forgers have excellent penmanship"). When John reminds his mother to take the doctor's tablets, Lucille replies in a complete non sequitur that faith in God is more important: "What about Moses and the tablets he left us? With the prescriptions right on them?" And, of course, there's her implication that if John had only played football instead of studying, he'd have turned out okay.

Some critics have also seen a homosexual subtext in John's snide character. He does indeed resemble the stereotype of the sophisticated gay repulsed by his parents' tackiness, but that could just as easily be part of the general anti-intellectualism of the film. In many ways, John comes off as a pod person out of *Invasion of the Body Snatchers*, an alien who can't comprehend the simple, honest things that mean so much to ordinary humans like Dan and Lucille.

What's odd about the film, and makes it infamously awful, is that Dan and Lucille aren't the salt-of-the-earth characters the script would seem to require. Lucille's devotion to Dan seems neurotic, almost the stereotype of the smothering mother of pop Freudianism; Dan is a small town Babbitt closer to a clueless boob than to a voice of morality. Dan is convinced that his local American Legion post is a bulwark against communist

4. Red Scare

takeover, and he's proud about how supposedly smart and knowledgeable he, his friends and the local paper's anticommunist editorials are. It plays as if McCarey was undercutting his own film.

Big Jim McLain (1952) Jim McLain (John Wayne) and Mal Baxter (James Arness) are HUAC investigators dedicated to subpoenaing commies and damn proud of it; as far as Jim's concerned, "Any member of the Communist Party after 1945 is committing high treason." The only down side is that every time they drag the commie filth into the light to face HUAC's relentless interrogation, the rats escape justice by taking the Fifth. Nevertheless, Wayne's voice-over assures us that every American owes HUAC a debt of gratitude for its work.

HUAC's new assignment for the guys is to subpoena Reds in Hawaii. Jim and Mal soon discover that the men who have been publicly exposed as communists are red herrings to distract attention from a secret cell working on nefarious plots against America. As they track down leads to the real Reds, they hear personal testimony from several people about the unimaginable vileness that is communism.

One man, Lexiter (Paul Hurst), has no qualms about informing on his Red son, telling Jim that he stopped speaking to his kid on the grounds that there's no way to reach a man who's rejected God. One communist's ex-wife, who now works as a nurse in a leper colony, tells Jim that communism is a crime against humanity, and she'd no more help her husband now than she would touch a leper — then she catches herself and laughs.

The communists dose Mal with truth serum to find out what he knows. Mal has a bad reaction and

As *Big Jim McLain* (1952), John Wayne lets us know that the difference between real Americans and no-good commies is that "we don't hit the little guy."

dies. Jim keeps pushing and his investigation enables the police to wire a meeting of the top party brass in the islands. The Reds plot to end the investigation by having a few more sacrificial lambs confess, leaving the cell free to carry out its plan to cripple the supply lines to Korea. The plan includes having a communist labor leader incite strikes on the waterfront, and having a doctor unleash plague-infected rats to keep the dock workers away.

Having everything down on tape, Jim and the cops bust up the cell and Mal's killers go to jail. The other Reds escape justice by invoking the Fifth Amendment at HUAC's next hearing. Watching troops board ships for Korea gives Jim hope that America will triumph.

The Korean War plays a large role in the film's worldview. Mal, a Korean War veteran, equates American Reds to the North Koreans; Jim tells his girlfriend that while he's heard lots of psychological crap about why some guys turn to communism, when you're in a war zone, it doesn't matter why the enemy is shooting at you. And of course, the Hawaiian scheme shows that the fight against Reds in America is the same battle going on in Korea — and as Mal's death shows, it can be just as dangerous.

Pearl Harbor also looms large in *Big Jim McLain*. Jim makes two visits to the *Arizona*, one of the ships sunk during the attack, and the trailer for the movie warns us that "the island we fought so hard to protect, not so long ago, is in danger again." HUAC, in short, is the bulwark standing between us and another sneak attack by the Reds in our midst.

I Led Three Lives (1953–56) Reading Herb Philbrick's *I Led Three Lives* today gives the impression that the American Communist Party was the most boring conspiracy ever conceived by the mind of man.

The bestselling memoir recounts how the young, idealistic Philbrick joined a pacifist organization prior to World War II only to be puzzled when it took on unrelated causes such as Negro rights, an end to poll taxes, and housing rights (an inflammatory issue in a time when attempts to provide housing in Detroit for black war workers sparked riots). Eventually, Philbrick learned that the group was a communist front and reported them to the FBI, who asked him to stay on as an informer. Philbrick agreed out of patriotism (some sources say he was a paid informant) and became a full Party member, even though he knew that being identified as a communist would destroy his life, since the FBI can't reveal they have agents inside the party.

What follows is nine years of talk, talk, talk: Pro-war propaganda after Russia joins the Allies, anti–American propaganda after World War II, endless classes on communist theory and endless anecdotes of how Philbrick cleverly chooses the right response to whatever new wind blows out of the Central Committee. The commies that he hangs with talk a lot about overthrowing the state but they never take action or do anything criminal; Philbrick continues compiling dossiers and photos until he testifies at the Smith Act trials, then resumes his normal life. Or as normal as you can get when you're a bestselling author, professional witness and TV show character.

Philbrick's failure to witness any espionage or criminal activity doesn't stop him from labeling the Communist Party as the prime mover behind pre–World War II isolationism

4. Red Scare

(which it wasn't), the loss of China, North Korea and (in an updated 1970s edition) Vietnam, Henry Wallace's defeat in 1948's presidential election (the Reds infiltrated his campaign and somehow conned Wallace into running on a radical left-wing platform) and JFK's assassination (because if party members who knew Oswald was a Red had reported him as loyal Americans would have, the FBI would have caught Oswald first).

In *I Led Three Lives*, communists are everywhere: College students, your next-door neighbors, anyone can be a closet Red, which is to say an enemy of America. The FBI, on the other hand, is completely aboveboard. It has no interest in liberal organizations except those infiltrated by communists and never does anything unethical.

The TV series based on the book veers even further into the world of political paranoia, pitting Philbrick (played by Richard Carlson) against an American Communist Party that seems interchangeable with James Bond's SPECTRE. Members are routinely trained to use explosives, coldbloodedly murder informers and federal agents, maintain a cadre of hired enforcers and spy on their own people. Absolute obedience is expected from all operatives.

The opening narration describes each episode as "a fantastically true story from the files of Herbert A. Philbrick who for nine frightening years did lead three lives — citizen, communist, counterspy." The stories don't look anything like Philbrick's tedious accounts, but that was explained by the producers as grafting true stories from other federal agents onto Philbrick's life.

Carlson's Philbrick provides more voice-over narration during each episode, delivered in a tense tone as if it were his last message before his execution. Worried about being exposed in one episode, he reminds himself, "You've been at the edge of the cliff before, the one you see yourself fall over every week in a dream. How long before it isn't a dream?"

In "Civil Defense," communists infiltrate local civil defense programs to learn what they'll have to overcome when Russia invades. In several episodes, Comrade Herb is caught up in commie efforts to get nuclear research secrets; in others, he has to stop assassination plans where the targets range from Congressmen to former party members about to turn state's evidence. In other episodes, he smashes phony charities that serve as commie fund-raising tools or confronts commie propaganda, a classification that included advocating peace, opposing the nuclear arms race and concern for minorities.

In one typical episode Comrade Bob tells Herb that Comrade Zack has been falsely accused of assaulting anticommunist labor leader Richard Black — he has an iron-clad alibi — and needs a lawyer. Herb hires Jeff, a straight-arrow attorney, but soon realizes that the alibi, fellow traveler Mrs. Penrose, is perjuring herself. If the court detects the lie, Jeff will take the blame; if the ruse succeeds, Zack goes free and the party can blackmail Jeff by framing him for suborning perjury. Herb, however, tricks Zack into exposing the false alibi, after which Jeff walks out on the case. Zack attacks a prosecution witness out of desperation and gets jailed.

In the "Newsreel" episode mentioned earlier, the party plots to smear America with doctored newsreels showing that police break strikes with violence, that politicians are idiots, that America discriminates against minorities and that the country is using germ warfare in Korea (a then-current allegation). Although unnerved by the knowledge that this party cell has already killed one FBI counterspy, Herb nonetheless convinces the plan's mastermind to get extra mileage out of the newsreel company by making sabotage training films for new recruits. Herb then switches the training film with a regular newsreel and when it airs, the FBI can bust the company for advocating violent attacks on government in defiance of the Smith Act.

The Complete Directory to Prime Time Network and Cable TV Shows speculates on whether audiences really bought this as a realistic drama about communist subversives or enjoyed it as an improbable spy thriller. Either way, it gave viewers three solid years of political paranoia to entertain themselves. In the early 1960s, Philbrick also appeared in the short film *What Is Communism?*

The Fearmakers (1958) After two years of torture and unsuccessful brainwashing as a Korean War POW, Alan Eaton (Dana Andrews) leaves an army hospital for home despite the fact that what is now known as PTSD still gives him occasional fainting spells and backflashes. A public relations man before the war, he intends to have his partner, Baker, buy him out, then take a long vacation. When Eaton visits the office, he finds out that Baker is dead and that he used Eaton's power of attorney to sell the entire firm to a man named McGinnis (Dick Foran). Eaton turns down McGinnis' offer to rejoin the firm and leaves the building, ignoring the odd presentation he hears in one room: "That's how we'll deal with the Jews. Next, the labor unions."

When Eaton's old friend Senator Walder (Roy Gordon) hears about this, he tells Eaton that McGinnis is bad news, distorting the results of opinion polls to benefit his clients. Eaton considers that a betrayal of the public trust; he's even more alarmed when Walder tells him that some of those clients are pushing for "peace at any price," the kind of peace that leads to "another Munich."

Eaton: "You mean McGinnis is using Eaton Baker to peddle propaganda — treason!"

When Eaton learns that Baker may have been murdered, it's the last straw: He takes McGinnis up on his offer and discovers the firm is using its slanted polls to dabble in politics. Eaton admits to Lorraine (Marilee Earle) — McGinnis' secretary and Eaton's new love interest — that he's fudged a few statistics in his time, but he sees a big difference between doing it to sell soap or cigarettes and doing it to sell politicians.

With Lorraine's help, Eaton keeps digging for answers. Finally he sneaks into McGinnis' office to find the raw data for one of his surveys, which could provide hard proof that he's cooking the results to advance a political agenda. Eaton overhears McGinnis planning a nuclear disarmament campaign and accuses him of peddling fear to control America. McGinnis gloatingly admits it, adding that he'll soon be able to swing elections, first for Congress, then the White House. And Eaton can accuse him all he likes — who's going to believe a "brainwashed psycho"?

A PTSD attack leaves Eaton helpless, so McGinnis and his henchmen drive Eaton and Lorraine to somewhere they can be disposed of. McGinnis fakes another fainting spell, which leaves the bad guys off-guard enough for him to crash the car. As the cops arrive, he takes down McGinnis on the footsteps of the Lincoln Memorial "for Clark

4. Red Scare

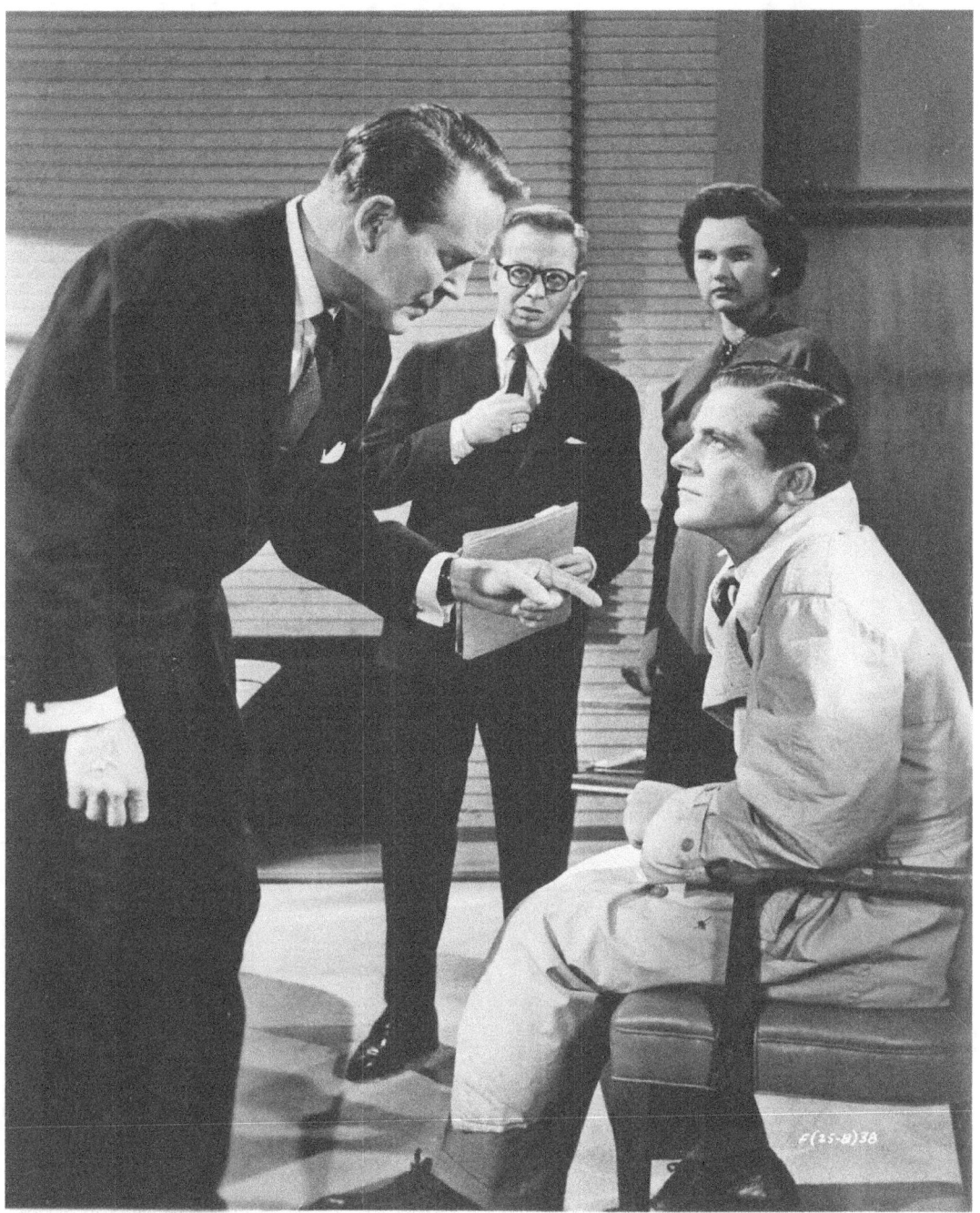

Corrupt PR flak McGinnis (Dick Foran) confronts ethical pollster and Korean War veteran Alan Eaton (Dana Andrews) while Barney (Mel Tormé) and Lorraine (Marilee Earle) watch in 1958's *The Fearmakers*.

Baker and a lot of guys in Korea." He then tells Lorraine ominously that "you can't fool all the people all the time, but nowadays you don't have to fool all the people."

Seen today, *The Fearmakers* seems slightly comical with its abhorrence at the idea of PR being used for politics and its outrage that polling research might be slanted to benefit the people paying for it. Post–World War II America, however, had become very aware of the power of advertising to manipulate consumers, and Madison Avenue had been the subject of both dramas (*The Hucksters*) and comedies (*Will Success Spoil Rock Hunter?*). By showing the dangers of public-relations to our national fiber, *The Fearmakers* fits right in.

The fifties were the high point for movies about the communist fifth column. While commies would play bad guys for years to come, the six cities would shift the focus from infiltration to James Bondian "spy vs. spy" battles. Even so, fifth-column movies would continue well up to the fall of the Soviet Union 30 years later.

5

Communist Fifth Columnists After 1960

Although communists continued to play the villain's role in movies and TV long after HUAC, McCarthy and the blacklist had lost their power, the movies rarely gave us the kind of fifth-column conspiracies we saw in *The Red Menace* or *I Led Three Lives*. The trends of the time pushed the movies in other directions.

One was Bond — James Bond. *Dr. No* (1962) and its sequels would make spies cooler and more entertaining than they'd ever been, and considerably less serious. Bond-style films had much more interest in excitement and beautiful women than in explaining the flaws in communist doctrine and why it was incompatible with Americanism. Bond also proved that groups such as SPECTRE worked just as well as villains as SMERSH (the Soviet agency Bond battled in most of Ian Fleming's books).

More serious spy films were less inclined to see the Cold War as good vs. evil; the USSR might be bad, but contrary to *The Red Menace*, America and the West weren't utopia, particularly in the dubious world of the Cold War. *The Spy Who Came In from The Cold* (1963) shows British intelligence treating its agents like pawns, and being as willing to sacrifice them as any chess player. *Dr. Strangelove* (1964), Stanley Kubrick's glorious Cold War satire, has an American general trigger nuclear war over fears the communists are polluting his bodily fluids by fluoridation (which had indeed been a bugaboo for the far right when it was introduced); the film suggests that the leaders on both sides are idiots.

Another factor was the feeling that the Cold War needn't be a doomsday struggle after all. Bond's best-known television counterpart, *The Man from U.N.C.L.E.*, presented a Russian working side by side with an American spy. *The Russians Are Coming, the Russians Are Coming* (1966) parodies the fears of the day by having a Russian sub stranded on the New England coast. The locals panic, but everyone eventually finds common ground

That being said, the sixties did contribute their share of political paranoia about communism.

Red Nightmare (1962) Produced by Jack Webb for the Department of Defense, this short film warned viewers that if they snooze, they lose their country, much the same way *Strange Holiday* did two decades earlier.

Webb, appearing on-camera and narrating, tells us that small-town resident and factory worker Jerry Donovan (Jack Kelly) is a typical American, taking his freedom so much for granted that he blows off his Army Reserve meeting because he wants to watch TV, and ducks a PTA meeting out of sheer laziness. To shake Jerry up, Webb gives him a "red nightmare" in which his town becomes a Soviet state with no Bill of Rights, no outside contact without a permit and mandatory output quotas at the factory. Jerry's teenage daughter is moving to a collective farm for the good of the state; his younger children condemn Jerry for his lack of loyalty. ("You should have trained me to think more along Party lines.") A furious Jerry drags them to Sunday school, but the church is now a science museum stuffed with false tributes claiming the great inventions for Russia, to Jerry's outrage ("The telephone was invented by Alexander Graham Bell—an American!").

Jerry's persistent pushback against the new order results in his being arrested, then sentenced to death by a kangaroo court as "an ugly diseased remnant of the bourgeois class." When he wakes up, he finds himself with a fresh appreciation of his responsibilities and starts taking them seriously. The show concludes with a montage of American symbols (picnics, D.C. monuments, etc.).

While the message is the same as *Invasion USA* and *Strange Holiday*, the set-up is odd. Webb informs us that the USSR has built a model American town for spies to learn the American way of life so they can pass for real Americans when they come here to advance the Red master plan. That town is merged with Jerry's own, which is why Jerry's first clue to his situation is a local commissar lecturing spies on their infiltration duties.

Why did Webb think this made more sense than having Reds just take over the town? Who knows? It is however, the first film to use the concept of such a training ground, which Pat Frank introduced to fiction in his 1956 novel *Forbidden Area*.

The Manchurian Candidate (1962) The movie opens with icy Army officer Raymond Shaw (Laurence Harvey) forcing his platoon out of a Korean brothel and onto patrol—where they're captured thanks to the treachery of Chang Li (Henry Silva), their Korean scout.

Months later, Shaw returns to Washington to receive the Congressional Medal of Honor for taking down a machine-gun nest single-handedly, saving almost his entire platoon and leading the survivors to safety. Shaw is horrified that his mother (Angela Lansbury) and stepfather, Senator Iselin (James Gregory), show up and milk the ceremony as theater for Iselin's campaign for a vice-presidential nomination. Shaw gets some revenge by telling his domineering mother that his new job will be working for a reporter aggressively opposed to Iselin's right-wing politics, which include McCarthyite lies about how many communists are working in the government.

Meanwhile, Major Ben Marco (Frank Sinatra), formerly Shaw's captain, suffers terrible nightmares in which the platoon is stuck in a hotel lobby, waiting to fly home and forced to listen to a garden club lecture ... except it sometimes turns into a lecture hall where Chinese and Soviet communists watch Dr. Yen Lo (Khigh Dhiegh) explain that Shaw is now a brainwashed assassin. To prove it, Yen Lo has Shaw strangle one of the platoon members.

Marco's superiors blame his nightmare on battle fatigue, since by Marco's own admis-

5. Communist Fifth Columnists After 1960

sion, Shaw is "the kindest, warmest, bravest, most wonderful human being I've ever known in my life." Dr. Yen arrives in America, contacts Shaw and places him in a trance by exposing him to the queen of hearts, which represents his "hated and loved" mother. Yen tests Shaw's programming by having him murder his employer.

Marco keeps telling the Army that something's wrong; he *knows*, for instance, that Shaw is a cold-blooded bastard, even though he simultaneously believes him the most wonderful, kindest, etc. Forced to take leave, he meets Rosie (Janet Leigh), who falls for him (so implausibly fast that a lot of viewers assume she's part of whatever's going on), and then visits Shaw. When he recognizes Shaw's servant as Chang Li, Ben pounds the crap out of him until the cops drag him away. Rosie bails him out.

Shaw tells Marco that another platoon member has written him about having similar nightmares and they wonder if their memories have been altered. The military begins to agree and begins piecing together the outline of what really happened. Meanwhile, at a costume party, Mrs. Iselin reveals herself to Shaw as his communist handler and hypnotizes him. After she leaves, Shaw's long-lost love, Josie (Leslie Parrish) — daughter of Iselin's arch-foe, Senator Jordan (John McGiver) — enters the room in a queen of hearts costume. Shaw helplessly falls in love with her all over again, and when Marco meets them the next day, they're married. Unfortunately, Mrs. Iselin's next assignment for her son is to murder Jordan, who's determined to keep Iselin off the ticket. Josie discovers the killing and Shaw obeys his order to murder any witnesses.

Marco tries deprogramming Shaw, but Shaw reports dutifully to his mother to learn the master plan: Shaw, a crack shot, will gun down Iselin's running mate, after which Iselin will deliver a Soviet-crafted speech that will rouse the nation to hysteria and "sweep us into office with powers that will make martial law look like anarchy." Mrs. Iselin tells Shaw that the Soviets assumed that using her would bind the Iselins to them more tightly. Instead, she intends to repay them for destroying Raymond's soul by grinding the communists into the dust.

Despite Marco's best efforts he arrives too late to stop the shooting — but his deprogramming worked, and instead of his designated target, Shaw shoots his mother and Iselin. He tells Ben nobody else could have stopped them, then shoots himself. (In the novel, Ben orders Shaw to kill himself, rather than have a Medal of Honor winner's reputation tarnished by a trial.)

The term "brainwashing" was coined by Edward Hunter in 1950, to explain how China was using thought-control techniques to transform its entire population into drones. Hunter actually distinguished brainwashing — ordinary indoctrination — from "brain-changing," which he described as using Pavlovian conditioning to "change a mind radically so that its owner becomes a living puppet ... new beliefs and new thought processes inserted into a captive body." Brainwashing, however, soon became the term of choice for both varieties of control.

This concept raised the stakes in the Cold War — not just a battle for territory or physical power but for the mind itself. But critics of the idea said it made the communists too scary and all-powerful. Psychiatrists pointed out that the Reds weren't turning people into zombies and that their supposedly advanced methods were nothing but standard techniques of indoctrination and intimidation.

Nevertheless, when Korean POWs made statements against the United States, the idea that they had been brainwashed, and that this involved something more than mere torture, seemed to explain how they could have switched sides. Several psychiatrists pointed out that none of the men who returned after brainwashing became loyal communists or turned against America, but brainwashing of POWs became a plot element in many fifties movies—*The Rack*, *The Bamboo Prison*, *Toward the Unknown* and *The Fearmakers*—and novels such as *The Brainwashed Pilot*. The possibility that advanced psychological techniques could reprogram people's minds became a permanent part of pop culture.

The Manchurian Candidate was the first movie to put brainwashing front and center, and to link it to a bigger, more audacious fifth-column plot than the movies had attempted before, putting a Soviet agent into the White House. Like *Big Jim McLain*, the movie presents the possibility that anticommunists are actually another face of the enemy, but rather than proving how evil and duplicitous the Reds are, the movie uses the idea to skewer McCarthyism and the anticommunist witch hunts. Small wonder the movie was condemned by both the American Legion and the Communist Party; the Legion suggested it was proof how far communists had infiltrated the movie industry.

Forbidden Area introduced the idea of sleeper agents several years earlier: The spies arriving in America retain their own minds, but brainwashing has burned their cover personalities so deeply into their consciousness, they can't slip up. *The Manchurian Candidate* made it a staple of pop culture, with brainwashed agents occurring in books, TV and film over the years; the name of the movie itself is now a synonym for a politician whose strings are being pulled by the bad guys.

What Is Communism? (196?) Although YouTube identifies this Herb Philbrick lecture as a 1950s short, it was clearly made after the Cuban missile crisis, which Philbrick refers to frequently; in his view, this was a solid win for the USSR, because now that we've dropped our guard, they're free to put even more missiles in Cuba. Philbrick warns us that commies are treacherous, lying, atheist evil monsters; college student protests are all communist-inspired; and the American Communist Party "is not an American political party like any other. It is an outlaw organization taking its orders and instructions from another government to do everything possible to destroy our government. It's an international criminal conspiracy" and every front organization or labor union the Reds take over puts them one step closer to their goal of total global domination.

The Outer Limits: "The Hundred Days of the Dragon" (1963) Somewhere inside China, a scientist demonstrates a serum that makes human flesh so pliable that facial features can be completely remade. At the command of leader Li Chin-Sung (Richard Loo), a Red Chinese agent is transformed into an exact double of presidential candidate William Selby (Sidney Blackmer); the Chinese then murder Selby and replace him. Once in the White House, "Selby" begins making peace overtures to Chin-Sung's brutal regime, while plotting to replace the executive staff and key figures in business, labor and the media

5. Communist Fifth Columnists After 1960

with more duplicates. Vice-President Ted Pearson (Phillip Pine) is among those who become suspicious, not only because of "Selby's" shifting politics but because of little personal things, such as "Selby" suddenly showing himself a crack shot on a hunting trip.

Pearson's double tries and fails to eliminate him, and the vice-president pieces together the truth. Obtaining a sample of the drug, he causes the president's face to revert to putty at a major gala, revealing the deception. As the new acting president, Pearson opts not to launch a nuclear attack on China, deciding the cost would be too high.

The Outer Limits was a science fiction anthology series that ran for two years in the sixties and has been revived a couple of times since. This tale of intrigue was more mundane than usual, with the false-face formula the only science-fictional element. While "Red China" generated its share of spy movies during the sixties — in the James Bond films, it was the mastermind backing *Goldfinger* (1964) and trying to provoke a U.S.–USSR war in *You Only Live Twice* (1967) — it provided far fewer film fifth columnists than the Soviet Union.

Mission: Impossible (1966–1973) For seven seasons — plus an eighties revival series and three theatrical films — the Impossible Mission Force operated as a black ops team tackling missions so difficult and sensitive that if any of them were caught or killed, "the secretary will disavow any knowledge of your actions." Two episodes of the show are particularly noteworthy for fifth-column themes:

In "The Carriers" (11/19/66), the IMF members infiltrate the mock–American town that the USSR uses as a training base, teaching spies about American slang, baseball and gender roles. When IMF agent Cinnamon (Barbara Bain) hits on teacher Passik (Arthur Hill), for instance, he informs her that American women never make the first move.

The team's mission? Thwart Passik's plan for a bio-weapon attack on the United States. Posing as trainees, they discover that he plans to infect his current class of 200 spies with a deadly septicimic bacteria that will become contagious some time after they arrive in America. Needless to say, Our Heroes manage to stop the plot and infect Passik with the disease.

In "The Town" (2/18/68), team leader Jim Phelps (Peter Graves) is on holiday when he stops off in a small town to check his car for engine trouble. When he sees a young woman drop a concealed gas gun, he's immediately dragged off to be paralyzed by the town doctor (Will Geer). It turns out that the entire community consists of enemy agents — "Doc" mentions that they've been around for a number of years — and the gas gun will be used in their latest mission, murdering a defector newly arrived in Los Angeles. When IMF agent Rollin (Martin Landau) shows up looking for Jim, Doc tells him that Jim had a heart attack. Jim, however, manages to signal Rollin by blinking, so Rollin calls in the IMF team to rescue Jim, stop the assassination and break up the spy operation.

The Seventies

Political paranoia about the Soviets continued to recede in the seventies. The USSR and U.S.A. negotiated missile cuts and adopted a policy of detente that toned down the

Cold War rhetoric; President Nixon recognized communist China's government, after years of the U.S. insisting that Taiwan was the "real" government of the mainland.

In addition, the American side looked less and less like utopia after the Watergate scandal exposed the corruption in our own government. Then the Church Committee/Commission hearings lifted the veil on the CIA's activities, including attempted assassinations, spying on left-wing American groups and destabilizing democratic but unfriendly governments. American spies no longer looked like a noble bulwark protecting us from Soviet aggression.

The Death of Me Yet (1971) This television pilot movie came up with a twist on the *Forbidden Area* training town: Paul Towers (Doug McClure) is a Soviet agent who trained to become a perfect American, then used that training to disappear and start a new life as a regular, law-abiding U.S. citizen. Unfortunately, Chalk (Darren McGavin), a ruthless American spymaster, locates Towers, the only man in America who can identify a top Soviet agent (Richard Basehart). Towers is forced to fake his death and begin spyhunting with Chalk, sustained by the hope that someday he'll succeed and can return to his "real" life.

Fear on Trial (1975) This TV drama was one of the first films to tackle the real-life political paranoia of the fifties, focusing on the true story of John Henry Faulk (William Devane), a folksy, homespun radio personality of the early 1950s. As detailed in *American Trials of the 20th Century*, Faulk ran for head of the American Federation of Television and Radio Artists in 1955 on a platform opposing both communists and blacklists and condemning Aware, Inc., a vetting service that checked performers for any possible communist taint. Aware informed CBS that he had "a significant communist front record" and in 1957, the network blacklisted him.

With the help of attorney William Nizer (George C. Scott), Faulk fought back. Nizer proved in court that Aware had no evidence showing Faulk to be a communist, and that his opposition to Aware was the prime motive for the company pushing to blacklist him. In 1962, the jury rendered a $3.5 million judgment in Faulk's favor, which was cut to $350,000 on appeal the following year.

The Front (1976) Directed by Martin Ritt and written by Walter Bernstein—both victims of the blacklist—this film tackles the same era in the form of fiction rather than docudrama: Bookie and unsuccessful writer Howard Prince (Woody Allen) agrees to submit scripts for a writer friend who's been blacklisted (a common practice at the time). Before long, Howard's a celebrated TV writer secretly taking work from several different clients, and a friend to TV star Hecky Brown (Zero Mostel). Then, Hecky goes on the blacklist and has to settle for cheap nightclub engagements to put bread on the table, while HUAC pressures Howard to testify. After Hecky kills himself in frustration at his destroyed career, Howard is told to give Hecky's name to the committee, since it won't hurt anyone. He refuses, goes to jail, and becomes a hero to the anti-blacklist left.

Telefon (1977) *Telefon* shows how a Soviet fifth-column thriller could still be made in the age of detente. Rather than a threat from the top of the Kremlin, the villain is Dalchimsky (Donald Pleasence), a file clerk affiliated with a hardline faction opposed to the thaw in the Cold War. After a violent purge of the hardliners, Dalchimsky heads to

5. Communist Fifth Columnists After 1960

America with plans to activate Telefon, a cadre of sleeper agents planted in America 20 years earlier and brainwashed so that even they believe their own cover stories as regular Americans. Once in America, Dalchimsky begins triggering the Telefon sleepers with a code phrase that compels them to launch attacks on American infrastructure and military sites, even though many of the targets are decades out of date.

The generals who originally conceived the Telefon project would rather not admit its existence to the USSR's current leadership, but they can't risk Dalchimsky causing an international incident either. Their solution is to send Borzof (Charles Bronson), a military intelligence officer with a photographic memory (so he can learn the Telefon sleepers without a written copy), to America, where he's to stop Dalchimsky's rampage with the help of Barbara (Lee Remick), a Soviet undercover agent.

Borzof doesn't know that Barbara has an added mission, to kill him once Dalchimsky is eliminated so that the secret of Telefon remains buried. And nobody on the Russian side knows that Barbara is actually a CIA double agent. She tells her American superiors that Borzof is effectively on the U.S. side in this, but she's ordered to kill him anyway, to maintain her standing with the KGB. Her superiors consider calling in the FBI to help crack Telefon, but decide it will only be an excuse for the Bureau to resume spying on law-abiding left-wingers.

As they seek to thwart an insidious operation, Grigori and Barbara (Charles Bronson, Lee Remick) find each other obnoxious and irritating in *Telefon* **(1977).**

Borzof and Barbara eventually realize that Dalchimsky is picking his targets in order to spell out his own name (Dallas, Apalachicola, Los Angeles ...), and they use that to anticipate and take him out. By this point, they've fallen in love, and Barbara tells her bosses she's not going to execute Borzof. More than that, the two agents tell their respective superiors they're not giving up the names of the remaining sleepers, who will continue to live law-abiding lives if left alone. The same goes for the two spies — and if either side comes after them, Borzof remembers all the names and could reactivate Telefon at any time.

The Eighties

After Ronald Reagan became president in 1980, America's perception of the Soviets become somewhat schizoid, as the book *Friend or Foe?* observes. That's not surprising, given that Reagan's policy combined tough talk about the "evil empire" and massive defense spending with a willingness to meet with the USSR and eventually negotiate an arms-reduction treaty.

The Osterman Weekend (1982) falls into the seventies camp where our side is as big a threat as the enemy. The original 1970s novel by Robert Ludlum was a fine piece of fifth-column paranoia in which Fassett, a CIA official, recruits reporter John Tanner to learn which of his friends is the secret head of Omega, a Soviet operation gathering blackmail material on U.S. business leaders in order to trigger a financial collapse when the time comes. Tanner's skeptical, but can't live with the possibility that one of his buddies is not who he seems to be.

When the friends gather for a weekend together, they all look suspicious. It turns out most of them are in a scheme to hide money from the IRS overseas, but one of them really is the head of Omega. Except the real head is Fassett, sacrificing his underling to convince the CIA that Omega has been destroyed. Tanner and America win out in the end, but the weekend of suspicion has ruined his relationship with the surviving friends.

Made a decade later, the film's political perspective is wildly different: Fassett (John Hurt) is a CIA agent obsessed with avenging his wife's murder at KGB hands, unaware that the agency's politically ambitious director, Danforth (Burt Lancaster), arranged the execution as part of a complicated deal with the other side. Fassett's fixation has led him to uncover the existence of Omega — here a Soviet terrorist plot involving bio-weapons — and as in the book, he recruits Tanner (Rutger Hauer) to find which of his friends is involved.

As in the book, Fassett and Tanner play a number of mind games to smoke out Omega, but the results are far more violent, with most of Tanner's circle getting killed. And the real twist is that Omega doesn't exist: Fassett knows Danforth is responsible for his wife's death, and has orchestrated the spy hunt to enable him to kidnap Tanner's wife and child to force him to expose Danforth's power-hungry agenda on his TV show. With the help of his last surviving friend, Tanner launches a plan to destroy Danforth, take

5. Communist Fifth Columnists After 1960

down Fassett and save his family. Everything goes according to plan, and at the end of the film Tanner turns to the TV audience (and us) and warns us to think for ourselves instead of watching TV. (The movie-makers apparently thought this was a powerful statement to end on, but it's completely anticlimactic.)

On the solidly anticommunist side of the scale we have the most paranoid film of the Reagan era, *Red Dawn* (1984), set in a near future when the USSR has invaded Poland, communist satellites in Cuba and Nicaragua have overthrown the governments in El Salvador and Honduras, Mexico has collapsed into civil war and the European left has pushed for the removal of nuclear weapons from Western Europe, which led, in turn, to the dissolution of NATO. America now stands alone.

The story is set in a small farming town where parachutists suddenly descend outside the high school. Before the community realizes that they're not Americans, Red forces have begun butchering the townsfolk and using firearm registration records to locate and eliminate any gun owners in the area. The invaders soon have control of the area, setting up prison camps for anyone who refuses to collaborate. A handful of teenagers escape into the wilderness and begin a guerilla war against the invaders (calling themselves the Wolverines after the high school teams) much to the distress of Bella (Ron O'Neal), the local military commander who sees his troops mowed down by repeated sneak attacks. Despite heavy losses, the kids eventually drive the occupying force out of town and years later, the war is finally won.

How did the war start? Midway through the film, a fighter pilot (Powers Boothe) who crashes near the town fills the kids in on what happened: Cuban fifth columnists infiltrated America's Strategic Air Command bases posing as workers, and somehow kept the military from realizing that the attack was underway until too late (the exact details are left unexplained). With the infiltrators in place, commercial charter flights dropped hundreds of Soviet troops into the Rockies to hold the passes, nuclear missiles took out a few major centers such as Washington, D.C., and Cuban and Nicaraguan troops drove up through Mexico and invaded, leaving the United States divided between occupied territory and Free America for years.

The film is very much a product of its time, not just in its general anticommunism but in the details of its anticommunism. The idea of Nicaraguan troops driving right through Texas reflects Reagan's warning that communist-controlled Nicaragua (which had kicked out a U.S.–backed dictator in the late seventies) was a dangerous enemy just a two-day drive from the Texas border. The film's opening draws on then-topical issues such as the European opposition to Reagan's anti–Soviet posturing (the pilot tells the Wolverines that Europe is sitting the war out) and Reagan treating El Salvador's repressive government as a valuable ally against communism.

Despite its politics, *Red Dawn* comes across quite light on message compared to *Invasion USA* thirty years earlier. The only political point seems to be that gun control is bad and so are the communists, and there's no sign of American communists collaborating with the invaders. When one of the Wolverines asks Jed (Patrick Swayze) the difference between them and the Reds, his response is simple: "We *live* here!"

Some critics thought the film's portrayal of heroic resistance had more in common with movies about left-wing partisans in European wars. Bella compares the Wolverines to the Afghans fighting the Soviet invasion of Afghanistan — a much more appealing right-wing comparison — but also to the Vietcong, even suggesting to his superiors that they should borrow from America's Vietnam War playbook and try to win hearts and minds instead of cracking down harder. His superior's curt response is that in Vietnam, the Americans lost. (How the remake announced for late 2010 will approach this — given that America is currently fighting an insurgency in Iraq and Afghanistan — is anyone's guess.)

Several other movies of this period featured the idea of a Soviet attack on American soil (though they don't rate high enough in paranoia to get much expansion here). In *Invasion USA* (1985), special agent Chuck Norris has to stop a Soviet strike force sowing disorder via terrorist attacks on American citizens, blowing up shopping malls and Christmas parties. In the TV movie *World War III* (1982), the Soviet response to an American grain embargo (a common tactic at the time) is to send a strike force to seize the Alaska pipeline and cut off the flow of oil. As a small band of Americans attempt to hold the line, leaders on both sides try to negotiate a solution ... but they fail and both sides launch their missiles.

Secrets of the Red Bedroom (1986) has Geena Davis and Linda Hamilton among the young Russian women trained to go out and seduce secrets of American men — though here the goal is commercial and industrial spying, not government (which is indicative of how far things had changed). *Amerika* (1987) was a TV miniseries that showed the U.S.A. under the heel of a Soviet occupation, ten years after the war was over (no explanation was offered as to how we fell).

Pack of Lies (1987), a drama set during the 1960s, presents spying on communist as much more painful than *I Led Three Lives* ever did. British housewife Barb Jackson (Ellen Burstyn) is best friends with Helen Shaeffer (Teri Garr), her American across-the-street neighbor. Stewart (Alan Bates) a security official, asks to use the Jackson house to spy on a possible criminal; after the man is seen visiting the Shaeffers, Stewart explains that obviously the government needs to watch them too and before long a full-fledged base is set up in the Jackson house. Stewart already knows the Shaeffers are spies, but doesn't tell Barb they're the real target.

For Barb, this is all kinds of Hell: She lies to her closest friend, has to wonder, over and over, if her friend has been using her all along, and considers painfully whether the right thing to do wouldn't be to warn Helen of what's happening. After the Shaeffers are arrested, Helen tells Barb's daughter she'll never forgive Barb for the betrayal. Barb dies of a heart attack shortly afterwards.

No Way Out (1987) This film works a variation on the Soviet mole who can become a perfect American, but this serves mostly to add a twist to what's otherwise a remake of *The Big Clock* (1948).

No Way Out opens with Naval officer Tom Farrell (Kevin Costner) under interrogation. Flashbacks show us how Farrell became the lover of Susan (Sean Young), the mistress of Defense Secretary David Brice (Gene Hackman). Unaware of Susan's affair, Brice makes Farrell his liaison with military intelligence.

5. Communist Fifth Columnists After 1960

When Brice discovers that Susan is cheating on him, they fight and he accidentally kills her. Brice's devoted aide Pritchard (Will Patton) — a gay man in love with his boss — suggests they blame the killing on Yuri, a possibly apocryphal Soviet mole who arrived in America in his teens and "for all intents and purposes, he can pass as an American." Alleging that Yuri is Susan's lover and the killer makes the case a military intelligence matter under Brice's jurisdiction.

Brice assigns Farrell to find Yuri. Farrell knows full well that if the investigation identifies him as Susan's lover, he'll be framed as both a spy and a murderer. As the net tightens, Scott learns that Brice is the killer. When he and Brice confront each other, Brice suggests the solution for both of them is to have Pritchard take the fall. Unable to bear the betrayal, Pritchard shoots himself. Unfortunately for David, an old Polaroid unmasks him as the real killer and he runs.

As we return to the opening scene, we learn that the interrogators are actually KGB and that Farrell really is Yuri. Offered the chance to return to the USSR as a hero, he instead walks out and drives away.

Little Nikita (1988) is an entry on the not-a-threat side. Although Jeff Grant (River Phoenix) doesn't know it, his parents are actually Soviet sleepers sent to this country years before, but because they were never activated, they've embraced their cover identities as their "real" life.

Despite his parents' objections, Jeff applies to the Air Force Academy; when a standard background check turns up his parents' death dates. FBI agent Parmenter (Sidney Poitier) figures out that they're spies, using names taken from American grave markers. Parmenter realizes they'll be natural targets for Scuba (Richard Lynch), a renegade Soviet agent murdering sleepers in hopes that the KGB will pay him to stop (because if the government figures out who the victims are and realizes how many sleepers the Russians have over here, the bad press could kill an important summit meeting). Parmenter owes Scuba for his partner's murder, so he begins watching the Grants, as does the KGB's Karpov (Richard Bradford).

When your parents are Soviet sleepers, who do you trust? For Jeff (River Phoenix) it's his girlfriend Barbara (Lucy Deakins) in 1988's *Little Nikita*.

Screen Enemies of the American Way

Eventually Parmenter tells Jeff the truth. Scuba then kidnaps Jeff's parents, so Karpov forcibly enlists Jeff's help to stop Scuba. In the final showdown, Karpov and Parmenter, despite their mutual antagonism, destroy Scuba together and allow the Grants to resume their American lives.

A lot of earlier Cold War films show Soviets switching sides when they get a taste of American life, but it was always because America was *better*— better politics in *The Red Menace*, better music, food and clothes in 1957's *Silk Stockings* and *Jet Pilot*. In *Little Nikita*, there's little discussion of American superiority; the Grants have simply come to love their lives the way any immigrant might. When Karpov forces them into the field to help him against Scuba, their objection is that they've been out of the game for twenty years, rather than any moral qualms at working with the KGB again. Jeff's response when Parmenter tells him the truth is that he's proud of his parents for building a business and a family.

The Experts (1988) was the 1980s' take on the *Forbidden Area* concept of the Soviets training spies in a mock–American town. In this comedy, it turns out that the town of Indian Falls has become a sinecure where many of the trainees have been living since the fifties, and the KGB's "Mr. Smith" (Charles Martin Smith) discovers the cultural training is correspondingly dated. ("Can you recommend a sushi bar?" "I don't go to bars, and I don't drink sushi.")

Smith's solution is to offer New York nitwits Travis and Wendell (John Travolta, Arye Gross) funding for their dream of opening a nightclub, provided they do it in his small, old-fashioned "Nebraska" town. Secretly, he plans to use them to educate Indian Falls on the slang, attitudes and lifestyles of present-day America, the better to infiltrate with.

Arriving in what they assume is the American heartland, the guys are horrified by their hick surroundings, and the townsfolk are just as unenthused about Travis and Wendell's style and attitudes. Things pick up, though, when the guys meet Bonnie (Kelly Preston) and Jill (Deborah Foreman), and when shipments of consumer goods they've ordered arrive from New York, introducing the town to the pleasures of Sony Walkmans, videotaped movies and color television.

When the guys realize that Smith has brought them behind the Iron Curtain, they start planning to escape back to the U.S.A. The authorities decide to have them executed, but the townies can't bring themselves to do something so un–American and let the guys live. Then Wendell and Travis learn that some of the other residents, horrified at the capitalist consumerism sweeping the town, have convinced their superiors to shut the project down, plunging people who have lived happy lives in 1950s America into the modern Soviet Union. Wendell and Travis revise their escape plans to take the entire population back to America where the U.S. government finds the perfect home for the defectors: a small town in Nebraska where nothing has changed since the 1950s.

Opposite: Travis and Wendell (John Travolta, left, and Arye Gross) unwittingly give Soviet spies a crash course in American pop culture in *The Experts* (1988).

Here we have the *Silk Stockings* theme that the difference between America and Russia can be explained by the relative quality of our consumer goods. There's no discussion of ideology, and the prospect of transplanting a townful of Soviet agents to America doesn't disturb anyone.

The House on Carroll Street (1988) is a historical drama set during the 1950s and that casts a critical eye on the anticommunism of the time. Emily Crane (Kelly McGillis) is a magazine editor called before HUAC because of her work with a civil rights group. When she refuses to name the people who have worked with the group, Crane gets blacklisted, then fired. She finds a new job working for an elderly Carroll Street matron (Jessica Tandy) and discovers the HUAC counsel, Ray Selwyn (a scene-stealing Mandy Patinkin), visiting a neighboring house, talking to the Germans there. When she asks a translator who works there about it, Selwyn has the young man killed.

With the help of Cochran (Jeff Daniels) the FBI agent assigned to watch her, Crane discovers that Selwyn is having various Nazi war criminals brought into the country to provide information to our intelligence services. (With a sick sense of humor, Selwyn has used the names of dead Jews for their cover identities.) Despite Selwyn's attempts to have Crane killed, she and Cochran ultimately arrest the Nazis. Selwyn falls to his death trying to kill Crane.

Guilty by Suspicion (1991) is a much more realistic portrayal of the blacklist, though not a very interesting one (nothing in the movie comes as a surprise, given the premise). Scriptwriter David Merrill (Robert De Niro) is on top of the world, respected by his peers and in demand with studio heads. Then he's told that to keep working, he'll have to go before HUAC and explain his presence at Communist Party meetings back in the thirties, even though he was never a member. ("I think I got thrown out for arguing.")

When Merrill refuses, the blacklist kicks in: Friends shun him, Broadway won't look at his plays and even Monogram, one of the worst of the Poverty Row studios, won't touch him. Finally, Merrill goes before HUAC and tries to resolve things — but balks at naming anyone else as a communist, even a dead friend they ask him about. While this destroys his career, it does inspire his close friend Bunny (George Wendt), who was on the brink of naming names, to refuse to cooperate with the committee. As in *The Front* and *The House on Carroll Street*, refusing to testify is the mark of a hero, in contrast to *Big Jim McLain*, where it was the brand of a traitor.

After the Fall

The collapse of the Soviet Union seems to have put an end to the fear of communist infiltration in film; when *The Manchurian Candidate* was remade in 2004, the villain was a multinational corporation.

When Russians do turn up, they're less likely to be commies than gangsters or secessionists, though bogeyman-style, they work just as well in those roles. In *Hired Gun* (2009), the Russian Mafia provides a joint Arab terrorist and neo–Nazi conspiracy with

5. Communist Fifth Columnists After 1960

a nuclear bomb; in the television series *Seven Days*, Chechen separatists — Chechnyan separatist terrorism was in the news a lot at the time — were recurring villains.

However, as post-communist Russia's government has become more of a saber-rattler, the old fears seem to have resurfaced. During the 2008 presidential campaign, Sen. John McCain's response to the Russia-Georgia clash was, "We have reached a crisis, the first probably serious crisis internationally since the end of the Cold War." Quite a statement for a period that included Bosnia, the first Gulf War, 9/11 and the occupation of Iraq.

In 2010, the eighth season of *24* showed Russians working with militant Muslims to sink a peace treaty between America and a hostile Islamic state, even to the point of backing an Islamic terrorist attack on New York. And later in that year, the movies gave us *Salt*.

Evelyn Salt (Angelina Jolie) is a happily married, well respected CIA agent operating under the supervision of her friend Ted Winter (Liev Schrieber). When she debriefs Orlov, (Daniel Olbrychski) a Russian defector, he claims that a Russian mole plans to murder the Russian president during a trip to New York, and that Salt is the designated shooter.

Winter doesn't believe this but security chief Peabody (Chiwetel Ejiofor) isn't about to take chances by letting Salt run loose. Salt, terrified that her husband Mike's life is at risk, escapes the CIA offices and returns home only to find that Mike (August Diehl) has vanished. The CIA hunts Salt, but she eludes them. The next day Salt makes it through the security net around the Russian president and guns him down. Peabody captures her, but can't understand why she didn't kill him too when she had the chance.

Salt soon escapes and goes to meet Orlov. In reality, Orlov is the leader of a network of sleepers who've been replacing Americans visiting Eastern Europe since the 1960s; Lee Harvey Oswald was one of the first Americans to be replaced, JFK's assassination one of the project's first successes. The project replaced the original Evelyn Salt in childhood. Even though the USSR is gone, the network is still dedicated to giving Russia world supremacy. The assassination, Salt learns, is the opening act for Day X, the master plan for crippling American power.

Salt finds Mike at Orlov's headquarters, and watches him get executed without batting an eye. Satisfied as to her loyalty, Orlov sketches his plan for infiltrating the White House and seizing control of America's nuclear arsenal. Salt then kills him and the other sleepers with him; her love for Mike outweighs her loyalty to her motherland, and while she had no way to stop Orlov killing him, she's determined to exact revenge.

Posing as a loyal Day X agent, Salt infiltrates the White House where another sleeper seemingly attacks President Lewis (Hunt Block). The Secret Service and Winter, who's reporting on the hunt for Salt, rush Lewis into a secure underground bunker. Worried that the attack was Russian payback for Salt killing their president, Lewis sets up for a nuclear missile launch, just in case. Winter — another sleeper — knocks out the president and kills his guards.

Salt breaks into the bunker to find Winter carrying out the heart of the Day X plan — missile strikes on Tehran and Mecca that will engulf America in an all-out war with the Arab world. Winter trusts Salt enough to let her get close, but then a news broadcast reveals the Russian president is alive, and was only paralyzed by spider venom (from arachnologist Mike's supply). This tips Winter off to Salt's true allegiance, but nevertheless, she succeeds in aborting the launch and later kills him. Peabody takes her into custody, but she reminds him that the rest of the sleepers are out there, and with Mike dead, she has no purpose in life other than hunting them down. Peabody lets her escape and the hunt begins.

Like *Telefon*, this movie shows how films can employ Cold War conspiracies regardless of the current Russian government. It also illustrates, yet again, how interchangeable bogeymen can be. Orlov assures Salt that the fall of Soviet communism doesn't matter because they're still working for the same country; there's no suggestion he plans to engineer a turn back to communism.

While this might indicate the Russian Bear is stirring old paranoia up, it's noteworthy that like the 2010 season of *24* and the film *Hired Gun*, the film shows that the real attack on America will come from the Islamic world. Apparently Muslims are still the ultimate bogeyman in the post–9/11 era.

6

Muslim Fifth Columns in America

Surprisingly, Muslim fifth columns are not a big subject in movies.

Since 9/11, many pundits have claimed that American Muslims constitute a fifth column, just like the Japanese 60 years earlier: They won't assimilate, their religion requires them to kill unbelievers, and they could take over just by outbreeding the white people, as they've supposedly already done in Europe. And just like the Japanese (and the Catholics and the Jews), American Muslims' real loyalty is to an outside master: If their religion requires them to kill infidels and impose Islamic law on America, they won't hesitate.

This view of Islam hasn't shown up as much in films, despite the fact that since the 1970s, Muslim terrorists have been appearing in films as dependably as Nazis. As Jack Shaheen points out in *Reel Bad Arabs*, they are often pure bogeymen, in stories that have no connection to the Middle East:

- In *Back to the Future* (1985), Doc (Christopher Lloyd) partners with Libyan terrorists to provide him with plutonium to power his time machine. They murder him when they realize he's not building them a nuclear bomb.
- In regional productions of the musical *It's a Bird ... It's a Plane ... It's Superman*, the Chinese communist villains of the original Broadway show are often replaced by Arab terrorists.
- In the 1986 *Rambo* cartoon, the Arab terrorist Noma works in the terrorist cartel S.A.V.A.G.E. alongside ninjas, Nazis and bikers.
- In *Patriot Games* (1992), which adapts Tom Clancy's novel about an Irish terrorist group, the Ulster Liberation Army takes refuge in Libya at Palestine Liberation Organization bases. (Shaheen points out that the story uses a fictitious Irish group but has no problems identifying a specific Palestinian organization.)

The fifth-column angle was only present in a few films before 9/11, however. While more films have approached Islamic terrorism from that vantage point since 2001, Hollywood seems more cautious about indicting all Muslims as evil than it was with the Japanese. Some films, such as *Rendition* (2007) and *Civic Duty* (2006), portray political paranoia as a bigger problem than terrorism.

Pre–9/11

Much as *Rising Sun* sprang from the fear of Japan's economic clout, and the possibility that Japan would eclipse the United States, *Rollover* (1982) and *Network* (1976) both dealt with fears of Arab financial power after OPEC (the Organization of Petroleum Exporting Countries) managed to maintain a united front on oil prices that sent gasoline costs spiking up in the seventies. That the Arabs invested a lot of their new oil wealth in America only added to the paranoia, even though at the time *Network* came out, 90 percent of overseas investment came from Western Europe.

Network is primarily known for its portrayal of a television network so desperate for ratings, it will try anything to draw viewers, such as hiring terrorists to commit attacks for a reality show. However, it also expresses a raging political paranoia about Arab investment reminiscent of World War II fears of Japanese buying land and far-right fears about "international Jewish bankers."

Howard Beale (Peter Finch), an unstable TV news anchor, informs his audience that the network's parent company, CAA, is being bought by a holding company that's "buying it for the Arabs.... [They] are going to own what you read and what you see.... We all know Arabs control $16 billion in this country.... There's a hell of a lot we don't know about because all of those Arab petrodollars are washed through Switzerland and Canada and the biggest banks in this country.... The Arabs are simply buying us."

Beale adds that this is possible because the Arabs have "screwed us out of enough American dollars" to buy up America's biggest companies and they "already own half of England." Beale's rant triggers widespread public opposition to the sale, which prompts the government to intervene and prevent it.

Similar fears run through *Rollover*. Early on, a TV interviewer asks banker Maxwell Emory (Hume Cronyn) if the millions of dollars America has paid OPEC for oil doesn't pose an unprecedented risk for the American economy. Emory replies that our interests and the Middle East's are linked; the Arab nations are our trustworthy partners.

Emory is lying: He knows for a fact that the Arabs are shifting their wealth out of dollars and into gold (they consider it a safer investment), which will cripple America's economy. The Arabs are keeping this secret to avoid hurting the dollar's value while they're still invested in it; when one businessman learns what's going on, they have him murdered.

The main plot of the film involves a business and romantic alliance between the businessman's ambitious widow, Leigh Winters (Jane Fonda), and banker Hubb Smith (Kris Kristofferson). Leigh wants to impress her husband's board with a showpiece project that will convince them to make her the new CEO. She and Hubb go hat in hand to Saudi investors for funding, which Leigh finds humiliating.

When Leigh learns about the Arab financial plan, she tries using the knowledge to negotiate better terms on the loan. They respond with another murder attempt, which fails (for no other reason than she's the protagonist), so they pull all of their investments out of dollars immediately, destroying the world financial order. Sitting amidst the economic ruins, Leigh and Hubb agree to start over together.

6. Muslim Fifth Columns in America

The more familiar use for Arab villains in this period was of course terrorism, and some terrorist films did see American Muslims as a potential fifth column. In *Wanted: Dead or Alive* (1986), Middle Eastern students attending college in California are shown to be part of Malek Al-Rahim's (Gene Simmons) terrorist network, which launches its campaign by blowing up a cinema playing *Rambo*.

The Siege (1998) presents us with a network of Islamic infiltrators that ranges from chop-shop owners to college professors. New York–based FBI agent Hubbard (Denzel Washington) and his Lebanese-born partner Haddad (Tony Shalhoub) are called in when terrorists take a busload of passengers hostage. The bomb turns out to be a fake. Having gauged the government's response time, the terrorists detonate a real bomb a few days later, taking out another bus in full view of the media.

The FBI investigates with the help of CIA agent Kraft (Annette Bening), who frequently obstructs the investigation with warnings national security is at stake. Kraft tells Hubbard they should ignore the Fourth Amendment and hunt the terrorists without a warrant ("They believe they have a warrant from God—your laws don't mean shit to them!"). Hubbard refuses to step outside the law. College professor Samir Nazhde (Sami Bouajila), Kraft's mole in the terrorist network (and also her lover), helps them bust one of the cells but the attacks continue.

After one attack destroys the FBI building, Gen. Devereaux (Bruce Willis) places the city under martial law, sets up internment camps for Arabs (both immigrants and citizens) and begins torturing prisoners for information. Kraft tells Hubbard that the terrorists were U.S.–trained for operations overseas and given visas afterwards to come to America; after Devereaux captured a prominent cleric linked to terrorism, the former allies turned to enemies.

Working together, Kraft and Hubbard use Samir to find the final cell in the network. As the organization collapses, Kraft discovers too late that Samir is playing a double game, plotting one final bombing. He laughs at her when she tries to talk him out of it, and he and Kraft die in a final shoot-out. Hubbard arrests Devereaux for torture.

The film's portrayal of a panicked reaction to Arab terrorism now looks rather prescient. It's tame in its portrayal of American Muslims compared to the anti–Japanese films of the 1940s (there's no suggestion all Muslims are terrorists or that the internment camps are a good idea) but a number of Arab spokesmen protested that portraying America's Arab community as riddled with terrorists would inflame hostility, and that no other minority would be portrayed this way. (It's certainly hard to imagine that if the IRA launched terrorist bombings in New York that we'd see a movie about interning Irish-Americans.) Another complaint is that the only Muslims seen practicing their religion are the terrorists.

Post-9/11

As with politically paranoid movies about Nazis, communists and far-right terrorists (discussed later in the book), movies about Islamic terrorism tend to assume much vaster

Denzel Washington has to cope with an Islamic terrorist fifth column in *The Siege* (1999), as well as the military putting New York under martial law.

6. Muslim Fifth Columns in America

networks than we've seen so far in the real world. This may be a genuine belief on the part of the filmmakers or simply a matter of story-telling—conspiracies look much more formidable than lone wolf terrorists, even though the lone wolves are probably harder to predict or prevent. It gives the movie or TV series a politically paranoid quality either way.

The War Within (2005), a drama exploring the motivations of a terrorist, scores low on the paranoid scale. Hassan (Ayad Akhtar), who was locked up in the aftermath of 9/11, is now working as a terrorist plotting the bombing of Grand Central Station. The movie shows a fair-sized terrorist network in place, but doesn't portray all or even most Arabs as killers; when Tariq's friend, Sayeed (Firdous Bamji), a doctor who's giving him room and board, discovers what Hassan is plotting, he reports him to the police (only to be arrested for "harboring" the terrorist). Hassan's sweetheart Duri (Nandana Sen) also tries to talk him out of his mission, but in the end he detonates the bomb, despite his own ambivalence, as she's trying to reach him and make one last appeal.

Sleeper Cell (2005) The tagline for this Showtime series was the sublimely paranoid "Friends. Neighbors. Husbands. Terrorists." The opening episode has Darwyn (Michael Ealy), an Islamic ex-con, recruited into a terrorist cell by Farik (Oded Fehr), a U.S. Army veteran. What Farik doesn't know is that although Darwyn is a Muslim, he's also a federal agent, assigned to infiltrate the cell and thwart an upcoming attack. Over the course of the season the episodes cover the occasional side missions, such as murdering a respected Islamic scholar who preaches against terrorism, and visiting the Mexican crimelord who's supposed to be providing funding for the operation.

The series portrays a network that's well beyond anything that real Islamic terrorists seem able to accomplish: They have access to weapons-grade anthrax and extensive contacts in the U.S. military. They take out the scholar with a drug that triggers a heart attack. In terms of their methods, they could as easily be SPECTRE.

In a special feature on the DVD, the creators point out that they've assembled a multi-racial cast (Darwyn is black, Tommy [Blake Shields] and Christiane [Alex Nesic] are white, Ilya [Henry Lubatti] is Bosnian Muslim, Christiane is French) much as real-world Muslims aren't all Arabs. The narration perversely notes that this makes infiltration even scarier since an Islamic terrorist could look like anyone.

The second season followed in the same vein: A new cell, plotting to detonate a dirty bomb, recruits Darwyn as the only member of Farik's team that escaped prison. Once again, he manages to foil the plot, but Gayle (Melissa Sagemiller), his significant other, dies.

24 (2001–10) When *24* started, it drew attention because it was filmed entirely in "real time": The 24 episodes covered 24 hours of story, less time for commercials. As several cast members have joked, it's the one show where they never change clothes in the entire season. It was tightly written, tense and different.

Before long, however, the show attracted more attention for its increasing use of torture whenever protagonist Jack Bauer (Kiefer Sutherland) decided it was the only way to get vital information. In the universe of *24*, this makes sense: It always produces information, nobody ever gives a false answer and it's rare for an innocent to get tortured.

THE WAR ON TERROR JUST CAME HOME.

peter krause
CIVIC DUTY

ARE YOU DOING YOURS?

6. Muslim Fifth Columns in America

24 also drew attention for its increasing use of Muslims as villains. The storyline most relevant to this book is the fourth season (2004–05) which shows Arab terrorists living among us for years as a fifth column.

As the season opens, we're introduced to the Araz family of Turkish immigrants: father Navi (Nestor Serrano), mother Dina (Shohreh Aghdashloo) and son Behrooz (Jonathan Ahdout). They live in Los Angeles alongside their white neighbors and by all appearances they're a typical immigrant family; at one point, one of their neighbors rebukes another for being suspicious just because they're Muslim.

Bad mistake: It turns out that the five years the family has spent living in America, building up its cover, have all been in preparation for one spectacular day of terror involving the kidnapping and execution of the secretary of state, the computerized meltdown of several nuclear plants, the downing of Air Force One and seizing control of the nuclear football.

Behrooz, however, has been unable to stay detached and focused on the mission during his stay in L.A.: He has an American girlfriend and can't bring himself to obey his parents and break up with her. When Dina realizes that Debbie (Leighton Meester) might have seen some of the terrorist operation while trailing after Behrooz, Dina invites her over, then kills her. Later in the season, we learn that the terrorist leader Marwan (Arnold Vosloo) has his own cover identity working for an electronics company

Civic Duty (2006) One of the films that suggests that paranoia is exactly that, *Civic Duty* stars Peter Krause as Terry Allen, a newly unemployed accountant constantly bombarded by bad news — economic meltdown, terrorist threat — who becomes seized by the fear that his new neighbor Gabe Hassan (Khaled Abol Naga) is about to launch a terrorist strike. Terry's wife Marla (Kari Matchett) scoffs at Terry's evidence — Hassan hangs out with other Middle Eastern men and drives a rented car — and the FBI isn't impressed either. Nevertheless, Terry tells his wife it's their duty to act as "the eyes and ears" and copes with his continuing unemployment by stalking Hassan, breaking into his house and continuing to find evidence (chemical equipment) and rejecting alternative explanations (Hassan's an environmental studies grad student who needs the equipment for research).

Finally Terry captures Hassan at gunpoint and tries to force him to confess. Hassan says he has nothing to confess, but after the death of his wife during the Iraq occupation, he'd be justified if he did want to strike back. Marla realizes what's going on and calls the police, who surround the apartment. Terry's FBI contact tries to talk him down by confirming that Hassan is clean; horrified, Terry tries to shoot himself, but Marla rushes in and winds up taking the bullet. The film ends with Terry in an asylum, where he hallucinates that the TV news has confirmed that he was right all along.

Rendition (2007) is a more mundane version of the same view: Anwar (Omar Metwally), an Egyptian-born American resident with an American wife (Reese Witherspoon)

Opposite: Peter Krause tries to do his *Civic Duty* (2006) and warn the cops that his Muslim neighbor is a terrorist; as it turns out, the threat is in his head.

is detained by the CIA in South Africa on the belief he's involved in the recent series of North African terrorist bombings. When the officials discover that Anwar, a chemist, had some experience with bomb-making as an ATF consultant, they become convinced he's the reason the attacks have recently become more successful. CIA official Corrine Whitman (Meryl Streep) has him taken by extraordinary rendition, held and delivered to Egyptian authorities. Here he's tortured until he confesses to his role (it's quite obvious he'd confess to anything by this point) until repentant CIA handler Douglas (Jake Gyllenhaal) releases him, gets him back to the States and reports the whole sordid mess to the press.

Traitor (2008) stars Don Cheadle as Samir Horn, an Algerian-born American Muslim working for a formidable Islamic terrorist network that's plotting a major attack. What neither the terrorists nor the American agents pursuing him realize is that Samir is an FBI double agent, working to crack the ring from the inside. Notably, the film gives a lot of prominence to Samir's Islamic beliefs, showing him quoting the Koran and performing other rituals of faith.

Given America's ongoing involvement in the Middle East, it's unlikely this will be the last Muslim fifth-column film that we see.

7

Invasion of the Body Snatchers

The science fiction section of this book starts with Jack Finney's short story and novel *Body Snatchers*.

It wasn't the first story to use the idea of an alien fifth column impersonating human beings. John Campbell's "Who Goes There?" used that notion in 1940, as researchers at an Arctic station realize that a shapeshifting alien could have replaced any one of them. Robert Heinlein's *Puppet Masters* preceded *Body Snatchers* by a couple of years.

It's Finney's "pod people," however, that became the ET fifth column people remember, and it's the 1956 film adaptation that's been remade three times, not *It Came from Outer Space* (which preceded it by three years) or *The Day Mars Invaded Earth*. And the way the four adaptations and the original story diverge from each other says something about their times, and about how SF body snatching can be adjusted to new themes and settings in a way that remaking *I Married a Communist* couldn't.

The Finney Story

Dr. Miles Bennell, a GP in Mill Valley, California, has two problems. One, Becky, his almost-girlfriend from high school, is back in town, newly divorced and available—but being divorced himself, Miles is skittish about jumping on the romance bandwagon again. (Back in the fifties, before no-fault divorce and "starter marriages," divorce was considered somewhat more disreputable than it is today.)

The second problem is that Miles' patient Wilma, a sensible, down-to-earth woman, swears her Uncle Ira has been replaced by an imposter, even though he has all of Ira's memories and physical features, right down to the scars. Mannie Kaufman, a local psychiatrist, tells Miles he's heard lots of similar cases. Becky tells Miles she has the same feeling about her father.

Jack Belecec, a local writer, shows Miles a body in his (Jack's) basement. Finney describes it as fully human but with an unlived look, as if empty of personality or life experience, and devoid of scars or fingerprints. Later, Jack's wife Theodora discovers that the body has become a duplicate of Jack. Remembering Becky's concerns about her father, Miles rushes over to Becky's house, discovers a similar duplicate there and takes Becky to hide out with him at the Belecec home.

Mannie convinces Miles, Becky and the Belececs that there's a rational explanation for everything. (Coming from a psychiatrist, this might have carried extra weight for readers in an era when psychotherapy was widely considered to have revealed the ultimate truths of the human mind.) Of course he's wrong, as the four protagonists discover when they find seed pods taking human shape in the Belecec basement. Jack connects the pods to a mysterious rain of seeds the previous summer, and one scientist's claim that the seeds were extraterrestrial. Miles calls a military buddy for help, but his friend tells him that by the time it reached anyone with the authority to act on it, it would be so far removed from first-hand it would sound like a crazy rumor.

Miles and his friends decide to flee, then realize they can't abandon their community. Running from the aliens — who now control Mill Valley — the Belececs are forced to separate from their friends, and Miles and Becky fall into enemy hands.

The alien imposters reveal that they're survivors of a dying world, who have adapted to drift across space as pods, then duplicate the inhabitants of new worlds by copying their unique atomic and electrical patterns (which causes the originals to disintegrate). They retain all the originals' memories and see themselves as the same people, but improved. The aliens insist that Miles and Becky will feel the same after transition, but Miles realizes the pod people are devoid of all emotion.

The aliens tell Miles that after the pods have replaced all Earth life, they'll eventually die, sending a new generation of pods into space and leaving a dead world behind (like their previous homes, the Moon and Mars). Manny's pod tells Miles that for his people, survival is an end in itself; wiping out humanity is no more personal than when humanity wiped out the passenger pigeon.

Miles and Becky escape town, stumble across a field where new pods are growing, and begin burning them before deciding that wiping out the pods is impossible. The Mill Valley pod people capture them, but then the remaining pods rise from the field and head into space. Miles guesses that other humans in other towns were also fighting, and that the pods have decided that humanity fights too hard to make Earth a good breeding ground for a survival-oriented species. The story ends several years later with Mill Valley's pod people starting to die off and new, human families moving in to replace them, to the delight of the Belececs, Miles and his new wife Becky. (Finney glosses over what the intervening years living alongside duplicates of their friends and neighbors must have been like.)

Finney's tale first appeared in serialized form in *Collier's Magazine* (with a slightly different ending where the FBI shows up to help Miles burn the pods), then came out in book form in 1955. It was rereleased in the seventies to accompany the 1978 adaptation, with a few changes and updates (and one in-joke, wherein the characters catch a film adaptation of Finney's *Time and Again*).

A great deal has been written about the message Finney and his screen adaptors were sending, but Finney told Stephen King (as recounted in King's *Danse Macabre*), "I have read explanations of the meaning of this story, which amuse me, because there is no meaning at all; it was just a story meant to entertain, and with no more meaning that that....

7. Invasion of the Body Snatchers

The idea of writing a whole book in order to say that it's not really a good thing for us all to be alike and that individuality is a good thing, makes me laugh." All he wanted to do, he told King, was write about a series of inexplicable events in a small town, including the idea of people claiming someone close to them was an imposter. Finney added that he had no idea when he started the book where it would lead.

If Finney's goal was to entertain, he succeeded: The book slides quietly from a few odd incidents and seemingly silly worries into an atmosphere of paranoia and fear. The creepiest part is that there's absolutely no malice in the pods: They have no evil agenda, no scheme of conquest, no particular interest in Earth at all. We're just the latest world they happened to land on.

The book does slow down for long expository sessions with a scientist explaining the pods and how they work. Given that *Body Snatchers* was written for a mainstream (rather than genre) audience, readers in the 1950s may have found it more interesting than now. The concept must have seemed far stranger then than it does to today's audience. When the film version came out in 1956, *Variety* said the weird premise might put off some filmgoers.

While the pods are supposedly emotionless, in two scenes where Miles confronts pod people, they seem quite angry. In an another scene later in the book, after his transformed patients have assured him that their fears were groundless, Miles hears them mock his gullibility and compares them to a black shoeshine man he once overheard secretly sneering at his customers; that must have been a powerful image for readers back in the days of segregation, but the gloating pods don't sound emotionless at all.

There's no reason to doubt Finney's disclaimer about having no deep meaning in mind, but emotionally the book is very much about something: Miles' determined struggle to preserve the community he loves and calls home.

Characters in Finney's stories were often frustrated with a modern world they found to be cold, bloodless and emotionally sterile compared to the days of old. In *The Third Level*, a modern psychiatrist becomes a farmer in small-town Iowa, 1894, and glories in the tight-knit, friendly community; in *Of Missing Persons*, a man tries to escape modern society for life in an agrarian space colony; *I'm Scared* has humanity reject the present so thoroughly that time itself is bent. The time-traveling protagonist of Finney's *Time and Again* decides to stay in the 19th century, which he sees as more passionate, more alive, more real than the present.

In *Body Snatchers*, Miles expresses the same unhappiness while using a rotary phone: They may be more efficient than an old-fashioned switchboard operator, but an operator who knew the town and knew Miles' schedule would be able to route calls to him wherever he was.

Rotary phones aside, Mill Valley is the dream community many Finney characters long for, a small town where everyone knows everyone and they all watch out for each other. One of the signs of infiltration is that pod people don't keep up their homes, gardens or stores, in order to discourage unwanted visitors. The happy ending is not Miles' marriage or the pods leaving the planet, but town itself returning to normal.

SCREEN ENEMIES OF THE AMERICAN WAY

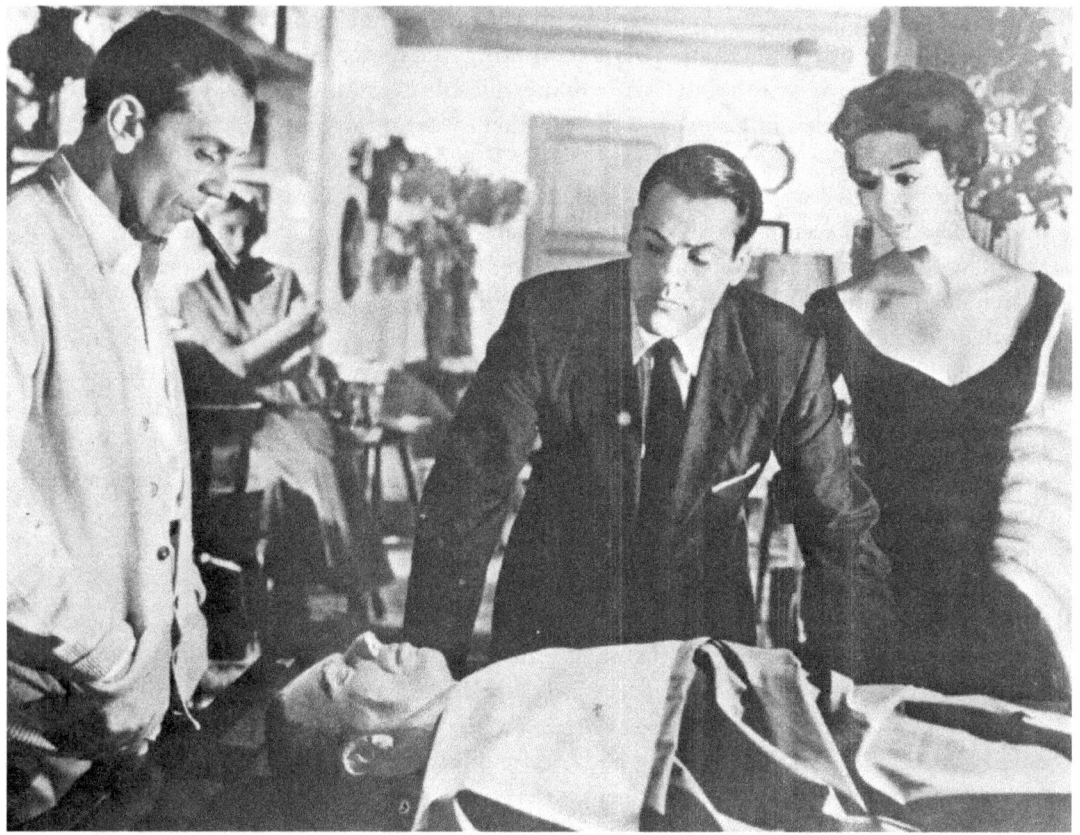

King Donovan, Kevin McCarthy and Dana Wynter encounter a pod in the process of becoming human in *Invasion of the Body Snatchers* (1956).

Each of the four *Body Snatchers* movie adaptations has a slightly different emotional core.

Invasion of the Body Snatchers (1956) Standing on the country club steps, small-town doctor Miles Bennell (Kevin McCarthy) tells his girlfriend Becky (Dana Wynter) that if he's right, people in town fall asleep and never wake up as themselves. Becky asks how he'd know if she were different, and he kisses her with a smile.

Less than an hour of running time later, he kisses her again — and knows she is no longer human. Where Finney's novel found its heart in fighting for community, the 1956 screen version finds it in fighting, unsuccessfully, to preserve love.

The film opens with Miles frantically trying to convince a pair of psych-ward doctors that he is absolutely sane and that his bizarre account should be taken seriously. Via flashbacks we see Miles returning to his hometown, Santa Mira, after several weeks away and launch into the filmed version of Finney's story: Becky's return, the troubled patient, the corpse in the Belicec house, the discovery of the pods.

As the leads grasp what's happening, Miles gives a speech to Becky that doesn't come

7. Invasion of the Body Snatchers

from the novel (though it's certainly in the spirit of Finney): "In my practice, I see how people have allowed their humanity to drain away ... only it happens slowly instead of all at once. They didn't seem to mind ... We harden our hearts, grow callous ... Only when we have to fight to stay human do we realize how precious it is to us ... how dear ... as you are to me."

Later, Dr. Kaufman (Larry Gates) and the transformed Jack Belecccs (King Donovan) assure Miles that it's better to become a pod because you live free from pain. When Miles replies that there's no love in the body snatchers either, Kaufman scoffs: "You've been in love before. It didn't last. It never does."

Miles and Becky overcome their captors, though Miles can't bring himself to kill them, and try to slip out of town by pretending they've already been taken over. They see the pod people transporting truckloads of pods out of town (or stuffing them into cars to visit relatives), then Becky screams at seeing a dog almost hit by a car. The pod people realize they're human and swarm after them.

Miles and Becky hide out in an old mine tunnel; hearing singing, Miles tracks down

There's hope! Kevin McCarthy and Dana Wynter hear the sounds of real human beings in *Invasion of the Body Snatchers* **(1956) — or so they think.**

the source (which Becky tells him shows they're not "the only ones left who know what love is") only to discovers it's the radio from the radio of a truck being loaded with pods from a greenhouse. When he returns to the tunnel, an exhausted Becky tells him they have to sleep; heroically, he carries her from the tunnel, kisses her passionately ... and knows she's been replaced.

This is the big departure from Finney, where Miles and Becky made it to a happy-ever-after ending. It's also a big logic gap in the film: There's no sign of any pods in the mine to replace Becky, and based on how slowly the pods grow, Becky wasn't alone long enough to be duplicated. Dramatically, though, it certainly works.

Miles flees from her, recounting to the doctors in voice-over, "I never knew what horror was until I kissed Becky." The pod people, satisfied that Miles will never convince anyone of their presence, let him run and Miles ends up on the freeway, screaming out "You're next!" to passing motorists.

Back in the present, the two doctors agree that Miles is an obvious loonie; then a driver comes in with severe injures from a crash — and an EMT mentions that the truck was piled high with weird, giant seed pods. Realizing the truth, the doctors direct a cop to have all traffic out of Santa Mira stopped, and an exhausted Miles sags against the wall in relief.

Director Don Siegel's original plan for the ending involved Miles wearily collapsing by the side of the road, gasping out warnings in his despair; a crowd surrounds him, but are they human or pod people? This was revised to have Miles standing and screaming on the freeway, but producer Walter Wanger vetoed this, tacking on the prologue and epilogue, despite Siegel's objections that he'd prefer to keep the tone at the start of the film completely normal.

This is the best of the four *Body Snatchers* adaptations, a solid, well-made film that drives home the creepiness of the premise even without special effects. As in the book, this fifth column isn't infiltrating us to conquer America or because they hate our freedoms; they just want to survive. The pods don't even think of themselves as imposters; the sense of self carries over from the original, so they believe they *are* the same person, just improved by the liberation from emotion. They show a bland affability when dealing with Miles and a total lack of emotion when they think they're unheard.

Meanings

Even without any underlying message, Finney's novel makes for a great story. The *Body Snatchers* films, however, have irresistibly drawn people eager to find meanings, whether or not they were intended. The Communist Party in *I Married a Communist* is not a symbol or a metaphor, it's a literal communist conspiracy and can't be mistaken for anything else. The pod people, by contrast, have no overt ties to commies, Nazis or anyone else, so they can be interpreted much more freely.

Siegel himself said that the movie was about losing feeling, losing passion, and the

7. Invasion of the Body Snatchers

possibility that some people, as Miles points out in the movie, are happier and more comfortable that way. Newspaper reviews at the time took much the same view.

In 1957, however, Italian critic Ernesto Laura said that the movie appeared to be an American portrayal of communist subversion, an interpretation that became widely accepted. Miles' voice-over comment after Becky is podded ("The girl I loved was an inhuman enemy bent on my destruction.... To survive [they] must take over every other man") is certainly close to the rhetoric in anticommunist movies of the era. Author Mike Davis has said that the film "completely fit all the descriptions my teachers and elders were telling me about what Communism was like." Siegel's own suggested title, *Sleep No More*, has been seen by some as a reference to the "eternal vigilance" that's said to be the price of freedom, although Siegel said it had more to do with his longstanding insomnia.

On the other hand, Miles' speech about losing ourselves day by day has been taken as proof that the film's message is anti-conformity. In *Seeing Is Believing*, Peter Biskind argues that the message of the film is pro-individual, anti-groupthink, rejecting conformity of any sort.

As noted above, where Miles in Finney's *Body Snatchers* triumphs when his community survives, Miles in this movie fails when Becky is podded. Miles fears the pods because they kill love; it's as a couple that he and Becky face the menace, and it's when they separate that she dies. Film teacher Nancy Steffen-Fluhr, however, has suggested that the movie shows a fear of sexual commitment — why else does Miles know fear when he kisses Becky? (of course, this overlooks that he's kissed her before without any fear)—and that the distinction Siegel makes between living with passion and becoming a pod is really a contrast between active machismo and less aggressive, more stereotypically feminine qualities.

Invasion of the Body Snatchers (1978) This remake follows the plot of the Siegel film fairly closely: Space spores drift down onto San Francisco, where they begin replacing various individuals. The odd incidents gradually draw the attention of health inspector Matthew Bennell (Donald Sutherland); lab worker Becky (Brooke Adams), his best friend; and the Belicecs (Jeff Goldblum, Veronica Cartwright). A psychiatrist, Kibner (Leonard Nimoy), assures them it's nothing, but the nightmare begins to develop. One particularly paranoid moment is when Matt tries to call outside the city, without giving his name, and the operator tells him, by name, that he shouldn't bother.

Special effects-wise, the scene where the pod almost takes over Matthew goes on far too long. There's also a misfired pod — a dog with its owner's face — that doesn't make much sense since we see no signs of other duplication errors (the dog-man jolts Becky out of pretending to be emotionless in the same way the endangered dog did in 1956). A special sound effect, the hideous screech the pod people give out upon sighting a human, worked for some filmgoers but came off laughable to others.

The biggest change in the plot comes with Becky's death: Becky crumbles into dust as Matt holds her, and her duplicate appears a second later. In a scene reminiscent of the book, Matt takes out his anger on a pod warehouse. We cut back at the end to alien-

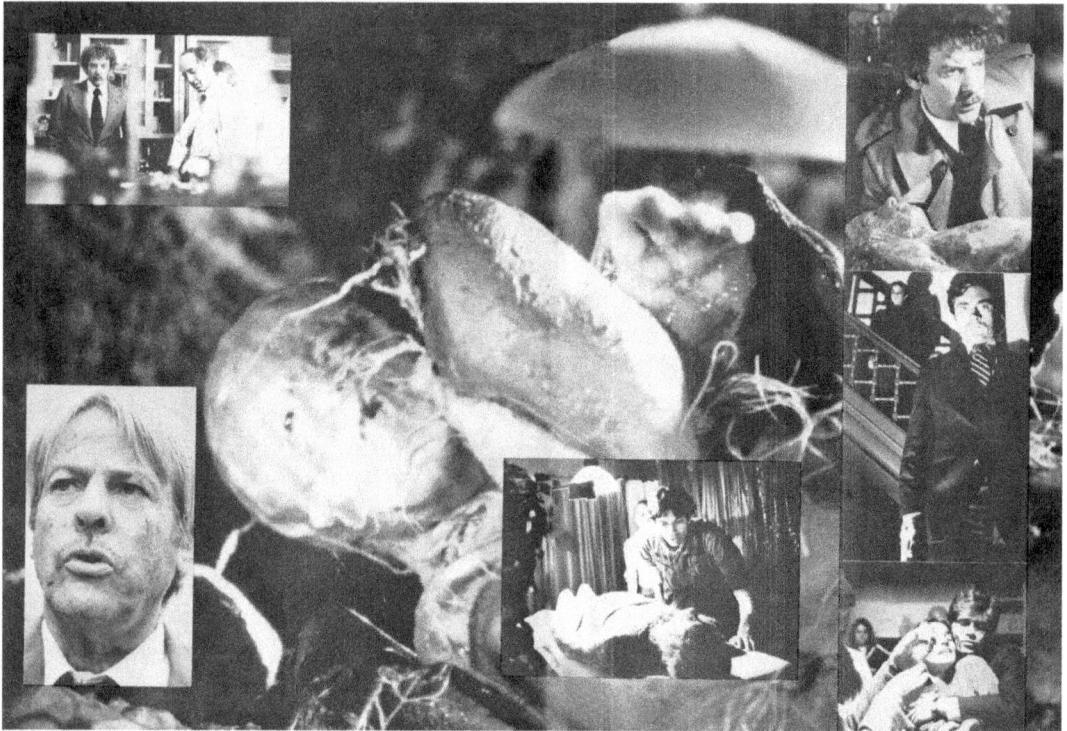

A two-page spread from the press kit for the 1978 film, with stills against a background of a developing pod. At the bottom left is Kevin McCarthy in his cameo role.

dominated San Francisco where Nancy Belicec, posing as a pod person, finds Matt. Unfortunately, he *is* a pod and when he sees she isn't, gives forth the scream.

In his DVD commentary, Philip Kaufman, the film's director, said he saw this as a sequel to the original—what happens 20 years after—including the 1956 version's star Kevin McCarthy showing up in traffic screaming, "You're next!" This doesn't make much sense since fresh pods are shown drifting from space at the start, and it's hard to believe they've spent the previous 20 years here without accomplishing more. (And as science fiction film critic Baird Searles once put it, has Miles been running in traffic for two decades?)

Although the plot is similar, the emotional core of the book is different, and so is the setting: San Francisco, the home of sixties counter culture. Several critics concluded that this *Body Snatchers* was about the death of the counter-culture, or its transformation into a new conformity; one writer compared the pod takeover to a cult that rejects society, drops out of the mainstream and ends up committing suicide.

Kaufman's DVD commentary suggests that it's more about creeping corporate-imposed conformity, and that setting it in the home of Haight-Ashbury and the summer of love made for more of a contrast. During a scene where Becky's pod-person husband, Geoffrey, sits woodenly watching commercials, Kaufman comments that this is precisely

7. Invasion of the Body Snatchers

The second *Invasion of the Body Snatchers* (1978) is all imaginary, psychiatrist Leonard Nimoy (back to camera) tells Jeff Goldblum, Donald Sutherland, Veronica Cartwright and Brooke Adams. He is, of course, wrong, even before becoming a pod person.

what the media want, viewers who will passively watch whatever they put on. At Matt's office during the ending scenes, the pod people continue with their everyday jobs, since they still believe themselves the same people, but when they're between tasks, they sit and stare at the walls blankly until there's more work.

"Everything in *Body Snatchers* has largely come to pass," Kaufman says. "We're living in a world largely controlled by pods." He adds that Kibner, the psychiatrist, represents the feel-good therapy of the day, the shrinks who tell us "everything is okay, but we know it's not okay."

Some critics saw the San Francisco setting as indicating a theme of big-city alienation—if your neighbors became pods, would you know them well enough to tell?—but in point of fact, it's the opposite. The movie's emotional core is a small group of friends struggling to hold together in the face of the pods. Film critic Pauline Kael wrote that the original film was about the right of normal folks to be normal, where this film is about "the right of freaks to be freaks." Santa Mira in the 1956 version is a wholesome community stuffed with average, middle-class Americans; Matthew and his friends are charmingly eccentric. Becky gets a laugh out of Matt by making her eyes quiver goofily (it's not easy to describe in print, sorry); Nancy embraces all manner of crackpot pseudoscience; Jack Belicec, instead of the successful writer of the first film, supports himself by running a mud bath and cries silently at his lack of success.

Matt isn't in love with Becky in this version, but he loves her as a friend, and hurts just as much when she dies. The movie's pod people do reiterate the 1956 statement about love never lasting, but it seems out of place since Matt and Becky aren't lovers; it's friendship that's at stake, and their friendship that will be destroyed.

Unlike the 1956 pod people, these fifth columnists are so dead to emotion, they can't even fake it. Once Becky's husband is podded, he's emotionally distant, brushes her off and obviously doesn't care for her; it's only the inconceivability of what's happened that keeps her from believing it. When Miles and Becky enter the city's red-light district while on the run, the human sleaziness is a relief compared to being surrounded by pods.

Body Snatchers (1994) Unlike the Kaufman version, the plot of this remake diverges from the start, as teenaged Marti Malone (Gabrielle Anwar) accompanies her family — father Steve (Terry Kinney), kid brother Andy (Reilly Murphy), stepmom Carol (Meg Tilly), "the woman who replaced my mother" — to dad's EPA assignment, helping an Army base dispose of toxic waste. In a voice-over, Marti informs viewers that "if we'd known what was waiting for us, we'd have run."

Marti's unhappy to be living on base, but soon makes a friend in Jenn (Christine Elise), the base commander's cynical, rebellious daughter, and acquires a boyfriend in Tim (Billy Wirth), a chopper pilot. Other developments are more ominous:

- Base doctor Major Collins (Forest Whitaker) asks Steve if chemical waste could trigger paranoia, which would explain why he's seeing people terrified of their own families, or afraid to go to sleep.
- All the kids in Andy's day-care art class draw identical pictures; Andy later tells Marti uneasily that they tried to make him take a nap.
- Jen's alcoholic mother becomes stone-cold sober.

Then Andy touches his mother one night and her body crumbles — but it happened while they were alone and a replacement Carol is right there, so no one believes Andy, or worries that Carol now talks in a monotone. Carol plants pods to take over the family, but Marti awakens in time to save them. Unaware that Carol's been changed, Steve tells her they need to run, but she replies, "Where are you going to go? Where are you going to run? Where are you going to hide? Nowhere. Because there's no one like you left ... I know you're frightened, I know you're scared, I know you're confused ... all that fear, all that confusion is going to melt away."

The Malones run but Carol uses the scream to set the neighbors on their trail. (A lawsuit resulted from director Abel Ferrara lifting the scream from the 1978 film without authorization; he told an interviewer that he assumed it had been part of the original novel.) Later, Steve guides Andy and Marti back through the base housing, telling them to show no feeling — but he's already been podded, and leads them into a trap. Marti reluctantly kills her father, then she and Andy are recaptured and taken to the base hospital to be podded. Tim rescues them — which requires ignoring everyone else being

7. Invasion of the Body Snatchers

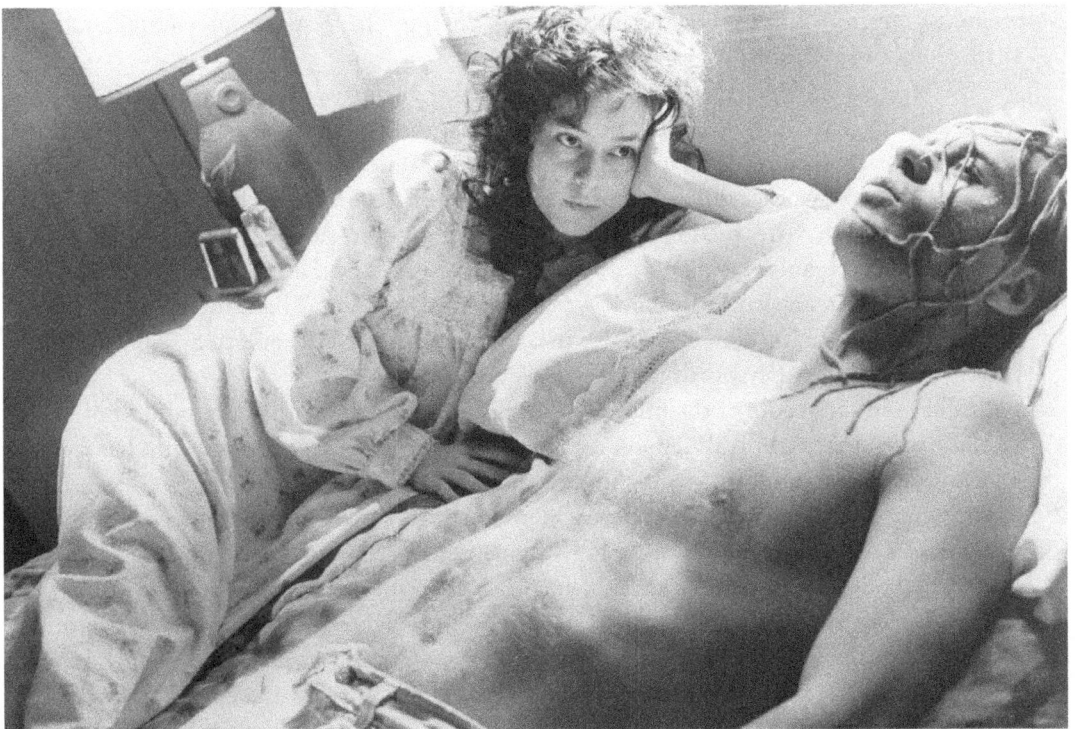

Carol (Meg Tilly) watches patiently as her husband (Terry Kinney) becomes the latest pod person in *Body Snatchers* (1994).

dragged to their doom — and they take off in Tim's helicopter. Andy, however, has become a pod person, and Marti has to throw her beloved brother to his death.

Tim unleashes his weaponry on the truckloads of pods being shipped to other bases and Marti observes that "our reaction was mostly human.... Revenge, hate, remorse, despair, pity and most of all fear. I remember feeling all those things as I watched the bombs explode." The movie ends with them landing at another base — but is the stone-faced soldier waving for them to land just disciplined or is he a pod?

Robert H. Solo, producer of the 1978 version, returned to the Finney story in what he hoped would launch a science fiction franchise, with a follow-up story planned for Washington, D.C. (which was indeed the setting later producers used for 2007's *The Invasion*). Stuart Gordon, the first director and scriptwriter, wanted to open focusing on Steve (so that when Marti turns out to be the protagonist, it's a surprise) but the decision to use a voice-over put an end to that. Gordon also proposed having the pods look completely alien under the human skin, but it was decided this veered too far from the Finney concept.

Eventually, Abel Ferrara, better known for street-tough stories such as *Bad Lieutenant*, took over from Gordon (disputes about the merits of the two directors and their approaches are covered extensively in the book *They're Here...*). All of which shows that whatever meaning is found in the finished film emerged from many interactions, rather than an auteur's vision.

What does emerge? A theme of opposition to conformity, which is reinforced by setting events on a military base. Like previous films, the pods insist their way is superior and more peaceful, but it's an authoritarian peace produced through conforming to the group, rather than peace through the loss of emotion. Gen. Platt (R. Lee Ermey) tells Collins the pods have learned in their spacefaring that group survival is everything, individual survival meaningless. Collins replies that the individual always matters, but Platt tells him the human way is doomed — pod unity is superior. The military setting also gives the pods more freedom to operate: In one scene, when Marti questions some soldiers about their actions, they brush her off with, "Following orders."

The emotional core of the film, the thing Marti fights for, is her family. It's not perfect, the way Finney's Mill Valley seems to be — Marti squabbles constantly with her father and loathes her stepmother — but she loves her dad and adores her brother. Like Miles, she's going to lose them both, and even more horribly, since Miles never had to kill the pod version of Becky (the filmmakers had an intense debate over the decision to have Marti kill Andy). Small wonder that the final attack on the pods is portrayed as pure rage, rather than the heroic struggle of the Finney novel or Matt's sobbing in the 1978 film.

The Invasion (2007) In every adaptation of *Body Snatchers*, the pod people assure us our lives will be better once they remove our emotions. *The Invasion* is the first version to imply that they're right — we really would be better off as emotionless pods than human.

Like the 1956 film, this is structured as a flashback. The movie opens with Washington psychiatrist Carol Bennell (Nicole Kidman) looting drugs and caffeinated drinks from an empty pharmacy to stay awake, then jumps back to a space shuttle breaking up and scattering pieces across the Southwest. Carol's ex-husband Tucker (Jeremy Northam) arrives at one of the crash sites with a CDC team investigating some alien spores on the shuttle, and cuts himself on the metal. That night, spore-cells spread through his body and cover him with a slime sheath.

Tucker shows up in DC the next day and tells Carol he wants to spend more time with their son, Oliver (Jackson Bond). Carol agrees to let Oliver visit Tucker for the weekend, though she tells her platonic-but-wishes-he-was-more friend Ben (Daniel Craig) she's uneasy about Tucker's sudden interest. At the office, Carol's patient Wendy (Veronica Cartwright) tells Carol her abusive husband has changed strangely: He doesn't yell at her, their dog hates him, and when it attacked him, he broke its neck without batting an eye. (In the tradition of countless horror movies, dogs in *Invasion* sense and hate the infected.)

Tucker next meets with pharmaceutical executives asking them to mass-produce a vaccine for the upcoming flu season; the meeting lets him spread the virus by having infected waiters puke into the water jugs. Carol drives Ollie to Tucker, sees a woman screaming "They're here!" struck by a car and sees the police watch without emotion. At dinner with Ben and the Belicecs (Josef Sommer, Celia Weston), Czech diplomats in this version, Carol talks to Yorish (Roger Rees) who tells her if we ever read a newspaper and don't find it full of terrible acts, it will be a sign people are no longer human.

7. Invasion of the Body Snatchers

As the infection spreads, Carol acquires a sample of infected cells; Ben and his friend Steve (Jeffrey Wright) analyze it and discover that the disease is an intelligent alien virus capable of rewriting human DNA. A frightened Carol rushes to collect Oliver, but Tucker traps her and spits in her face, assuring her she'll be fine when she wakes up. Carol flees and winds up on a subway car full of stiff, emotionless passengers — all of whom, Carol realizes, are normal humans trying to pass. As she crosses the city, she discovers the infected are using drastic tactics, such as suicide jumps off tall buildings, to provoke a reaction from the fakers.

A call from Oliver makes Carol realize he's immune to the virus, which means his blood might be the basis for a cure. She and Ben set off to rescue him, but split up when Ben has to lead a posse of the infected away. As Carol rescues Oliver, we see glimpses of the news that show hostile nations signing peace treaties and universal healthcare and nuclear disarmament becoming a reality. When Tucker catches Carol, he taunts her that infection is doing more good for people than her practice ever did, and that once she changes, she'll no longer put him third behind Oliver and her career. (For someone who's free of emotion, he comes off as extremely pissed.) Carol and Oliver escape and we catch up to the opening scene.

Ben, now infected, leads the posse to confront Carol in the pharmacy, telling her that the infection is ending poverty, war, murder and rape, creating a world "where no one can hurt each other, exploit each other — there is no other. Deep down, you know that fighting us is fighting for the wrong things." But when Carol asks about Oliver, Ben admits that immune humans won't be allowed to live. Carol grabs a gun and starts shooting.

With Steve's help, Carol reaches an Army base that's become a haven for the uninfected. Oliver's blood becomes the basis for a vaccine, which the military sprays across the country; days later, Ben and Carol are together, but the newspapers show that we're once again human, committing violence and destruction the way we always have.

In interviews on the DVD, *The Invasion*'s creators say they went with a viral form of invasion because they saw pandemics as the great fear of the 21st century. As a result, the movie feels less like an adaptation of Finney and more like a remake of *Robin Cook's Invasion* (1997). This considerably undercuts the horror compared to the first three movies, since infection doesn't kill the victims, only takes them over. Unlike the other Finney adaptations, the protagonists all survive.

Perhaps the low body count makes it easy for the movie to side with the body snatchers. Under the influence of the virus, the world is at peace and utopia is on the horizon, and unlike the other movies, there is no downside to the transformation. While the Kaufman pods might be too listless to make war on each other, it's hard to imagine them passing universal healthcare either; nor does *Invasion* show much of Gen. Platt's "the race is everything" thinking. If anything, Ben's "there is no other" seems to imply there's some sort of hive mind, though it's never spelled out.

In contrast, the infected cite Carol's psychiatric practice as a perfect example of how clumsily and ineffectively humans try to improve things; prescribing antidepressants is a poor substitute for utopia. It's true, immune humans will be killed, but that's treated less as immoral and more as a personal tragedy; if it wasn't Oliver, it's possible Carol wouldn't have objected.

As a result, even though nobody dies and the world returns to normal, *Invasion*'s ending comes off as the darkest of any version: In winning, we've lost. *Nobody* has any argument in favor of staying human, even as simple as *The Faculty*'s "I'd rather be scared" (as covered in the next chapter).

Emotionally, the Carol-Ollie relationship is the core of the film, but *Invasion*'s approach gives it a different spin from any other Finney film: The real terror for Carol is not that Ollie will become a pod person, it's that he'll be killed because he can't become one.

This is also the only film where the government does anything effective against the body snatchers. Even though Steven does the research, it's the military that spreads the vaccine and saves the day.

At press time, this was the last adaptation of Finney (though this author would bet good money there will be another sooner or later) but there's a lot more science fictional fifth columns to come in our next chapter.

8

Brain Eaters, Human Duplicators and Other Science Fictional Fifth Columns

Finney's pod people are science fiction's best and most memorable fifth column, but even in the movies, they weren't the first, or the only alien infiltrators.

An earlier SF body snatcher film, *It Came from Outer Space* (1953) is unusual in that it opts for trust over paranoia. The movie is set around the small Arizona town of Sand Rock, which considers astronomer-science writer John Putnam (Richard Carlson) its resident flake. When a meteor crashes nearby, John discovers it's a spaceship, but the crater wall collapses and buries it before he can show anyone. The locals think he's crazy to call for guarding the crater, but later, John and his girlfriend Ellen (Barbara Rush) see a one-eyed blob on the road back to town.

John discovers that the aliens are shapeshifters who have replaced his friends George and Frank (Joe Sawyer, Russell Johnson). But the aliens assure him it's a temporary imposture — "We cannot, we would not take your souls or minds or bodies. Don't be afraid." (A few years later, this would have seemed a deliberate twist on *Invasion of the Body Snatchers*.) However, if he doesn't give them enough time to finish their mission, terrible things will happen.

As the evidence of an alien presence accumulates, Sheriff Matt Warren (Charles Drake) tells John that if the aliens can change shape, "I couldn't be sure you were John Putnam." John replies, "That's right.... Wouldn't it be a fine trick if I were an alien from another world, come here to give you a lot of false leads?"

An alien duplicate of Ellen lures John to the mine where the aliens are repairing their ship. They tell John that they crashed on Earth by mistake, and will be gone soon. When John tells Matt, the sheriff refuses to believe their good intentions. What if they're lying? What if they've replaced more townies than John knows?

When John tells Ellen's duplicate that Matt is going to storm the mine, "Ellen" tries to kill him for what she believes is his betrayal. John survives and confronts the aliens at the worksite, where his duplicate tells him that he'd sooner destroy the ship they've worked on for a thousand years than let it fall into human hands. John convinces them not to give up, and to free their human captives, then he seals off the mine they're working in. This gives the aliens time to complete their repairs and leave. John tells the townies that while it was too soon for the two worlds to meet, "there will be other nights, other stars for us to watch.... They'll be back."

John Putnam (Richard Carlson) finds a crashed spaceship in a supposed meteor crater and realizes that *It Came from Outer Space* (1953).

This film, based on a story by Ray Bradbury (Bill Warren's book *Keep Watching the Skies!* has a detailed discussion of how much can be credited to Bradbury and how much credit goes to screenwriter Harry Essex), is unusual for showing that our fear of the aliens among us is injustified: Unlike Miles' patients or the kids in *The Faculty*, Sand Rock has nothing to be afraid of. Of course, they have no way to know that; John compares the sheriff's fear of the aliens to arachnophobia, but from Matt's point of view, the aliens are kidnapping and replacing innocent people. There's no more reason to believe them than to believe the pod people when they tell Miles and Becky that being podded is an improvement. (A 1995 remake, *It Came from Outer Space II*, follows the same plot, but makes it the basis for a far more boring movie.)

Invaders from Mars (1953) Another predecessor of the *Body Snatchers* film, this stands out from the pack for its distinctive visual style and by giving us a child's eye view of an alien fifth column.

David (Jimmy Hunt) is a boy with a passion for astronomy and two loving parents, George (Leif Erickson) and Mary (Hillary Brooke). Waking during a storm, David sees

8. Brain Eaters, Human Duplicators and Other SF Fifth Columns

The backs of the *Invaders from Mars* (1953) have visible zippers, but Bill Warren in *Keep Watching the Skies!* has described how terrifying this kid's-eye view of alien infiltration was in his childhood.

a flying saucer descend ("Gee whiz!"), landing out of sight on the sandy lot behind his parents' farmhouse. George, an engineer on a top-secret military rocket project, feels an obligation to check out the sandlot; the next thing we see is the lot without George, and a hole in the sand slowly filling itself up.

When Mary reports him gone, the cops assure her that George is just absent-minded (she retorts, "He's an engineer, not a comic book scientist!"). The cops go out to the sandy area. The sand falls away under the officers, swallowing them.

George returns home, transformed: Instead of his usual friendly manner, he's hard, authoritarian and angry, refusing to answer questions. When David points out an odd scratch on the back of his neck, George knocks him to the floor. The two cops, now stiff and wooden, tell the family they're dropping the matter and discuss the "important work" they're doing with George. Mary jokes that it sounds like they're plotting.

After David's playmate Kathy (Janine Perreau) gets taken over, he tries to find an adult to help him, but they either refuse to believe him or they're possessed. The enslaved chief of police has David locked away until his mother, who's also been taken, comes to pick him up. Fortunately Dr. Blake (Helena Carter), a psychiatrist, is impressed enough by David to contact Kelston (Arthur Franz), an astronomer who's befriended David. Kelston vouches for David's reliability; when Mary shows up, Blake claims David has polio and takes him into quarantine.

Kelston tells David and Blake his theory: After Mars grew too cold to support life, the Martians moved their civilization into space, where they're served by synthetic mutants. Now that Earth is preparing to enter space, the Martians see it as a threat to their sphere of interest and want to squelch our space program.

The alien puppets begin a campaign of sabotage while the military, alerted by Kelston, prepares for a counter-attack on the buried ship. David learns that the Martians control people by a crystal implanted in their brains, and that the side effects have killed Kathy. Surgery to remove the crystal is just as risky, making David ambivalent when his parents are caught and prepped for surgery.

The military men break into the buried Martian ship, but the assault is blocked by the Martian technology, which can open and reseal passages instantly. Blake and David are caught and dragged before a giant Martian head — "mankind developed to its ultimate intelligence" — but escape before being implanted with crystals. As David flees, he flashes back to his experiences. Then the Army detonates the ship — and David wakes up during a thunderstorm to find himself safe at home. It was all a dream. His babble baffles his parents ("The big green head had a raygun!") but they convince David he was only dreaming. He returns to his bedroom but through the window he sees a familiar saucer descending. (The British release replaced this with a scene of Kelston and Blake telling David his parents came through the operation fine.)

As *Keep Watching the Skies!* points out, this is a child's-eye view of fifth-column paranoia: David's parents are turned into monsters, his friends are taken over and every authority figure is working against him. The mood is enhanced by director William Cameron Menzies' set design: The police station, for example, consists of little beyond a

8. Brain Eaters, Human Duplicators and Other SF Fifth Columns

front desk, a jail cell and a big clock on the wall, the items that might most impress themselves on a small kid in a dream.

It Conquered the World (1956) This is one of the few movies (along with *The Brain Eaters*) to feature a willing human collaborator with the alien takeover.

At the start of the movie, Dr. Paul Nelson (Peter Graves) is overseeing a satellite launch, despite warnings from physicist Tom Anderson (Lee Van Cleef) that an extraterrestrial intelligence is watching our venture into space with disapproval. Three months later, Tom shows Paul a radio he claims communicates with Venus, then he tells his wife Claire (Beverly Garland) that a Venusian is riding the satellite back to Earth to save humanity.

When the satellite lands, the alien kills all electrical power in the area so that phones, planes, cars and, illogically, watches no longer work. The alien sends out batlike creatures which inject their victims with implants that render them emotionless and obedient; Tom singles out the local police chief, the mayor, the general running the satellite project and Paul and his wife Joan (Sally Fraser) for takeover. Paul kills the creature that attacks him, but the other attacks succeed and the enslaved general places the area under martial law.

A shot of Beulah from *It Conquered the World* (1956)

Tom tries to convince Paul that the Venusian will help us rise above hate and bitterness, but Paul replies, "Your hands are human but your mind is enemy. You're the greatest traitor of all time." Paul sees the alien puppets kill whoever gets in their way, then finds Joan waiting for him at home with another bat-creature. He destroys it, but Joan confirms that the process is irreversible and her humanity is lost forever. Paul reluctantly kills her.

Claire can't convince Tom he's on the wrong side so she takes a shotgun and tries to kill the alien. It kills her instead. When Tom hears her dying screams over his radio, it finally turns him against the Venusian. He arrives at its lair in the middle of the military attack and burns the alien to death with a blowtorch, dying in the attempt. Paul concludes that if there's any hope for man, it has to come from us ourselves, not an outside force.

Claire (Beverly Garland) and Beulah in *It Conquered the World* (1956). The inferior 1966 remake at least provided the creature's given name: *Zontar, the Thing from Venus*.

While this film is low-budget and frequently flawed, it has the advantage of a good cast and, like *Invasion of the Body Snatchers*, a no-escape set-up: Once the alien takes you, there's no hope. Like the 1994 *Body Snatchers*, it takes this one step further by forcing the protagonist to kill someone he cares about.

Azalea Productions remade this as *Zontar, the Thing from Venus* (1966), one of several

8. Brain Eaters, Human Duplicators and Other SF Fifth Columns

AIP remakes from that company. The remake replicated this almost scene for scene (though with poorer actors) so there's no point in reviewing it here.

I Married a Monster from Outer Space (1958) Traveling home from his bachelor party, small-town resident Bill Fowler (Tom Tryon) sees a body in his road, and stops his car. Once he steps into the road, an alien confronts him and Bill vanishes. Next morning he arrives late to his wedding with a glazed look and a brooding manner. In a storm that night, lightning reveals Bill's face is just an illusion concealing the alien under it.

A year later, Bill's wife Marge (Gloria Talbott) still isn't pregnant and she's baffled by how Bill has changed; at one point she tells him it's like he's been replaced by a twin brother. The changes trouble her enough that she follows Bill one night and sees the alien step out of his body, which becomes inert and unmoving.

Marge tells her godfather, Police Chief Collins (John Eldredge), what she saw, and he tells her to sit tight until he comes up with a plan. She has no idea that Collins is another alien, as are several of Bill's friends. After Dr. Wayne (Ken Lynch) gives Bill's buddy Sam oxygen after a near-drowning, Sam dies because he's an alien (oxygen is toxic, forcing them to use a breathing apparatus). Marge reports back to her godfather, who tells her he'll have her committed if she talks about aliens; she realizes he's one of them. Marge discovers the phone lines and the telegraph office are both under alien control so she can't contact anyone outside town, and the police have the roads blocked off.

Marge pushes "Bill" for the truth and he tells her that radiation from his home world's dying sun wiped out their women. The male survivors have been scouring the universe for a habitable planet and Earth is one of the few they've found; once they figure out how to sire alien babies via human women, the space fleet will descend and take over.

Gambling that Wayne isn't one of the invaders, Marge goes to him for help, and discovers that he's figured out the truth too. They realize that the one place they can find humans is among fathers in the maternity waiting room (where expectant fathers would sit, smoke and fret in the days before it became accepted for them to be there at birth). There they recruit a posse. (As Bill Warren points out in *Keep Watching the Skies!*, it's certain that all the town women are human, but the movie never suggests turning to them for help.)

The men fight their way into the spaceship where they find the prisoners strapped into what are apparently duplicator machines; pulling them free kills the alien imposters. Collins dies telling the fleet to give up on Earth and Bill expires telling Marge that he was just learning to understand this human experience of emotion.

The film is unusual for giving its alien fifth columnists individual personalities: Bill feels guilty about seizing Earth, other aliens kill us like cockroaches and the alien who marries the town party girl clearly loves his sex life. Unlike the Finney films, only a dozen humans are taken, but this proves enough to control the town (reminiscent of the anti-communist cliché that it only takes a small cadre to seize power).

The Brain Eaters (1958) Robert A. Heinlein's novel *Puppet Masters* (1951) was one of the landmark SF handlings of the alien-infiltrator concept. Set in the near future, it has federal agents of a super-secret spy service investigate the site of a flying saucer landing. The word from the area is that everything is fine, but the first agents sent to investigate never report back.

The latest crew of investigators discover that the ship was occupied by mind-controlling alien slugs and their ET host bodies, and the slugs are now taking over humans. Despite the government's best efforts to control the infestation, the slugs conquer a sizable part of the country until the good guys develop a bio-weapon that kills them off. The book ends on a spaceship heading to the slugs' home on Titan, ready to destroy them and free their hosts — but knowing, also, that we may face worse challenges in space and only a constant willingness to fight will keep us free.

The book is much more a straight invasion story than Finney's later tale of paranoia (and it also tapped into the then current interest in flying saucers) but Heinlein adds several touches to the alien invader formula. One of the first danger signs is that men around the crash site don't respond to Mary, a stunningly sexy agent — because the slugs, of course, don't have human sex drives. After the invasion, public nudity becomes the norm so that people can spot anyone ridden by a slug.

Heinlein said in 1957 that the book "is a thinly disguised allegory, a diatribe against totalitarianism in all its forms. Each writer has his personal philosophy; included in mine is an intense love of personal freedom and an almost religious respect for the dignity of the individual." The book specifically compares life in slug-controlled territory to life behind the Iron Curtain; humans who serve the slugs voluntarily are compared to communist collaborators. The metaphor may be why the slugs' idea of entertainment consists of forcing humans into sex games, gladiatorial combat and other degrading activities suitable to conquerors.

In 1958, AIP released *The Brain Eaters*, which triggered a lawsuit from Heinlein for ripping off his novel (the case was settled out of court). In the film, a mysterious, indestructible 50-foot-high cone appears in the woods outside the town of Riverdale (no relationship, presumably, to Archie Andrews' hometown). Residents start turning up dead and there are stories of a "fiery chariot" in the sky (which makes no sense given the slugs are actually subterranean). Blustering Senator Powers (Jack Hill) arrives to expose the "spaceship fairy tale" and meets the mayor's son Glenn Cameron (Alan Frost) and Kettering (Ed Nelson), a scientist studying the cone. Kettering believes it's a fuel section dropped by a spaceship, but can't explain the tunnel inside the cone or figure out where the tunnel goes.

Powers and the local doctor (Doug Banks) visit Mayor Cameron (Orville Sherman); a few seconds earlier, we saw Cameron struggling unsuccessfully to shoot himself. Their arrival turns him more aggressive and assertive. When Powers claims federal authority over the spaceship investigation, Cameron pulls his gun and tries to kill Powers; instead, the mayor gets shot and the good guys find a big dead slug on his back. The autopsy reveals

Opposite: Despite the title, *The Brain Eaters* (1958) don't actually eat brains, they simply take control of them. According to Professor Cole (Leonard Nimoy), the end result will be utopia, but don't believe him.

CRAWLING, SLIMY THINGS TERROR-BENT ON DESTROYING THE WORLD!
the Brain Eaters
STARRING EDWIN NELSON · JOANNA LEE · ALAN FROST · Produced by EDWIN NELSON
Directed by BRUNO VESOTA · Story and Screenplay by GORDON URQUHART · AN AMERICAN INTERNATIONAL PICTURE

that if the bullets hadn't finished the mayor, the slug would have killed him by dissolving his brain with acid if they'd tried to remove it.

The slugs have been possessing hosts all over town, including Kettering's girlfriend Alice (Joanna Lee), then using those hosts to put slugs on more victims. Powers announces a civil defense test to justify bringing in the military without alerting the slugs that he's onto them. The alien slaves make sure that, as usual, neither his telegrams nor his radio broadcast reaches Washington.

Near the cone, Glenn and Kettering discover a dying scientists babbling the word "carboniferous." Kettering realizes that the slugs date back to Earth's Carboniferous Period and have been living in the subterranean coal beds from that era (no explaining how they built the cone down there, what they parasitized inside the rocks or what that fiery chariot was). Fighting the slug-ridden cops guarding the cone, the guys follow the interior tunnel down to a cavern where they meet a graybeard named Prof. Cole (Leonard Nimoy — yes, the same Nimoy who gained SF immortality several years after this film). Cole claims that he voluntarily joined up with the aliens because they can create a world of complete harmony: "There is no conflict of purpose here as there is among mankind. We do not engage in combat, no violence of any kind.... We shall force upon man a life free of strain and turmoil." Unimpressed, Kettering shoots him, then he and Glenn flee the angry slugs.

Kettering works out a plan to electrocute the slugs by hooking the cone up to a power line. When Alice confronts him on the cone as he's completing the set-up, he vows to find some way to free her mind. Repulsed by the thought of betraying her masters, she shoots him. The slugs begin crawling out from below but Powers manages to trigger Kettering's trap and destroy them, along with Kettering and Alice. He then vows to hunt down the remaining slug-puppets.

An authorized adaptation of *Puppet Masters* came to the screen in 1994.

The Day Mars Invaded Earth (1963) This dull film opens with Dr. Fielding (Kent Taylor) landing a communications device on Mars; it explodes, sending out a powerful radio signal. Fielding then takes a vacation outside Los Angeles with his estranged wife Claire (Marie Windsor) and their children Judi (Betty Beall) and Rocky (Gregg Shank).

Shortly after arriving at their vacation home, David discovers doubles of the entire Fielding family wandering around the estate; other members of the family have the same experience. This bafflement continues for what seems like a very long time, then the doubles confront the family and tell them they're Martians, and Mars doesn't want further contact with Earth. Shortly afterwards, we see the family leaving to return to the city, then the film cuts to a shot of piles of ash (human remains) being washed away in the swimming pool. The Martians triumphed, "Fielding" is a fifth columnist and the probe will be sabotaged.

Other than having the aliens win, this is mind-bogglingly tedious. It is, however, unusually intelligent for an alien fifth column to replace an entire family up front, eliminating the "He's not my husband!" problem that crops up so often.

The Human Duplicators (1965) Glenn Martin (George Nader), an NIA agent, is called in to learn why several trusted scientists have turned against their employers, stealing

8. Brain Eaters, Human Duplicators and Other SF Fifth Columns

valuable equipment and, in one case, showing superhuman strength and invulnerability to bullets. Martin's boss suspects Red China or the USSR, but Martin doesn't buy either story. To add to the mystery, a scientist shot during a theft turns up dead with no bullet holes in him.

The trail leads to Prof. Dornheimer (George Macready), a scientist now working as a consultant for those he considers brilliant enough to deserve it. Martin learns that Dornheimer's hi-tech research is geared toward creating androids and at one point tells his girl Friday Gale (Barbara Nichols) to look out the window: "Hundred and hundreds of people—who's to say how many of them were androids ... imagine what it would mean if androids were infiltrating our society, our government, the military ... a silent, secret invasion."

That is, of course, exactly what's happening: Kolos (Richard Kiel), an agent of the Galactic Masters, has been sent here to infiltrate human society and prepare Earth for conquest. He used Dornheimer's research to create androids, then replaced Dornheimer himself—but not the professor's blind daughter, Lisa (Dolores Faith), whom Kolos has fallen for.

Martin discovers Dornheimer's android-making lab, only to be captured and duplicated himself. The duplicate reports to Martin's boss that Dornheimer was a dead end, but Gale becomes suspicious and discovers the imposture. Back at the lab, the Galactic Masters order Kolos to replace Lisa with another android. Sensing his reluctance, the other androids, led by the Dornheimer duplicate, turn on Kolos. They tell him they've been programmed to the point they're now superior to him, free of the pathetic emotions that are making him weak, and they warn that after they destroy him, his masters are next.

Gale reaches the laboratory and frees Martin, who uses the equipment she brought to destroy most of the androids. Martin's duplicate survives, but remains loyal to Kolos. He and Dornheimer destroy each other (although the androids are bulletproof, they shatter if you hit them hard). Kolos concedes defeat and tells the humans he will advise his masters against invasion, even though they will destroy him—but since he, himself, is only an android, his destruction matters not.

This is alien infiltration filtered through the James Bond formula, which had a huge influence on all kinds of films and other media during the sixties.

The Thing (1982) John W. Campbell's "Who Goes There?" is a classic SF short story. A research team in the Antarctic discovers a spaceship whose alien occupant can shift shape to take the form of any living creature, or multiple creatures since it reproduces by division. Realizing the threat this poses to humanity, the men work to destroy it—but can they succeed when some of them may have already been replaced?

In 1951, this inspired *The Thing from Another World*, in which a military Arctic expedition discovers a crashed spaceship and unwittingly releases its occupant. In this case, it's a plant-based life-form ("An intelligent carrot? The mind boggles!") that tries to kill the flyboys with sheer brute strength and cunning. The movie has little to do with Campbell, but does make for great viewing.

SCREEN ENEMIES OF THE AMERICAN WAY

Kolos (Richard Kiel) can't help falling for Lisa (Dolores Faith), even though he's only an android, and his feelings interfere with his plans to conquer Earth, in *The Human Duplicators* (1965).

The 1982 *The Thing* was considerably more faithful, with director John Carpenter giving us a fine piece of infiltration paranoia. It begins at a U.S. Antarctic base when a chopper from the nearby Norwegian station flies in, shooting at a running dog. When the chopper lands, the gunman fires at the Americans, then blows up his own chopper before the base crew members kill him in self-defense. Chopper pilot MacReady (Kurt Russell) visits the Norwegian camp, where everyone has died violently. Does it have anything to do with the mysterious object they were thawing out of the Antarctic ice?

After the dog is placed in the pen with the other sled dogs, the men catch it killing and duplicating them. They realize what they're up against — and that the dog ran around free long enough that any of them could have been replaced by the alien. The fear of infiltration proves as deadly a threat as the alien itself. One man has to be locked up when he snaps; MacReady shoots a suspected alien who turns out to be human; and one of the aliens frames MacReady as the shapeshifter.

MacReady discovers the alien building a spaceship, which the men destroy. The

8. Brain Eaters, Human Duplicators and Other SF Fifth Columns

alien responds by destroying the station's generator; with no heat, the men will freeze but the alien can return to suspended animation until a relief crew arrives.. MacReady blows up the alien, along with the base, leaving him and the one other survivor facing certain death from freezing — but the world is safe.

Strange Invaders (1983) In 1958, a spaceship arrives in the American town of Centerville and captures the townspeople. Twenty-five years later, Charles Bigelow's (Paul LeMat) ex-wife Margaret (Diana Scarwid) tells him that she's returning to Centerville for her mother's funeral and asks him to take care of their daughter Elizabeth (Lulu Sylbert). When Margaret doesn't return or contact them, Charles goes looking for her.

Charles finds Centerville mired in the 1950s; the folks there claim they have never heard of Margaret or her family. While he sits at the coffee shop, something blasts his car with lightning; panicked, he steals a convenient car, and barely survives when a bug-eyed alien blasts that vehicle too.

Returning to New York, Charles contacts Benjamin (Louise Fletcher), a government UFO researcher who assures him that aliens are a myth and Centerville has been a ghost town for 25 years. When Charles sees a photo of the alien on a tabloid newspaper cover, he contacts the writer, Betty Walker (Nancy Allen), who tells him she yanked the photo from their old files to illustrate a made-up story. The aliens, however, assume she knows something; one of them cons its way into her apartment where her neighbor finds it. It kills the neighbor, but when the police arrive, the body is gone. Betty flees to Charles for help.

Margaret returns and warns Charles that the aliens want Elizabeth; sure enough, the ETs abduct the girl and pursue Betty and Charles. Benjamin meets them and reveals that the government granted the aliens the use of Centerville as a base in return for various unspecified favors. The lease is almost up, and Charles and Betty risk disrupting the arrangement by their meddling.

Undeterred, the couple leave to meet Willie (Michael Lerner), the man who took the old photo of the aliens. They find him in a mental institution, where he's been confined for 25 years, ever since he started telling people that aliens disintegrated his family in Centerville. Willie escapes and joins them on the trip to Centerville, and the trio successfully sneak past Benjamin's security patrols.

In Centerville, they learn that the aliens came here to study Earth so that their leaders could make a "final decision" about our planet. The aliens plan to take Elizabeth, a human-alien hybrid (Margaret's an alien, who broke the rules by marrying Charles), back with them, though neither she nor her parents wants that. Margaret and Elizabeth use their powers to free the girl and her father from the alien spaceship, which then departs, restoring the Centerville inhabitants it replaced 25 years earlier, as well as other "disintegrated" people such as Willie's family and Betty's neighbor.

This rather pointless film has all the elements of a 1950s alien-infiltration movie (including 1950s screen actor Kenneth Tobey as one of the aliens) but seems to have no idea what to do with them. It doesn't work as a straight film, but it's not funny enough for a parody either (and unlike *The Experts* it makes little use of having a 1950s town preserved into the present).

SCREEN ENEMIES OF THE AMERICAN WAY

Invaders from Mars (1986) This remake of the Menzies film updates the concept: Instead of objecting to our entering space, the Martians want to stop us from sending more probes to their planet. As in the original, a spaceship crashes behind David's (Hunter Carson) house, and his dad George (Timothy Bottoms) comes back creepily calm after going to check it out. Before long, Dave's mom Ellen (Laraine Newman) is the same way, as are the police and science teacher McKeltch (Louise Fletcher), and they're all insisting that David take a walk with them back to the sand behind his parents' house....

Fortunately, the school nurse (Karen Black) begins to realize that David isn't imagining things. Despite the Martian agents' efforts to stop them, she and David contact the local military base, which mounts an expedition into the ship. At the end of the fight, David is fleeing his controlled parents when he suddenly wakes up and realizes it was all a dream. But then the ship appears outside — and when he rushes into his parents' room, whatever he sees there causes him to scream.

While the special effects in this film are light years beyond the original, the realistic look is a poor substitutes for Menzies' dream visuals, and the film never attains the paranoid creepiness of the first film.

They Live (1988) Nada (Roddy Piper) is a drifter living in an L.A. shantytown but still believing in the American dream, in contrast to his bitterly cynical friend Frank

An alien invader in *They Live* (1988) stands exposed in front of a subliminal broadcast. Despite the film's flaws, the movie's economic-exploitation theme remains timely.

8. Brain Eaters, Human Duplicators and Other SF Fifth Columns

(Keith David). Frank's steel-worker union granted huge concessions to keep a mill open; then it closed anyway, once the bosses had secured themselves some huge bonuses.

Odd pirate broadcasts warning of danger ("They want us asleep!") interrupt the camp's TV; Nada discovers Gilbert (Peter Jason), one of the camp leaders, is involved, broadcasting from a neighborhood church. After a police strike force busts up the operation, Nada finds sunglasses at the pirate station that reveal sublims everywhere—TV broadcasts, magazines, on our money—advising us to "Submit," "Obey," "Marry and Reproduce" plus "This is your god" on money. The glasses also show many Los Angelenos are actually aliens; Nada's response is to grab a gun, go into a bank and start shooting every ET he sees, which doesn't endear him to the authorities. Frank suspects him of going crazy until Nada forces him to wear the shades.

Gilbert reveals that the aliens are businesspeople who see Earth as a market to be exploited much as Europe and America exploit the Third World. The ETs have taken over the government and the corporate sector with the help of the rich, who see no reason to rock the boat since they're getting steadily richer. Anyone who fights back is either killed or bought off.

The resistance launches an attack on one of the broadcast towers that the aliens use to keep us from seeing the sublims or their true faces. One by one, the resistance falls in the attempt until only Nada remains; he succeeds and everyone suddenly sees the truth, just before the credits roll.

The idea that the world as we know it is being run by the infiltrators is an old one in SF. Henry Kuttner's short story "Don't Look Now" (1948) has a man explain how Martians are manipulating us to create most of our technology, which is for their use, not ours (they trigger wars because that spurs technology and invention). Eric Frank Russell's "Into Your Tent I'll Creep" (1957) posits that dogs are a highly intelligent alien race whose members have convinced humanity to care for them, feed them and even pick up their poop.

This John Carpenter film merges that idea with familiar themes of economic exploitation (which makes it surprisingly timely to view nowadays), but unfortunately doesn't do much with it. Far too much of the film is spent on mindless action, and Piper is a very poor actor.

Seedpeople (1992) This clichéd recycling of *Invasion of the Body Snatchers* opens with Tom Baines (Sam Hennings) in a hospital, trying to tell a federal agent about his nightmarish experiences despite the objections of Tom's worried doctor. Baines tells how he returned to his hometown of Comet Valley shortly after a meteor shower. Staying at his ex-girlfriend Heidi's (Andrea Roth) boarding house, he discovers that her sister Kim (Holly Fields) is convinced that housekeeper Mrs. Santiago (Anne Betancourt) is an imposter, as is Kim's father.

Needless to say, she's right. The meteor shower was actually a rain of alien seed pods; the plants that grow out of them shower passersby with what looks like semen and transforms them into rather comical aliens (but able to shift back to their human faces as well). Crazy Doc Roller (Bernard Kates) has figured it out, but he doesn't know who to trust, and nobody takes the crackpot seriously. However, a few attacks by the seedpeople convince Tom that Kim and Doc aren't crazy.

Having discovered that ultraviolet light is lethal to the aliens, Tom and Roller set up a trap; then Heidi and her boyfriend, posing as seedpeople, steal a truck containing the unhatched seeds. They arrive at the trap, but it shorts out, and Doc dies trying to hook up the power cord. Mrs. Santiago drives off with the truck; Tom jumps on top of it and begins smashing seeds as Santiago climbs out and attacks him in alien form. The truck goes over the cliff and most of the seeds burn.

Back in the hospital, Tom informs the agents that Doc is dead—at which point the agent and the doctor both relax. Heidi enters from the waiting room and Tom realizes that like the others in the room, she is now one of the seedpeople....

Charles Band's Full Moon has been providing direct-to-video low-budget horror and SF for years, often quite successfully (the *Trancers* and *Puppet Master* series). This lame recycling was not one of their triumphs.

Tribulation 99: Alien Anomalies Under America (1992) Craig Baldwin's bizarre mockumentary reveals that centuries ago, the planet Quetzal on the far side of the sun exploded (forming the asteroid belt); the survivors traveled by flying saucer to Earth where they took up residence in the hollow space inside our planet.

The aliens, whose accessways to the surface lie in South and Central America, take an interest in that part of the world, using artificial imposters to replace key leaders. After they replace President Arbenz of Guatemala, he revives the human-sacrifice practices of pre–Columbian America. Guatemala's nationalization of United Fruit and its plans to redistribute its land among the poor are actually a cover for building more sacrificial pyramids. The United States, unable to tolerate this atrocity, overthrows Arbenz, although alien activity still claims the lives of more than 100,000 Guatemalans.

Later, alien activity spreads to Cuba, where the Quetzalians set up Castro, a synthetic lifeform, as the leader of a supposed communist revolution. The Bay of Pigs plan is intended to overthrow the alien tyranny, but Kennedy refuses to commit support—a foolish mistake, since the aliens later kill him ("No lone human being could possibly hit a distant moving target two times within 1.8 seconds!"). Castro, not being truly alive, survives all our attempts to destroy him, and goes on to frame some of the Cubans fighting him as terrorists. They're later liberated by Oliver North and other Americans dedicated to fighting the aliens.

Under Nixon, the government investigates possible alien infiltration into the Democratic Party only to be accused of committing a simple burglary. Undeterred, the aliens make their agent Salvador Allende the leader of Chile, from where he can disrupt the Earth's orbital axis. Fortunately, American businesses realize the threat and alert our government, which manages to have a naval ship on hand when Chile's military rise to destroy Allende.

In the eighties, the Grenadan government is overthrown by psychic vampires using Atlantean technology, forcing another American intervention "to exorcise the Grenadan menace!" The aliens then turn to Nicaragua, where earthquakes destabilize the country

8. Brain Eaters, Human Duplicators and Other SF Fifth Columns

and the nation's leader, Somoza, is unable to provide relief because the battle against the ET Sandinista cultists is consuming all his resources. Somoza's situation worsens when President Carter foolishly blames Somoza rather than the aliens for thousands of Nicaraguans disappearing. Fortunately, Ronald Reagan is elected in 1980, and he begins supplying the Contras with "humanitarian weapons" to fight back against the Sandinistas.

In El Salvador, the government declares war on clerics who have taken up practicing witchcraft. Even though we provide money to support the government's efforts, the death toll keeps rising. In Panama, trustworthy Gen. Noriega is replaced by a lookalike "grotesque, voodoo-spouting freak" which forces the United States to invade and battle his army of zombies.

While American efforts have thwarted the aliens so far, their plan to irradiate the world's oceans, use the water to melt the polar icecaps and wipe out all surface life through flooding remains in place. The clock is ticking: Can we stop the Quetzal menace in time?

Using news clips, photos and movie scenes, Baldwin takes America's long history of intervention in South America—such as our support of right-wing dictatorships and their human rights violations, including genocide and death squads—and portrays it as one cohesive struggle against the aliens from Quetzal and their fifth column. It has to be seen to be believed.

The movie didn't originate the idea of a planet on the far side of the sun (an SF staple for decades) or of a hollow Earth, a concept that goes back to 1692, when Sir Edmund Halley proposed it. One later version of the idea, published as a series of essays by Richard Shaver in *Amazing Stories* starting in 1943 (and later collected as *The Hidden World*), presents a similar vision to Baldwin's (and apparently claimed it quite seriously to be true): The alien Titans arrived on Earth millennia ago and bred an army of subservient "robot" races (but fully biological robots) that gave rise to many of the myths of ancient times. To escape harmful radiation from the sun, the Titans initially moved underground; when even that proved inadequate to protect them, they left for another world, leaving the robots behind. In time the degenerate robots took over the underground world and used its machinery to wreak havoc on the surface. Their crimes included giving FDR his fatal brain hemorrhage at the end of World War II and driving Oswald to murder JFK, according to later editions of *The Hidden World*.

The Puppet Masters (1994) This follows the basic outline of Heinlein's novel, but with many of the details (the near-future setting, the full nudity) removed. As in Heinlein, a security chief called the Old Man (Donald Sutherland), his son Sam (Eric Thal) and xenobiologist Mary (Julie Warner) investigate a rumored spaceship crash and discover the aliens (rather than slugs, they resemble small, flying manta-rays) have established a beachhead among the humans in the town. As in the book, lack of interest in Mary is a sign of non-humanness.

The humans, even small children, try to stop the trio from reporting back to base, but fail. At the Old Man's headquarters, however, he discovers one of the other agents is already infected. The agency struggles to capture the creature and its host, but instead it captures Sam, takes him over and forces him to transport parasite cocoons to high-level government targets. Fortunately the agency catches Sam before he can plant one near the president.

The Old Man interrogates and tortures the parasite, even though Sam shares its pain. As usual, the alien claims that their way is better, and reveals the parasites are a hive mind: "You won't be lonely when you're one of us. No one will be." Electroshock forces the parasite off Sam, who's debilitated by the disconnection.

The aliens breed fast enough that before long, a large part of the country is under their control, and the troops sent to take it back have been taken over too. Mary consoles Sam, but he discovers she's been taken and is only seeking to re-implant a parasite. She flees to the alien hive in the occupied territory, pursued by Sam who rescues her and kills her parasite. They also find and rescue a boy who's been imprisoned since his parasite dropped dead; it turns out the boy had encephalitis, which inflames brain tissue and is thereby fatal to aliens whose bodies are completely brain tissue. Using the disease as a weapon wipes out the aliens, but the last survivor takes over the Old Man; Sam manages to electrocute it, ending the menace.

Given this was made just a couple of years after the USSR collapsed, it's perhaps not surprising that this ignored Heinlein's totalitarian metaphors. It's better than *The Brain Eaters* but quite unremarkable.

Men in Black (1997) This movie takes the idea of an alien fifth column and plays it for comedy, starting with an early scene where Agent K (Tommy Lee Jones), who works for the government's Division 6, horns in on a police bust of illegal aliens. To the bafflement of the cops, he lets most of the illegals rush over the border, then exposes one of the people involved as a genuine space alien.

Later on in the movie, new recruit Agent J (Will Smith) learns that aliens have been arriving on Earth for decades but has carefully hidden them by the federal government, in the equivalent of a witness protection program: They live as diamond merchants, postal workers, dogs, etc.; pretty much anyone could be an ET. A chart in Division 6 HQ showing every alien on Earth reveals that Sylvester Stallone, Al Roker, Sen. Newt Gingrich and Dionne Warwick are all aliens.

Village of the Damned (1995) It's a typical day in the California town of Midwich — until a mysterious shadow falls on the town and everyone falls asleep, as does anyone who enters the town for the next few hours. The sleep passes and everything's back to normal (other than accidents like the man who fell asleep on his grill and burned to death) … until a few weeks later, when every fertile woman turns out to be pregnant, regardless of her sex life or fertility. Verner (Kirstie Alley), a government researcher, announces that the federal government is treating this as a medical emergency and will pay for either abortions or free prenatal care for the mothers. She attends the mass birth; when one child is stillborn, she takes the corpse away.

The remaining children are all silver-haired, blue-eyed and grow up amazingly fast. They're also telepathic, devoid of emotion and ruthless: When Barbara (Karen Kahn) accidentally burns baby Mara (Lindsey Haun) with overheated food, Mara compels Barbara to stick her hand into a boiling pot of soup. After Barbara gets out of the hospital,

8. Brain Eaters, Human Duplicators and Other SF Fifth Columns

Mara pushes her mother to commit suicide (which makes no sense, since the children's retaliation is otherwise eye-for-an-eye). Verner convinces the government to study the children and their power instead of taking action against them.

One child, David (Thomas Dekker), tells Barbara's husband Allan (Christopher Reeve) that the stillborn girl was to be his mate (the others are equally divided between the sexes) and perhaps because of her absence, David develops emotions. Mara tells him later that this is not acceptable. Although the children share a group-mind, David doesn't seem to be part of that, either.

Verner tells Allan that there have been similar births around the world, but in all other cases, they were in small, third-world towns where the residents killed the babies immediately. She tells him the possibilities are some sort of spontaneous mutation, a government experiment or "xenogenesis," an alien species born on Earth — and shows him the corpse of an ET to prove which idea she favors. (The implication seems to be that it's the stillborn baby, though it doesn't look much like the others.) She convinces him to serve as teacher to the children in the abandoned barn they've made into a group home, so that he can keep tabs on them.

Mara tells Allan that "the lifeforce" has placed both of them on this planet but coexistence is impossible: Either the children dominate, or humanity destroys them. She goes on to say that they're ready to leave Midwich and found their own breeding colonies, and that she knows he'll help them because he can't bring himself to act against his daughter.

The night they plan to leave, violence erupts. A fanatical religious mob tries to burn the kids out, but after the leader is forced to burn herself to death, the mob runs away. Cops show up to shoot down the kids, but the children compel the police to turn the guns on themselves. The children learn about their stillborn sibling and punish Verner by forcing her to use a scalpel to vivisect herself.

Allan, having learned to mask his thoughts from the children, shows up at the barn with a bomb in his briefcase, and tries to send David out to the car before it goes off. Mara and the children try to break through his defenses; then David's mother, who knows what Allan plans, shows up and takes David outside while the children focus on Allan. Allan's will breaks a second before the bomb goes off, wiping out the children — but David survives.

John Wyndham's fine SF novel *The Midwich Cuckoos* (referring to cuckoos laying eggs in other birds' nests) first came to the screen as *Village of the Damned* in 1960 (not included here because it's a British production). John Carpenter's remake makes several for-the-worse changes, such as David having the capacity for emotion.

That being said, this still remains a story of infiltration. Similar to the later *Threshold* series, the aliens who created the children have solved the problem of colonizing or invading by making us breed colonists for them. In the Wyndham book, the aliens put the town to sleep in order to artificially inseminate the women; in both the original and remake films, the sleeping serves no point (since the aliens apparently do it by some impregnation ray from space, there's no reason for the townspeople to be asleep).

The Faculty (1998) One of the best ET fifth-column films, *The Faculty* gives the *Body Snatchers* formula a teen spin. First Coach Willis (Robert Patrick) is approached by someone mysterious, then that night he attacks Principal Drake (Bebe Neuwirth) in the halls. She almost escapes, then maternal Mrs. Olson (Piper Laurie) attacks her too.

The next day Stan (Shawn Hatosy), the star quarterback, tells his girlfriend Delilah (Jordana Brewster) — head cheerleader and editor of the school paper — that he's going to quit the team and concentrate on academics, which doesn't suit Delilah at all. We also meet Delilah's wimpy photographer Casey (Elijah Wood); Stokely (Clea DuVall), a Goth, science-fiction geek and supposed lesbian; Southern transfer student Marybeth (Laura Harris) and Zeke (John Hartnett), a rebel constantly hitting on shy teacher Burke (Famke Janssen), and selling Scat, a "designer drug" that's mostly caffeine.

Casey finds an odd creature on the football field; when he puts it into an aquarium, it grows into a sharp-toothed eel-creature that can create offspring by budding. Olson, Willis and Drake begin converting the rest of the faculty and start drinking water by the gallon. The kids notice things getting weird, but the bodies they find (people who didn't survive the transition to alien) disappear, the cops who investigate get possessed and nobody else believes them. Stokely jokes to Casey that the faculty members are becoming pod people; after she explains the Finney reference, he asks if it could be true. Stokely points out there are no pods around, but suggests other alternatives, like the slugs from *Puppet Masters*.

Circumstance brings the six teens together, but none of them believe the truth until a teacher attacks them with superhuman strength. Even dismemberment doesn't kill him, but he does drop dead after Zeke stabs him with a straw full of Scat. The sextet leaves the school, wondering who they can trust. As usual, the radio stations, the roads and the cops are under alien control so no word can get out.

The kids discover the aliens need water to live and the caffeine in the Scat kills them by drying them out. Stokely says that killing the alien queen could destroy the entire hive and free their hosts (which isn't true of either *Puppet Masters* or *Invasion of the Body Snatchers*); Delilah favors running instead; Casey points out the aliens have taken over the school in two days: Where could they run that would be any safer?

Then the teens begin to point suspicious fingers at each other: Why has Stan quit football? If Stokely's a lesbian, why is she hitting on Stan? Why is Zeke suddenly revealing himself as a genius? They agree to test themselves by taking Scat, but Delilah, who's possessed, destroys Zeke's supply and flees. The others figure Drake is the queen and kill her with Scat, but nothing changes; Stan gets possessed ("There's no pain ... it's better!") and traps them in the gym. Delilah attacks Casey, telling him that since her father's death, nothing has made her as happy as the transformation.

Stokely is worried that humanity will lose as it did in *Body Snatchers* (which isn't true of Finney — which we've seen her reading — or the original movie); he hides with Marybeth and jokes that she used to think "the only alien in this high school was me." Marybeth asks if it isn't tiring being on the outside — and reveals that she's the alien queen. She joins with Delilah in hunting the remaining teens. Marybeth tells Casey she's

A lot of high-schoolers think their teachers are evil monsters; in *The Faculty* (1998), it's true. Kevin Williamson's screenplay makes frequently inaccurate SF references, but does a good job of showing fifth-column paranoia playing out in high school.

hurt that they don't appreciate her gift of a world where everyone fits in, a world where the jock won't be mocked for studying and the class wimp needn't be afraid. Casey tells her he'd sooner be afraid, and traps Marybeth long enough to finish her off with Scat, ending the entire infestation. The authorities deny all the crazy stories about aliens, but that doesn't stop Casey from becoming a celebrity and Delilah's new boyfriend. Stokely and Stan become a couple and Zeke takes up football and an affair with Burke.

Despite screenwriter Kevin Williamson's unfamiliarity with the Finney novel, this movie does a great job using body-snatching as a metaphor for high school alienation, as reflected in Marybeth's description of the utopia she's bringing us. This is also one of the few movies in which the protagonists entertain serious doubts about each other (Becky and Miles never wonder if the other is a pod person until it happens) which reflects, again, the discomfort at each other stepping out of their roles in the high school hierarchy.

The Astronaut's Wife (1999) Spencer Armacost (Johnny Depp) returns from a space mission where he was out of contact with Earth for two minutes. His wife Jillian (Charlize Theron) is baffled when he tells her that he's quitting NASA and moving them to New York for an office job. Not long afterwards, his fellow astronaut from the mission drops dead of a coronary; his wife subsequently kills herself. Spencer rapes his wife (telling her she was all he thought about during those two minutes) and she becomes pregnant with twins. Jillian has a past history of mental troubles (it appears to be depression); dissatisfied with life in New York, lonely and troubled by Spencer's behavior, she finds herself sliding into depression and drinking.

Reese (Joe Morton), a NASA official, tells Jillian that when Spencer returned, all his vital signs and his signature were off— not enough to trigger any warning bells, but enough that Reese is convinced there's something wrong. When Jillian arranges a meeting with Reese, her sister, worried by her behavior, tells Spencer, who intercepts Reese and his briefcase full of proof. Reese isn't seen again, but Jillian discovers a tape he made spelling out his theory: Rather than travel physically across space, aliens transferred their minds into the two astronauts.

Afraid that the twins might be alien spawn, Jillian contemplates taking an abortifacent, but Spencer beats her up when he catches her. (He also reminds her that with her history, she could easily wind up back in a mental hospital.) When Jillian recovers, she lures Spencer into a trap and electrocutes him, but the energy inside him jumps into her. Several years later, she's remarried and one of the twins is not a human (at least mentally). The ending shot suggests that Jillian may not be 100 percent human either.

This film uses the *Midwich Cuckoos* concept but, like *Rosemary's Baby* (1968), infuses it with the fears of an expectant mother about everything that's happening to her body. The idea of a woman giving birth to something not quite human has cropped up before in such films as *Demon Seed* (1977), *It's Alive* (1974) and the telemovie *The Stranger Within*. *The Astronaut's Wife* is one of the weakest renditions of the idea.

Invasion of the Pod People (2007) This direct-to-DVD film from The Asylum was released to coincide with *The Invasion*. (The Asylum is known for what some have dubbed

8. Brain Eaters, Human Duplicators and Other SF Fifth Columns

"Mockbusters," such as releasing *Transmorphers* at the same time *Transformers* hit the big screen.)

An asteroid strike demolishes Monterey, California, and sends meteorites streaking down into Los Angeles as well. The meteorites produce plants that form duplicates of the first person who touches them. The pods duplicate members of an L.A. modeling agency and their clients, then murder them. The originals don't disintegrate, which is why they have to be killed. The duplicates are friendly and fun-loving and into sex, which results in a lot of girl-on-girl action on screen.

Melissa (Erica Roby), an agency staffer, realizes what's happened, but gets trapped by the pod people and forced to touch a plant. A cop intervenes, killing the duplicates and saving Melissa — but at the end of the movie, one of her co-workers learns too late that the plant Melissa touched has replaced her after all.

This was a cheap, exploitative variation on Finney, though it does show how flexible the body snatchers concept can be, since it has little purpose here other than to rationalize an all-girl sex party mid-movie. Although the pods give the standard speech about how they're a higher life-form and better than the originals, it's undercut by the graphic footage of one of the first duplicates beating its human original to death.

9

Invaders, X-Files and Dynamators
Alien Fifth Columns on Television

The first TV series to give us an alien fifth column was *The Invaders*, which ran on ABC from January 1967 to March, 1968.

The first episode opens with weary architect David Vincent (Roy Thinnes) parking for a nap in the middle of an all-night drive; he's awakened by the arrival of a flying saucer. He returns to the site the next day with the police and his partner Alan. There's no sign of the saucer, and a honeymooning couple camped nearby tell the police they saw nothing. Vincent returns later to talk to them and notices that one of the husband's fingers sticks out at an odd angle. When he tries to beat information out of the guy, the man knocks him out, starts glowing and drives away with his wife.

To his horror, Vincent awakens in a mental hospital under a fake name — but it's not the aliens who placed him there, it's his partner, who found Vincent and institutionalized him to avoid negative publicity for their business (this was the best twist in the entire series). That night, an elderly patient burns down the hospital and almost kills Vincent.

Still convinced he saw a UFO, Vincent checks out the honeymooners' home address in a small town that a developer is buying up lock, stock and barrel. Vincent suspects the town will become a beachhead for the aliens, explores it and discovers that the local power plant is chockfull of alien machinery. He summons Alan as a witness.

What Vincent doesn't realize is that the alien fifth column has already taken over the town. One woman, Kathy, flirts to distract him from Alan's arrival; when he catches on, she tells him that only some of her people have the problematic finger. (Publicity for the show emphasized the finger as the giveaway sign, but the series did more with the fact the aliens don't bleed and have no heartbeat.) Kathy tells Vincent he might as well give up now, because her people won't fail.

The aliens remove their equipment from the power plant and kill Alan, but they decide that killing Vincent now that he has such a high profile as a UFO alarmist would raise too many questions. From that moment on, Vincent's goal in life is to alert the world to the alien threat.

Producer Alan Amrer said that the tone he was shooting for was the fear that "[t]hey're here among us now ... in your city ... maybe on your block. They're invaders ... alien

9. Invaders, X-Files and Dynamators

beings from another planet ... but they look just like us! Take a look around. Casually. No sense letting them know you're suspicious. The new neighbors across the street. The substitute teacher. That too-pretty secretary in your husband's office. Any one of them might be an invader from outer space. How can you tell?"

In practice, this came off less paranoid than later ET infiltration stories (*Threshold, Invasion, War of the Worlds*) because while Vincent's adversaries take human form, they don't duplicate or replace real people (though they *can* control them with hypnosis and brainwashing). As a result, even though the aliens are not offered as a metaphor for Soviet infiltration, many episodes could easily be part of a conventional spy series. In "The Leeches," a squad of aliens kidnaps human geniuses to steal their knowledge; in "Vikor," an embittered Korean War vet collaborates with the invaders. In "The Prophet," Vincent explains his investigation of a phony preacher by telling the man's associates that the minister is "an agent for a foreign power." Even a story about a school train-

David Vincent (Roy Thinnes) flees an alien spaceship in this publicity shot for the 1967 TV Series *The Invaders*. The opening credits told us the aliens wanted Earth because their world was dying, but that was never stated in the show.

ing the emotionless invaders to simulate human feelings ("Ivy Curtain") could have been a spy training camp *à la The Experts*.

Another difference from later series is that even though Vincent defeats multiple alien plans, *The Invaders* places more emphasis on proving the aliens' existence than stopping them. Even the show's intro asserts that Vincent's goal is "to prove to a disbelieving world that the nightmare has already begun." In *Threshold* and *Dark Skies*, the heroes are actively hiding the truth about the invaders, but the primary goal is to block their attack; in *X-Files*, Mulder and Scully are constantly thwarted by higher authorities determined to bury the truth. Vincent doesn't face a conspiracy, just a complete lack of belief and a government where reports get swallowed up in the limbo of committee reviews.

Unfortunately, the show is wildly inconsistent about this. In some episodes, Vincent asserts that finding one more witness would turn the tide and convince the authorities; in others, he gets multiple witnesses and doesn't use them, or asserts that no amount of testimony will convince the authorities. In "The Trial," Vincent unmasks an alien before a respected judge, a prosecutor and a cop, but makes no attempt to use them to prove his case. In some episodes, the aliens murder eyewitnesses; in others, Vincent tells eyewitnesses that the Invaders won't kill them because without hard evidence, no one will take them seriously.

This may partly reflect the nature of TV science fiction back then. Serious SF was a small-screen rarity, and contemporary serious SF even rarer; a lone alien hunter fighting the threat may have been easier to swallow than a show presenting a coordinated government strike force. And lone drifters who travel from town to town, meeting a new guest cast every week, had been a successful format for shows including *Route 66* and *The Fugitive* (like *The Invaders*, a Quinn Martin production), and would continue on into the seventies with *Then Came Bronson, The Incredible Hulk* and *The Immortal.* Vincent fits right in.

Things did change somewhat in the second-season episode "The Believers," which introduces a small band of allies who have met the aliens (none of the guest stars from previous shows, though) and are working with Vincent to thwart them. Despite the fact that the Believers' backer, Edgar Scoville (Kent Smith), is a powerful, well-connected millionaire, there was no greater effort to get the government to listen and the stories stayed much the same. In "Counter Strike" the Believers did take a pro-active stance, crashing the saucers by disrupting their navigation, but that was the exception. Of course, it's the nature of a TV series to stay the same week after week. While later series such as *X-Files* would attempt multi-season story arcs, that wasn't something to expect in the sixties.

There are a few moments of real paranoia in *The Invaders*: In "Nightmare," a woman starts to realize that many of the people around her are aliens; in the creepy opening of "Doomsday Minus One," a man trying to escape from a phone booth can't understand why everyone around is ignoring his calls for help.

After David Vincent left the screen, there wouldn't be another series about alien infiltration until the late eighties, but TV movies, many of them pilots, took up the slack.

The Aliens Are Coming (1980) has electrical aliens taking over human bodies in order to prepare the way for an ET colony, starting by taking over a hydroelectric dam as a power worker. An astrophysicist working for the government leads the opposition.

Annihilator (1986) has a newspaper editor (Mark Lindsay Chapman) discover the reason for his girlfriend's personality change after her vacation: She's been replaced by a "dynamator," a super-strong, glowing-eyed robot. Chapman destroys her, gets accused of her murder and discovers everyone from her vacation plane flight has been replaced by dynamators. A woman who helps him turns out to be a dynamator as well. With only the flight passenger list to guide him, he sets out to learn and thwart the dynamators.

Twilight Zone: "A Day in Beaumont" (1986) In 1955, astronomer Kevin Carlson

9. Invaders, X-Files and Dynamators

(Victor Garber) and his girlfriend Faith (Stacy Nelkin) see a burning object hurtle through the sky to Earth, moving too slowly to be a meteor. At the impact site, they find a flying saucer with a crew of humanoid insects that pursues the couple, narrowly missing their car with shots from their ray weapons. When the couple arrives in nearby Beaumont, the sheriff (Kenneth Tobey) tells them it was a crashed jet fighter, something the local paper confirms.

Carlson brings the sheriff back to the crash site to prove otherwise, and they find it cordoned off by the Air Force. The man in charge, Major Whitmore, has a deformed hand (the little finger sticks out) that convinces Carlson he's not human, so Carlson backs off. A photographer takes flash pictures of the sheriff and Whitmore, and each flash gives Carlson and Faith a quick glimpse of the two men as aliens.

Carlson tries to call the FBI, but the lines are out; he turns to the local newspaper for help, but realizes the publisher has a deformed finger too. He and Faith try driving out, but the saucer captures them with a tractor beam. Inside the ship, the sheriff and the other fifth columnists confront Carlson; Faith tells him she's been "reprogrammed," and pulls off a mask to show an insect face beneath, as do the men. Carlson vows that the human spirit will not be broken — but the old men inform him that that doesn't mean much as he's an alien too, temporarily brainwashed into thinking he's human as part of their war-game scenario for the real invasion of Earth.

In the conclusion, it's 1955 in Beaumont, and a young man rushes into the diner, claiming to have seen a flying saucer — but this time, Carlson is the sheriff. (Whether this means the fifth column is in place for the real invasion or if it's simply another war game is anyone's guess.)

This sci-fi equivalent of the *Forbidden Area* training village is rife with in-jokes, including the town name (for Charles Beaumont, one of the writers on the original *Twilight Zone*) and that of the hero (Richard Carlson being the star of *It Came from Outer Space*), the use of several stars from 1950s SF (John Agar, Kenneth Tobey, Jeff Morrow) and visual touches such as giant pods being loaded into a truck. The plot sends up this style of film considerably better than *Strange Invaders* did.

The Invaders (1995) was a sequel to the original TV series in which the aliens David Vincent fought are still around, attempting to pollute Earth to the point that it's comfortable for their biology (something added to the original mythos). Nolan Wood (Scott Bakula) learns that the hallucinations that destroyed his marriage and career and then got him jailed for manslaughter are due to an alien mind-control implant. Because of his childhood autism, the implant doesn't control him but gives him a telepathic link to the aliens. When the invaders destroy an experimental pollution-free train, the link helps Wood and his allies (his son and an emergency room doctor) save the passengers.

This attempt to relaunch the series (which included Roy Thinnes reprising his role as David Vincent) added some visual touches: Instead of disintegrating on death, alien bodies dissolve into blood and flies. After years of *X-Files*, however, it looked like a cheap knock-off.

Robin Cook's Invasion (1997) is more a straight alien invasion story than a paranoid exercise, though the victims of alien mind control (from touching black meteorites that trigger a virus implanted in earthly life millennia ago) do become a fifth column, building "the Gateway" to bring their masters to work. (Surprise! They lose.)

Target: Earth (1998) has Detective Sam Adams (Christopher Meloni) discover that aliens have transformed humans into mind-controlled Implants who are preparing a base for the alien invaders to teleport into. Sam blows up the base and apparently the fleet, but some of the Implants remain. (The cop has also been framed for murder, though they forget that at the end.)

The Lake (1998) When Jackie Ivers (Yasmine Bleeth) visits her estranged, dying father Steve (Stanley Anderson), she finds her old home town hides secrets. A man she runs over in her car shows up unharmed; Steve is not only in excellent health, he's suddenly loving and affectionate; their neighbor Maggie (Marion Ross) tells Jackie that her husband has been replaced by an imposter, then denies it. To top it all off, Jackie and her old boyfriend Jeff (Linden Ashby) find the mayor throwing people into a vortex in the nearby lake.

Steve finally confesses to Jackie that the townsfolk are parallel-world counterparts of the people she grew up with; their Earth is dying, so they're passing through a gate to replace the population on ours. Steve, however, loves Jackie as much as his real daughter; they head to the cops, but their duplicates capture them. Steve sacrifices his life to help Jackie escape, and she and Jeff reach the state police. The cops scoff at this crackpot theory until they meet their own duplicates. But it may not matter, for more gateways are opening all over the country....

The first post–*Invaders* series was *War of the Worlds* (1988–90), a sequel to the 1953 film *The War of the Worlds*. In the opening episode we learn that after Earth bacteria wiped out the Martian invaders of the movie, their bodies were buried on government land. When leaking drums of radioactive waste are dumped there too, the radiation revives the Martians and enables them to take over human bodies; inside their human shells, they're immune to bacteria. The disguised aliens set out to find and resurrect more of their kind.

The Martian plots — opposed by a government strike force — included efforts to overcome their vulnerability to disease in their exposed forms, to develop new weapons against humanity and to infiltrate the human opposition. As usual, the invasion and the opposition were kept secret from the public, who had also blotted out the traumatic memories of the original invasion. The second season dropped the body-snatching angle as a new wave of invaders arrived on Earth, killed one of the government team members and forced them to go rogue, without official support. The attempt to boost ratings by shaking things up didn't work at all.

The X-Files (1993–2002) In 1993, when the FBI assigned agent Dana Scully (Gillian Anderson) to work with Fox "Spooky" Mulder (David Duchovny) on closing some of the FBI's X-Files (cases that were never solved), it touched off TV's longest-running drama of political paranoia, mingling government conspiracies with alien fifth columns preparing the way for colonizing the planet.

9. Invaders, X-Files and Dynamators

In the pilot episode, Mulder (obsessed with the paranormal and UFO activity since his sister was abducted by a spaceship years earlier) and Scully (a brilliant doctor and confirmed skeptic) discover hard proof that extraterrestrials are implanting control modules in human beings, though Scully, as she would for much of the series, considers alternative explanations. At the end of the episode we learn that the government was already aware of the alien activity.

Much of the first season (and subsequent seasons) involves stand-alone cases featuring mutants, psychics, body snatchers and other menaces (some of which were played for humor rather than spookiness), but further evidence of the conspiracy kept turning up. By the end of the first season, Deep Throat (Jerry Hardin), Mulder's government contact, had revealed that extraterrestrials have been landing on Earth for decades, and that the government was using alien genes to create human-alien hybrids. "The Sydicate," a conspiracy within the government, had been hiding the truth and had enough power to pull strings within the FBI, much to the frustration of the X-Files' overseer, Skinner (Mitch Pileggi). The front man for the Syndicate was a chain-smoking, never named individual (William B. Davis), a former friend of Mulder's father.

At the end of the first season, the agents acquired proof of the genetic-engineering project, but Deep Throat gave up the proof to save Mulder's life, after which the Syndicate killed him and ordered Skinner to shut down the X-Files unit. The following season, when it became obvious that the X-File investigations were the one thing that worried the Syndicate, Skinner had the office reopened. The Cigarette-Smoking Man wasn't happy, but refused to let his cohorts execute Mulder, warning them (much as the Invaders concluded about David Vincent) that Mulder's death would draw too much attention and turn his quixotic quest into a wider crusade. The fact that the Cigarette-Smoking Man was, in fact, Mulder's real father (a revelation that dribbled out over the course of the series) may have factored into it.

Over the next few seasons, the agents encountered a colony of clones planted by aliens, including several clones of Mulder's sister Samantha; discovered an oozing black oil that was actually an alien intelligence capable of taking over human bodies; visited villages populated by human-alien hybrids; and battled an Alien Bounty Hunter.

Eventually the shape of the conspiracy became clear (or reasonably so). The Roswell crash had shown the government that aliens were plotting to infest the entire world with the black-oil creatures, taking humanity over as happened on countless other worlds. To buy time, the Syndicate began using Axis experiments on creating human-alien hybrids to breed a slave race for the alien colonists, with the understanding that the invasion would be postponed until the hybrids were ready. As proof of good faith, members of the conspiracy gave up their own family members for alien experiments; Fox's father, a member of the Syndicate, had sent Mulder's sister Samantha. Unlike the others, however, the senior Mulder believed resistance wasn't futile, and that they should only collaborate until we could develop a virus that will protect humanity against the oil. A vaccine had been developed by a rebel faction of aliens fighting the "oileans" but the Syndicate decided they were safer working with the colonizers than trying to resist them.

Screen Enemies of the American Way

In the sixth season, the agents discovered that one abductee — Cassandra, the Cigarette-Smoking Man's wife — was the success the Syndicate had been hoping for, a perfect human-alien hybrid. That was bad news, because once the aliens realized they'd succeeded, colonization would begin. The rebel faction, however, moved in and killed the hybrids and the members of the Syndicate (though the Cigarette-Smoking Man escaped) before it could turn Cassandra over.

The alien threat wasn't held back long, however: By the eighth season, the aliens had launched a backup plan, genetically engineering former abductees into super-soldiers, incredibly strong, invulnerable and controlled by implants in the backs of their necks. The X-Files team discovered that the super-soldiers included members of the American government who were now directly under alien domination, forming a "shadow government" to prepare for colonization.

The only hope for humanity was Scully's son (by Mulder, it was assumed) William: When Scully was abducted earlier in the series, it had been by the military, genetically engineering her to create a superhuman. William had some degree of psychic power, and aliens and various human factions believed that he had the potential to stave off the invasion. Scully ultimately gave William up for adoption for fear that he'd otherwise be killed.

In the final episode, Mulder located the military base that served as the shadow government headquarters, only to be arrested for supposedly killing a super-soldier. With the court stacked against him, a guilty verdict was inevitable, but Skinner led his fellow X-Files agents — by this point the department included Doggett (Robert Patrick) and Reyes (Annabeth Gish) along with Scully — to free him. Mulder and Scully went on the run but the supposedly dead Cigarette-Smoking Man confronted them and told them that despite everything they'd done and attempted to do, the full invasion was still scheduled for 2012, supposedly the endpoint of the Mayan calendar (it actually isn't). His prediction drove home Mulder's bitter comment earlier in the episode: "I thought my victories mattered — only I realized nobody was keeping score."

With the shadow government against them and the invasion apparently inevitable, Scully and Mulder agreed to keep fighting, somehow — and on that note, the series ended. (A movie followed several years later, but it was a stand-alone story unconnected to the grand arc.)

Synopsizing doesn't capture how the truth about the conspiracy gradually and murkily unwound over the years. Nor does it capture the constant conspiratorial, paranoid atmosphere, where people who started as allies such as United Nations official Marita Covarrubias (Laurie Holden) turned out to be agents of the Syndicate. Shapeshifting aliens could turn out to be anyone, and Mulder and Scully are constantly warned that the conspiracy goes higher than anyone realizes. Even people on the inside didn't see the whole picture: In one episode, the head of Area 51 admits he has no idea if aliens and UFOs exist and asks Mulder to tell him the truth.

Opposite: David Duchovny stars in the ultimate paranoid fantasy series: *X-Files*, where the man behind the curtain is only standing in front of another curtain.

At the end of the fourth season, Mulder sees a chance to bring proof of the ET presence on Earth to the public, in the form of a buried alien corpse. Then a Defense Department official tells Scully that everything in the X-Files is a massive government fraud designed to distract people from various covert defense operations; the corpse has been genetically engineered by the government and will be stolen before it can be examined in depth, all in the hope of pushing Mulder to go public with what he's seen and muddy the waters even further. All of this turned out to be a lie, but for several episodes the following season, Mulder was genuinely convinced that the X-Files and all UFO investigations were fake.

The series constantly alludes to other conspiracies or alleged conspiracies such as Kennedy's assassination. One conspiracy theorist makes the off-hand remark "I had breakfast with the man who shot Kennedy today." A woman in a flashback episode claims the government killed JFK, and also plants surveillance Bibles in Gideon Bibles, giving them an eye in every hotel room in the country. "Musings of a Cigarette-Smoking Man" shows the Cigarette-Smoking Man assassinating JFK and Martin Luther King as well as arranging the 1980 Olympic triumph of the U.S. hockey team. But the episode is based on one character reading a magazine article about the Cigarette-Smoking Man, and therefore not canonical.

Author Peter Knight has suggested that the series fits perfectly with the role of conspiracy theory today: *X-Files* is a world where our government is not on our side, history and events are not what we've been told they are, and even if specific people turn out to be innocent and suspicious events have a legitimate explanation, there are other conspiracies and conspiracies behind conspiracies, and everyone in the know understands that nothing is ever what it seems.

Dark Skies (1996–1997) John Loengard (Eric Close) and his fiancée Kim Sayers (Megan Ward) are bright, idealistic young workers in the John F. Kennedy administration. Then John discovers the existence of Majestic 12, a secret agency created in 1947 after the alien crash at Roswell revealed the existence of the Hive, alien parasites who can take over human bodies (they arrived here riding the bodies of an alien humanoid race Majestic calls the Greys).

John and Kim are drafted into Majestic, whose leader Col. Bach (J.T. Walsh) is dedicated to keeping the threat hidden from the American people, something the new recruits disagree with. When John realizes that President Kennedy doesn't know about Majestic either, he attempts to warn Kennedy before the Hive can take him over; the upshot is that Lee Harvey Oswald, a Hive agent, assassinates the president (and is in turn eradicated by the Hive-controlled Jack Ruby). Later in the series, John testifies before the Warren Commission about the assassination; Bach discredits him but RFK becomes interested enough to start investigating, which leads to his own murder.

One of the Hive's mind-controlling "ganglia" takes him over but John frees her from Hive control. John and Kim go on the run, trying to find proof of the conspiracy, hunted by Steele (Tim Kelleher), a Majestic agent turned Hive killer, and by Majestic itself, which is determined to keep the secret. Over the course of the season we learn that one of the

9. Invaders, X-Files and Dynamators

goals of the space program was to reach a wrecked Hive ship on the Moon; that Howard Hughes' increasing isolation began when he realized the existence of the alien threat; and that the Gulf of Tonkin incident actually covered up a strike against an alien base.

When Kim realizes that Majestic is keeping the Vietnam War going to siphon off funds for its off-the-books operations, her outrage leads to her succumbing to the Hive and she starts working with Steele. In the final episode (the series was canceled after its first season), Steele assumes the name of Charles Manson. Bach discovers, too late, that the Hive can now control people through electronic implants that Majestic can't detect, and gets murdered by his immediate subordinate. In the present day, Loengard, aboard an alien ship, finally goes to confront the Hive.

The idea that shadowy forces control the course of history is a popular one in conspiratorial circles — the founding of the United States and the French Revolution have been both been credited to the manipulations of the Freemasons, for example. This series, which had an announced five-year plan to follow Loengard into the 21st century, takes a science-fictional approach to the same belief.

Animorphs (1998–99) Based on a highly successful children's book series by Katherine Applegate, *Animorphs* opens with five teens discovering a crashed alien ship. The dying alien pilot reveals that Earth has been invaded by the Yeerks, parasitic Controllers that take over the bodies of others. With no other help at hand, he gives the kids an edge by sharing his power to duplicate the shape of any animal once they touch it.

They need it: Many of the local adults and some kids have been taken by the Controllers, and Visser Three (Richard Sali), the head of the local Yeerk infestation, inhabits an alien body with the same shapechanging powers as the Animorphs. The kids have to fight the Yeerks — including a supposedly social organization known as the Sharing which they use to recruit new hosts — keep their human identities secret and avoid falling under Yeerk control themselves.

The Nickelodeon series ended with the battle unfinished; the book series continued with the Yeerks exposed, some of the Animorphs dead and the rest of the kids going into final battle with a Yeerk battle cruiser.

First Wave (1998–2001) Former thief Cade Foster (Sebastian Spence) had an idyllic life as a security consultant with a beautiful, loving wife until he was targeted by the First Wave of the alien Gua, advanced scouts for an invasion, studying humanity and its weaknesses by taking human form and infiltrating human society. When Cade learned what was going on, the Gua murdered his wife and framed him, forcing him to run not only from the aliens but the police.

Cade's only allies in the fight against the Gua are Joshua (Roger R. Cross), a Gua who questions their militaristic ways, and Crazy Eddie (Rob LaBelle), a conspiracy theorist who helps him figure out the fifth column's agenda by studying the lost prophecies of Nostradamus. The Gua infiltrators have placed themselves in positions of power and authority (although like the Invaders, they don't replace real humans) but Cade continues to confront and spike their various plans for crushing humanity.

In the third and final season, the aliens prepare to welcome their war leader Mabus to Earth at which point the Second Wave will launch the attack. But, Cade has new allies: Jordan Radcliffe (Traci Lords), a wealthy survivor of one of the Gua schemes, and the Raven Nation, a Believers-like organization that Jordan had organized to help Cade in his fight (the name was another Nostradamus reference). With the help of his friends Cade successfully thwarts the invasion, leaving him free to start a new life with Jordan.

Threshold (2005) In the first episode of this series, a mysterious alien signal explodes over a freighter. Many of the crew die and the handful that remain are transformed: stronger, faster, and obsessed with the need to create more "Infected." Dr. Molly Caffrey (Carla Gugino), a specialist in drafting federal contingency plans, is informed that Threshold, her plan for alien invasion, has just been activated.

Caffrey and her team discover that the signal transforms the double helix of the DNA molecule into a triple helix, leading to their physical and mental transformation. Caffrey's theory is that rather than cross space to colonize Earth, the aliens are "bioforming" it, transforming us into them (as happened earlier in *Village of the Damned* and *The Astronaut's Wife*). One of the infected, however, tells her the alien agenda is positive: Radiation from a stellar explosion will wipe out life on Earth if our DNA isn't enhanced to resist it.

This form of fifth column recruitment proved particularly difficult to fight: The signal could be spread by cellphone, by computer image, coded into music or spread through bioformed food. In the episode "Pulse," the Threshold team is only able to stop transmission by using an electromagnetic pulse to short out every electrical device in one-third of Miami. Caffrey and her teammates Lucas (Robert Patrick Benedict) and Cavennaugh (Brian Van Holt) were all partially exposed to the signal (which led to weird dreams about the alien homeworld); at one point Lucas became almost completely infected. In another episode, a close friend of Molly's is infected, and Molly has to order her killed.

As in many other shows, the government actively suppressed any evidence of the invasion, a policy Molly and her team disliked, particularly Fenway (Brent Spiner), a brilliant scientist and former sixties radical. While Threshold's superiors lacked the sinister agendas Scully and Mulder contended with in *The X-Files*, Washington bureaucracy and power plays proved almost as challenging, as various politicians and officials demanded to know what Threshold was up to or attempted to micromanage its operations. The show ended with the invasion still in process, but in a final dream, Molly learned that humanity will triumph, though she won't live to see it.

Invasion (2005) This ABC series debuted the same year as *Threshold*; in contrast to *Threshold*'s more *X-Files* approach, *Invasion* does a good job with a traditional fifties–SF infiltration premise, stretched out to the length of a TV season.

In the opening episode, as the town of Florida City endures a major hurricane, young Rose (Ariel Gade) sees lights falling into the nearby waters. Everyone assures her she imagined it, except her crazy uncle Dave (Tyler Labine), who blogs that it may be the first sign of a UFO invasion.

Dave is right. Several people in town are taken by the creatures, including Rose's mom Mariel (Kari Matchett), the town preacher and others. It turns out that the aliens

9. Invaders, X-Files and Dynamators

turned Sheriff Tom Underlay (William Fichtner), Mariel's husband, into one of their "hybrids" years before, after a plane crash that almost killed him and did kill his first wife. The military knows of the invasion and is secretly working to capture and control the hybrids, but so slowly that many Florida City residents end up transformed. One episode shows the high school's social structure is reorganizing based around who's human and who's hybrid.

Although Tom feels torn between the human and hybrid sides and wants to keep some sort of peace between them, the military is a lot more ruthless and so are some of the aliens. In the final episode, the hybrid Szura (James Frain) attempts to force the transformation of the entire town; he fails and Tom kills him. Had the show survived, Tom would have learned that his first wife had survived the plane crash as a hybrid and was now working with the military as head of the hybrid-control project.

V (2009) The original *V* presented a world in which seemingly benevolent aliens arrived on Earth with the intent of stealing our resources and using us as a food supply. After exposing plots to steal their science — plots secretly set up by the aliens themselves as a ruse — the "Visitors" not-so-reluctantly seized control of the world's governments.

In the 2009 remake, the Visitors' public arrival is more benevolent, but federal agent Erica and priest Frank soon learn that the aliens have been among us for years in sleeper cells doing ... what? For that reason, members of the Resistance can't be sure who to trust. (The Visitors have a similar problem, due to a fifth column of their own people working to undermine the occupation.) At the time this book was finished, the full significance of the Visitors' schemes and the scope of their infiltration were not yet clear.

10

Sexual Politics and the War Between Men and Women

Sexual infiltration plays a role in a lot of movies.

The bad girl seducing the hero for his money. The kind, loving husband who plots to murder his wife for the insurance or turns out to be a foreign spy, as in *Conspirator*. The fear that the person to whom we've given our heart is showing us a false face. That's usually the subject of film noir or romantic dramas — but when it's an organized, systematic attempt to seize power, it becomes a gendered fifth column.

Dr. Goldfoot and the Bikini Machine (1965) Inept secret agent Craig Gamble (Frankie Avalon) is stunned when Diane (Susan Hart), a beautiful Southern belle, comes on to him and invites herself up to his apartment. He's more stunned when she suddenly turns on him and walks out, now speaking with a French accent.

The reason? Diane's an artificial creation of Dr. Goldfoot (Vincent Price), a criminal scientist who plans to use his female robots to seduce some of *the* richest men, steal their money and use the loot to take over the world. Daphne made a play for Craig because Goldfoot's inept assistant Igor (Jack Mullaney) misdirected her; once Goldfoot takes control, Diane resumes her original mission, the seduction of millionaire Todd Armstrong (Dwayne Hickman). In only a few days, Diane is married to Todd, and he's signing over property to her left and right; Craig, however, warns him that something fishy is going on, so he refuses to sign the power of attorney that would give Diane full control of his finances. Goldfoot captures the guys and locks them in his torture dungeon to coerce cooperation (this involves a number of in-jokes from earlier AIP movies, such as Todd being strapped under the death-trap from Price's *Pit and the Pendulum*), but the guys escape. Goldfoot and Igor flee, but at the end of the movie, we see the mad doctor continuing his evil activities.

As writer Annalee Newitz has pointed out, the idea of a sinister female robot goes back to *Metropolis* (1927) where the villainous Rotwang (Rudolf Klein-Rogge) replaces the labor activist Maria (Brigitte Helm) with a robot double who discredits Maria with her wild, dissipated behavior. The Bikini Machines and similar robots embody the male suspicion that a seemingly loving woman only wants his money, or worse, his life. The fembots in the Austin Powers films, for instance, are seductive killers with guns in their breasts; the fembots in *The Bionic Woman* or the Girl Bombs in the second Dr. Goldfoot film are equally murderous.

At the same time, they're also a male fantasy: beautiful woman completely under a

10. Sexual Politics and the War Between Men and Women

man's control, whether it's Dr. Goldfoot or Dr. Evil in *Austin Powers, International Man of Mystery*. When Diane fails him, Goldfoot sets her to work scrubbing floors; he administers electric shocks when she doesn't work hard enough, which makes no sense since she doesn't have independent thought. The theme song assures us that when Goldfoot creates a robot "Then she behaves/Just like a slave."

Dr. Goldfoot and the Girl Bombs (1966) In this follow-up, Goldfoot's latest line of sexy androids come with bombs attached, in order to seduce, then kill nine of the top ten NATO generals. Goldfoot himself will replace the tenth general, his lookalike, and with no one to challenge his decisions, he will trigger a nuclear war between NATO and the USSR, after which Goldfoot and his backer — the Red Chinese government — will divide the world between them. Needless to say, it doesn't quite work.

The Million Eyes of Sumuru (1967) At the opening of this movie, Sumuru (Shirley Eaton) narrates as the sons of the world's richest man carry their father's coffin to its burial — at which point an explosion wipes them out. One of Sumuru's female agents watches as Sumuru warns us: "Other eyes may be on you now — I have a million eyes."

Sumuru, we learn, employs an army of female agents with the goal of ultimately taking down male authority and creating a worldwide utopia ruled by women. To this end, her agents have married 11 of the wealthiest men in the world, giving Sumuru control, through their husbands, of money enough to accomplish her goal. She needs one more conquest to have everything in place, but President Boong (Klaus Kinski) has proven impossible to control. Now, she intends to have him assassinated.

British Intelligence recruits American adventurers Tommy Carter (Frankie Avalon) and Nick West (George Nader), to stop her; Carter seduces Sumuru's assassin, but one of Boong's female guards, a Sumuru plant, shoots Boong. Fortunately, it turns out that Boong was just an impersonator providing an added level of security. Carter and West lead the military against Sumuru, whose island lair eventually explodes — but is it possible she could have survived?

Sax Rohmer created Sumuru in the belief that after China went communist, Cold War politics made it complicated to work with Chinese supervillain Fu Manchu. Sumuru — ageless, and ethnically unidentified — leads an all-girl cult that rejects marriage as male-dominated and focuses on breeding children without benefit of clergy in order to build a new civilization.

The movie turns all this into a Bond knockoff right down to Sumuru — who decrees that execution is the punishment for her followers who fall in love — melting into West's arms and telling him she needs a man to take her and dominate her.

Invasion of the Bee Girls (1973) When a prominent government scientist has a fatal coronary in a motel room in the middle of sex, federal agent Neil Agar (William Smith) assumes that checking out the death will be routine. Julie (Victoria Vetri), a research assistant, assures Agar that the research institute staff has little to do in their small town of Peckham, so the community is a hotbed of sex games and adultery.

Within two days, however, more dead bodies have turned up, not all scientists, but all male and all apparently killed by over-exertion during sex. The police warn the men of Peckham to stop having sex, particularly one-night stands, until they figure out what's causing this. The suggestion goes over about as well as you might expect. Meanwhile, the victims' frumpy wives receive mysterious phone calls, then visit entomologist Dr. Harris's (Anitra Ford) lab where they're covered in some sort of royal jelly and transformed into sexy (and horny) women with multifaceted insect eyes.

A chance remark about men dropping like flies steers Neil and Julie to the truth: Dr. Harris is transforming women into a hybrid super-race of bee women (though it's hard to see why — other than their eyes, they don't have any special powers). As queen bees, they could reproduce indefinitely once they were fertilized, but Harris's radiation treatment sterilizes them, so the frustrated urge to breed translates into an insatiable sex drive.

This is one of the great bad movies. The sexual paranoia in this film could be seen as a metaphor for the consequences of promiscuous sex (it would certainly have been seen as an AIDS metaphor a decade later), or women turning to each other when men cheat on them (the scenes of the women together in the lab have undeniable lesbian overtones). But that would probably be giving it more credit than it deserves.

The Stepford Wives (1978) This adaptation of Ira Levin's best-seller opens with aspiring New York photographer Joanna Everhart (Katharine Ross) reluctantly relocating with her husband Walter (Peter Masterson) and their kids to Stepford, a bucolic bedroom community where nobody locks their doors. As they drive into town, the local cops nod knowingly to Walter, fully aware what's ahead.

Joanna is astonished that the Stepford women are uniformly submissive, vacuous housewives who handle all household chores, talk in the bland tones of a spokesmodel displaying a new product (and without about as limited a vocabulary) and are also consumed with passion for their husbands. She's also annoyed to realize that Walter joined the town's Men's Association even before she agreed to move to Stepford

On the bright side, Joanna meets and bonds with fellow New Yorker Bobbie Marco (Paula Prentiss). The two women try to form a consciousness-raising group, and Charmaine (Tina Louise) — a tennis enthusiast who employs a maid instead of cleaning house herself — signs on. The other women resist, insisting they can't spare the time from caring for their families, but eventually a few wives agree. At the first meeting, Joanna and Charmaine discuss the strains in their marriage, then Kit (Carole Mallory) reveals her secret guilt: She was so busy washing clothes yesterday that she didn't have time to bake anything. The meeting dissolves into commercial soundbites ("If you don't have time, *make* time — for Easy On!").

Joanna learns that her neighbor Carol (Nanette Newman) used to be an active feminist, but Carol insists she's happier building her life around Ted. Then Charmaine transforms into yet another Valium-calm Stepford wife, happy to let her husband plow up her beloved tennis court so he can have a swimming pool. Wondering if there are drugs in Stepford's water, Joanna has an ex-boyfriend analyze it (it's harmless), and tells Walter she wants to return to New York. He convinces her to compromise on moving to another small town.

In *Invasion of the Bee Girls* (1973), a mad scientist turns human women into sexy, sexually insatiable women who exhaust their lovers to death.

To Joanna's horror, overnight Bobbie becomes another of the Stepford pod people and tells Joanna, "Dave works hard all day and what was he coming home to? A slob!" Walter tells Joanna she's worried about nothing and pushes her into therapy; Joanna eventually tells her shrink that she's convinced the Men's Association is doing something monstrous to the women: "If I'm wrong I'm insane — and if I'm right it's worse than if I'm wrong ... There will be somebody with my name, and she'll cook and clean like crazy but she won't take pictures and she won't be me."

The doctor tells Joanna to take her kids and run, but when she returns home, the children are gone. She looks for them at Bobbie's house and discovers the new Bobbie is actually an automaton. As usual, the phones are jammed and the roads blocked off, but Joanna's not leaving anyway until she reclaims the kids. Joanna tracks them to the Association building, but it's just a trap: One of the men confronts her and mockingly tells her that what's about to happen is nothing she wouldn't do herself if she had the option to replace Walter with a younger, better-looking, completely obedient man. Trying to escape, Joanna confronts her big-breasted android duplicate, which strangles her with a stocking. In the closing scene, robot Joanna, as blandly 1950s as the other women, dutifully goes shopping.

The film was a success that made "Stepford" as instantly recognizable a reference as Peyton Place was once — though in pop culture, it doesn't refer to sexism but to the supposed soullessness of the suburbs (move to small bedroom communities and become a robot!). Peter Knight says in *Conspiracy Culture* that a number of feminist writers had referred to modern culture and society as "brainwashing" women and portrayed society as actively conspiring to put women in their place, but also stating that the language of conspiracy should not be taken literally. In *The Stepford Wives*, it *is* literal: The women of Stepford are domestic slaves not because culture imposes it on them or because it's a life choice, but because they're robots who have no alternative but to obey.

The fembots differ from Goldfoot's Girl Bombs and Dr. Evil's fembots, being all male fantasy with none of the threat; fembots might seduce you and kill you, but Stepford Wives can't do anything but seduce you. For a man who'd prefer an obedient sex-robot for a spouse to a living woman with her own mind, there's no drawback to replacing the real wives.

In addition to the 21st century remake discussed below, *The Stepford Wives* generated three TV sequels. In *Revenge of the Stepford Wives* (1980) the men control their wives with drugs to keep them submissive, a scheme exposed when a female reporter comes to town. In *The Stepford Children* (1987) the parents replace misbehaving kids with perfect robot duplicates appropriate to perfect suburban families. In *The Stepford Husbands* (1996) a female scientist shows businesswomen how her brainwashing treatment can keep their less successful spouses compliant and cooperative (foreshadowing the treatment of overachieving women in the 2004 *Stepford Wives* remake).

Amazons (1984) When Congressman Barstow (William Schallert) enters a Washington, D.C., hospital for appendicitis, it appears quite routine — until a woman enters the phrase "stallion kill" in his file. A short while later, Barstow becomes insanely violent and

10. Sexual Politics and the War Between Men and Women

dies. The attending doctor, Sharon Fields (Madeleine Stowe), is stunned to discover that Barstow's file shows an allergy to antibiotics, which she can't believe she missed. She suspects the real cause is some unexplained chemicals found in Barstow's body, chemicals which she later learns can drive their victim crazy with fear.

With the help of pathologist Jerry (Peter Scolari) and suspicious cop Lt. Monaco (Jack Scalia), Fields learns that many powerful men in a variety of fields died with the drugs in their blood. They discover that several hospital staffers, including the administrator, Cosgrove (Jennifer Warren), are part of a conspiracy of women descended from the ancient Amazons. In the centuries since Hercules and his men overran their homeland and took them away in chains, the memory of their heritage has been passed down mother-to-daughter, in the hope that someday they will regain their power. They're close to doing it too: The men on the death list have been replaced by their wives or female subordinates, and Stowe, the favored candidate in the next presidential election, has a female vice-president who's one of the Amazons.

Cosgrove and her fellow Amazons try to stop Fields and Monaco from getting the information to the authorities, but in the final battle with the good guys, they wind up dead, and Stowe's vice-president is soon arrested. However, some of the daughters of the imprisoned Amazons remain free, and their fight against the race of men will go on....

The Stepford Wives (2004) In this much inferior remake, Joanna Eberhart (Nicole Kidman) is the president of a TV network whose male-bashing reality shows cost one contestant his marriage; this drives him to shoot his wife, her new lover, and Joanna. To minimize the bad PR, the network fires Joanna, who moves with her family to Stepford, an ultra-exclusive, ultra-expensive gated community.

The plot proceeds with less subtlety and more slapstick humor than the original as Joanna, Bobbie (Bette Midler) and Roger (Roger Bart)—a sarcastic homosexual who moved to Stepford with his more conservative partner—discover the town's oddities, including the submissive wives and the 1950s-style fashions on the women. A woman at the town dance keels over with sparks coming out of her head; a remote control found in a male neighbor's house controls his wife (though Joanna doesn't realize that); and Joanna discovers that all the housewives of Stepford are former high-powered executives.

Inevitably, Bobbie and Roger fall under the Stepford spell. Joanna confronts her husband Walter (Matthew Broderick) at the Men's Association where he tells her that the menfolk, all computer geniuses, have created a nanotech implant that reprograms their women into perfect wives. And guess who's next?

At the dance the next night, Joanna is perfectly obedient, but in reality, Walter couldn't bring himself to reprogram her. While she distracts Mike (Christopher Walken), the association director, Walter destroys the nanotech system, freeing the women. Mike attacks Walter, but Joanna smashes Mike's head and discovers he's a robot. It's Mike's wife Claire (Glenn Close) who's the real brains behind Stepford: Unhinged when the original Mike cheated on her, she decided to create a utopia where marriages would be perfect. ("Where would people never notice a town full of robots? Connecticut!")

Six months later, Joanna, Bobbie and Roger have turned their experience into fame, fortune and success; Joanna says she and Walter (smiling offstage) are finally happy because they've learned it's "not about perfection." As for the men of Stepford, they're now reduced to the ultimate punishment: doing the domestic chores for their wives.

The idea of men replacing professional high achievers with submissive hausfraus is a neat updating of the original (and makes the men marginally less monstrous than the murderers of the first film) but the film is more sexist: Joanna comes across as an arrogant bitch who belittles her husband and badly needed a comeuppance. The film is also inconsistent about how Stepford Wives are made. If the women are brainwashed, why are there robot bodies around the lab, and how does one wife pop money out of her mouth like a walking ATM?

11

The Master Race

This chapter deals with SF stories in which the fifth column is not body snatchers but *Homo superior*, the next step up in evolution (whether that step be biological or mechanical)

Tales of Tomorrow: "Conqueror's Isle" (1953) In SF writer Nelson Bond's short story "Conqueror's Isle" (1946), a pilot crashes on an isolated island that turns out to be the hiding place for the next step in evolution, a super-intellectual, super-human race of man that has every intention of gently, but firmly replacing regular humans. The pilot tells his story and is committed by a military doctor — who, we learn in the last paragraph, is secretly one of the neohumans.

Bond adapted his story for the radio adventure series *Escape* in 1949, then for *Tales of Tomorrow* in 1953. It would not be the last story to present the possibility that the master race is walking among us.

The Creation of the Humanoids (1962) Decades after a two-day nuclear war wiped out 92 percent of humanity, the survivors depend on robots to keep society running. Initially, "Clickers" were crude and truly robotic in appearance, but the latest models are bald with grayish-green skin and appear more like an android than a robot. They handle all the dirty work from food services to bureaucracy, leaving humans free for more inspired pursuits — and are close to outnumbering humans.

That doesn't suit Cragis (Don Megowan), who worries that humanity is losing the ability to fend for itself and that the robots could become our masters, particularly since society's computers are linked to the Clicker recharge station, so that over time the robots could download all human knowledge. The existence of the almost-human R-96 androids only adds to fears that someone will build an R-100, fully human.

Cragis' organization, the Order of Flesh and Blood, resorts to everything from lobbying the government to bombing a pro-robot newspaper to stop the oncoming wave. Despite their efforts, society remains unimpressed. Cragis' sister Esme (Frances McCann) has divorced her husband and married an R-94.

Cragis would be even more upset if he knew that scientist Dr. Raven (Don Doolittle) has begun transferring the minds of newly deceased humans into R-96 bodies, creating Clickers who think they're human, except during the hour they spend at Raven's laboratory each day recharging. For some, the transition is too big a shock, and one of the unstable ones strangles Raven.

While visiting Esme, Cragis meets her friend Maxine (Erica Elliott), a pro-robot reporter. They find themselves drawn to each other despite their different views. As they discuss plans for a life together, they find themselves compelled to visit Raven's lab, where they enter a recharge booth: They're both R-96s.

Cragis promptly updates the Clickers there about the Order's plans — the main reason the plans keep failing — and the growing suspicions within the order that he's a traitor. The Clickers confirm that they've used his information to block the Order: Contacting a printing company computer to make sure that fliers for a rally arrive late, guaranteeing that a restrictive anti–Clicker bill will get lost in the bureaucracy. Esme's husband, one Clicker says, is using sleep-programming to make her increasingly sympathetic to their agenda.

A younger Raven enters and tells Cragis and Maxine the truth about their new condition. Cragis, it turns out, died six months ago from a cerebral hemorrhage brought on by overwork (death memories are erased during the mind-transfers to ease the shock). Maxine died three months later, the result of one of the Order's terrorist bombings (Cragis is not proud of this).

Raven explains that his death was prearranged to escape capture and execution by the government, which would have destroyed the formulas he carries in his memory. The Clickers' prime directive is to serve and protect humanity: Given that radiation-induced sterility makes human extinction inevitable, transferring human minds to humanoid bodies is the only solution. Soon, Raven tells Cragis, they'll be ready for him to announce that the mind-transfer is available to everyone, presenting it as a chance to achieve immortality.

Even though Raven convinces Cragis that his new body isn't soulless, Maxine is despondent that she'll never be able to bear children. Raven replies that with a few simple operations, he can elevate them to R-100, fully human and capable of propagating a new race. Turning to the audience, he adds that we can be sure he succeeded — otherwise, we wouldn't be here.

A curious film that takes many of the themes of fifth-column movies, such as the replacement of humans by androids. But in this case the replacements are truly for our own good — though this doesn't make the idea of Esme's loving husband brainwashing her in her sleep any less creepy. Regrettably, the movie is mind-numbing in its stiff performances and bad dialogue.

Futureworld (1976) In 1973's *Westworld*, the humanoid robots populating an Old West amusement park malfunction and begin gunning down the paying guests. At the beginning of *Futureworld*, we learn that newspaper reporter Chuck Browning (Peter Fonda) delivered an explosive scoop on the disaster; now he gets a call from Frenchy (Ed Geldard), a man offering info for an equally spectacular follow-up story. Chuck arrives to find Frenchy dying, gasping out the name of the Delos Corporation, which controlled Westworld.

Soon afterward, Delos executive Duffy (Arthur Hill) reveals that robots in all of Delos' amusement parks (including medieval, futuristic and Roman settings) went haywire, but the company has now invested $15 million upgrading to the point where the

11. The Master Race

parks are now foolproof. To reassure the public, Delos is throwing a major reopening party to be attended by prominent business and government leaders and the press, including Chuck and TV journalist Tracy Ballard (Blythe Danner).

In between enjoying the wonders of Futureworld (holographic chess and sex androids), Chuck becomes convinced that Delos is hiding something. He discovers that the entire staff is robotic, but Duffy assures him that's neither secret nor bad, since the complex will be run without the human error that caused the Westworld disaster.

Of course, something *is* going on: Delos agents take sleeping guests to have their bodies scanned down to the last detail, and Chuck tells Tracy that many prominent figures have been invited to the parks. They learn from a friendly tech, Harry (Stuart Margolin), that not only the staffs but the maintenance crews are all androids, and that there are parts of the complex only the androids can enter. Harry gets around this by using an android eye to enter the hidden sector, where the technicians are creating exact duplicates of the V.I.P.s currently visiting — and also Chuck and Tracy. As they watch, the duplicates come to life as servants of Delos and go to kill their originals.

After the reporters leave the secret lab, Duffy captures Chuck and explains that since human beings are ruining the world, the latest androids from Delos — all self-aware and intelligent — have decided to take it over. Tracy kills Duffy only to discover he's a duplicate too. The reporters' android duplicates catch up to them, and it's kill or be killed, but ultimately Chuck and Tracy survive (and prove they're both real by a kiss). They leave the next day, posing as their duplicates. The fake Tracy shows up to warn Delos, but too late to stop Chuck and Tracy from leaving with the truth.

This was followed in 1980 by the TV series *Beyond Westworld*, which took the *Futureworld* concept of android doppelgangers but ignored the movie itself, harking back to *Westworld*. In the opening episode, Simon Quaid (James Wainwright), who assisted in the creation of the Westworld androids, dreams of using them to build a perfect society, controlled by androids and overseen by himself. He never accepted the androids' designer selling the plans to Delos and triggered the Westworld massacre to destroy the park and cover the theft of 200 androids he plans to use to accomplish his goals. Quaid uses one of the androids to take over a nuclear sub; in subsequent episodes, he tries taking over an oil company, providing a revolutionary with a nuclear bomb in return for sanctuary in his country, and putting a mind-control implant in a state governor's head. Five episodes were made, but only three aired.

Prey (1998) Dr. Sloan Parker (Debra Messing) is an anthropologist studying human genetics. After Parker's mentor Coulter (Natalija Nogulich) — an expert in the genetic basis of violence — agrees to testify against the murderous Lynch (Roger Howarth), Lynch escapes and kills her. Parker learns Coulter had genetic evidence showing that many serial killers are genetically distinct from Homo sapiens: They're a new species living among us, and could potentially replace us.

As the escaped killer continues his murder spree, Parker allies with Tom Daniels (Adam Storke), a federal agent hunting the man. Tom reveals that he himself is part of the new super-race, but opposes his fellows' fondness for treating ordinary humans as prey. The new race — "Dominants" — are smarter and more aggressive than Homo sapiens, with some degree of psychic ability, and convinced that as the superior race, they are entitled to subjugate and kill us. They've also figured out how to genetically engineer humans into their own kind. Some groups of Dominants, like Tom, wish to co-exist with humans, and some human groups wish to collaborate with the new master race.

Frankenstein (2004) New Orleans detectives Carson O'Connor and Michael Sloane (Parker Posey, Adam Goldberg) thought it couldn't get much worse than tracking "The Surgeon," a killer who murders his victims, then dissects them with professional skill and removes one or two of their organs. The detectives were wrong.

First came the discovery that the most recent victim had two hearts — not to mention multiple other improvements such as extra lymph glands and bones far stronger and denser than a human skeleton — making him the next step up in human evolution.

Then O'Connor met Deucalion (Vincent Perez), who claimed to be a composite life-form created by Dr. Helios, a renowned New Orleans surgeon. Helios created Deucalion more than two centuries before, which became the origin of the Frankenstein legend. He tells O'Connor that the Surgeon is another of Helios' creations, yearning to die but unable to overcome his natural instinct for self-preservation — so while conducting his experiments, at some level he's hoping the cops will finish him off.

While the cops and Deucalion hunt the Surgeon, the movie cuts away periodically to Helios (Thomas Kretschmann), a coolly arrogant genius who informs his dinner guests that he believes the best way to oversee genetics and cloning is to put control of them into the hands of men of vision. His vision, unfortunately, is a world where his creations have replaced Homo sapiens. A number of them already exist in human society, including cops (one of whom is the Surgeon) and a priest who hopes that bridging the gap between the neo-men and God will help them to attain a human soul. When Helios, who has enhanced his own body with genetic engineering, discovers that the priest has moral qualms about Helios' agenda, the doctor murders him.

O'Connor and her partner discover that the Surgeon is their colleague Detective Harker (Michael Maadsen). Deucalion tells O'Connor that Helios has been preparing for 200 years to replace humanity with his new race; if they do not fight him together, he may succeed.

This failed pilot was based on a Dean Koontz novel, but Koontz disliked the results and had his name taken off it. Koontz continued the story in further novels and graphic novels.

12

Satanic and Supernatural Infiltration in Film and Television

Along with science fiction, horror has also contributed to filmdom's fifth columns.

It's not surprising. Paranoia is a common element of horror fiction, as is the idea that something is lurking below the surface: Your friends, your neighborhood, reality itself is not what it appears.

The fear of Satanism and witchcraft has been a recurring element in Christianity since the Catholic church began hunting witches in the 14th century. The idea that Christian communities are riddled with these subversive enemies of God, and that they form an organized network of Satanic servants, is part of this fear.

This fear has continued even into the late twentieth century. Conservative Christian author Hal Lindsay titled one of his works, written in 1972, *Satan Is Alive and Well on Planet Earth*.

The roots of the fear include a belief among some conservatives that anything non–Christian must be Satanic; that anything that goes wrong in their lives can be explained as the work of Satan attacking true Christians; and that many trends in society, from teaching evolution to gay marriage, can be blamed on Satan's influence.

Rumors that Procter and Gamble have vowed to devote part of their profits to the Church of Satan have persisted for more than 20 years, despite the company's denial and the lack of any evidence. (According to Snopes.com, the company sued several Amway distributors for spreading the rumor.) Similar accusations have been made against McDonalds and other companies.

In the late eighties, it took only a few shreds of dubious evidence to convince prosecutors, police and the public that vast networks of Satanic cultists scattered through day-care centers across America were molesting children and sacrificing their pets to the dark powers (the book *Satan's Silence* covers this nightmare in detail). Put all that together and it's no surprise that the movies have milked Satan for material.

Rosemary's Baby (1968) Slowly, slowly, the evidence accumulates that everyone around Rosemary Woodhouse, even her husband, are part of some secret organization. It seems she's just paranoid, but in the end it turns out she's right.

The movie starts innocuously as Rosemary and her husband Guy (Mia Farrow, John Cassavetes) learn that the death of a tenant in the elegant Branford Building gives them a chance to move into a huge rent-controlled apartment. They snap it up, despite warnings from their friend Hutch (Maurice Evans) that the building's lurid past includes murder, cannibalism and Satanism.

Rosemary befriends Terri (Angela Dorian), a drug addict saved from the streets by kindly Branford residents Minnie and Roman Castevet (Ruth Gordon, Sidney Blackmer). After Terri kills herself, the Castevets turn to the Woodhouses for emotional support. Rosemary soon finds herself seething over the way the Castavets insist on spending all their time with her and Guy. On the plus side, Guy's unsuccessful acting career picks up when a fellow actor goes blind and Guy is asked to take over a plum role.

After eating Minnie's odd-tasting chocolate dessert, Rosemary hallucinates being raped by something monstrous and wakes with scratches on her back. Guy tells her he bedded her after she passed out drunk, and soon afterwards, her doctor confirms that she's pregnant.

The Castevets steer Rosemary to Dr. Sapirstein (Ralph Bellamy), a top obstetrician who puts her on a course of herbal tonics and warns her to ignore advice from books or friends and listen only to him. Rosemary suffers agonizing pain and loses weight, but Sapirstein assures her it's normal, and the pain will pass. When it doesn't, Hutch becomes worried, but a sudden illness renders him comatose, then kills him.

When Rosemary finally tells her friends about her pains, they confirm that the agony isn't normal and urge her to get a second opinion. This infuriates Guy, who tells Rosemary they can't insult a doctor as important as Sapirstein that way. Rosemary is outraged that Guy cares more about the doctor than his wife, but the pain disappears in the middle of the argument, so she stops worrying. Then one of Hutch's friends gives her a cryptic last message from Hutch: When Rosemary deciphers it, it reveals that Roman is the son of an infamous Satanist, and she becomes convinced the Castevets want to sacrifice her baby in a black mass.

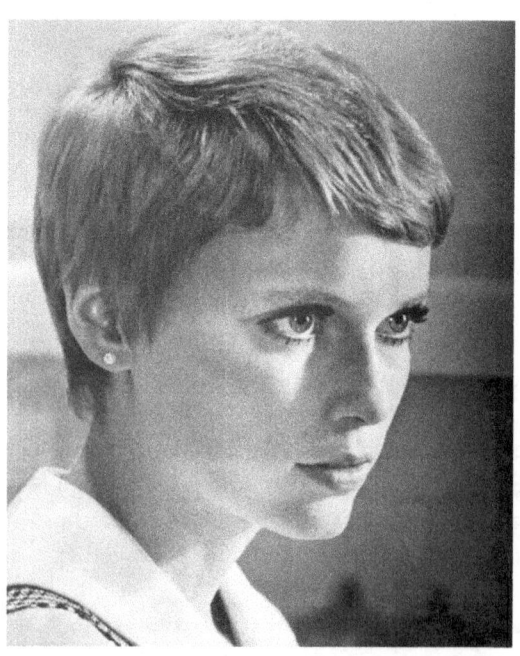

A publicity shot of Mia Farrow from *Rosemary's Baby* (1968), the film in which a Satanist fifth column plots to overthrow the laws of God and Man.

When she asks Guy to move to a new apartment, he refuses, and throws out her black magic reference book. The Castevets leave on a cruise, but Rosemary doesn't feel safe and continues studying the occult. She learns that the actor Guy replaced could have been blinded by sorcery — and that would imply that Guy is part of the cult. She goes to Sapirstein, only to realize he's part of the coven too, so she turns in desperation to her

12. Satanic and Supernatural Infiltration in Film and Television

old doctor. When he hears her story, he calls Sapirstein and Guy to drag poor, disturbed Rosemary back to the Branford.

When Rosemary goes into labor, Sapirstein sedates her. After she wakes, she's told baby Adrian was stillborn, but she suspects he was really taken for a sacrifice. When she hears a baby crying at the Castevets,' she sneaks over to find a party in progress and her baby in a cradle. Rosemary rushes over to claim him only to recoil in horror, crying, "What have you done to his eyes?"

A Satanist says, "He has his father's eyes."

Rosemary was right about the Satanist conspiracy, but wrong about the motive: Satan himself impregnated her, to create a son who will topple the existing order and overturn the laws of God and man. (The term Antichrist would have been appropriate, but it didn't enter pop culture until *The Omen* a decade later.) Roman tells her it would be much better for Adrian if he had his mother to care for him, and reluctantly Rosemary agrees, gently rocking his cradle. (The Ira Levin novel has Rosemary hoping that a mother's nurturing care can overcome Satanic nature, but there's no hint of this in the film.)

Director Roman Polanski asserted that he meant the movie to be ambiguous as to whether Satan really targeted Rosemary and Adrian, or whether Rosemary might have fantasized the whole thing. If that was the case, Polanski failed miserably: While it's true we never see Adrian up close, the closing scenes make no sense if the conspiracy isn't real.

What we have, instead, is a story of paranoia and infiltration from an expectant mother's point of view. The movie takes normal fears — is my doctor reliable? will my husband be there for me? will my baby turn out okay?— but in Rosemary's case, the answer is always no. She's surrounded by a fifth column subverting not only America but God and Christianity, with agents who can be elderly retirees, struggling actors or prominent doctors.

In a 2002 interview, Levin said he felt somewhat guilty that *Rosemary's Baby* had promoted the idea of Satanists in the modern world — inspiring other movies such as *The Exorcist* and *The Omen*— and giving credence to the idea that Satan existed (and thereby, he believed, fueling the rise of the religious right). While Levin probably overstated his influence, certainly a number of horror films showed the influence of *Rosemary's Baby* in their presentation of Satanists lurking around us.

The Devil's Child (1997) and *Omen IV* (1991) both have women bearing Satan's child discover that Satanists lurk all around them, manipulating them to make sure they give birth to the demonic infant (both movies have the ob/gyn in on the plot).

End of Days (1999) has detective Jericho Cane (Arnold Schwarzenegger) assigned to protect the woman chosen by Satan (Gabriel Byrne) to bear the Antichrist. Increasing numbers of people including many of his fellow cops turn out to be Satanic agents.

Other films took more distinctive slants on occult fifth columns.

The Dead Don't Die (1975) is a supernatural thriller (though not actually very thrilling) set in 1930s Chicago. Don Drake (George Hamilton) agrees to find the man who murdered his sister-in-law and framed Don's brother Ralph (Jerry Douglas) as the killer. The answers lie with Varek (Ray Milland), a voodoo master raising the dead as his slaves (Ralph soon becomes one of his pawns) and plotting to use his sorcery to enslave the city's power brokers, the first step to taking over America. Ultimately, Varek escapes through the help of one of his zombie puppets, leaving Don with no proof that any of this happened.

The TV series *Kindred: The Embraced* (1996) spun off from the successful role-playing game *Vampire: The Masquerade*. The premise of the game is that vampires once ruled humanity, only to be overthrown and hunted down; to preserve themselves, they live among us secretly, taking blood only from volunteers. The number one rule for all vampires, whatever their clan (corporate Ventrue, Toreador aesthetes, Gangrel drifters, etc.) is never to betray the masquerade that protects them.

In the opening episode of *Kindred*, cop Frank Kohanek (C. Thomas Howell) discovers that his lover is a vampire, and the former lover of Julian Luna (Mark Frankel), the vampire leader of Los Angeles. When the vampires brand her as a threat to the masquerade, she kills herself to protect Frank from their wrath. Frank discovers that the vampires are woven into Los Angeles' social, business and political scene (his own partner is one of them)—but the paranoia aspect wasn't really developed, as the vampires weren't out to "embrace" more humans, and Frank was more likely to wind up working with Julian to take down the more murderous undead.

Left Behind (2000) This film is based on the first book in the best-selling Christian fiction series. It opens with ace reporter Buck Williams (Kirk Cameron) reporting on a miraculous formula created by Israeli scientist Chaim Rosensweig (Colin Fox) that can transform deserts into verdant gardens—and not a moment too soon, since the world is on the brink of a massive food shortage. An enemy attack by unstated adversaries (in the book it's a combined assault by Ethiopia and Russia) darkens the Israeli skies but to Buck's astonishment, the planes crash and the bombs and missiles don't detonate when they hit.

Returning to New York, Buck meets an old friend, conspiracy theorist Dirk Burton (Jack Langedijk), who warns him that Rosensweig's formula is part of a conspiracy by international banker Jonathan Stonegal (Daniel Pilon). Dirk also presents Buck with what he claims is Stonegal's plan for world domination. Buck isn't convinced but later we see Stonegal working with Nicolae Carpathia (Gordon Currie), a Romanian politician, secretary general of the United Nations and prominent peace activist in some sort of shady deal which Carpathia believes will bring peace to the Mideast. When one of Stonegal's associates asks him if the Arabs will play ball, Stonegal replies, "When their children start starving, they'll make peace."

On the way back from Israel, dozens of people on Buck's plane vanish. Shell-shocked, the survivors land and discover that the disappearances stretch across the world. Buck meets the pilot's daughter Chloe (Janaya Stephens) and assures her he'll let her know if he discovers anything. He then goes to meet Dirk, even though nothing in Dirk's story ties to the disappearances. He finds Dirk dead, his apartment ransacked. A hidden gunman destroys Dirk's computer but Buck gets away with a computer disc.

The disc, which Buck deduces ties in with the vanishings, turns out to contain the

12. Satanic and Supernatural Infiltration in Film and Television

plans for the attack on Israel, a design for a rebuilt Temple in Jerusalem and a lot of details about global crop deficits. Later, he meets with Alan (Philip Akin), a federal agent who tells him that while the government has officially embraced Carpathia's theory (fallout from decades of nuclear testing somehow caused the vanishings), behind the scenes, everyone's worried.

With Alan's help, Buck pieces together Stonegal's plot: After Rosensweig gives his formula to the UN for the benefit of the world, Stonegal and his allies in banking will call in various loans to bankrupt the UN. That gives them control of the formula and with it, the world food supply; how they plan to eliminate everyone else growing food is left unexplained, probably because it doesn't make much senses. Buck decides he needs to warn Rosensweig, but as he's about to get into Alan's car, a woman on the street distracts him. A car bomb kills Alan.

Buck learns the real cause of the vanishing: The Rapture, an event based on an interpretation of Revelation that predicts true Christians will be taken up to Heaven before the End Times begin, sparing them the horrors of living under the Antichrist. When he arrives at the UN, he and Rosensweig tell Nicolae about Stonegal. Nicolae's response is to bring them, Stonegal and his ally Cothran (Tony De Santis) together with several politicians from around the world.

Carpathia announces that as secretary general he will divide the world into ten regions, with the politicians ruling over them. Stonegal and Cothran have been trying to exploit him, and so do not get to share in the goodies. To drive this home, Carpathia takes a gun from the security guard, shoots both men and wills everyone in the room to believe that Stonegal shot Cothran, then himself, after his plans were revealed.

Having accepted Jesus as his savior Buck isn't affected by Carpathia's mind-whammy, but isn't about to show it. Carpathia tells Buck that the timing is perfect: Buck's story on the conspiracy's plans to exploit Carpathia will help secure his position at the apex of power. Buck realizes that Carpathia is the Antichrist who will rule over the world for the seven years of tribulation (The secretary general position isn't exactly the apex of power, but Timothy LaHaye, the co-author of the *Left Behind* novels, comes from the right-wing position where the UN is a diabolical threat to American independence).

As blogger Fred Clark has pointed out, this movie doesn't make a lot of sense: Buck starts digging into the Stonegal case as if he just knows it had some connection to the Rapture, which he can't (especially as it doesn't, except in the sense that both the Antichrist's rise to power and the Rapture are on the end times checklist). Still the conspiratorial aspects seem to qualify Carpathia as a true fifth columnist, seizing power for evil as much as Senator Iselin did in *The Manchurian Candidate*.

In the sequel *Left Behind: Tribulation Force* (2002), Carpathia tightens his grip on the reins of power, taking over Buck's news network, censoring unfriendly reports and "reluctantly" agreeing to oversee the transition to a single world currency to make it easier to manage the economic chaos following the Rapture (this is another part of the events to come according to some, but not all, interpretations of Revelation). Buck and his friends try to warn people about Carpathia's true nature, but find it difficult to convince anyone that Carpathia, the savior of all mankind in its hour of need, could have a hidden agenda.

Supernatural (2005) This series focuses on Sam and Dean Winchester (Jared Padalecki, Jensen Ackles), whose father dedicated his life to hunting supernatural forces. Sam eventually rejected that life, went to college and planned to settle down with his girlfriend. After she's murdered by the same supernatural forces that killed the Winchesters' mother, he reluctantly rejoins Dean on the hunt.

In the fourth episode, "Phantom Traveler," the brothers discovered a demon possessing plane pilots and causing havoc for no other reason than the joy of destruction. They learn that demons constantly possess human vessels to advance evil in secret, though there are ways to exorcise them. Demons constantly lurked in the shadows in the series, manipulating mortal minds and covertly scheming against humanity, particularly one malevolent, yellow-eyed demon who had designs on Sam, who possessed supernatural powers of his own.

One demon, Ruby (Katie Cassidy), allied herself with Sam, convincing him to work to stop Lilith (Rachel Pattee), a demon of great power possessing the body of a small girl. Lilith's goal is to break the 66 seals that have bound Satan; if she succeeds, the Apocalypse will begin. Ruby eventually helps Sam to kill Lilith — which he discovers is the final seal, the one thing that will ultimately release Satan. The fifth season had them working to stop Lucifer and the Four Horsemen from bringing about the end of the world, a battle that was still in progress at the time of writing.

13

Miscellanea

Corporate Takeovers, Secret Societies and the JFK Assassination

While the thrust of this book is infiltration from outside forces, sometimes political paranoia focuses itself inward.

The idea that some subgroup of Americans is subverting the republic to its own ends, without being part of some outside agency, has cropped up again and again in history. Munitions manufacturers cause wars to boost profits. Secular humanists plot to drive God out of the schools. The CIA killed Kennedy. Neoconservatives orchestrated 9/11. The patriarchy isn't simply sexist, it's an organized conspiracy to keep women down.

Conspiracy theories by themselves don't qualify for this book, but some movies portray the internal conspiracies as interchangeable with more conventional fifth columns, sinister conspiracies out to seize control of the American government and the American people.

Corporate Skullduggery

The President Vanishes (1934) With a European war in the offing, a cabal of industrialists decides that they could make even more money as government contractors, providing America enters the war; this will also give them a seat at the table when the spoils of war are divided afterwards. Of course, a lot of Americans will die if they push us into the war, but as one of them says, World War I "gave us the greatest year of prosperity we ever had.... Four hundred thousand casualties are nothing."

The one obstacle they see is that President Stanley (Arthur Byron) is adamantly opposed to war. Their solution is a massive publicity campaign built around the theme that America's honor is at stake, and to redeem it, we must fight! The cabal also backs the fascist Gray Shirts, who assault pacifist speakers and antiwar demonstrations under the leadership of religious zealot Lincoln Lee (Edward Ellis). When Lee's followers meet in a parking garage, he reminds them that "a greater cause than ours was born in a stable!"

The mix of money, political influence and brute force guarantees the Senate will vote for war by a veto-proof majority—but on the eve of the vote, Stanley disappears. All thought of war is dropped as the government searches for its leader, with Secretary of War Lewis Wardell (Edward Arnold), secretly part of the cabal, leading the hunt.

It turns out the disappearance was Stanley's last-ditch attempt to avert war with the help of a few trusted friends: After a week, he intends to be found in the Grey Shirt headquarters, apparently kidnapped by the warhawks, thereby discrediting them. The plan almost goes astray and leaves the president dead, but in the end he triumphs and peace is preserved.

Years before President Eisenhower warned about the dangers of the military-industrial complex, there was a widespread suspicion that munitions makers actively promoted war for their own ends. This suspicion grew out of the First World War (1934's *The Man Who Reclaimed His Head* offers this version of history) and continued on into the thirties, when Gen. Smedley Butler openly accused business leaders of launching wars for profit (he also claims to have spiked a corporate conspiracy to overthrow FDR by refusing to participate). That attitude suffuses this movie, in which high-level political scheming is backed up by fascist thugs in the street, though most of the plot is devoted to a murder mystery — no surprise since it was written by mystery writer Rex Stout (anonymously).

The idea of blaming wars on the corporations that profit from them would crop up later in the century in *JFK* (1991) and *Loose Change* (2009).

As *Voodoo Histories* points out, the underlying assumption behind this theory is that "Who benefits?" is the key question, and who benefits from war besides the warmongers? The catch is, this ignores all the people in Europe who supported World War I in the belief that it would be a short, glorious war offering heroism, excitement and adventure. The fact that their dreams of glory didn't match the reality of Verdun doesn't make those dreams any less sincere.

The Manchurian Candidate (2004) In this remake, Major Ben Marco (Denzel Washington) is a Desert Storm veteran tormented by recurring nightmares about a firefight that would have wiped his platoon out if not for the heroism of Raymond Shaw (Liev Schreiber), now a Congressman. The nightmares are Marco's true memories resurfacing: A conspiracy run by the Manchurian Global Corporation and Raymond's mother, Sen. Eleanor Shaw (Meryl Streep), brainwashed the platoon to remember a battle that never happened in order to kick-start Raymond's political career. Sen. Shaw is a post–9/11 authoritarian who equates liberal Sen. Jordan's (Jon Voight) concern for the Bill of Rights to saying that keeping suicide bombers off buses is unconstitutional. Believing that her gender has denied her shot at the White House, Shaw has pulled strings to make Raymond the Republican vice-presidential candidate.

Marco befriends Raymond, and they try to uncover the truth about what happened to them in Kuwait. What they don't know is that Ben's been brainwashed too: During a major political event, he will assassinate the Republican presidential candidate, allowing Raymond to step into his place and win on a wave of sympathy. Even after Ben learns the truth, he's unable to stop himself from going through with the killing — except that at the last minute, he finds the force of will to take out Raymond and his mother instead.

This weak remake lacks the black humor of the original film and also drops novelist

13. Miscellanea

Richard Condon's interplay of paranoid poses and hidden agendas: Unlike the phony anticommunist Iselins in the original film, Eleanor Shaw is exactly what she appears to be, a right-wing authoritarian rather than a terrorist sleeper. (Ben's girlfriend, on the other hand, is a military-intelligence agent assigned to watch over him, the kind of suspicion so many people had about Janet Leigh in the original.)

In the DVD interviews, director Jonathan Demme and screenwriter Daniel Pyne said they revamped the original because communism was no longer the big global threat and "corporate totalitarianism is probably the new philosophy that's scariest." Critic Roger Ebert agreed that corporate control of America is much more believable that a communist takeover in the original.

The flaw, though, is that we can imagine what the communists could gain from controlling the White House; since we never learn anything of Manchurian Global's agenda, we're left to guess what they wanted that normal corruption and cash donations couldn't buy them. Perhaps Pyne's view that Eleanor is the real threat ("I don't see Manchurian Global as the enemy, I see Eleanor Shaw as the enemy") explains it.

Dollhouse (2009–2010) In this TV series, the Rossum Corporation has the technology to wipe personalities from our minds and imprint new ones. "Dolls" sign up for five-year hitches (in some cases they're coerced into it) during which they will receive whatever personality their owner pays for. Typically it's a sex fantasy (a doll makes the perfect, ideally responsive girlfriend with whatever personality you desire) but they're also used as investigators, thieves, bodyguards (etc.), perfectly tailored to the situation. Episodes focused on Echo (Eliza Dushku), a doll who retains some of her imprinted personalities between jobs, and Ballard (Tahmoh Penikett), an FBI investigator convinced, despite official skepticism, that the Dollhouse exists and working to expose it.

The first season hinted that Rossum had bigger plans for the Dolls than just money. It also established that Rossum can create Dolls with two implanted personalities: A cover personality and a "sleeper" for emergencies. Ballard's girlfriend Mellie (Miracle Laurie), for example, can be triggered to become a lethal fighting machine as soon as she hears the right code phrase.

In the second season episode "The Public Eye," Sen. Perrin (Alexis Denisof) has acquired Madeline — Mellie's real identity, now that she's free of her Rossum contract — as a witness at his upcoming Congressional hearing on Rossum and the Dollhouse. Dollhouse executive DeWitt (Olivia Williams) sends Echo and Ballard (who went to work for her in return for freeing Madeline) to discredit Perrin and rescue Madeline; since it's believed that Perrin's wife Cindy (Stacey Scowley) is a Doll working for one of Rossum's branches playing some sort of scheme against the others, DeWitt equips Ballard with a device to deactivate Dolls.

When Ballard activates the device, it turns out that Perrin is the Doll and Cindy his handler. When he finally reaches the Congressional hearing in the next episode, "The Left Hand," Perrin denounces the rumors of the Dollhouse as a vicious smear by Rossum's competitors and brands Madeline as a former mental patient. In one stroke, Rossum eliminates the rumors about its operations and grooms Perrin as a prospective presidential candidate. (It didn't do them much good — Echo, Ballard and some of the other characters took Rossum down at the end of the second season.)

Loose Change 9/11: An American Coup (2009) This is the latest revision in a series of Dylan Avery documentaries (though a largely fact-free one, which is why it's listed here) arguing that the United States government staged 9/11 in order to justify the invasion of Iraq and advance a neoconservative agenda in the Middle East.

The film opens by arguing that governments have always done this sort of thing: The Nazis started the Reichstag fire in 1933 in order to justify a crackdown on communists (a communist was accused of the crime) and FDR knew about Pearl Harbor but let it happen to bring America into World War II. After more history highlights such as the Manhattan Project (presumably to emphasize how well the government keeps secrets) and the Kennedy assassination, Avery brings in the Gulf of Tonkin incident, a supposed attack by North Vietnamese vessels on American ships that President Johnson cited to justify committing ground troops to Vietnam.

From this, Avery springs to 9/11, which he argues makes no logical sense unless we assume it was an inside job. The first version of this film asserted that the planes that supposedly hit the World Trade Center and the Pentagon had been spotted still flying around, which proved they'd been replaced by remote-controlled drones; subsequent versions, including this one, dropped that idea, but made a variety of other claims, such as the impossibility of a plane crash doing that much damage to the Pentagon, regardless of what any eyewitnesses might have said.

Avery's points have been refuted, but he asserted in one interview that the inaccuracies in some versions were intentional: People would have to research them to find the facts, and research will guide them to the overall truth of his thesis. Other conspiracy theorists have argued that the film is so riddled with flaws that it must be a plant to make the entire 9/11 "truth" movement look like fools. (UFOlogists have made the same arguments about some of the crazier UFO believers: The government planted them as a disinformation ploy.)

Exactly who makes up the sinister conspiracy is unclear: While Avery starts out by fingering the neoconservative Project for a New American Century, he goes on to imply that the "stranglehold on America" still exists under Obama. This leaves us with a boogeyman vague enough that it could be anyone from the military-industrial complex to the Illuminati.

Even Avery's opening history is dubious: Most historians believe that while the Nazis exploited the Reichstag fire, they didn't set it, and while FDR was aware the Japanese were planning an attack, there's little evidence he knew it would be on Pearl Harbor.

The Kennedy Assassination

Executive Action (1973) opens with a group of conservative businessmen in 1963 trying to convince Texas businessman Ferguson (Will Geer) that JFK is taking the country

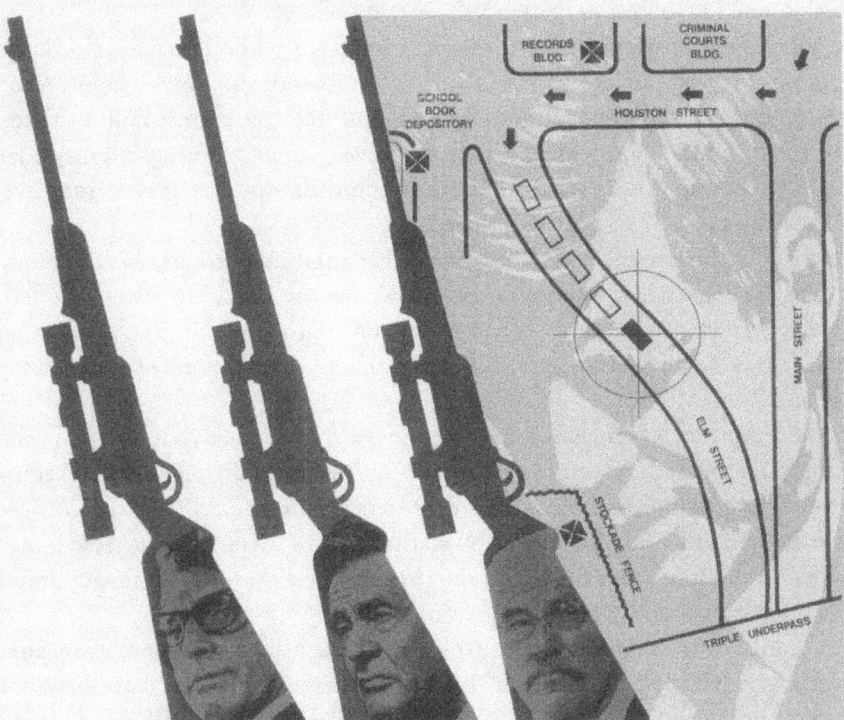

Executive Action (1973) reveals that we were duped by an Oswald imposter. Corrupt capitalists took out JFK to keep the war going.

in the wrong direction. To win the '64 election, Farrington (Burt Lancaster) says, Kennedy will negotiate an arms treaty with Russia, pull out of Vietnam and support the civil rights movement; these decisions will destabilize the country by (for example) leading to angry whites starting a race war which the government can use to justify martial law. Farrington recommends assassinating Kennedy and pinning the blame on a lone gunman; Ferguson agrees to sign on if he becomes convinced it's truly necessary.

The schemers begin training a three-man hit team while selecting ex–Marine and CIA agent Lee Harvey Oswald to take the fall. An Oswald imposter (James Mac Coll) will stage scenes that make Oswald look like an unstable communist radical; false Secret Service agents in Dealy Plaza will help with the cover-up; and a thirty-minute telephone outage in DC will keep the authorities from coordinating a response until everyone involved gets away.

The conspirators are thinking big: One of Farrington's partners says the population boom in the Far East will cause major problems for the U.S., but using Vietnam as a power base will enable America, guided by the conspirators, to trim the population back to 5.5 billion. The same techniques will be used to cull the numbers of America's blacks, Hispanics and poor whites.

Ferguson signs on when he becomes convinced that Kennedy's moving in the direction Farrington predicted. After the assassination, Oswald, realizing he's been set up, tries to get away before he can be killed. He's captured, but to the relief of the conspirators, Jack Ruby shoots him. The movie ends by stating that 18 material witnesses to the assassination died in the four years following the shooting and that it's statistically impossible this could have happened by chance.

The Kennedy assassination has provoked more conspiracy theories than any event in recent history. Multiple "nonfiction" books about the conspiracy have been written, some simply poking holes in the official verdict, others blaming JFK's assassination on Castro, the CIA, Howard Hughes, the Soviets or the Mafia (there are also several books refuting the conspiracy theories). William Manchester in *Death of a President* suggests that conspiracy theories are attractive because they are more emotionally satisfying than accepting that one lone gunman could cause such a tragedy. *Executive Action* was the first fictional movie to present JFK's death as a conspiracy; unlike the later *The Parallax View* (1974) or *Winter Kills* (1979) it deals with the real assassination rather than a fictionalized version.

The claims about dead witnesses are a standard part of JFK conspiracy lore (cropping up in *The Parallax View* as well), though the movie offers no suggestion about why they were killed. Were they all lying or hushed up? Did they see something they never told anyone? If so, why worry they were going to talk later? If the conspirators knew these witnesses were about to spill the beans, wouldn't monitoring and murdering them require many more people, increasing the odds of a security leak? Nevertheless, some conspiracy theorists have claimed as many as 100 deaths linked to the cover-up, which sounds now like a forerunner of the "Clinton death list" of the 1990s.

The Parallax View (1974) opens with the assassination of Senator Carroll, witnessed

13. Miscellanea

by hack reporter Joe Frady (Warren Beatty). Although some of the witnesses claim that a second shooter was involved, the Warren Commission–style investigation concludes that it was a lone gunman, acting out of frustration and rage.

Three years later, Lee (Paula Prentiss) — another witness and Joe's former lover — tells Joe that except for her, every witness who disagreed with that verdict is now dead. Even though every death was ruled an accident, she believes she's next. Joe, unimpressed, kicks her out. The next day, Lee dies while driving extremely drunk; even though that would be in character for her, Joe becomes suspicious.

Joe travels to a small town to investigate the drowning of one witness during a fishing trip. The affable sheriff (Kelly Thordsen) tells Joe that the man was caught when the local hydroelectric dam discharged some water, and invites him up to the dam to talk to a witness. When they reach the dam, the sheriff attacks Joe, admitting the trip was a ruse to trap him. In the struggle, the sheriff's the one who dies, leaving Joe free to search his house. The only possible clue is a set of papers from the Parallax Corporation.

Joe's editor Bill (Hume Cronyn) scoffs at Joe's theories and suggests the corrupt sheriff tried to kill Joe in the belief that Joe was doing an exposé. Undeterred, Joe shows a personality test from the Parallax file to a psychiatrist, who tells him it's designed to spot angry, violent people. He helps Joe shape his answers to fit, and an FBI buddy of Joe's helps him create a cover identity.

Carroll's former aide Austin Tucker (William Daniels) contacts Joe with a photo of a waiter he believes was the second gunman. They go out on Tucker's yacht to talk, but a bomb destroys the boat, killing Tucker. Joe is also listed as dead; he tells Bill, who's no longer skeptical, that this is the perfect cover for him to assume his new ID and infiltrate Parallax. Parallax, however, hasn't been fooled and poisons Bill to induce a fatal heart attack, eliminating the one person who knows Joe's real agenda.

Joe's phony test results and fabricated antisocial biography soon convince a Parallax recruiter he's a natural for them. At the corporate offices, Joe spots the man Tucker identified, follows him to the airport and watches him place a suitcase on a baggage cart. Joe buys a ticket for the flight and discovers there's a Senator on board, so he aborts the flight with a bomb scare. After the passengers disembark, the real bomb goes off.

Parallax gives Joe his first assignment, under a more experienced partner. Joe contrives to send his partner out of town, leaving him free to tail another Parallax agent to a political rally. After a gunman murders the candidate, Joe pursues the killer, only to find himself locked in. The police arrive, spot Joe trying to flee, and shoot him. An investigative commission concludes that Joe was the assassin, that he was mentally disturbed, and that he acted entirely alone.

This is one of the few paranoid thrillers where the bad guys win, reflecting the cynicism of the Watergate era and the multiple assassinations of the previous decade. Parallax here isn't just a bogeyman, it's a complete cipher: There's no hint what their goals are, who's behind them and whether they're run by the Soviets or the CIA or are purely corporate.

JFK (1991) Like most Americans, New Orleans District Attorney Jim Garrison (Kevin

Costner) is shocked at JFK's murder. When Garrison learns that Lee Harvey Oswald spent time in New Orleans, he prepares to gather information for Oswald's trial, until Oswald's death takes care of that.

Garrison, however, finds several loose ends, such as Banister (Ed Asner), a Big Easy ex-cop with ties to the CIA's anti–Castro operations. Garrison discovers that Banister assaulted his sidekick Jack Martin (Jack Lemmon) after the shooting merely for reminding Banister of his association with Oswald. Later, Sen. Long (Walter Matthau) assures Garrison that even the world's best marksman couldn't have placed three accurate shots so fast, and Oswald was far from that good (in point of fact, one of the shots missed).

Three years later, despite protests from his neglected wife (Sissy Spacek), Garrison is still on the case, frustrated that witnesses with credible testimony indicating multiple shooters have been ignored, as has the evidence that Oswald worked for military intelligence. Garrison has also discovered that one, possibly more people impersonated Oswald earlier in '63 to create the image of a crazed assassin, an image he says has been constructed "like some dummy corporation in the Bahamas."

As Garrison and his staff put together the evidence of conspiracy and cover-up, X (Donald Sutherland), a retired military officer, provides the motive. He reveals that JFK's plan to withdraw from Vietnam once he'd won re-election had enraged conservatives, as well as the military contractors who were making millions off the war. The CIA also hated Kennedy for refusing to support the Bay of Pigs invasion, for firing revered agency head Allen Foster Dulles, and because it controlled some of the contractors who would lose big money if the war wrapped up.

X backs up his claims with facts (that is, factual within the world of the film): The Dallas motorcade violated every rule of presidential security, and the conspiracy contrived to send the Cabinet overseas and shut down the Washington phone lines, guaranteeing that nobody could interfere with the hit. Troops had been placed on alert in case riots broke out after the shooting.

As Garrison gets closer to the truth, the conspirators fights back. Witnesses turn up dead, Garrison's offices are bugged, and well-connected people intimidate Garrison's staff (one staffer is told flat out that the Cubans killed JFK and the only way to prevent war is to let the cover-up stand). Media reports smear Garrison as either a crackpot or a politician building his reputation. Garrison's aide Bill (Vincent D'Onofrio) quits, telling Garrison that it's impossible for a combined Mafia-CIA-military operation (Garrison asserts matter-of-factly that the Mafia were only involved "at a very low level") to have operated in perfect secrecy. Garrison never counters this other than with vague assertions such as, "All it takes is one Judas on the inside."

Eventually Garrison brings charges against alleged conspirator Clay Shaw (Tommy Lee Jones), a New Orleans homosexual with CIA ties. Despite the judge ruling key evidence inadmissible, Garrison forges ahead, pointing out that two other peace activists, Robert F. Kennedy and Martin Luther King, were also assassinated, and that multiple "political murders" of witnesses have been passed off as suicides, car accidents or cancer (Jack Ruby claimed he'd been injected with cancer to kill him); he also calls J. Edgar

Hoover and LBJ accessories to the crime. He describes the American people as a Hamlet still haunted by their father's ghost, while the killer has seized the throne in a *coup d'etat* which, among other things, led us to commit ground troops to Vietnam for years, wasting millions in military spending and costing thousands of lives on both sides.

Ultimately, the jury finds Shaw not guilty. Garrison vows to keep digging and takes a certain pride in being the only man to bring prosecution charges against anyone involved in the conspiracy.

Oliver Stone's movie, based on Garrison's own account and a book by Jim Marrs (who would later go on to suggest that JFK was killed to cover up the government's contact with extraterrestrials), is certainly absorbing (even at three and a half hours, it's watchable) and well-made, but it's as far removed from facts and accuracy as *G-Men vs. the Black Dragon*. Rather than single out any of the many alleged forces conspiring against Kennedy, Stone simply indicts them all. Criticism of Garrison is taken much the same way that criticism of HUAC was taken in *Big Jim McLain* and *I Was a Communist for the FBI*: The flak is proof of how much of a threat Garrison is to America's enemies.

The Silencer (1999) FBI Agent Jason Wells (Brennan Elliott) is assigned to pose as a professional killer to infiltrate the Group, a ruthless terrorist network. Working with Simmons (Michael Dudikoff), a world-weary professional assassin, Wells learns that their mission for the Group will be to assassinate ambitious left-wing Senator Cayton (Michael St. John Smith). To Wells' surprise the assassination goes ahead without him or Simmons pulling the trigger, but the evidence still points to Wells as the shooter.

With Simmons' help, Wells learns the truth: The Group doesn't exist. The man behind the killing was Wells' FBI superior Donovan (Terence Kelly), a member of D5, a black ops unit that J. Edgar Hoover created within the FBI years earlier. D5's original goal was to spy on anyone Hoover considered a subversive; later, Hoover used it to gather blackmail information on his challengers. Eventually it branched out into assassinations, murdering JFK and Martin Luther King. (The movie asserts that Hoover didn't directly order the killings, but covered them up afterwards.) Cayton, a critic of the FBI, was the latest victim. Wells brings Donovan to justice and Simmons turns away from murder and settles into a law-abiding life with the woman he loves.

These aren't the only films where a JFK conspiracy appears. The mockumentary *Tribulation 99* offers the theory that Oswald's uncanny marksmanship proves he was an extraterrestrial, but that film isn't serious. *Winter Kills* is adapted from a Richard Condon novel in which Kennedy's father had him killed when he realized that Kennedy was starting to act out of principle. And as the entry on *X-Files* notes, that film makes multiple references to a conspiracy behind the shooting.

Military

Seven Days in May (1964) With President Jordan Lyman (Fredric March) preparing to sign a nuclear disarmament treaty with the Soviet Union, Gen. Scott (Burt Lancaster) has come out publicly against the idea that "a piece of paper will take the place of missile sites and Polaris submarines." His devoted subordinate Col. Jiggs Casey (Kirk Douglas) is amused to discover that at the same time, Scott is setting up a heavy betting pool involving many of the military's top brass.

Before long, other incidents make the pool seem much less amusing. Col. Henderson (Andrew Duggan) tells Jiggs that recent training exercises seem less concerned with defending the country from Soviet attack than seizing it back; a Congressman makes an ominous reference to a military drill scheduled to take place in seven days; Scott is meeting secretly with a prominent TV newsman. Coupling these incidents with other information, Casey becomes convinced that Scott plans to block the treaty by a military takeover, using the drill to explain the troop movements.

Lyman and his advisors are skeptical and demand proof; Casey and drunken Sen. Clark (Edmond O'Brien) set out to find it. Clark discovers a secret, black-budget base Scott has set up in the Southwest, but the troops hold him incommunicado. When he finally returns to Washington, he doesn't have any proof. Scott later assures Lyman that the president approved construction, and he has the documentation to prove it.

Casey is unable to find any evidence, but does secure embarrassing love letters from his and Scott's former lover, Eleanor (Ava Gardner). One investigator gets a signed statement from Admiral Barnswell (John Houseman) that Scott approached him about the treasonous plan, but the investigator's plane (with the signed statement aboard) crashes.

Lyman can't bring himself to smear Scott with the letters, even though he has no other options. When he meets with Scott, the general makes it clear he believes he's expressing the will of the people and acting for America's greater good, and that Lyman can't sway him from his course. Fortunately, a crash investigator finds Farnsworth's statement and Lyman uses it to demand the resignations of Scott's allies. Scott remains defiant, but realizes his power is gone.

The trailer for the movie says, "Even though people say it can't happen here, this movie is the story of how it could happen here." Film buffs have suggested that Scott is based on Generals Curtis LeMay or Edwin Walker, though he shows some of MacArthur's arrogance as well.

The Enemy Within (1995) In this remake of *Seven Days in May*, President Forster (Sam Waterston) has proposed big military spending cuts in order to provide more social services and infrastructure improvements. (This reflects the political climate between the end of the Cold War and 9/11, when people spoke of a "peace dividend."). Col. Casey (Forest Whitaker) realizes that Slam Dunk, a sports betting pool run by Gen. Lloyd (Jason Robards), chairman of the Joint Chiefs, is actually the code name for a top-secret wargame involving close to 100,000 troops fighting to take over a small nation. The scope and secrecy of Slam Dunk make Casey suspicious.

He's right to be: Lloyd, in conjunction with a cabal inside Forster's cabinet, is plotting to depose the president and impose martial law. Forster and his chief of staff Corcoran (Dana Delany), an old friend of Casey's, remain unconvinced until the attorney general dies of a sudden heart attack (we know, but they don't, that he was poisoned when he decided to oppose the takeover). The trio discovers that the plan is for the cabinet to invoke the 25th Amendment, declaring the president incompetent to serve, after which the vice-president will step in and the troops will move into the streets to keep everything orderly.

Despite Casey's best efforts, the conspirators destroy all the evidence and execute the witnesses who might be willing to testify. Lloyd tells Forster to step down, but Casey plays a trump card: He's created a computer trail proving he's part of the conspiracy, and if the plan goes ahead, he'll speak to the media and reveal everything, including the names of the real conspirators. Realizing their guns have been spiked, the conspirators agree to resign.

Secret Societies

The Brotherhood of the Bell (1970) Professor Andrew Paterson (Glenn Ford) initiates college student Philip Dunning (Robert Pine) into the Brotherhood of the Bell, a secret society at the College of St. George whose members number among America's most powerful men. Paterson's mentor, Harmon (Dean Jagger), tells Philip that if he ever needs anything in his career, his brothers will do what they can to help — and in return, some day, he will have to repay them with a favor. ("Continuity depends on one thing — obedience, absolute obedience.") After the ceremony, Paterson tells Philip that he's now part of the country's ruling class.

Shortly afterward, the Brotherhood calls on Paterson for his favor: convince his friend Horvathy (Eduard Franz) to drop his application for a prestigious teaching position that one of the members covets. The selling point is that the Brotherhood has a list of the people who helped Horvathy defect from Eastern Europe, and will send it behind the Iron Curtain — a death sentence for everyone on it — if Horvathy doesn't cooperate.

To Paterson's horror, Horvathy kills himself (this comes off as such an overreaction that I expected the Brotherhood to be behind it, but it wasn't). Paterson's father-in-law Harry (Maurice Evans) takes him to visit federal agent Thaddeus Burns (Logan Field) in a sparsely furnished office in one of L.A.'s federal buildings (Burns explains it's sparse because it's only used for covert meetings). Burns reveals that the government is already aware of the Brotherhood, which has been around for 200 years.

When Paterson returns to work, he finds his secretary gone and his office locked up for a week. Dean Fielder (William Smithers) tells him that the wing is being repainted and suggests that Paterson take a week off. Paterson checks back with the feds only to be told there's no Burns working there, and that if they wanted a covert meeting, they wouldn't use an office in a federal building. Harry claims the meeting never happened and suggests that Paterson is cracking up over Horvathy's death. Then Fielder tells Paterson that the college foundation wants major budget cuts, and his entire department has been shut down.

Paterson tells Harmon that the punishment isn't fair, since he's never asked the Brotherhood for a single favor. Harmon replies, "You have never competed for one thing in the past 22 years": Paterson's own successful career and his father's construction company (a multimillion-dollar corporation) were both the gifts of the society. Despite Harmon's warning, Paterson goes public and names names, but the local district attorney dismisses the existence of a "white, Anglo-Saxon Mafia" and Harmon tells the media that such a society couldn't possibly be kept secret.

Andrew's life continues to go downhill: Forged documents make his father look like a tax fraud, and the stress triggers a heart attack. Andrew's wife shoots a prowler who turns out to be a neighbor, and finally walks out on Andrew. Paterson goes on Bart Harris's (William Conrad) right-wing TV talk show, where he finds unexpected and unwanted supporters: A black man says the Brotherhood of the Bell is just a euphemism for the white power structure that controls everything; a woman says Paterson is a red herring distracting people from the cabal of Jews that really runs the country; Harris suggests the Bell is a Catholic conspiracy.

Things turn around when Fielder tells Andrew he believes him, because while the rest of the staff have new jobs, "it was as though your name was on an invisible national blacklist." To convince anyone else, he says, Andrew will have to find a witness with nothing at stake. Paterson then goes to see Philip, telling him that the price for what the Bell offers is too high to pay, and that if they act together, this is their chance to get out. Philip eventually agrees and they head to the authorities to begin tearing down the Brotherhood.

Suspicions of a covert society manipulating all human affairs is one of the oldest forms of political paranoia; as noted in the introduction, paranoia about Freemasons and the Illuminati (in reality, a minor European branch of the Freemasons) goes back more than 200 years. Other supposed threats include the Trilateral Commission, the Council on Foreign Relations and the Knights Templar (who are frequently linked with the Freemasons).

This is the only time that branch of paranoia has made it into the movies; the Brotherhood of the Bell (supposedly based on Yale's Skull and Bones) has the political clout to ruin lives, provide jobs and cover up anything.

Nowhere Man (1995–96) After years of globetrotting, photojournalist Tom Veil (Bruce Greenwood) is riding high, with a beautiful wife, Alyson (Megan Gallagher), and a major gallery show. After a dinner, he steps outside for a smoke ... and when he returns, Alyson insists she's never seen him before, as does everyone else in the restaurant. Not only that, Veil's IDs are gone, his credit and ATM cards no longer work, and his best friend turns up dead. Tom's studio belongs to someone else and his wife is married to someone he's never met.

Unsurprisingly, Tom winds up in a mental hospital where the director, Dr. Bellamy, turns out to be part of the Organization, the same conspiracy that erased him (and apparently had Alyson as one of its agents). Their goal: acquiring the negative of "Hidden Agenda," a photograph Tom took in the jungle showing U.S. forces hanging women and kids.

13. Miscellanea

How did they erase Tom? Was Alyson really just an agent for the Organization? What was the significance of Hidden Agenda? Escaping from the hospital, Tom sets out to hunt down the answers, constantly hounded by the Organization. Its branches stretched everywhere: prosecutors, doctors, teachers, reporters, anyone could be agents. As the UPN series progressed, it became obvious they also had extensive mind-control capabilities. In "Calloway," Tom meets a fellow inmate at Bellamy's asylum who now believes himself to be an Organization agent.

Slowly the evidence accumulated that Tom's own memories weren't reliable: The site of Hidden Agenda turned out to be not the jungle but a wood outside Washington; the executed men were not Latin Americans but American Senators (who have since been replaced by doubles); and in the closing episode, Tom discovered that he wasn't Tom Veil but a federal agent, Gemini, charged with investigating the Hidden Agenda executions. Or so it appeared.

Nowhere Man's **Tom Veil (Bruce Greenwood) gets his identity erased in the UPN series, then discovers it was never his identity to start with.**

Producer Lawrence Hertzog says on the DVD set that his goal was to do a version of the classic BBC show *The Prisoner* (in which shadowy captors play games with a defiant ex-spy played by Patrick McGoohan) but to give it more of a human element. The actual explanation of the mystery didn't interest him, Hidden Agenda being simply a McGuffin to set up a kind of *Twilight Zone* anthology with Veil as the central character (which explains why several episodes could have fitted into *The Fugitive* or *The Incredible Hulk* without much effort, one drifter being much like another). However, he soon realized that he'd raised questions and people would be annoyed if he didn't answer at least some of them; Fox pushed him to answer more, eventually insisting on a season-ending explanation. Had the show been renewed, Tom would have assumed Gemini's identity to continue work against the Organization, even though he still wasn't sure Gemini was him.

Traveler (2007) This short-lived summer replacement series has three buddies — Jay, Tyler and Will Traveler — visit New York the summer after graduation; Traveler convinces his friends to race through a museum on inline skates, right past the security. A moment later, the museum is torn apart by a bomb — and the security cameras have Jay and Tyler racing out as if they were responsible. To make matters worse, both their fathers have shadows in their past that could have pushed the boys to make the terrorist strike — and when they look for Will, he's gone, his things are gone from their rooms, and none of the photographs they have from grad school provide any evidence he existed at all.

The remaining seven episodes had the boys struggling to stay away from the cops, while trying to unravel the mystery behind the frame-up. Will turns up alive and together they discover that the conspiracy involves Tyler's father and a mysterious sub-unit operating within Homeland Security, the Fourth Branch. But the evidence, and a captured Fourth Branch agent, are destroyed before they can prove their innocence.

Right-Wing

Betrayed (1988) The murder of a Jewish talk radio host (loosely based on the killing of New York radio host Alan Berg) prompts the FBI to send Kathy Weaver (Debra Winger) into the heartland to learn if white supremacist farmer Gary Simmons (Tom Berenger) is behind it. Weaver discovers that Simmons is a veteran, a loving father, a hard-working farmer — and a white supremacist who believes violent action is the only way to stop the "Zionist Occupied Government" and its "nigger police" from crushing decent heterosexual Christian white people. Most members of his community feel the same way, as Kathy discovers when they kidnap a black man and hunt him to death through the woods. (Gary argues that since they gave him a gun before letting him run, it's self-defense when they kill him.)

Despite Gary's views, Weaver falls in love with him, but her superior at the bureau, Michael (John Heard), browbeats her into continuing to spy on him, as she's now the best chance to learn what he and his allies are up to. Weaver agrees, and pretends to join Gary's movement, attending Klan rallies and participating in a bank robbery. She shoots and almost injures a guard during the robbery, but Michael assures her there's no moral dilemma — in a war, there's always collateral damage.

Eventually, Weaver learns of Gary's plan: an all-out attack by the terrorist network involving a political assassination, the destruction of a major power plant, and terrorist bombings in Chicago, Harlem and San Francisco's gay district. Gary, however, has learned her real agenda, and takes her with him to the assassination — that of Jack Carpenter (David Clennon), a politician siding with the far right for political gain — with the intent of blaming the killing on a federal agent. Weaver shoots her husband first, but a second gunman kills Carpenter, giving the far right a martyr and a replacement candidate milking Carpenter's death for political advantage. Michael assures Weaver that they've smashed the network but she replies that someone in the bureau tipped Gary off about her; no matter how many they catch, there are countless more out there. Grieving for Gary, she walks away from her job, even knowing the network may want revenge.

Director Costa-Gavras (whose other political thrillers include *Z* and *Missing*) says

13. Miscellanea

on the DVD that he finds obvious organizations such as the KKK and the American Nazi Party "less frightening than the far greater number of simple people who adhere to those ideas. They're everywhere, and we don't know who they are." The film creepily presents seemingly nice, salt-of-the-Earth Americans as being at the same time right wing terrorists who yearn to wipe out the "mud people." Like *Pack of Lies*, it suggests that it is possible to form an attachment to the bad guys while despising their politics.

While it's certainly not paranoid to say that far-right terrorists exist, this presents a network far more sophisticated and coordinated than exists in reality, where "lone wolves" such as Timothy McVeigh or Jim Adkisson (who shot up a Unitarian Church in 2008 out of a desire to "kill all liberals") seem to do the most damage. It was also quite prescient in showing the Internet's potential as a recruiting tool for extremists.

Arlington Road (1999) When college professor Michael Faraday (Jeff Bridges) finds young Brady Lang (Mason

Who *Betrayed* who when FBI agent Debra Winger married loving white supremacist Tom Berenger in hopes of thwarting his terrorist agenda?

Gamble) injured in the street from a fireworks accident, he rushes him to the hospital. When he meets the boy's parents, engineer Oliver Lang and his wife Cheryl (Tim Robbins, Joan Cusack), Michael feels ashamed to learn they've been living on his block for two months and he hasn't spoken to them before.

Michael and his girlfriend Brooke (Hope Davis) befriend the Langs; we also learn that Michael's field is terrorism studies, something of particular interest since his wife Leah (Laura Poe) died in a shootout during a botched attack on what had inaccurately been identified as a militant compound. Michael is still friends with his wife's partner Whit (Robert Gossett), but disagrees openly with the FBI view that most terrorists are lone wolves — for example, one devastating attack on a federal building (a thinly fictionalized account of the 1995 Murrah Building bombing) was blamed on a man who had no experience with munitions, no history of radical politics and no reason to attack the government.

Michael soon begins to notice inconsistencies about the Langs — the plans in Oliver's study don't look like the building he's supposedly designing — but Whit thinks he's paranoid and Brooke thinks he's obsessed with carrying on Leah's work. Michael keeps digging and discovers that Oliver is William Fenimore, a farmboy who served time as a teenager for pipebombing a government office. Oliver tells him he bombed the office after the government diverted the farm's water supply, ruining them and driving his father to suicide — and that he's no longer the same angry boy: "Did you ever do anything wrong when you were sixteen? Crash the car? Screw the wrong girl? Are you going to tell your kid everything you did when you were sixteen?"

Brooke, however, discovers Oliver picking up suspicious parcels in a nearby parking garage; Cheryl catches her spying, and Brooke dies in a fatal car "accident." The Langs are so supportive after her death that Michael realizes his suspicions were ridiculous — until he discovers someone is tapping his phone, and that all the messages on his answering machine the afternoon of Brooke's death were erased. With his suspicions renewed, Michael discovers a link between Oliver and the federal bombing incident — but when he gets home, the Langs have kidnapped his son Grant (Spencer Treat Clark) to prevent him from calling the authorities. Oliver adds that Michael would be dead already if he hadn't saved Brady's life.

Michael tries unsuccessfully to rescue his son, and realizes that the FBI building where Whit works is Oliver's target. He pursues a bomb-laded van into the building's parking lot, but when the feds inspect the van, it's empty. Whit points out that the only unauthorized person on the premises is Michael, and Michael realizes, too late, that the real bomb is in his trunk.

We cut to the media rattling off the body count (184) and the evidence that Michael was a lone wolf terrorist flashing out at the FBI as payback for his wife's death; in interviews, every ambiguous comment Michael ever made to his students is recalled to prove it. The film ends with the Langs awaiting their next assignment.

The extremists here are pure bogeyman: Other than one reference to "godless society," the Langs' beliefs go unmentioned (the director says he didn't want to make the film a

13. Miscellanea

Jeff Bridges checks out his neighbors in *Arlington Road* (1999). As Oliver (Tim Robbins) says, "There are millions like us, ready to spread the word." Peter Krause in *Civic Duty*'s poster strikes a similar pose.

soapbox) so they could just as easily be German subversives, Red conspirators or Islamic militants.

Interviews on the *Arlington Road* DVD say the message is also about suburban isolation and how little we know about who's living next door to us. ("A greater danger may live right across the street.... We really know less and less of what our neighbor is like.") This is a fine sentiment of political paranoia in this context.

Criminal Conspiracies

The Invisible Monster (1950) In this Republic serial, the Phantom Ruler (Stanley Price) smuggles four men from dictatorships into the United States, promising them citizenship; once they're here, he tells them they will either help him in his plans for world conquest or he'll ship them back home to face firing squads. His plan is to steal enough money to mass-produce his invisibility formula and create an invisible army. Placing his reluctant henchmen in industries where they have skills, he forces them to either steal or provide him with information to do the job invisibly. Repeatedly, however, he runs into trouble from insurance investigators Lane Carson (Richard Webb) and Carol Richards

(Aline Towne). Eventually, despite the Ruler's best efforts, Land and Carol bring him to justice and smash his plans.

The infiltration element is minor — this is much more of a straight crime drama — but it's sufficient to make a note of it.

Universal Soldier III: Unfinished Business (1998) *Universal Soldier* (1992) was an action film in which the government resurrected the American war dead as unstoppable cyborgs. We got both a TV-movie sequel and a theatrical sequel that went in different directions: The television sequel *Universal Soldier II* (1998) has the sinister Mentor plotting to sell off the "UniSol" forces to the highest bidder.

In this follow-up, reporter Veronica Roberts (Chandra West) learns that in addition to cyborgs, Mentor (Burt Reynolds) has found a way to create "sleepers," resurrectees who appear to be alive and normal. In order to carry out a multimillion-dollar gold robbery, Mentor turns the security chief into a Sleeper. Veronica and her friends manage to expose Mentor's schemes on TV, so he kills himself—to be resurrected later by the UniSol program. And he already has an army of Sleepers waiting for his commands....

This looked suspiciously like a pilot, taking the *Universal Soldier* name in a direction that could involve week-to-week exploits battling the various Sleepers.

Alias (2004–09) When this series began, Sydney Bristow (Jennifer Garner) thought she was serving her country by working for SD-6, an elite, super-secret branch of the CIA. When she told her fiancé what she did for a living and SD-6 had him killed, she realized she was wrong.

SD-6 is actually part of the Alliance, an international consortium of various criminal and subversive factions, and it includes multiple offices throughout the United States. Working with her estranged father (Victor Garber) a CIA agent, and Vaughn (Michael Vartan), her CIA handler, Sydney continues operating as an SD-6 agent while secretly doing her best to make sure that SD-6 and its leader Arvin Sloane (Ron Rifkin) gain nothing useful from her missions.

Sydney and her allies eventually destroy SD-6 in the second season of the show, but the show remained rife with conspiracies, spies and double-agents. Sydney's best friend was replaced by an agent for the Russian K-Directorate; Vaughn married a woman (while Sydney was believed dead) who was an agent for the sinister Covenant; Vaughn turned out to be involved with the secret group Prophet Five; and in the fifth season, Sydney learned that Prophet Five was running the Shed, a supposed CIA black ops team similar to SD-6 when she joined. Despite all the treachery and deceit, Vaughn and Sydney survived, eventually married and retired from the spy game.

Appendix 1

Film Credits

Wherever possible, credits were taken directly from the screen.
Other sources can be found in the bibliography.

ACROSS THE PACIFIC   (1942, Warner Bros., 97 minutes)
Cast: Capt. Rick Leland (Humphrey Bogart), Alberta Marlow (Mary Astor), Dr. Lorenz (Sydney Greenstreet), A.V. Smith (Charles Halton), Joe Totsuikio (Victor Sen Yung), Sugi (Roland Got), Sam Wing On (Lee Tung Foo), Captain Morrison (Frank Wilcox), Col. Hart (Paul Stanton), Canadian Major (Lester Matthews), Court-Martial President (John Hamilton), Man (Tom Stevenson), Capt. Harkness (Roland Drew), Dan Morton (Monte Blue), Capt. Higito (Chester Gan), First Officer Miyuma (Richard Loo), Clerk (Keye Luke), T. Oki (Kam Tong), Mitsuko (Spencer Chan), Filipino Assassin (Rudy Robles)
Credits: Director: John Huston; Screenplay: Richard Macauley, from *Aloha Means Goodbye* by Robert Carson; Producers: Jerry Wald, Jack Saper; Photography: Arthur Edeson; Art Directors: Robert Haas, Hugh Reticker; Editor: Frank Magee; Music: Leo Forbstein.

THE ALIENS ARE COMING   (3/2/80, NBC, 100 minutes)
Cast: Dr. Scott Dryden (Tom Mason), Leonard Nero (Eric Braeden), Gwen O'Brien (Melinda Fee), Joyce Cummings (Fawne Harriman), Timmy Garner (Matthew Laborteaux), Harve Nelson (Ron Masak), Sue Garner (Caroline McWilliams), Eldon Gates (John Milford), Russ Garner (Max Gail), Chuck Polchek (Ed Harris), Lt. Col. John Sebastian (Hank Brandt), Bert Fowler (Laurence Haddon), Patrolman Ashley (Gerald McRaney), Frank Foley (Curtis Credel), Nurse (Peter Shuck), Patrolman Strong (Richard Lockmiller), Dr. Conley (Sean Griffin), Technician (Chris O'Brien), Intern (Tom Lowell), Teacher (Nancy Priddy), Waitress (Lorna Thayer), Floyd (John Gilgreen), Student (Laurie Beach), Waiter (Dirk Olthof), Guard (Tom Pittman)
Credits: Director: Harvey Hart; Screenplay: Robert W. Lenski; Producer: Philip Saltzman; Photography: Jacques R. Marquette; Art Directors: George B. Chan, Norman R. Newberry; Editor: James Gross: Music: William Goldstein.

ALL THROUGH THE NIGHT   (1942, Warner Bros., 107 minutes)
Cast: "Gloves" Donahue (Humphrey Bogart), Leda Hamilton (Kaaren Verne), Pepi (Peter Lorre), Epping (Conrad Veidt), Sunshine (William Demarest), Mrs. Donahue (Jane Darwell), Barney (Frank McHugh), Madame (Judith Anderson), Starchy (Jackie Gleason), Waiter (Phil Silvers), Spats Hunter (Wallace Ford), Marty Callahan (Barton MacLane), Joe Denning (Edward Brophy), Steindorff (Martin Kosleck), Annabelle (Jean Ames), Miller (Ludwig Stossel), Mrs. Miller (Irene Seidner), Forbes (James Burke), Smitty (Ben Welden), Anton (Hans Schumm), Sage (Charles Cane), Spence (Frank Sully), Deacon (Sam McDaniel)
Credits: Director: Vincent Sherman; Screenplay: Leonard Spigelgass, Edwin Gilbert, from a story by Leonard Q. Ross and Leonard Spigelgass; Executive Producer: Hal Wallis; Photography: Sid Hickox; Art Director: Max Parker: Editor: Rudi Fehr; Music: Adolph Deutsch.

AMAZONS   (1984, ABC, 90 minutes)
Cast: Dr. Sharon Fields (Madeleine Stowe), Rosalyn Joseph (Tamara Dobson), Lt. Tony Monaco (Jack Scalia), Kathryn Lundquist (Stella Stevens), Dr. Diane Cosgrove (Jennifer Warren), Congressman Stan Barstow (William Schallert), Jerry Menzies (Peter Scolari), Dr. Thompson (Nicholas Pryor), Vivian Todd (Leslie Bevis), Stowe (Jordan Chaney), James (Greg Monaghan), Kevin (Stephen Shellen), Governor Price (Hansford Rowe), Baker (Jessie Lawrence Ferguson), Nurse Franklin (Suzanne Kent), Roger (Robert Harrison), Marge Webster (Morgan Lofting), Martin (Paul Cross), Rossi (Carl LaRocco), Attendant (Wesley Thompson), Woman Newscaster (Paula Russell), Reporter

(John Walsh), Anchorman (Edward Beimfohr), Victim (Nick DeMauro), Moderator (Donald Craig), Desk Sergeant (Ron Prince), Mailman (Fred Dennis), Tracy (Heather Hepler), Amy (Chrystal DeWoody), Christine (Jessica Weisman), Kelly (Amy Benesh), Deidre (Misty Hall), Marsha (Danielle Michonne)

Credits: Director: Paul Michael Glaser; Screenplay: David Solomon; Story: David Solomon, Guerdon Trueblood; Producer: Stuart Cohen; Photography: Dean Cundey; Production Design: Dean Mitzner; Editor: Patrick Kennedy; Music: Basil Poledouris.

ANNIHILATOR (4/7/86, NBC, 100 minutes)

Cast: Richard Armour (Mark Lindsay Chapman), Layla (Susan Blakely), Cindy (Lisa Blount), Alien Leader (Brion James), Sid (Earl Boen), Prof. Alan Jeffries (Geoffrey Lewis), Angela Taylor (Catherine Mary Stewart), Elyse (Nicole Eggert), Eddie (Barry Pearl), Pops (Paul Brinegar), Susan Weiss (Channing Chase), Celia Evans (Barbara Townsend), Henry Evans (Glen Vernon), FBI Agents (Richard Partlow, Biff Yeager), Patti (Toni Attell), Policemen (James Parks, Greg Collins), Man in Coat (Roger LaRue), Cammie (Stanley Bennett Clay), Nervous Woman (Lola Fisher), Agents (Jerry Boyd, Al Pugliesse), Coroner (Martin Clark), Trucker (John Durbin), Airline Agents (Donald Hayes, Helen Anderson), Supervisor (William Jackson), Bum (Gary Burden), Girl (Julie Harris)

Credits: Director: Michael Chapman; Screenplay: Roderick Taylor, Bruce A. Taylor; Producers: Thomas C. Chapman, Alan C. Pederson; Photography: Paul Goldsmith: Art Director: Kirk Axtell; Editor: Frank Mazzola; Music: Sylvester Levay.

THE ARGYLE SECRETS (1948, Eronel Productions, 64 minutes)

Cast: Harry Mitchell (William Gargan), Marla (Marjorie Lord), Lt. Samson (Ralph Byrd), Panama (Jack Reitzen), Winter (John Banner), Miss Court (Barbara Billingsley), Jor McBrod (Alex Fraser), Scanlon (Peter Brocco), Pierce (George Anderson), Gil (Mickey Simpson), Pinky (Alvin Hammer), Nurse (Carole Donne), Mrs. Rubin (Mary Tarcai), Melvyn (Robert Kellard), Gerald (Kenneth Greenwald), Dr. Van Selbin (Herbert Rawlinson)

Credits: Director-Screenwriter: Cyril Endfield; Assistant Director: Clarence Eurist; Producer: Alan H. Posner; Photography: Mack Stengler; Art Director: Rudi Feld; Editor: Gregg Tallas; Music: David Chudnow.

ARLINGTON ROAD (1999, Screen Gems/Lakeshore Entertainment, 117 minutes)

Cast: Michael Faraday (Jeff Bridges), Oliver Lang (Tim Robbins), Cheryl Lang (Joan Cusack), Brooke Wolfe (Hope Davis), Whit Carver (Robert Gossett), Brady Lang (Mason Gamble), Grant Faraday (Spencer Treat Clark), Dr. Archer Scobee (Stanley Anderson), Nurse (Vivianne Vives), Orderly (Lee Stringer), Troopmaster (Darryl Cox), Delivery Man (Loyd Catlett), Phone Technician (Sid Hillman), Hannah Lang (Auden Thornton), Daphne Lang (Mary Ashleigh Green), Ponytail Girl (Jennie Tooley), Student Kemp (Grant Garrison), Student O'Neill (Naya Castinado), Leah Faraday (Laura Poe), Buckley (Chris Dahlberg), Merks (Gabriel Folse), Hutch Parsons (Hunter Burkes), Ma Parsons (Diane Peterson), Parsons at 16 (Hans Stroble), Parsons at 18 (Josh Ridgway), Parsons Girl (Michelle Du Bois), Reporters (Steve Ottesen, Harris Mackenzie), Detective (John Hussey), Camp Officials (Charles Sanders, Todd Terry), Party Girl (Gina Santori), FBI Guards (Denver Williams, Willie Dirden), FBI Van Agents (Paul Pender, Charlie Webb, Billy D. Washington), Reporters (Cindy Hom, Dave Allen Clark), Charles Bell (Ken Manelis), Bomb Site Reporter (Deborah Swanson), Student (Homer Jon Young), Pilots (Robin Simpson, Doug Frances)

Credits: Director: Mark Pellington; Screenplay: Ehren Kruger; Producers: Tom Gorai, Marc Samuelson, Peter Samuelson; Co-Producers: Jean Higgins, Richard S. Wright; Photography: Bobby Bukowski; Production Design: Therese DePrez; Editor: Conrad Buff; Music: Angelo Badalamenti.

THE ASTRONAUT'S WIFE (1999, Mad Chance Productions, 110 minutes)

Cast: Spencer Armacost (Johnny Depp), Jillian Armacost (Charlize Theron), Sherman Reese (Joe Morton), Natalie Struck (Donna Murphy), Alex Struck (Nick Cassavetes), Doctor (Samantha Eggar), NASA Director (Gary Grubbs), Shelly McLaren (Blair Brown), Jackson McLaren (Tom Noonan), Allen Dodge (Tom O'Brien), Shelly Carter (Lucy Lin), Pat Elliot (Michael Crider), Calvin (Jacob Stein), Wide-eyed Kid (Timothy Wicker), Excited Fourth-Grader (Brian Johnson), Paula (Sarah Dampp), Spencer's Doctor (Charles Lanyer), Doctor (Carlos Cervantes), Reporter (Conrad Bachman), Dr. Petrotta (Rondi Reed), Yuppie Shark (Seth Barrish), Dried-Up Socialite (Ellen Lancaster), Waiter (Julian Barnes), Women (Priscilla Shanks, Jennifer Burry, Susan Cella, Linda Powell), Screaming Girl (Lyndsey Danielle Bonomolo), Guard (Elston Ridge), Maitre D' (Robert Sella), Video Reporter (Samantha Carpel), Taxi Driver (Lahai Fahnbulleh), Doorman (Stephen

Berger), Waiter (Michael Luceri), Storage Facility Client (Ben Van Bergen), Pilot (Edward Kerr), Twins (Cole Mitchell Sprouse, Dylan Thomas Sprouse)

Credits: Director-Screenwriter: Rand Ravich; Producer: Andrew Lazar; Photography: Allen Daviau; Production Design: Jan Roelfs; Editors: Steve Mirkovich, Tim Alverson; Music: George S. Clinton.

THE BATTLE CRY OF PEACE (1915, Vitagraph, 9 reels)

Cast: John Harrison (Charles Richman), Emanon (L. Rogers Lytton), Charley Harrison (James Morrison), Mrs. Harrison (Mary Maurice), Mrs. Vandergriff (Louise Beaudet), John Vandergriff (Harold Hubert), Poet Scout (Jack Crawford), The Master (Charles Kent), Magdalen (Julia Swayne Gordon), Vandergriff's Son (Evart Overton), Alice Harrison (Belle Bruce), Virginia Vandergriff (Norma Talmadge), Dorothy Vandergriff (Lucille Hamill), Butler (George Stevens), Columbia (Thais Lawton), The War Monster (Lionel Braham), George Washington (Joseph Kilgour), Ulysses S. Grant (Paul Scardon), Abraham Lincoln (William J. Ferguson), Hudson Maxim, Tefft Johnson, Harry S. Northrup, James Lacksye

Credits: Director: Wilfred North; Producer-Screenwriter: J. Stuart Blackton, based on *Defenseless* by Hudson Maxim; Cinematographers: Leonard Smith, Arthur T. Quinn, Frank Tyrell.

BETRAYAL FROM THE EAST (1944, RKO, 82 minutes)

Cast: Eddie Carter (Lee Tracy), Peggy Harrison (Nancy Kelly), Tanni (Richard Loo), Yamato (Abner Biberman), Jimmy Scott (Regis Toomey), Kato (Philip Ahn), Capt. Bates (Addison Richards), Purdy (Bruce Edwards), Araki (Hugh Hoo), Omaya (Victor Sen Yung), Kurth Gunther (Roland Varno), Jack Marsden (Louis Jean Heydt), Girl (Rosemary La Planche), American Boys (Steve Winston, Chris Drake), Narrator (Drew Pearson), Purser (Harold Fong), Newsie (Fred Carpenter), Miss Morita (Jean Wong), Japanese Agent (Spencer Chan), Gloria (Mary Halsey), Peg (Patti Brill), Jeannie (Margie Stewart), Girl (Virginia Belmont), Drunk (Sammy Blum), Joe (Victor Wong), Ito (Alfred Song), Waitress (Early Cantrell), Japanese Consul (Key Chang), Capt. Yasuda (Peter Chong), Policeman (Alan Ward), Brunzman (Henry Victor), Holtzig (Erick Hanson), Taxi Driver (Weaver Levy), Dr. Kabeneshki (Paul Fung), Fortune Teller (Grace Lem), Helga (Fay Wall), Keller (Hermine Sterler), Wilhelm (Howard Johnson), Bellhop (George Lee), Immigration Officer (Lee Phelps), Waiter (Manuel Lopez), Desk Clerks (Guy Zanett, Manuel Paris), With Edmund Glover, Isabelle La Mal, Chester Conklin, Sherry Hall, Russell Hopton, Bryant Washburn

Credits: Director: William Berke; Screenplay: Kenneth Gamet, Aubrey Wisberg, adapted by Wisberg from the book by Alan Hynd; Producer: Herman Schlom; Photography: Russell Metty; Art Directors: Albert S. D'Agostino, Ralph Berger; Editor: Duncan Mansfield; Music: Roy Webb.

BETRAYED (1988, United Artists, 127 minutes)

Cast: Cathy Weaver (Debra Winger), Gary Simmons (Tom Berenger), Michael Carnes (John Heard), Gladys Simmons (Betsy Blair), Shorty (John Mahoney), Wes (Ted Levine), Flynn (Jeffrey DeMunn), Al Sanders (Albert Hall), Jack Carpenter (David Clennon), Dean (Robert Swan), Sam Kraus (Richard Libertini), Rachel Simmons (Maria Valdez), Joey Simmons (Brian Bosak), Duffin (Alan Wilder), Rev. Johnson (Clifford A. Pellow), Lyle (Ralph Foody), Betty Jo (Shawn Schepps), Toby (Dolores Drake), Buster (Stephen E. Miller), Ellie (Suzie Payne), Gary's Buddy (Chris Kubasik), Bartender (Timothy Jerome), Del (Jack Ackroyd), Hank (Howard Siegel), Young Guy (Ruston Harker), Engineer (Howard Storey), Man at Gate (Bill Dow), Nazi (Leslie Stolzenberger), Minister (Terry David Mulligan), Carpenter's Aide (Fred Keating), Man with Glasses (Dan Conway), Man in Thirties (Will Zahrn), Hunted Man (Kevin C. White), Man in Bar (Jefferson Wagner), Reporter (Joel Daly), Guard (Bob Herron), Band Members (Eric Geisreiter, Ed Johnson, Wayne Lawson, Reid Seibert, Vic Vogt), Bureau Guard (Frank Harmon), Bureau Chief (Wally Marsh), Grandfather (Leroy R. Horn), Radio Callers (W. Wayne Arrants, Mimi Besinger, Bill Corsair, Judith C. Jacobs, Joyce Leigh Bowden, Rodger Parsons, Mary Sharmat)

Credits: Director: Costa-Gavras; Screenwriter: Joe Eszterhas; Producer: Irwin Winkler: Photography: Patrick Blossier; Production Design: Patrizia Von Brandenstein; Editor: Joele Van Effenterre; Music: Bill Conti.

BIG JIM MCLAIN (1952, Warner Bros., 90 minutes)

Cast: Jim McLain (John Wayne), Mal Baxter (Jim Arness), Nancy Vellon (Nancy Olson), Madge (Veda Ann Borg), Sturak (Alan Napier), Robert Henreid (Hans Conried), Gelster (Gayne Whitman), Poke (Hal Baylor), Olaf (Gordon Jones), Edwin White (Robert Keys), Lt. Comdr. Clint Grey (John Hubbard), Mrs. Nomaka (Madame Soo Yong), Chief Liu (Himself), Phil Brigs (Red McQueen), Lexiter (Paul Hurst), Mrs. Lexiter (Sara

APPENDIX 1

Padden), Muscleman (Zinko Simunovich) Rev. Ito (Bishop Kinai Ikuma), With Joel Trapido, Sam Mokuaki, Charles Baptiste, Rennie Brooks, Ralph Honda, Akiru Fukunaza, Al Kealoha Perry

Credits: Director: Edward Ludwig; Screenplay: James Edward Grant, Richard English, Eric Taylor; Producer: Robert Fellows; Photography: Archie Stout; Art Director: Al Ybarra; Editor: Jack Murray; Music: Emil Newman, Arthur Lange, Paul Dunlap.

BLACK DRAGONS (1942, Monogram, 64 minutes)

Cast: Colomb (Bela Lugosi), Dick Martin (Clayton Moore), Dr. Bill Saunders (George Pembroke), Alice (Joan Barclay), Hanlin (Robert Frazer), Ryder (Robert Fiske), Wallace (Edward Piel), Van Dyke (Irving Mitchell), Colton (Kenneth Harlan), FBI Agent (Frank Melton), The Dragon (I. Stanford Jolley), Kearney (Max Hoffman, Jr.), Stevens (Joseph Eggenton), Cabby (Bernard Gorcey)

Credits: Director: William Nigh; Story & Screenplay: Harvey Gates; Producers: Sam Katzman, Jack Dietz; Photography: Art Reed; Art Director: David Milton; Editor: Carl Pierson; Music: Lange & Porter.

BODY SNATCHERS (1994, Warner Bros., 87 minutes)

Cast: Marti Malone (Gabrielle Anwar), Steve Malone (Terry Kinney), Carol Malone (Meg Tilly), Andy Malone (Reilly Murphy), Tim Young (Billy Wirth), Jenn Platt (Christine Elise), Gen. Platt (R. Lee Ermey), Mrs. Platt (Kathleen Doyle), Dr. Collins (Forest Whitaker), Pete (G. Elvis Phillips), Platt's Aide (Stanley Small), Teacher (Tonea Stewart), Gas Station Soldier (Keith Smith), Gas Attendant (Winston E. Grant), MP Captain (Phil Nelson), MPs (Timothy P. Brown, Thurman L. Combs, Allen Perada, Rick Kangrga, Michael Cohen), Soldier (Sylvia Small), Red (Adrian Unveragh), Neighbor (Johnny L. Smith), Medic (Candy Orsini), Man in Infirmary (Marty Lyons), Pod Soldier (Kimberly L. Cole), GIs (James P. Monoghan, Craig Lockhart), Alien Woman (Darien Taylor)

Credits: Director: Abel Ferrara; Screenplay: Stuart Gordon, Dennis Paoli, Nicholas St. John; Story: Raymond Cistheri, Larry Cohen, based on *The Body Snatchers* by Jack Finney; Producer: Kimberly Brent; Co-Producer: Michael Jaffe; Photography: Bojan Bazelli; Production Design: Peter Jamison; Editor: Anthony Redman; Music: Joe Delia.

THE BRAIN EATERS (1958, AIP, 60 minutes)

Cast: Dr. Paul Kettering (Ed Nelson), Glenn Cameron (Alan Frost), Sen. Walter Powers (Jack Hill), Alice Summers (Joanna Lee), Elaine (Jody Fair), Dr. Hyler (David Hughes), Dan Walker (Greigh Phillips), Mayor Cameron (Orville Sherman), Prof. Cole (Leonard Nimoy, billed as Leonard Nemoy), Doctor (Doug Banks), Telegrapher (Henry Randolph)

Credits: Director: Bruno VeSota; Screenplay: Gordon Urquhart; Producer: Ed Nelson; Photography: Larry Raimond; Art Director: Burt Shonberg; Editor: Carlo Lodato; Music: Tom Johnson.

THE BROTHERHOOD OF THE BELL (9/17/70, CBS, 100 minutes)

Cast: Prof. Andrew Paterson (Glenn Ford), Vivian Paterson (Rosemary Forsyth), Chad Harmon (Dean Jagger), Harry Masters (Maurice Evans), Mike Paterson (Will Geer), Dr. Konstantin Horvathy (Eduard Franz), Bart Harris (William Conrad), Philip Dunning (Robert Pine), Jerry Fielder (William Smithers), Thaddeus Burns (Logan Field), Betty Fielder (Lisabeth Hush), with James McEachin, Leon Lontoc, Dabney Coleman, Virginia Gilmore, Joe Brooks, Robert Clarke, Marc Hannibal, Scott Graham

Credits: Director: Paul Wendkos; Producer-Screenwriter: David Karp; Photography: Robert B. Hauser; Art Director: William Craig Smith; Music; Jerry Goldsmith; Editor: Carroll Sax.

CIVIC DUTY (2006, Landslide Pictures/Sepia Films, 94 minutes)

Cast: Terry Allen (Peter Krause), Marla Allen (Kari Matchett), Agent Tom Hilary (Richard Schiff),

In *Body Snatchers*, Gabrielle Anwar is the protagonist as the action takes place at a military base.

184

Film Credits

Gabe Hassan (Khaled Abol Naga), Lt. Lloyd (Ian Tracey), Bank Teller (Vanesa Tomasino), Loan Officer (Laurie Murdoch), Postal Clerk (Michael Roberds), Nurse (Agam Darshi), Anchor Brett Anderson (Mark Brandon), Anchor Tricia Wise (Brenda M. Crichlow), Anchor Susan Harwood (Val Cole), Reporter Chad Winslow (Mark Docherty), Legal Analyst (Michael St. John Smith), Gov. Bradley (P. Lynn Johnson), Policeman (Bruno Verdoni), Reporter (Benita Ha), Golf Announcer (Alan Duncan), Radio Announcers (Brian Carey, Judy DeAngelis), Computer Voice (Jessica Wachsman), Phone Operator (Cheryl Uphill), Sniper (Eli Rothman)

Credits: Director-Editor: Jeff Renfroe; Screenplay: Andrew Joiner; Producers: Tina Pehme, Kim Roberts, Peter Krause, Andrew Joiner, Andrew Lanter; Photography: Dylan MacLeod; Production Design: Rick Willoughby; Music: Eli Kratzberg.

CONFESSIONS OF A NAZI SPY (1939, Warner Bros., 102 minutes)

Cast: Edward Renard (Edward G. Robinson), Schneider (Francis Lederer), Schlager (George Sanders), Dr. Kassel (Paul Lukas), Attorney Kellogg (Henry O'Neill), Hilda Keinhauer (Dorothy Tree), Erika Wolf (Lya Lys), Mrs. Schneider (Grace Stafford), British Agent (James Stephenson), Mrs. Kassell (Celia Sibelius), Werner Renz (Joe Sawyer), Krogman (Sig Rumann), Hintze (Lionel Royce), Wildebrandt (Henry Victor), Helldorf (Hans von Twardowsky), Westphal (John Voigt), Capt. Richter (Frederick Vogeding), Greutzwald (Willy Kaufman), Capt. Straubel (Robert O. Davis), Capt. Von Eichen (William Vaughn), Klauber (George Rosener), Judge (Frederick Burton), Mrs. McLaughlin (Eily Malyon), Passenger (Bodil Rosing), Narrator (John Deering)

Credits: Director: Anatole Litvak; Screenplay: Milton Krims, John Wexley, based on articles by Leon G. Turrou; Photography: Sol Polito; Art Director: Carl Jules Weyl; Editor: Owen Marks; Music: Leo F. Forbstein.

THE CREATION OF THE HUMANOIDS (1962, Genie Productions, 75 minutes)

Cast: Captain Kenneth Cragis (Don Megowan), Maxine Megan (Erica Elliot), Esme Cragis Milos (Frances McCann), Dr. Raven (Don Doolittle), Pax (David Cross), Mark (Richard Vath), Court (Malcolm Smith), Acto (George Milan), Lagan (Dudley Manlove), Hart (Rod Hammond), Orus (Gil Frye), Dr. Moffitt (Pat Bradley), Ward (William Hunter), Cop (Paul Sheriff), Kelly's Duplicate (Alton Taber)

Credits: Director: Wesley E. Barry; Screenplay: Jay Simms; Producers: Edward J. Kay, Wesley E. Barry; Photography: Hal Mohr; Art Director: Ted Rich; Editor: Leonard W. Herman.

DANGEROUS HOURS (1920, Paramount, 7 reels)

Cast: John King (Lloyd Hughes), Sophia Guerni (Claire DuBrey), May Weston (Barbara Castleton), Boris Blotchi (Jack Richardson), Dr. King (Walt Whitman), Michael Regan (Lew Morrison), Andrew Felton (Gordon Mullen)

Credits: Director: Fred Niblo; Screenplay: C. Gardner Sullivan, based on *A Prodigal in Utopia* by Brian Oswald Donn-Byrne; Producer; Thomas H. Ince; Cinematography: George Barnes.

THE DAY MARS INVADED EARTH (1963, Twentieth Century–Fox, 70 minutes)

Cast: Dr. David Fielding (Kent Taylor), Claire Fielding (Marie Windsor), Dr. Web Spencer (William Mims), Judi Fielding (Betty Beall), Frank (Lowell Brown), Rocky Fielding (Gregg Shank). With: Henrietta Moore, Troy Melton, George Riley.

Credits: Director-Producer: Maury Dexter; Screenplay: Harry Spalding; Photography: John Nickolaus Jr.; Editor: Jodie Copelan: Music: Richard La Salle.

THE DEAD DON'T DIE (1975, NBC, 74 minutes)

Cast: Don Drake (George Hamilton), Jim Moss (Ray Milland), Vera LaValle (Linda Cristal), Lt. Reardon (Ralph Meeker), Frankie Specht (James McEachin), Levenia (Joan Blondell), Perdido (Reggie Nalder), Ralph Drake (Jerry Douglas), Receptionist (Milton Parsons), Priest (William O'Connell), Miss Adrian (Yvette Vickers), Prison Chaplain (Brendan Dillon), Prison Guard (Russ Grieves), Newspaper Man (Bill Smillie)

Credits: Director: Curtis Harrington; Screenplay: Robert Bloch; Producer: Henry Colman; Photography: James Crabe; Art Director: Robert Kinoshita; Editor: Ronald J. Fagan; Music: Robert Prince.

THE DEATH OF ME YET (1971, ABC, 74 minutes)

Cast: Edward Young/Paul Towers (Doug McClure), Joe Chalk (Darren McGavin), Sybil Towers (Rosemary Forsyth), Robert Barnes/Dr. Shevlin (Richard Basehart) Alice (Meg Foster), Hank Keller (Dana Elcar), Marilyn Keller (Jean Allison), George Dickman (Steve Dunne), Nylec (Allen Jaffe), Jerry (Sam Edwards), Redstone (John Kroga), Easley (Ivan Bonar)

Credits: Director: John Llewellyn Moxey; Screenplay: A.J. Russell, from the novel by Whit Masterson; Producer: Aaron Spelling; Photography: Tim Southcott; Art Director: Tracy Bousman; Editor: Art Seid; Music: Pete Rugolo.

Appendix 1

The Devil's Child (1997, ABC, 100 minutes)
Cast: Nikki DiMarco (Kim Delaney), Alex Rota (Thomas Gibson), Ruby (Colleen Flynn), Tim (Matthew Lillard), Ezra Hersch (Tracey Walter), Eva (Gia Carides), Max (Martin Davidson), Father Darcy (Christopher John Fields), Lena (Ivana Milavich), Todd Gilman (Larry Holden), Mrs. DeMarco (Grace Zabriskie), Young Nikki (Rachael Bella), Detective Rapp (Henry Sanders), Dr. Zimmerman (Paul Bartel), Nurse (Laura Hinsburger), Sam (Nick Roth), Holly (Maya Rudolph), Dr. Haft (Lauren Tom)
Credits: Director: Bobby Roth; Screenplay: Pablo F. Fenjves; Story–Co-Producers: Pablo F. Fenjves, Laurence Minkoff; Producer: Mark S. Glick; Photography: Shelly Johnson; Production Design: Glenda Ganis; Music: Christopher Franke; Editor: Henk Van Eeghen.

Dr. Goldfoot and the Bikini Machine (1965, AIP, 90 minutes)
Cast: Dr. Goldfoot (Vincent Price), Craig Gamble (Frankie Avalon), Todd Armstrong (Dwayne Hickman), Diane (Susan Hart), Igor (Jack Mullaney), DJ Pevney (Fred Clark), Robots (Patti Chandler, Mary Hughes, Salli Sachse, Luree Holmes, Sue Hamilton, Laura Nicholson, Marianne Gaba, China Lee, Issa Arnal, Deanna Lund, Pam Rodgers, Leslie Summer, Sally Frei, Kay Michaels, Jan Watson, Arlene Charles)
Credits: Director: Norman Taurog; Screenplay: Elwood Ullman, Robert Kaufman; Story: James H. Nicholson; Producers: James H. Nicholson, Samuel Z. Arkoff; Co-Producer: Anthony Carras; Photography: Sam Leavitt; Art Director: Daniel Haller; Editors: Ronald Sinclair, Fred Feitshans; Music: Les Baxter.

Dr. Goldfoot and the Girl Bombs (1966, AIP, 95 minutes)
Cast: Dr. Goldfoot (Vincent Price), Bill Dexter (Fabian), Franco (Franco Franchi), Ciccio (Ciccio Ingrassia), Rosanna (Laura Antonelli), Goldfoot's Assistant (Moana Tahi), Col. Benson (Francesco Mule)
Credits: Director: Mario Bava; Screenplay: Louis M. Heyward, Robert Kaufman; Story: James H. Nicholson; Producers: Fulvio Lucisano, Louis M. Heyward; Photography: Antonio Rinaldi; Art Director: Gastone Carsetti; Editor: Ronald Sinclair. Music: Les Baxter.

The Enemy Within (1994, HBO, 86 minutes)
Cast: Col. Mackenzie "Mac" Casey (Forest Whitaker), Gen. R. Pendleton Lloyd (Jason Robards), President William Forster (Sam Waterston), Betsy Corcoran (Dana Delany), Defense Secretary Charles Potter (Josef Sommer), Jake (George Dzundza), Sarah McCann (Isabel Glasser), Vice President Kelly (Dakin Matthews), Lt. Dorsett (William O'Leary), Jean Casey (Lisa Summerour), Honor Guard Sergeant (Rory Aylward), Tracker (Greg Brickman), Pentagon Security Officer (David Combs), President's Secretary (Patricia Donaldson), Dr. Jarvis (Denise Dowse), Reporters (Yolanda Gaskins, Jayne Hess), Bowman (Chuck Hicks), Protective Services Guard (Leonard Kelly-Young), Priest (Archie Lang), Agriculture Secretary Spencer (Barry Lynch), Jack Giddings (Ryan MacDonald), Todd Casey (Willie Norwood, Jr.), Treasury Secretary Monroe (Anthony Peck), Attorney General Arthur Daniels (Lawrence Pressman), Fletcher (George Marshall Ruge), Reporter #1 (Steven Ruge), Lt. Lonner (Michael Buchman Silver).
Credits: Director, Jonathan Darby; Screenplay: Darryl Ponicsan, Ron Bass, based on *Seven Days in May* by Rod Serling and the novel *Seven Days in May* by Fletcher Knebel, Charles W. Bailey; Producer: Robert A. Papazian; Photography: Kees van Oostrum; Art Director, Erik Olsen; Editor: Peter Zinner; Music: Joe Delia.

Executive Action (1973, Wakeford/Orloff, 91 minutes)
Cast: Farrington (Burt Lancaster), Foster (Robert Ryan), Ferguson (Will Geer), Paulitz (Gilbert Green), Jalliday (John Anderson), Team A Gunmen (Paul Carr, Richard Bull, Lee Delano), Tim (Colby Chester), Team A Chief (Ed Lauter), Smythe (Walter Brooke), Team B Riflemen (John Brascia, Hunter Von Leer), Depository Clerk (Sidney Clute), Stripper (Deanna Darrin), McCadden (Lloyd Gough), TV Commentator (Graydon Gould), Car Salesman (Richard Hurst), Man at Rifle Range (Robert Karnes), Oswald Imposter (James Mac Coll), Art Mendoza (Jacquin Martinez), Policeman (Sandy Ward), Team B Leader (William Watson)
Credits: Director: David Miller; Screenplay: Dalton Trumbo; Story: Donald Freed, Mark Lane; Producer: Edward Lewis; Photography: Robert Steadman; Art Director: Kirk Axtell; Editor: George Grenville; Music: Randy Edelman.

The Experts (1988, Paramount, 83 minutes)
Cast: Travis (John Travolta), Wendell (Arye Gross), Bonnie Grant (Kelly Preston), Jill (Deborah Foreman), Yuri (James Keach), Illyich (Jan Rubes), Jones (Brian Doyle-Murray), Smith (Charles Martin Smith), Mrs. Smith (Mimi Maynard), Aunt Thelma

Film Credits

(Eve Brent), Sparks (Rick Ducommun), Gil (Steve Levitt), Nathan (Tony Edwards), Doc Benson (Jack Ammon), Billy Smith (Marc Reid), Kathy Smith (Robyn Simons), Old Timers (Joseph Golland, Imbert Orchard, John Boylan), Floyd (Nigel Harvey), Lawyer (Ron Chabidon), Lovers (Roman Podhora, Caroline Healy), Elmo (Adrien Dorval), Taxi Driver (Alex Bruhanski), Operator (Sandy Tucker), Journalists (Ella Levykh, Michael Levykh), Guards (Marek Czuma, Andrei Grigoriev), Sheriff (Frank C. Turner), Huge Guy (Dan Zale), Soda Jerk (Robert Sidley), Stewardess (Narda Singh), Prison Guard (Filonov Sergey), Butcher (Gary Snider), DC-4 Pilot (Michael C. Bogle), DC-4 Co-Pilot (John Watson)

Credits: Director: Dave Thomas; Screenplay: Nick Thiel, Steven Greene, Eric Alter; Story: Steven Greene, Eric Alter; Producer: James Keach; Photography: Ronnie Taylor; Production Design: David Fischer; Editor: Bud Molin; Music: Marvin Hamlisch.

THE FACULTY (1998, Dimension films, 104 minutes)

Cast: Delilah (Jordana Brewster), Stokely (Clea DuVall), Marybeth (Laura Harris), Zeke (Josh Hartnett), Stan (Shawn Hatosy), Nurse (Salma Hayek), Burke (Famke Janssen), Olson (Piper Laurie), Casey's Dad (Chris McDonald), Drake (Bebe Neuwirth), Coach Willis (Robert Patrick), Gabe (Usher Raymond), Furlong (Jon Stewart), Tate (Daniel Von Bargen), Casey (Elijah Wood), F%#* You Girl (Summer Phoenix), F%# You Boy (Jon Abrahams), Mrs. Brummel (Susan Willis), Meat (Pete Janssen), Tattoo Girl (Christina Rodriguez), F%# Ups (Danny Masterson, Wiley Wiggins), Knowles (Harry Knowles), Tina (Donna Casey), Mr. Lewis (Louis Black), Freshmen (Eric Jungmann, Chris Viteychuk), PE Teacher (Jim Johnston), Casey's Mom (Libby Villari), Officers (Duane Martin, Katherine Willis), Hornet Mascot (Mike Lutz), Brun Coach (Doug Aarniokoski)

Credits: Director: Robert Rodriguez; Screenplay: Kevin Williamson; Story: David Wechter, Bruce Kimmel; Producer: Elizabeth Avellan; Photography: Enrique Chediak; Production Design: Cary White; Editor: Robert Rodriguez; Music: Marco Beltrami, Alex Steyermark.

THE FALL OF A NATION (1916, National Films)

Cast: Charles Waldron (Arthur Shirley), Virginia Holland (Lorraine Huling); with Flora MacDonald, Percy Standing, Paul Willis, Philip Gastrock

Credits: Director: Bartley Cushing; Screenplay: Thomas Dixon.

THE FEARMAKERS (1958, United Artists, 83 minutes)

Cast: Captain Alan Eaton (Dana Andrews), Jim McGinnis (Dick Foran), Lorraine Dennis (Marilee Earle), Vivian Loder (Veda Ann Borg), Hal Loder (Kelly Thordsen), Sen. Walder (Roy Gordon), Rodney Hillyer (Joel Marston), Barney Bond (Mel Torme), Dr. Gregory Jessup (Oliver Blake), Army Doctor (Dennis Moore), Secretary (Janet Brandt), Stewardess (Fran Andrade), Conference Room Speaker (Robert Carson), Police Sergeant (Lyle Latell).

Credits: Director: Jacques Tourneur; Screenplay: Elliot West, Chris Appley, based on the novel by Darwin Teilhet; Producer: Martin H. Lancer; Photography: Sam Leavitt; Art direction: Serge Krizman; Editor: J.R. Whittredge; Music: Irving Gertz.

FIGHTING YOUTH (1935, Universal, 78 minutes)

Cast: Larry Davis (Charles Farrell), Betty Wilson (June Martel), "Cy" Kipp (Andy Devine), Carol Arlington (Ann Sheridan), Coach Parker (J. Farrell MacDonald), Tony Tonnetti (Edward Nugent), "Dodo" Gates (Phyllis Fraser), Herman (Herman Bing), Louis Markoff (Alden Chase), Football Players (Larry "Moon" Mullins, Jim Purvis), with Paul Schwegler, Dale Van Sickel, Jim Thorpe, Leslie Cooper, Howard "Red" Christie, Nick Lukats, Frank Sully

Credits: Director: Hamilton MacFadden; Screenplay: Henry Johnson, Florabel Muir, Hamilton MacFadden, based on an idea by Stan Meyer; Producer: Carl Laemmle; Photographer: Edward J. Snyder; Art Director: Ralph Berger; Editor: Bernard Burton; Music: Bakaleinikoff.

FRANKENSTEIN (2004, USA Network, 88 minutes)

Cast: Carson O'Connor (Parker Posey), Michael Sloane (Adam Goldberg), Deucalion (Vincent Perez), Victor Helios (Thomas Kretschmann), Erika Helios (Ivana Milicevic), Detective Harker (Michael Madsen) Angelique (Deborah Duke), Jenna (Ann Mahoney Kadar), Burke (Deneen Tyler), Detective Frye (Brett Rice), Patrick (Stocker Fontelieu), Vickey (Maureen Brennan), Rogers (Billy Louviere), Anthony O'Connor (Will Schierhorn), Watkins (Tom Nowicki), Fullbright (David Jensen), Nancy Whistler (Sandra Dorsey), Christine (Lauren Swinney), Sailor (Thirl Halston)

Credits: Director-Producer: Marcus Nispel; Screenplay: John Shiban; Photography: Daniel Pearl; Production Design: Gregory Blair; Editor: Jay Friedkin; Music: Norman Corbell.

THE FRONT (1976, Columbia, 95 minutes)

Cast: Howard Prince (Woody Allen), Hecky Brown (Zero Mostel), Florence Barnett (Andrea

Appendix 1

Marcovicci), Phil Sussman (Herschel Bernardi) Alfred Miller (Michael Murphy), Hennessey (Remak Ramsay), Myer Prince (Marvin Lichterman), Delaney (Lloyd Gough), Phelps (David Margulies), Sam (Joshua Shelley), Attorney (Norman Rose), Committee Counselor (Charles Kimbrough), Committee Chair (Josef Sommer), LaGattuta (Danny Aiello), Interviewer (Georgann Johnson), Hampton (Scott McKay), Hubert Jackson (David Clarke), Bank Teller (I.W. Klein), Bartender (John Bentley), Margo (Julie Garfield), Boss (Murray Moston), Harry Stone (McIntyre Dixon), Tailman (Rudolph Wilrich), Bookseller (Burt Britton), Principal (Albert M. Ottenheimer), Parks (William Bogert), Waiter (Joey Faye), Sandy (Marilyn Sokol), Director (John J. Slater), Girl (Renée Paris), Stagehand (Gino Gennaro), Myer's Wife (Joan Porter), Alfred's Children (Andrew Bernstein, Jacob Bernstein), Man at Party (Matthew Tobin), Date (Marilyn Persky), Young Man (Sam McMurray), FBI Agents (Joe Jamrog, Michael Miller), Nurse (Lucy Lee Flippin), Congressmen (Jack Davidson, Donald Symington), Federal Marshal (Patrick McNamara)

Credits: Director-Producer: Martin Ritt; Screenplay: Walter Bernstein; Photography: Michael Chapman; Art Director: Charles Bailey; Editor: Sidney Levin; Music: Dave Grusin.

FUTUREWORLD (1976, AIP, 104 minutes)

Cast: Chuck Browning (Peter Fonda), Tracy (Blythe Danner), Duffy (Arthur Hill), Dr. Schneider (John Ryan), Harry (Stuart Margolin), Gunslinger (Yul Brynner), Game Show Host (Allen Ludden), Mr. Reed (Robert Cornthwaite), Mrs. Reed (Angela Greene), Eric (Darrell Larson), Erica (Nancy Bell), Karnovski (Burt Conroy), Mrs. Karnovski (Dorothy Konrad), Takaguchi (John Fujioka), Takaguchi's Aide (Dana Lee), KGB Man (Alex Rodine), Bartender (Judson Pratt), Male Robot (Andrew Masset), Robot Clark (James Connor), Technician (Ray Holland), Steven (Mike Scott), Frenchy (Ed Geldard), Fantasy Technician (David Perkins), Holcombe (Charles Krohn), Arab (Hirsh Scholl), Guard (Barry Gilmore), Secretary (Catherine McClenny), Page (Barry Gremillion), Shorty (Jim Everhart), Hostess (Jan Cobbler), Reporter (Howard Finch)

Credits: Director: Richard T. Heffron; Screenplay: Mayo Simon, George Schenck; Producers: Paul N. Lazarus III, James T. Aubrey; Photography: Howard Schwartz, Gene Polito; Editor: James Mitchell; Music: Fred Karlin.

G-MEN VS. THE BLACK DRAGON (1943, Republic, 15 chapters)

Cast: Rex Bennett (Rod Cameron), Chang (Roland Got), Vivian Marsh (Constance Worth), Haruchi (Nino Pipitone), Ranga (Noel Cravat), Lugo (George J. Lewis), Marie (Maxine Doyle), Thug (Donald Kirke), Customs Inspector (Ivan Miller), Williams (Walter Fenner), Nicholson (C. Montague Shaw), Tony Mills (Harry Burns), Kennedy (Forbes Murray), Caldwell (Hooper Atchley), Gorman (Robert Homans), Fuji (Allen Jung)

Credits: Director: William Witney; Screenplay: Ronald Davidson, Joseph O'Donnell, William Lively, Joseph Poland; Producer: William J. O'Sullivan; Photography: Bud Thackery; Editors: Edward Todd, Tony Martinelli; Music: Mort Glickman.

HEADIN' FOR GOD'S COUNTRY (1943, Republic, 78 minutes)

Cast: Michael Banyan (William Lundigan), Laurie Lane (Virginia Dale), Clem Adams (Harry Davenport), Albert Ness (Harry Shannon), Commissioner (Addison Richards), Hilary Higgins (J. Frank Hamilton), Hugo Higgins (Eddie Acuff), Jim Talbot (Wade Crosby), Jeff (Skelton Knaggs), Nickolai (John Bleifer), Hank (Eddy Waller), Willie Soba (Charlie Lung), Gim Lung (Eddie Lee), Chuck (Ernie Adams), Japanese Officer (James B. Leong), Mrs. Nilsson (Anna Q. Nilsson), Flash (Ace), Boat Captain (Harrison Greene), Minnemook (Frank Lackteen), John Lane (Charles Miller), Meteorologist (Edmund Cobb), Weatherman (Howard Banks), Japanese Radio Operator (George Lee), Army Radio Operator (Jack Gardner)

Credits: Director: William Morgan; Screenplay: Elizabeth Meehan, Houston Branch; Story: Houston Branch; Photography: Bud Thackery; Art Director: Russell Kimball; Editor: Arthur Roberts; Music: Morton Scott.

HITLER'S DAUGHTER (1990, USA Network, 88 minutes)

Cast: Ted Scott (Patrick Cassidy), Sen. Leona Gordon (Kay Lenz), Sharon Franklin (Melody Anderson), Jill Breyer (Carolyn Dunn), Jim (Lindsay Merrithew), Elliott Benedict (George R. Robertson), Patricia Benedict (Veronica Cartwright), Dr. Baumann (Donald Davis), David Holland (Gary Reineke), Averill Rutledge (Clayton Ed McGibbon), Trautmann (Cec Linder), Berger (Nigel Bennett), Mitchell (Frank Adamson), Dolan (Tom Butler), Taylor (John Stoneham, Jr.), Dr. Wolf (Chris Mann), Nurse (Deborah Lobban), Melvin O'Neill (James Mainprize), Pizza Delivery Driver (Falconer Abraham), News Producer (Rex Hagon)

Credits: Director: James A. Contner; Screenplay: Sherman Gray, Christopher Canaan, based on the novel by Timothy B. Benford; Producer: Richard Luke Rothschild; Photography: Frank Tidy; Art

Film Credits

Director: Tony Hall; Music: Joel McNeely; Editor: Scott Smith.

THE HOUSE ON CARROLL STREET (1988, MGM, 101 minutes)

Cast: Emily Crane (Kelly McGillis), Cochran (Jeff Daniels), Miss Venable (Jessica Tandy), Hackett (Ken Welsh), Stefan (Christopher Rode), Salwen (Mandy Patinkin), Sen. Byington (Remak Ramsay), Salwen Aides (Charles McCaughan, Randle Mell, Jim Babchack), Senator (Michael Flanagan), Slote (Paul Sparer), Warren (Brian Davies), Maid (Mary Diveny), Teperson (Bill Moor), Woman in the House (Patricia Falkenhain), FBI Director (Frederick Rolf), Funeral Woman (Anna Berger), McKay (Cliff Cudney), Sackadorf (Alexis Yulin), Lt. Sloan (Trey Wilson), FBI Librarian (William Duff-Griffin), Conductor (George Ede), Gateman (John Carpenter), Porter (Jamey Sheridan), Barber (P.J. Barry), Hurwitz (Boris Leskin), Bistrong (Marat Yusim), Official (James Rebhorn), Boria (Howard Sherman), Simpson (John Randolph Jones), Stage Manager (David Hart), Mrs. Byington (Maeve McGuire), Byington's Daughter (Suzanne Slade), Byington's Son (Todd deFreitas), Office Boy (Gregory Jbara), Sam (James Tew), Manicurists (Polly O'Malley, Maureen Moore), Woman at Hearing (Alice Drummond), Xanthias (Tony Carreiro), Doinysus (Robert Stanton), Bartender (Daniel Mills), Receptionist (Melba La Rose), Man at Theater Bar (Stephen Gleason), Theater Goers (Christopher Cusack, Elizabeth A. Reilly), Sloan's Partner (Skip Rose), Sergeant (Frank Patton), Theater Manager (Gaylord C. Mason), Rabbi (Rabbi Morris S. Friedman), Waiter (John-Kenneth Hoffman)

Credits: Director-Producer: Peter Yates; Screenplay: Walter Bernstein; Producer: Robert F. Colesberry; Photography: Michael Ballhaus; Production Design: Stuart Wurtzel; Editor: Ray Lovejoy; Music: George Delerue.

THE HUMAN DUPLICATORS (1965, Woolner Bros. Pictures/Allied Artists, 82 minutes)

Cast: Glenn Martin (George Nader), Kolos (Richard Kiel), Dornheimer (George Macready), Gale Wilson (Barbara Nichols), Lisa (Dolores Faith), NIA Director (Richard Arlen), Austin Welles (Hugh Beaumont), Galaxy Being (Ted Durant), with Tommy Leonetti, Lonnie Sattin, John Indrisano

Credits: Director: Hugo Grimaldi; Screenplay: Arthur C. Pierce; Producers: Hugo Grimaldi, Arthur C. Pierce; Photography: Monroe Askins; Art Director: Paul Sylos; Editor: Donald Wolfe; Music: Gordon Zahler.

I MARRIED A MONSTER (1998, UPN, 90 minutes)

Cast: Nicholas Farrell (Richard Burgi), Kelly Drummond (Susan Walters), Steve (Tim Ryan), Linda Harris (Barbara Niven), Uncle Paul (Richard Herd), Bartender (Barney Martin), Bud Riley (Tim DeZarn), Sheriff Collins (Vaughn Armstrong), Deputies (Jason Van, Michael Bard Bayer, Scott Benefiel), Posse (Clement Blake, Jason D. Smith), Man (Dan Borowicz), Friends (Jonathan Breck, Brien Perry), Bridesmaids (Toshi Harrison, Leslie Harter), Woman (Christine Kludjian), Coroner (Ming Lo), Lifeguard (Hank Matt), Ellen (Sandra Phillips), Minister (Charles C. Stevenson, Jr.), Mrs. Drummond (Elaine Ward), Deliveryman (Miles Wiltshire), Nurses (Bonnie Brewster, Annie Hinton), Jim (Brady Finta), Bellman (Josh Garner), Flower Girl (Ashley Majoros), Clerk (Aloma Wright)

Credits: Director: Nancy Malone; Screenplay: Duane Poole, based on the movie *I Married a Monster from Outer Space*; Producer: Stu Segall; Photography: Geoff Schaaf; Production Design: Nigel Clinker; Editor: Ron Kobrin; Music: David Shire.

I MARRIED A MONSTER FROM OUTER SPACE (1958, Paramount, 78 minutes)

Cast: Marge Farrell (Gloria Talbott), Bill Farrell (Tom Tryon), Sam Benson (Alan Dexter), Harry Phillips (Robert Ivers), Ted (Chuck Wassill), Francine (Valerie Allen), Swanson (Peter Baldwin), Mac Brody (Ty Hardin), Dr. Wayne (Ken Lynch), Chief Collins (John Eldredge), Weldon (James Anderson), Helen Rhodes (Jean Carson), Schultz (Jack Orrison), Charles Mason (Steve London), Grady (Maxie Rosenbloom), Mrs. Bradley (Mary Treen), Minister (Arthur Lovejoy), First Girl (Scherry Staiger), Second Girl (Helen Jay), Ralph (Paul Manza), Caroline Hanks (Darlene Fields), Western Union Clerk (Tony di Milo)

Credits: Director-Producer: Gene Fowler, Jr.; Screenplay: Louis Vittes; Photography: Haskell Boggs; Art Directors: Hal Pereira, Henry Bumstead; Editor: George Tomasini.

I WAS A COMMUNIST FOR THE FBI (1951, Warner Bros., 84 minutes)

Cast: Matt Cvetic (Frank Lovejoy), Jim Blandon (James Millican), Eve Merrick (Dorothy Hart), Mason (Philip Carey), Ken Crowley (Richard Webb), Gerhardt Eisler (Konstantin Shayne), Joe Cvetic (Paul Picerni), Father Novac (Roy Roberts), Harmon (Edward Norris), Dick Cvetic (Ron Hagerthy), Clyde Garson (Hugh Sanders), Ruth Cvetic (Hope Kramer), Tom Cvetic (Frank

APPENDIX 1

Gerstle), Frank Cvetic (Russ Conway), Mrs. Cvetic (Kasia Orzazekski), Miss Nova (Ann Morrison), McIntyre (Paul McGuire), Chief Agent (Douglas Evans), Secretaries (Janet Barrett, Karen Hale), Thugs (Joseph Smith, Jimmy O'Gatty, Charles Horvath), Workers (Frank Marlowe, Brick Sullivan), Foreman (Mike Ross), Principal (Lenita Lane), Teacher (Alma Mansfield), Students (Ann Kimball, Paula Sowl), Wife (Grace Lenard), Jackie (Eric Neilsen), Jackie's Father (Roy Engel), Brown (Bill Lester), McGowan (John Crawford), Black Men (Ernest Anderson, Sugarfoot Anderson), Dobbs (Johnny Bradford), Brennan (Jimmy Gonzalez), Masonvitch (David McMahon), Irishman (Phil Tully), Union Chairman (Howard Negley), Picketers (Bobby Gilbert, James Adamson), Officer (Barry Reagan), Cahill (Lyle Latell), Brakeman (Chuck Coleman), Lawyers (Dick Gordon, William Bailey, Paul Bradley, Robert Shaw), Sen. Wood (William Forrest), Sen. Gray (Bert Moorhouse), with Theresa Harris, Charles Sherlock, Mary Alan Hokanson, Mildred Boyd, George Magrill, Gorilla Jones, Snub Pollard

Credits: Director: Gordon Douglas; Screenplay: Crane Wilbur: Producer: Bryan Foy; Photography: Edwin DuPar; Art Director: Leo K. Kuter; Editor: Folmar Blangsted; Music: William Lava.

THE INVADERS (1995, CBS, 200 minutes)

Cast: Nolan Wood (Scott Bakula), Dr. Ellen Garza (Elizabeth Peña), Jerry Thayer (Richard Thomas), Randy Stein (Richard Belzer), Amanda Thayer (Delane Mathews), Josh (Eric King), David Vincent (Roy Thinnes), Coyle (Terence Knox), Grace (Shannon Kenny), Suarez (Raoul Trujillo), Kyle (Mario Yedidia), Norma Winters (Elinor Donahue), Frankel (Lindsay Ginter), Lucinda (Judy Hain), Bus Driver (Lee Bayles), Postman (J. Marvin Campbell), Coyote (Luis Contreras), Erskine (William Duffy), Trucker (Frank Farmer), Paramedic (Craig Higgins), Reporter (Sally Hightower), Marty (Dean Hill), Trustee (Eugene Lee), Pipe (Don Pugsley), Cop (Al Rodrigo), Guard (Roger Rook), Espereanza (Julia Vera), Nurse (Susan Ware), Dr. Rysmiller (Lorine Dills-Vozoff), Billy (Todd Merrill), Dr. Singh (Duke Moosekian), Secret Service Man (Rick Fitts), Cops (Jim Holmes, Todd Stanton), Metrolink Worker (Nick Jameson), Aide (Hillary Matthews), Raymond (Roland Molina), Wood's Lawyer (David St. James), Security Man (Tegan West), with Debra Jo Rupp, Channon Roe, Jack Kehler, Jon Cypher, Todd Susman

Credits: Director: Paul Shapiro; Screenplay: James Dott; Executive Producers: James G. Hirsch, Robert Papazian, James D. Parriott; Photography: Alar Hivilo; Production Design: Rodger Maus; Editor: Daniel Cahn; Music: Joseph Vitarelli.

INVADERS FROM MARS (1953, 20th Century–Fox, 78 minutes)

Cast: David Maclean (Jimmy Hunt), Dr. Pat Blake (Helena Carter), Dr. Stuart Kelston (Arthur Franz), George Maclean (Leif Erickson), Mary Maclean (Hillary Brooke), Col. Fielding (Morris Ankrum), Sgt. Rinaldi (Max Wagner), Capt. Roth (Milburn Stone), Major Cleary (Bill Phipps), Desk Sgt. Finley (Walter Sande), Chief Barrows (Bert Freed), Officer Jackson (Douglas Kennedy), Officer Blaine (Charles Cane), Dr. William Wilson (Robert Shayne), Kathy Wilson (Janine Perreau), Brainard (Peter Brocco), Dr. Kelston's Secretary (Barbara Billingsley), Gen. Mayberry (William Forrest), Chief of Staff (Frank Wilcox), Sentry Regan (Richard Deacon), Martian in Globe (Luce Potter), Giant Mutants (Max Palmer, Lock Martin)

Credits: Director–Production Designer: William Cameron Menzies; Screenplay: Richard Blake; Associate Producer: Edward L. Alperson, Jr.; Photography: John Seitz; Art Director: Boris Leven; Editor: Arthur Roberts; Music: Raoul Kraushaar.

INVADERS FROM MARS (1986, Cannon, 99 minutes)

Cast: Linda (Karen Black), David (Hunter Carson), George (Timothy Bottoms), Ellen (Laraine Newman), General Wilson (James Karen), Young NASA Scientist (Bud Cort), Mrs. McKeltch (Louise Fletcher), Sgt. Rinaldi (Eric Pierpoint), Capt. Curtis (Christopher Allport), Old NASA Scientist (Donald Hotton), Officer Kenney (Kenneth Kimmins), Mr. Cross (Charlie Dell), Chief (Jimmy Hunt), NASA Scientist (William Bassett), Heather (Virginia Keehne), Kevin (Chris Hebert), Doug (Mason Nupuf), Ed (William Frankfather), MPs (Joseph Brutsman, Eric Norris), Corporal Walker (Debra Berger), Hollis (Eddy Donno), Johnson (Mark Giardino), Classmates (Daryl Bartley, Roy Mansano, Shonda Whipple, Amy Fitzpatrick, Shawn Campbell, Brett Johnson), Squad Leader (Dale Dye), Lieutenant (Douglas Simpson), Communications Officer (Lonny Low), Marine Officer (Scott Leva), Young Marine (Scott Wulff), Marines (Frederick Menslage, Michael McGrady, Lawrence Poindexter, J. Acheson, Matt Bennett, Aaron Scott Bernard), Demolition Man (Steve Lambert), Drones (Debbie Carrington, Margarite Fernandez, Joe Anthony Cox, Salvatore Fondacaro, Matt Bennett, Lonny Low, Douglas Simpson, Scott Wulff)

Credits: Director: Tobe Hooper; Screenplay: Dan O'Bannon, Don Jakoby, based on a screenplay by Richard Blake; Producer: Menahem Golan, Yoram Globus; Photography: Daniel Pearl; Production Design: Leslie Dilley; Editor: Alan Jakubowicz; Music: Christopher Young.

THE INVASION (2007, Warner Bros., 99 minutes)

Cast: Carol Bennell (Nicole Kidman), Ben Driscoll (Daniel Craig), Tucker Kaufman (Jeremy Northam), Oliver (Jackson Bond), Dr. Stephen Galeano (Jeffrey Wright), Wendy Lenk (Veronica Cartwright), Dr. Henry Belicec (Josef Sommer), Ludmilla Belicec (Celia Weston), Yorish (Roger Rees), Gene (Eric Benjamin), Pam (Susan Floyd), Carly (Stephanie Berry), Belicec's Aide (Alexis Raben), Richard Lenk (Adam LeFevre), Joan Kaufman (Joanna Merlin), Census Taker (Field Blauvelt), Dina Twain (Rhonda Overby), NASA Official (Reid Sasser), John (Brandon J. Price), Jan (Mia Arniece Chambers), Mrs. Cunningham (Ava Lenet), Dog Owner (Michael A. Kelly), Andy (Jeremiah Hake), Cop in Tunnel (Luray Cooper), Panicked Woman in Tunnel (Nanna Ingvarsson), Transit Cop (Jeff Wincott), News Vendor (Wes Johnson), Mrs. Robinson (Becky Woodley), Man in Rags (Parker Webb), Sobbing Team (Cloie Wyatt Taylor), Reporter (John Colton), Tucker's Colleague (John Leslie Wolfe), Butler (Michael Stone Forrest), Subway Guy (Tim Scanlin), Subway Girl (Tara Garwood), Sleep-Deprived Screamer (Genevieve Adell), Helpful Cop (Derren Fuentes), Crying Woman (Darla Mason Robinson), Street Cop (Brian Augustus Parnell), Boy in Train Station (Benjamin Bullard), Nurse (Jean H. Miller), Elderly Lady (Jean B. Schertler), Security Guard (James Bouchet)

Credits: Director: Oliver Hirschbiegel; Screenplay: David Kajganich; Producer: Joel Silver; Photography: Rainer Klausmann; Production Design: Jack Fisk; Editors: Joel Negron, Hans Funck; Music: John Ottman.

INVASION OF THE BEE GIRLS (1973, Centaur, 85 minutes)

Cast: Neil Agar (William Smith), Julie Zorn (Victoria Vetri), Dr. Susan Harris (Anitra Ford), Captain Peters (Cliff Osmond), Dr. Murger (Wright King), Herb Kline (Ben Hammer), Nora Kline (Anna Aries), Aldo Ferrara (Andre Phillippe), Stan Williams (Sid Kaiser), Gretchen Grubowsky (Katie Saylor), Harriet Williams (Beverly Powers), Harv (Tom Pittman), Joe (William Keller), Coroner (Cliff Emmich), Herm (Al Bordiggi), Barney (Jack Perkins), Girl (Susie Player), MPs (Lloyd McLinn, Don Hall, Steve Lefkowitz), Elvira Ferrara (Danielle Dupont), Rednecks (Mickey Carus, Herb Robbins, Gregory White), Motel Manager (John Nelson), Dr. Lyons (F. Stewart Wilson), Funeral Director (Dick Murphy), Bee Ladies (Mary Sweeney, Amanda Jefferies, Sharon Madigan, Renee Bond, Cathy Hilton)

Credits: Director: Denis Sanders ; Screenplay: Nicholas Meyer; Photography: Gary Graver; Art Director: Elayne Ceder; Editor: H&R Travis Editorial Services; Music: Charles Bernstein.

INVASION OF THE BODY SNATCHERS (1956, Allied Artists, 80 minutes)

Cast: Miles Bennell (Kevin McCarthy), Becky Driscoll (Dana Wynter), Jack Belicec (King Donovan), Teddy Belicec (Carolyn Jones), Dr. Daniel Kaufman (Larry Gates), Sheriff Nick Grivett (Ralph Dumke), Sally Withers (Jean Willes), Wilma Lentz (Virginia Christine), Uncle Ira (Tom Fadden), Driscoll (Kenneth Patterson), Sam Janzek (Guy Way), Jimmy Grimaldi (Bobby Clark), Mrs. Grimaldi (Eileen Stevens), Grandmother Grimaldi (Beatrice Maude), Aunt Eleda (Jean Andren), Dr. Ed Pursey (Everett Glass), Mac (Dabbs Greer), Baggage Man (Pat O'Malley), Proprietor (Guy Rennie), Martha (Marie Selland), Charlie Buckholtz (Sam Peckinpah), Grimaldi (Harry J. Vejar), Dr. Harvey Bassett (Richard Deacon), Dr. Hill (Whit Bissell)

Credits: Director: Don Siegel; Screenplay: Daniel Mainwaring; Based on the Novel *Body Snatchers* by Jack Finney; Producer: Walter Wanger; Photography: Ellsworth Fredericks; Production Design: Edward Haworth; Editor: Robert S. Eisen; Music: Carmen Dragon.

INVASION OF THE BODY SNATCHERS (1978, MGM, 115 minutes)

Cast: Matthew Bennell (Donald Sutherland), Elizabeth Driscoll (Brooke Adams), Jack Belicec (Jeff Goldblum), Nancy Belicec (Veronica Cartwright), Dr. David Kibner (Leonard Nimoy), Dr. Geoffrey Howell (Art Hindle), Katherine Hendley (Lelia Goldoni), Running Man (Kevin McCarthy), Taxi Driver (Don Siegel), Ted Hendley (Tom Luddy), Stahn (Stan Ritchie), Mr. Gianni (David Fisher), Detective (Tom Dahlgren), Boccardo (Gary Goodrow), Restaurant Owner (Jerry Walter), Chef (Maurice Argent), Barker (Sam Conti), Mr. Tong (Wood Moy), Mrs. Tong (R. Wong), Outraged Woman (Rose Kaufman), Beggar (Joe Bellan), Policemen (Sam Hiona, Lee McVeigh), Rodent Man (Albert Malbandian), Teacher (Lee Mines), Priest (Robert Duvall)

Credits: Director: Philip Kaufman; Screenplay: W.D. Richter, based on the novel *The Body Snatchers* by Jack Finney; Producer: Robert H. Solo; Photography: Michael Chapman; Production De-

Appendix 1

The transformation into pod people is much more tactile in the 1978 *Invasion of the Body Snatchers* than it was in the original film.

signer: Charles Rosen; Editor: Douglas Stewart; Music: Denny Zeitlin.

INVASION OF THE POD PEOPLE (2007, The Asylum, 85 minutes)

Cast: Melissa (Erica Roby), Samantha (Jessica Bork), Louise (Sarah Lieving), Billie (Danae Nason), Taylor (Shaley Scott), Vickland (Michael Tower), Andrew (David Schick), Casey (Amanda Ward), Alexander (Marat Glazer), Bailey (Lorraine Smith), Gianna (Teri Hunter Fruichantie), Zach (Leigh Scott), Pawn Broker (Elliot Salter), James (Justin Jones), Photographer (Nat Magnuson)

Credits: Director: Justin Jones; Screenplay: Leigh Scott; Story: Ron Magid, Jay Marks; Producer: Justin Jones, Leigh Scott; Photography: Bianca Bahena, Leigh Scott; Production Design: Steven B. Fish II; Editor: Kristen Quintrall.

INVASION USA (1952, Columbia, 73 minutes)

Cast: Vince Potter (Gerald Mohr), Carla (Peggie Castle), Mr. Ohman (Dan O'Herlihy), George Sylvester (Robert Bice), Ed Mulfory (Erik Blythe), Congressman (Wade Crosby), Bartender (Tom Kennedy), Mrs. Mulfory (Phyllis Coates), Fifth Columnist Leader (Aram Katcher), TV Newsman (Knox Manning), with Edward G. Robinson Jr., Noel Neill, Clarence A. Shoop

Credits: Director: Alfred E. Green; Screenplay, Robert Smith; Story: Robert Smith, Franz Spencer; Producers: Albert Zugsmith, Robert Smith; Photography: John L. Russell, Jr.; Art Director: James Sullivan; Supervising Editor: W. Donn Hayes; Music: Albert Glasser.

THE INVISIBLE MONSTER (1950, Republic, 12 chapters)

Cast: Lane Carson (Richard Webb), Carol Richards (Aline Towne), Burton (Lane Bradford), The Phantom Ruler (Stanley Price), Harris (John Crawford), Harry Long (George Meeker), Art (Charles Regan), Martin (Dale Van Sickel)

Credits: Director: Fred C. Brannon; Screenplay: Ronald Davidson; Associate Producer: Franklin Adreon; Photography: Ellis W. Carter; Art Director: Fred A. Ritter; Editors: Cliff Bell, Sr., Sam Starr; Music: Stanley Wilson.

IT CAME FROM OUTER SPACE (1953, Universal, 81 minutes)

Cast: John Putnam (Richard Carlson), Ellen Fields (Barbara Rush), Sheriff Matt Warren (Charles Drake), Frank Daylon (Joe Sawyer), George (Russell Johnson), Jane (Kathleen Hughes), Dave Loring (Alan Dexter), Pete Davis (Dave Willock), Dr. Snell (George Eldredge), Dr. Snell's Assistant (Brad Jackson), Toby (Warren MacGregor), Tom (George Selk), Sam (Edgar Dearing), Deputy Reed (William Pullen), Mrs. Daylon (Virginia Mullen), Dugan (Robert S. Carson), Lober (Dick Pinner), Man (Ned Davenport), Perry (Whitey Haupt)

Credits: Director: Jack Arnold; Screenplay: Harry Essex; Story: Ray Bradbury; Producer: William Alland; Photography: Clifford Stine; Special Photography: David S. Horsley; Art Directors: Bernard Herzbrun, Robert Boyle; Editor: Paul Weatherwax; Music: Joseph Gershenson.

IT CAME FROM OUTER SPACE II (1995, Sci-Fi Channel, 100 minutes)

Film Credits

Cast: Jack Putnam (Brian Kerwin), Ellen Fields (Elizabeth Peña), Stevie Fields (Jonathan Carrasco), Roy Minter (Bill McKinney), Alan Parson (Adrian Sparks), Dave Grant (Dean Norris), Linda Grant (Dawn Zeek), Carolee Minter (Lauren Tewes), Chance Madson (Mickey Jones), Kathy Parson (I'Lana B'Tiste), Zack (Jerry Giles), Ben Cully (Howard Morris), Desert Rats (Michael Ray Miller, Clement Blake), Hughy (Thomas Adcox), Mrs. Otis (Connie Sawyer), Mrs. Hughy (Bonnie Hellman), Onlooker (Richard Stay), Zack's Wife (Lauren Dow)

Credits: Director: Roger Duchowny; Screenplay: Ken and Jim Wheat, based on Harry Essex's screenplay from a Ray Bradbury story; Photography: Robert C. New; Production Design: Anthony Tremblay; Editor: Michael S. McLean; Music: Shirley Walker.

IT CONQUERED THE WORLD (1956, AIP, 71 minutes)

Cast: Dr. Paul Nelson (Peter Graves), Dr. Tom Anderson (Lee Van Cleef), Claire Anderson (Beverly Garland), Joan Nelson (Sally Fraser), Gen. Pattick (Russ Bender), Private Manuel Ortiz (Jonathan Haze), Sgt. Neil (Dick Miller), Pete Shelton (Charles B. Griffith), Ellen Peters (Karen Kadler), Monster (Paul Blaisdell)

Credits: Director-Producer: Roger Corman; Screenplay: Charles B. Griffith, credited to Lou Rusoff; Photography: Frederick West; Editor: Charles Gross; Music: Ronald Stein.

JFK (1991, Warner Bros., 206 minutes)

Cast: Jim Garrison (Kevin Costner), Rose Cheramie (Sally Kirkland), Doctor (Gary Taggart), Epileptic (Anthony Ramirez), Zapruder (Ray LePere), JFK Double (Steve Reed), Jackie Double (Jodi Farber), Nellie Connally Double (Columbia DuBose), Gov. Connally Double (Randy Means), Lou Ivon (Jay O. Sanders), Witnesses (E.J. Morris, Cheryl Penland, Jim Gough), Bar Patron (Perry R. Russo), Newsman (Mike Longman), Guy Bannister (Edward Asner), Jack Martin (Jack Lemmon), Bannister's Secretary (Ann Strub), Bill Newman (Vincent D'Onofrio), Lee Harvey Oswald (Gary Oldman), Liz Garrison (Sissy Spacek), Mattie (Pat Perkins), Jack Ruby (Brian Doyle-Murray), Numa Bertel (Wayne Knight), Bill Broussard (Michael Rooker), Susie Cox (Laurie Metcalf), Al Oser (Gary Grubbs), Marina Oswald (Beata Pozniak), Bill Williams (Gary Carter), LBJ (Tom Howard, John William Galt [voice]), David Ferrie (Joe Pesci), FBI Spokesman (Ron Jackson), Sen. Long (Walter Matthau), Jasper Garrison (Sean Stone), Virginia Garrison (Amy Long), Snapper Garrison (Scott Krueger), Elizabeth Garrison (Allison Pratt Davis), Lew Bowers (Pruitt Taylor Vince), Sgt. Harkness (Red Mitchell), Hobos (Ronald von Klaussen, John S. Davies, Michael Ozag), Clay Shaw (Tommy Lee Jones), Leopoldo (Tomas Milian), Angelo (Raul Aranas), Dean Andrews (John Candy), Prison Guard (John C. Martin), Willie O'Keefe (Kevin Bacon), Maitre d' (Henri Alciatore), George DeMorhenschildt (Willem Oltmans), Janet Williams (Gail Cronauer), Bill Williams (Gary Carter), Earlene Roberts (Roxie M. Frnka), JC Price (Zeke Mills), Sam Holland (James N. Harrell), Dodd (Ray Redd), Jean Hill (Ellen McElduff), Mary Moorman (Sally Nystuen), Julia Ann Mercer (Jo Anderson), Mercer Interrogators (Marco Perella, Edwin Neal), FBI Agents with Hill (Spain Logue, Darryl Cox), Hill Interrogator (T.J. Kennedy), Beverly Oliver (Lolita Davidovitch), Stripper (Carolina McCullough), Earl Warren (Jim Garrison), Mobster (J.J. Johnston), Oswald Imposter (Frank Whaley), Bolton Ford Dealer (R. Bruce Elliott), Man at Firing Range (Barry Chambers), Sylvia Odio (Linda Flores Wade), Will Fritz (William Larsen), TV Newsman #2 (Alec Gifford), French Reporter (Eric A. Vicini), Russian Reporter (Michael Gurievsky), British Reporter (Caroline Crosthwaite-Eyre), Garrison Receptionist (Helen Miller), Garrison Secretary (Maria Mason), DA Staff (Agnes Aurelio), Coroner (Harold Herthum), Frank (Wayne Tippit), X (Donald Sutherland), General Y (Dale Dye), Col. Reich (Norman Davis), Man with Umbrella (Errol McLendon), Gen. Lemnitzer (John Seitz), Board Room Men (Bruce Gelb, Jerry Douglas, Ryan MacDonald, Duane Grey), White House Men (George Robertson, Baxter Harris, Alex Rodzi Rodine, Sam Stoneburner), Officer Habighorst (Odin K. Langford), Newsman #3 (Bob Gunton), John Chancler (Nathan Scott), Miguel Torres (Jorge Fernandez), Jerry Johnson (John Larroquette), Jerry Johnson Sidekick (George Kelly) Stage Manager (Doug Jackson), FBI Agent at Airport (Murray Stokes), Samuel (Victor Kempster), Airport Police Sergeant (John St. Paul), Irvin F. Dymond (Roy Barnitt), Bailiff (Alvin Spicuzza), Judge Haggerty (John Finnegan), Clinton Witness (Carolyn T. Wright), Clinton Sheriff (Henry Tull III), Vernon Bundy (Walter Breaux), James Teague (Michael Skipper), Goldberg (Ron Rifkin), FBI Receptionist (Melodee Bowman), Dr. Peters (I.D. Brickman), Dr. McClelland (Joseph Nadell), Dr. Humes (Chris Robinson), Col. Finck (Peter Maloney), Bethesda Doctor (Chris Renna), Roy Truly (Johnny Brink), Kenny O'Donnell (David Benn), Dr. Rose (Hugh Feagin), General (Dalton Dear-

Appendix 1

born), Admiral Kenney (Merlyn Sexton), Pathologists (Steve F. Price Jr., Tom Bullock, Ruary O'Connell), FBI Agent at Autopsy (Christopher Kosiciuk), Shooters (John Reneau, Stanley White, Richard Rutowski), Powell (Bill Bolender), Patrolman Smith (Larry Melton), Carolyn Arnold (Carol Farabee), Bonnie Ray Williams (Willie Minor), Arnold Rowland (Ted Pennebaker), Marion Baker (Bill Pickle), Sandra Styles (Mykel Chaves), Tippet (Price Carson), Tippet Shooter (Gil Glasgow), Officer Poe (Bob Orwig), Foreman (Loys Bergeron), Reporter (Kristina Hare)

Credits: Director: Oliver Stone; Screenplay: Oliver Stone, Zachary Sklar, based on *On The Trail of the Assassins*, by Jim Garrison and *Crossfire* by Jim Marrs; Producers: Oliver Stone, A. Kitman Ho; Photography: Robert Richardson; Production Design: Victor Kempster; Music: John Williams; Editors: Joe Hutshing, Pietro Scalia.

JUNGLE HEAT (1957, United Artists, 75 minutes)

Cast: Dr. Jim Ransom (Lex Barker), Ann McRae (Mari Blanchard), Harvey Mathews (James Westerfield), Roger McRae (Glenn Langan), Kimi Grey (Miyoko Sasaki), Major Richard Grey (Rhodes Reason), Felix Agung (Glenn Dixon), Kuji (Bob Okazaki), Corporal (Jerry Frank), Kaem (Daniel Wong), Folger (Andrew Gross), Jules (Yun Kui Chang), Freight Agent Assistant (Kunio Fudimura), Expectant Mother (Leo Ezell)

Credits: Director: Howard W. Koch; Screenplay: Jameson Brewer; Producer: Aubrey Schenck; Photography: William Margulies; Production Design: Jack T. Collis; Editor: John A. Bushelman; Music: Les Baxter.

THE KAISER'S FINISH (1918, Warner Bros.)

Cast: Robert Busch/Crown Prince (Earl Schenck), Emily Busch (Claire Whitney), Kaiser (Louis Dean), Lt. Patin (John Sunderland), Carl Von Strumpf (Fred G. Hearn), Lewis Keene (Charles T. Parr), Little French Girl (Billie Wagner), Butler (Vic De Linsky)

Credits: Director: John Joseph Harvey.

THE LAKE (1998, NBC, 95 minutes)

Cast: Jackie Ivers (Yasmine Bleeth), Jeff Chapman (Linden Ashby), Maggie (Marion Ross), Herb (Robert Prosky), Steve Ivers (Stanley Anderson), Dylan (Haley Joel Osment), Louise (Caroline Lagerfelt), Denise (Susanna Thompson), Reade (Dewey Weber), Mills (Matthew Beck), Dr. Braden (Michael Winters), The Man (Carey Scott), Lt. Governor Chandler (Marc Gomes), Chief Ramirez (Geoffrey Rivas), Lt. Frank Thompson (David S. Dunard), Dr. Sanjay (Anjul Nigaia), CHP Officer (Anthony Moore), Sgt. Straughn (Blumes Tracy), Server (Katie Rich), Saleswoman (Amy Stock-Poynton), Janitor (Winston Rocha), Mayor's Aide (Carmen Mormino), Buddies (John Brandon, Fred Lerner), Beat Cop (Ben R. Scott), Forensics Guy (Thomas Crawford), Computer Guy (Artur Cybulski), Nurses (Monique Edward, Jo Farkas, Audrey Kissel), Technician (Benjamin Livingston), Bedridden Man (R.L. Talbiri), Newscaster (Holmes Osborne)

Credits: Director: David S. Jackson; Screenplay: Alan Brennert, J.D. Feigelson; Story: J.D. Feigelson; Producer: Andrew Gottlieb; Photography: Denis Maloney; Production Design: Kim Hix; Editor: Craig Ridenour; Music: Don Davis.

LEFT BEHIND (2000, Cloud Ten Pictures, 95 minutes)

Cast: Buck Williams (Kirk Cameron), Rayford Steele (Brad Johnson), Chloe Steele (Janaya Stephens), Bruce Barnes (Clarence Gilyard), Chaim Rosensweig (Colin Fox), Nicolae Carpathia (Gordon Currie), Hattie Durham (Chelsea Noble), Jonathan Stonegal (Daniel Pilon), Joshua Cothran (Tony De Santis), Dirk Burton (Jack Langedijk), Ivy Gold (Krista Bridges), Steve Plank (Thomas Hauff), Ken Ritz (Neil Crone), Carol (Sten Eirik), Gloria (Raven Dauda), Fitzhugh (Marvin Ishmael), Alan Tompkins (Philip Akin), Iren Steele (Christine MacFadyen), Raymie (Jack Manchester), Pastor Billings (Bishop T.D. Jakes), Girl on Plane (Marion Bennett), Chris (David MacNiven), Media Relations Officer (Thea Andrews), General (Terry Samuels), Old Man (Robert Levine), Soldier (Alan Rosenthal), Husband on Plane (Tufford Kennedy), Wife/Mother (Christine Donato), Elderly Woman (Fran Elliot), Old Drunk Lady (Lillian Lewis), Big Man (David Blacker), Zombie Man (Steve Behal), Young Mother in Road (Stacie Fox), Washroom Attendant (Peter Loung), Eric Miller (Chris Gillett), Tall Man (Richard Hardacre), Woman in Green Blouse (Katherine Trowell), Security Guards (Rufus Crawford, Tony Curtis Bondell), News Anchor (Sherry Hilliard), Passenger (Regan Moore), Buck's Assistant (Rebecca St. James), GNN Reporter (Bob Carlisle), UN Security Guards (Clay Crosse, Josh Penner, Marty Penner, Toby Penner), Baby (Ava Van Heerden)

Credits: Director: Vic Sarin; Screenplay: Alan McElroy, Paul Lalonde, Joe Goodman, based on *Left Behind* by Jerry Jenkins and Tim LaHaye; Producers: Peter Lalonde, Paul Lalonde, Joe Goodman, Ralph Winter; Photography: Gerigi Jiri Tirl; Production Design: Arthur W. Herriott; Music: James Covell; Editor: Michael Pacek.

LEFT BEHIND II: TRIBULATION FORCE (2002, Cloud Ten Pictures, 95 minutes)

Cast: Buck Williams (Kirk Cameron), Rayford Steele (Brad Johnson), Chloe Steele (Janaya Stephens), Bruce Barnes (Clarence Gilyard), Nicolae Carpathia (Gordon Currie), Hattie Durham (Chelsea Noble), Ivy Gold (Krista Bridges), Ben-Judah (Lubomir Myktiuk), Steve Plank (Chris Bondy), Irene Steel (Christie MacFadyen), Chris (David MacNiven), Young Man in Church (Jason Jones), Witnesses (Les Carlson, Louis Negin), House Speaker (Elias Zarou), WMF Representative (Rudy Webb), GNN Security Guard (Howard Jerome), Israeli Soldier (Lorn Eisen), Woman in Church (Jacqueline Leung), Angelic Woman (Cindy Gomez), Burned Fireman (Brian Kaulback), George (Adam David), Verna Zee (Sandi Ross), Older Man (Robert McKenna), National Guardsman (Eldridge Hyndman, Todd Faithfull), Commentator (David Ferry), Panelists (Susanne Sutchy, Karen Glave), Fire Chief (Roger Dunn), Henchman (Nicholas D. Tabarrok), Looters (Andrew Butcher, Joshua Wittig, Matt van Hart)

Credits: Director: Bill Corcoran; Screenplay: John Patus, Paul Lalonde, based on *Tribulation Force* by Jerry Jekins and Tim LaHaye; Producer: Michals D. Tabarrok, Peter Lalonde; Photography: Michael Storey; Production Design: Harold Thrasher; Editor: Michael Doherty; Music: Gary Koftinoff.

LET'S GET TOUGH (1942, Monogram, 62 minutes)

Cast: Muggs (Leo Gorcey), Danny (Bobby Jordan), Glimpy (Huntz Hall), Fritz Heinbach (Gabriel Dell), Phil (Tom Brown), Nora Stevens (Florence Rice), Pop Stevens (Robert Armstrong), Peewee (David Gorcey), Scruno (Sunshine Sammy Morrison), Skinny (Bobby Stone), Heinbach Sr. (Sam Bernard), Joe Matsui (Philip Ahn), Music Master (Jerry Bergen), Matsui (Moy Ming)

Credits: Director: Wallace Fox; Screenplay: Harvey Gates; Producers: Sam Katzman, Jack Dietz; Photography: Arthur Reed; Art Director: David Milton; Editor: Robert Golden.

LITTLE NIKITA (1988, Columbia, 98 minutes)

Cast: Jeff Grant (River Phoenix), Roy Parmenter (Sidney Poitier), Richard Grant (Richard Jenkins), Elizabeth Grant (Caroline Kava), Konstantin Karpov (Richard Bradford), Scuba (Richard Lynch), Verna McLaughlin (Loretta Devine), Barbara Kerry (Lucy Deakins), Brewer (Jerry Hardin), Bunin (Albert Fortell), Spassky (Ronald Guttman), Miguel (Jacob Vargas), Joaquin (Roberto Jimenez), Sergeant Leathers (Robb Madrid), Tom (Chez Lister), Tony (Bill Stevenson), Brett (Tom Zak), Drill Sergeant (Newell Alexander), Corporal Hogan (Ingrid Rhoads), Water-skier (Lisa McCullough), Diplomat (Richard Holden), Joe (Vojo Goric), DMV Clerk (Kim Strange), Customer (Lou Hancock), Spike (David M. Paynter), Bucky (Biff Wiff), Dolphin Trainers (Tasha Stewart, John Spafford), Dilys (Brooke Theiss), Tour Boat Guide (Jonathan McMurtry), Trolley Conductor (Charles T. Salter, Jr.), Trolley Passenger (Rick L. Nahera), Border Patrolman (Jim Parrott), TV Announcer (Arlin L. Miller), Soccer Announcer (Julio Medina).

Credits: Director: Richard Benjamin; Screenplay: John Hill, Bo Goldman; Story: Tom Musca, Terry Schwartz; Producer: Harry Gittes; Co-Producer: Art Levinson; Photography: Laszlo Kovacs; Production Design: Gene Callahan; Editor: Jacqueline Cambas; Music: Marvin Hamlisch.

LITTLE TOKYO, USA (1942, 20th Century–Fox, 64 minutes)

Cast: Michael Steele (Preston Foster), Maris Hanover (Brenda Joyce), Ito Takimura (Harold Huber), Hendricks (Don Douglas), Teru (June Duprez), Kingoro (George E. Stone), Satsuma (Abner Biberman), Marsten (Charles Tannen), Jerry (Frank Orth), Suma (Edward Soo Hoo), Shadow (Beal Wong), Mrs. Satsuma (Daisy Lee), Fujiama (Leonard Strong), Captain Wade (J. Farrell MacDonald), Oshima (Richard Loo), Okono (Victor Sen Yung), Mrs. Okono (Melle Chang), George "Sleepy" Miles (Millard Mitchell), Boy (Tommy Tucker), Announcers (Emmett Vogan, John Wald, Mel Ruick), Clerk (Lester Dorr), Police Sergeant (James Farley), Slavin (Emory Parnell), District Attorney (William Forrest), Consul (Nino Pipitone)

Credits: Director: Otto Brower; Screenplay: George Bricker; Producer: Bryan Foy; Art Directors: Richard Day, Maurice Ransford; Editor: Harry Reynolds; Music: Emil Newman.

LOOSE CHANGE 9/11: AN AMERICAN COUP (2009, Collective Minds Media, 98 minutes)

Narrator: Daniel Sunjata

Credits: Director-Screenplay-Editor: Dylan Avery; Producer: Korey Rowe; Music: Mike Cartier.

THE MANCHURIAN CANDIDATE (1962, United Artists, 126 minutes)

Appendix 1

Cast: Ben Marco (Frank Sinatra), Raymond Shaw (Laurence Harvey), Raymond's Mother (Angela Lansbury), Sen. John Dierkes Iselin (James Gregory), Dr. Yen Lo (Khigh Dhiegh), Eugenie Rose Chaney (Janet Leigh), Jocie Jordan (Leslie Parrish), Sen. Thomas Jordan (John McGiver), Chunjin (Henry Silva), Corp. Allen Melvin (James Edwards), Colonel (Douglas Henderson), Zilkov (Albert Paulsen), Berezovo (Madame Spivy), Berezovo (Nick Bolin), Secretary of Defense (Barry Kelley), Psychiatrist (Joe Adams), Holborn Gaines (Lloyd Corrigan), Medical Officer (Whit Bissell), Melvin's Wife (Mimi Dillard), Officer (Anton van Stralen), Gossfield (John Laurence), Silvers (Nicky Blair), Bobby Lembeck (Tom Lowell), Ed Mavole (Richard LaPore), Freeman (Irving Steinberg), Hiken (John Francis), Little (William Thourlby), Nominee (Robert Riordan), Gomel (Reggie Nalder), Gomel (Bess Flowers), Miss Gertrude (Miyoshi Jingu), Korean Girl (Anna Shin), Chairladies (Helen Kleeb, Maye Henderson), Reporters (Mickey Finn, Richard Norris, John Indrisano), Manager (Lou Krugg), FBI Men (Mike Masters, Tom Harris), Soprano (Mariquita Moll), Convention Chairman (Robert Burton), Secretary (Karen Norris), Nurse (Jean Vaughn), Policeman (Ray Spikers), Jiffy (Merritt Bohn), Photographer (Frank Basso), General (Harry Holcomb), Guests at Party (Julie Payne, Lana Crawford, Evelyn Byrd), Page Boy (Ray Dalley), Women in Lobby (Estelle Exterre, Mary Benoit, Rita Kenaston, Maggie Hathaway, Joan Douglas, Frances Nealy, Evelyn Byrd), Men in Lobby (Ralph Gambina, Sam Hogan), Chinese Men in Lobby (James Hagi, Lee Tung Foo, Raynum Tsukamoto)

Credits: Director: John Frankenheimer; Screenplay: George Axelrod, John Frankenheimer, based on the Richard Condon novel; Producers: George Axelrod, John Frankenheimer; Photography: Lionel Lindon; Production Design: Richard Sylbert; Editor: Ferris Webster; Music: David Amram.

MANCHURIAN CANDIDATE (2004, Paramount, 130 minutes)

Cast: Major Bennett Marco (Denzel Washington), Sen. Eleanor Shaw (Meryl Streep), Raymond Shaw (Liev Schreiber), Rosie (Kimberly Elise), Sen. Thomas Jordan (Jon Voight), Al Melvin (Jeffrey Wright), Eddie Ingram (Pablo Schreiber), Robert Baker (Anthony Mackie), Owens (Dorian Missick), Villalobos (Jose Pablo Cantillo), Wilson (Teddy Dunn), Atkins (Joaquin Perez-Campbell), Jameson (Tim Artz), Tokar (Robyn Hitchcock), Scouts (Antoine Taylor, Joseph Alessi), Scout Dad (Ray Anthony Thomas), Scoutmaster (Bill Irwin), TV Commentator (Al Franken), Gillespie (Paul Lazar), Eleanor's Aide (Danny Darst), Aides (Stephanie McBride, Molly Hickock, Victoria Haynes), Healy (Adam LeFevre), Secretary (Roger Corman), Official (Leona E. Sondreal), Vaughn Utly (Zeljko Ivanek), Florida Senator (Jim Roche), Becket (Ann Dowd), Wells (Obba Babatunde), Flores (Harry Northup), James Beattie Howard (Himself), Rawlins (Walter Mosley), Gordy (Gordon Brummer), Media Icon (Gayle King), Newscasters (Brad Holbrook, Stacey Newsome Santiago, Kristen Shaughnessy, Prue Lewarne, Forrest Sawyer, Ukee Washington, Ed Crane, Kaity Tong, Roma Torre-Lopez), Tyler Prentiss (William Meisle), Sen. Shaw (Dan Olmstead), Arabic Woman (Sakina Jaffrey), Atticus Noyle (Simon McBurney), Gen. Sloan (Charles Napier), Gen. Wilson (Robert Castle), Rear Admiral Glick (John Aprea), Robert Arthur (Tom Stechschulte), Mrs. Arthur (Jane DeNoble), Jocelyn Jordan (Vera Farmiga), David Donovan (Jude Ciccolella), Mark Whiting (Dean Stockwell), Jay Johnston (John Bedford Lloyd), Agent Anderson (David Keeley), Secret Service Agents (Christopher M. Russo, Michael C. Pierce), Col. Howard (Ted Levine), Col. Garret (Miguel Ferrer), Transcribers (Marin Ireland, Glenn Hartell), Night Clerk (Tracey Walter), Mirella Freeman (Alyson Renaldo), Rosie's Cousin (Edwidge Danticat), Rosie's Cousin's Mentor (Kenny Utt), Delp (Bruno Ganz), Reporters (Enrique Correa, David Neumann, Neda Armian), Security (Paul Johnson), FBI Agents (James McCauley, Be Be Winans, Darrell Larson), Agent Volk (Kate Valk), Comedian (Beau Sia), Library Clerk (Duana Butler), Library Patron (Big Jim Wheeler), Jordan's Aides (Lauren Roselli, Stephen Richardson), Rosie's Sidekick (Shing Ka), Kid (Malcolm Simpson), Kids in Play (Cassius Wilkinson, Josephine Demme, Gabriela Fung, Denzel Dellahoussaye, Aaron Scoenfeld, Geovonne Long, Jonathan Borst, Michael Shehata), Gov. Nelson (Tom Chapin), Churchgoer (Lewis "Jiggs" Walker), Jimmy (Joey Perillo), Guy with Shades (Buzz Kilman), Arthur's Mother (Marie Runyon), Arthur's Children (Eliza Simpson, Julie Adamy), Party Director (Andre Blake), Celebrity Soldier (Tymberly Canale Harris), Shaw Aides (Lilly McDowell, Josh Elrod), Bachman (Craig Branam), Pundits (Sidney Lumet, Reno, Anna Deavere Smith, Roy Blount Jr., Fab 5 Freddy)

Credits: Director: Jonathan Demme; Screenplay: Daniel Pyne, Dean Georgaris, based on George Axelrod's screenplay, based upon *The Manchurian Candidate* by Richard Condon; Producer: Tina Sinatra, Scott Rudin, Jonathan Demme, Ilona Herzberg; Photography: Tak Fujimoto; Production

Film Credits

Design: Kristi Zea; Editor: Carol Littleton, Craig McKay; Music: Rachel Portman.

THE MASTER RACE (1944, RKO, 96 minutes)
Cast: Von Beck (George Coulouris), Major Phil Carson (Stanley Ridges), Helena (Osa Massen), Andrei (Carl Esmond), Nina (Nancy Gates), Bartoc (Morris Carnovsky), Frank (Lloyd Bridges), Altmeier (Eric Feldary), Mrs. Varin (Helen Beverly), Capt. William Forsythe (Gavin Muir), Katry (Paul Guilfoyle), Sgt. O'Farrell (Richard Nugent), Schmidt (Ludwig Donath), John (Herbert Rudley), Baby (Gigi Perreau), George Rudan (Merrill Rodin), Matalie Rudan (Helene Thimig), Officers (Paul Kruger, George Blagoi, William Martin, Eric Mack, Fred Somers, Albin Robeling, Naum Coster, Gabriel Leonoff, Axel Anderson), Civilians (Max Linder, Virgil Johansen, Charles Legneur, Hans Hopf, Jack Davis, Ernest Brengk), Captain (Alan Ward), Pole (Bert Moorhouse), Alex (Sammy Blum), Grunning (John Mylong), Sentry (Bob Stevenson), Lieutenant (Harry Clay), Mrs. Matchet (Marie Lund), Porto (Russ Hopton), Lantz (Bryant Washburn), Haldec (Walter Soderling), Soldiers (Jimmy Jordan, Bob Robinson), Peter (Frank Mayo)
Credits: Director: Herbert J. Biberman; Screenplay: Anne Froelick, Rowland Leigh, Herbert J. Biberman; Story: Herbert J. Biberman; Producer: Robert Golden: Photography: Russell Metty; Art Directors: Albert S. D'Agostino, Jack Okey; Editor: Ernie Leadley; Music: C. Bakaleinikoff.

THE MILLION EYES OF SUMURU (1967, AIP, 86 minutes)
Cast: Nick West (George Nader), Tommy Carter (Frankie Avalon), Sumuru (Shirley Easton), Col. Baisbrook (Wilfrid Hyde-White), President Boong (Klaus Kinski), Louise (Patti Chandler), Mikki, (Salli Sachse) Erna (Ursula Bank) Zoe (Krista Nell) Helga (Maria Rohm), Inspector Koo (Paul Chang), Kitty (Essie Huang), Col. Medika (John Fong), Sumuru Guard (Denise Vareux, Mary Cheng, Jill Hamilton, Lisa Gray, Christine Lok, Margaret Cheung, Louise Lee)
Credits: Director: Lindsay Shonteff; Screenplay: Kevin Kavanagh; Story: Peter Welbeck, based on the stories by Sax Rohmer; Producer: Harry Alan Towers; Cinematography: John von Kotze; Art Director: Scott MacGregor; Editor: Alan Morrison; Music: Johnny Scott.

MINISTRY OF FEAR (1944 Paramount, 84 or 86 minutes)
Cast: Stephen Neale (Ray Milland), Carla Hilfe (Marjorie Reynolds), Willi Hilfe (Carl Esmond), Mrs. Bellane (Hillary Brooke), Prentice (Percy Waram), Cost (Dan Duryea), Dr. Forrester (Alan Napier), Rennit (Erskine Sanford), Newland (Thomas Louden), First Mrs. Bellane (Aminta Dyne), Blind Man (Eustace Wyatt), Martha Penteel (Mary Field), Newby (Byron Foulger), Dr. Morton (Lester Matthews), Mrs. Merrick (Helena Grant), Lady with Floppy Hat (Grayce Hampton), Woman at Admission Gate (Ottola Nesmith), Cake Buyer (Connie Leon), Cake Booth Lady (Jessica Newcombe), Fat Lady (Evelyn Beresford), Vicar (Frank Dawson), Mother (Anne Curson), Delivery Man (Harry Allen), Railroad Agent (Cyril Delevanti), Scotland Yard Men (Eric Wilton, Boyd Irwin, Colin Kelly, Frank Baker), Police Clerk (Bruce Carruthers), Officer (Arthur Blake), Executive (Edward Fielding), Bobby (David Clyde), Air Raid Warden (Wilson Benge), Men in Tailor Shop (Clive Morgan, George Broughton, Olaf Hytten), Maid (Hilda Plowright), Porter (Leonard Carey), with Frank Leigh, Francis Sayles, Matthew Boulton, Edmond Russell
Credits: Director: Fritz Lang; Screenplay: Seton I. Miller, based on the novel by Graham Greene; Associate Producer: Seton I. Miller; Photography: Henry Sharp; Art Direction: Hans Dreier, Hal Pereira; Editor: Archie Marshek; Music: Victor Young.

MISSION TO MOSCOW (1943, Warner Bros., 123 minutes)
Cast: Joseph E. Davies (Walter Huston), Mrs. Marjorie Davies (Ann Harding), Maksim Litivinov (Oscar Homolka), Freddie (George Tobias), Molotov (Gene Lockhart), Emien Davies (Eleanor Parker), Paul (Richard Travis), Major Kamenev (Helmut Dantine), Vyshinsky (Victor Francen), Von Ribbentrop (Henry Daniell), Mrs. Litvinov (Barbara Everest), Winston Churchill (Dudley Field Malone), Krestinsky (Roman Bohnen), Tanya Litvinov (Maria Palmer), Col. Faymonville (Moroni Olsen), Loy Henderson (Minor Watson), Mikhail Kalinin (Vladimir Sokoloff), Dr. Botkin (Maurice Schwartz), Madame Molotov (Frieda Inescort), Spendler (Jerome Cowan), Bukharin (Konstantin Shayne), Stalin (Manart Kippen), Lady Chilston (Kathleen Lockhart), Timoshenko (Kurt Katch), Dr. Schact (Felix Basch), Judge Ulrich (Frank Puglia), Grinko (John Abbott), Cordell Hull (Charles Trowbridge), Haile Selassie (Leigh Whipper), Paul Van Zeeland (Georges Renavent), Anthony Eden (Clive Morgan), Pierre Laval (Alex Chirva, Mrs. Churchill (Doris Lloyd), Member of Parliament (Olaf Hytten), Commentator (Art

Appendix 1

Gilmore), Vincent Massey (Don Clayton), Reporters (Duncan Renaldo, Nino Bellini), Ferdinand Schumann-Heink, Rolf Lindau, Peter Michael, George Davis, Jean Del Val), Speaker (Emory Parnell), Irish American (Pat O'Malley), Englishman (Mark Strong), Frenchman (Albert D'Arno), German (Rudolf Steinbeck, Richard Ryen, Ernest Golm), Italian (Gino Corrado), Southerner (Glenn Strange), Delegate Van deWater (Oliver Cross), Raymond (Ray Walker), President Roosevelt (Jack Young), Steward (Ernst Hausserman), Reporters (Frank Faylen, John Maxwell, Joseph Crehan), Young Men (Ross Ford, Warren Douglas), Friends (George Lessey, Wallis Clark), Guard (Hans Schumm), German Wife (Lisa Golm), Schufeldt (Henry Victor), Train Announcer (Louis Arco), Conductor (Alfred Zeisler), German Businessman (Erwin Kaiser), Naval Attaché (Pierre Watkin), Diplomat (Edward Van Sloan), Russian Women (Esther Zeitlin, Nina Blagol), Flower Girl (Tanya Somova), Soviet Official (Nikolai Gelikhovsky), Barkov (Michael Visaroff), Spadebeard (Sam Savitsky), OGPU Men (Nick Kobliansky, Gabriel Leonoff, Alex Akimoff, George Gleboff, Mike Tellegan, Adia Kuznetzoff, Demetrius Alexis, Henry Guttman), Soldier (Robert Baikoff), Petya (Mischa Westfall), Elderly Woman (Elizabeth Archer), Russian Servant (Rosa Margot), Natasha (Valya Terry), Ski Troop Lieutenant (Sandor Szabo), Mrs. Molotov (Lala DeTolly), Tukhachevsky (Ivan Triesault), Yagoda (Daniel Ocko), Radek (David Hoffman), Lord Chilston (Lumsden Hare), Shigemitsu (Peter Chong), Von Schulenberg (Robert C. Fischer), Trotsky (Sam Goldenberg)

Credits: Director: Michael Curtiz; Screenplay: Howard Koch; Producer: Robert Buckner; Photography: Bert Glennon; Art Director: Carl Jules Weyl; Editor: Owen Marks; Music: Max Steiner.

MY SON JOHN (1952, Paramount, 122 minutes)
Cast: Lucille Jefferson (Helen Hayes), Stedman (Van Heflin), Dan Jefferson (Dean Jagger), John Jefferson (Robert Walker), Dr. Carver (Minor Watson), Father O'Dowd (Frank McHugh), Chuck Jefferson (Richard Jaeckel), Ben Jefferson (James Young), Agent Bedford (Todd Karns), Drycleaner (Fred Sweeney), Government Worker (Douglas Evans)

Credits: Director-Producer-Story: Leo McCarey; Screenplay: Myles Connolly, Leo McCarey; Adaptation: John Lee Mahin; Photography: Harry Stradling; Art Directors: Hal Pereira, William Flannery; Editor: Marvin Coil; Music: Robert Emmett Dolan.

NO WAY OUT (1987, MGM, 106 minutes)
Cast: Commander Tom Farrell (Kevin Costner), David Brice (Gene Hackman), Susan Atwell (Sean Young), Scott Pritchard (Will Patton), Senator Duvall (Howard Duff), Sam Hessiman (George Dzundza), Major Donovan (Jason Bernard), Nina Beka (Iman), Marshall (Fred Dalton Thompson), Kevin O'Brien (Leon Russom), Mate (Dennis Burkley), Contras (Marshall Bell, Chris D.), Courier (Michael Shilio), Cup Breaker (Nicholas Worth), Ensign Fox (Leo Geter), Bellboy (Matthew Barry), Lt. Chadway (John Diaquino), Seaman Dufor (Peter Bell), Helmsman (Tony Webster)

Credits: Director: Roger Donaldson; Screenplay: Robert Garland; Based on *The Big Clock* by Kenneth Fearing; Producers: Laura Ziskin, Robert Garland; Photography: John Alcott; Production Design: Dennis Washington; Editor: Neil Travis; Music: Maurice Jarre.

THE ODESSA FILE (1974, Columbia Pictures, 130 minutes)
Cast: Peter Miller (Jon Voight), Roschmann (Maximilian Schell), Frau Miller (Maria Schell), Sigi (Mary Tamm), Klaus Wenzer (Derek Jacobi), David Porath (Peter Jeffrey), Gustav Mackensen (Klaus Lowitch), Alfred Oster (Kurt Meisel), Gen. Glücks (Hannes Messemer), Israeli General (Garfield Morgan), Simon Wiesenthal (Schmuel Rodensky), Werner Deilman (Ernst Schroder), Kunik (Günter Stract), Franz Bayer (Noel Willman), Marx (Martin Brandt), Dr. Schultz (Hans Caninenberg), Shapira (Heinz Ehrenfreund), Colonel (Alexander Golling), Salomon Tauber (Towje Kleiner), Gen. Greifer (Günter Meisner), Karl Braun (Gunnar Moller), Frau Wenzer (Elisabeth Neumann-Viertel), Gisela (Christine Wodetzky), Hoffman (Werner Bruhns), Medal Shop Proprietor (Til Kiwe), Lawyer (George Marischka), Wehrmacht Captain (Joachim Dietmar Mues), Landlord (Hans Wyprachtiger), Tauber's Voice (Cyril Shaps)

Credits: Director: Ronald Neame; Screenplay: Kenneth Ross, George Markstein, based on the novel by Fredrick Forsythe; Producer: John Woolf; Photography: Oswald Morris; Production Design: Rolf Zehetbauer; Editor: Ralph Kemplen; Music: Andrew Lloyd Webber.

THE OSTERMAN WEEKEND (1983, 20th Century–Fox, 102 minutes)
Cast: John Tanner (Rutger Hauer), Lawrence Fassett (John Hurt), Bernard Osterman (Craig T. Nelson), Richard Tremayne (Dennis Hopper), Joseph Cardone (Chris Sarandon), Ali Tanner (Meg Foster), Virginia Tremayne (Helen Shaver), Betty Cardone (Cassie Yates), Stennings (Sandy McPeak), Steve Tanner (Christopher Starr), Maxwell Danforth (Burt Lancaster).

Film Credits

Credits: Director: Sam Peckinpah; Screenplay: Alan Sharp, based on the book by Robert Ludlum; Producers: Peter S. Davis, William N. Panzer; Photography: John Coquillon; Editors: Edward Abroms, David Rawlins; Music: Lalo Schifrin.

PACK OF LIES (1987, CBS, 100 minutes)
Cast: Barbara Jackson (Ellen Burstyn), Helen Shaeffer (Teri Garr), Stewart (Alan Bates), Bob Jackson (Ronald Hines), Peter Shaeffer (Daniel Benzali), Powell (Peter Schofield), Malcolm (David Corti), Thelma (Margot Leicester), Sally (Jackie Downey), Club Manager (Peter Hughes), Waiter (Bruce Morrison), Telephone Man (Tim Barker), Vegetable Truck Man (Alan Renwick), Police Gas Man (Terry John)
Credits: Director: Anthony Page; Screenplay: Ralph Gallup, based on the play by Hugh Whitemore; Producer: Robert Halmi; Photography: Kenneth MacMillan; Production Design: Tony Curtis; Editor: Chris Wimble; Music: Stanley Myers.

THE PARALLAX VIEW (1974, Paramount, 102 minutes)
Cast: Joe Frady (Warren Beatty), Bill Rintels (Hume Cronyn), Austin Tucker (William Daniels), Lee Carter (Paula Prentiss), Sheriff Wicker (Kelly Thordsen), Deputy (Earl Hindiman), Will (Kenneth Mars), Linder (Chuck Waters), Jack Younger (Walter McGinn), Sen. Hammond (Jim Davis), Sen. Carroll (Bill Joyce), Assassin (Bill McKinney), Tucker's Aide (William Jordan), Spokesmen (Stacy Keach, Sr., Ford Rainey), Chrissy (JoAnne Harris), Schecter (Ted Gehring), Shirley (Lee Pulford), Gale (Doria Cook), George Hammond (Jim Davis), Organist (Joan Lemmo), Joy Holder (Alma Beltran), Goon (Richard Bull), Stewardess (Suzanne Cohane), Girl (Ronda Copland), Scoletta (Joseph Di Reda), Women (Patsy Garrett, Penelope Gillette), Sen. Gillingham (Robert Lieb), Herbert Moon (William Swan), Buster Himan (John S. Ragin), Lutz (Vernon Weddle)
Credits: Director-Producer: Alan J. Pakula; Screenplay: David Giler, Lorenzo Semple, Jr.; Photography: Gordon Willis; Production Design: George Jenkins; Editor: John W. Wheeler; Music: Michael Small.

PATRIA (1917, Pathé International, 15 chapters)
Cast: Patria Channing (Irene Castle), with Warner Oland
Credits: Directors: Paul Duckey, Leopold Wharton, Jacques Jaccard; Writers: Louis Joseph Vance, Charles Goddard; Producer: William Randolph Hearst.

THE PRESIDENT VANISHES (1935, Paramount, 83 minutes)
Cast: President Stanley (Arthur Byron), Secretary of War Lewis Wardell (Edward Arnold), Chick Moffat (Paul Kelly), Mrs. Alma Stanley (Peggy Conklin), Val Orcott (Andy Devine), Mrs. Stanley (Janet Beecher), Harris Brownell (Osgood Perkins), D.L. Voorman (Sidney Blackmer), Lincoln Lee (Edward Ellis), Mrs. Orcott (Irene Franklin), Richard Norton (Charles Grapewin), Sally Voorman (Rosalind Russell), Vice-President Molleson (Robert McWade), Edward Cullen (DeWitt Jennings), Martin Drew (Walter Kingsford), Roger Grant (Douglas Wood), Corcoran (Charles Richman), Skinner (Paul Harvey), Kramer (Harry Woods), Nolan (Tommy Dugan), Mrs. Delling (Martha Mayo), Senators (Charles K. French, William Worthington, William J. Holmes, Charles Meakin, Art Howard, Ed Lewis, Ed Mortimer, Emmett King, Edgar Sherrod, Henry Herbert), with Clara Blandick
Credits: Director: William A. Wellman; Screenplay: Carey Wilson, Cedric Worth; Producer: Walter Wanger; Photography: Barney McGill; Art Director: Sidney M. Ullman; Editor: Hanson Fritch.

THE PUPPET MASTERS (1994, Hollywood Pictures, 109 minutes)
Cast: Andrew Nivens (Donald Sutherland), Sam Nivens (Eric Thal), Mary Sefton (Julie Warner), Holland (Keith David), Graves (Will Patton), Jarvis (Richard Belzer), President Douglas (Tom Mason), Ressler (Yaphet Kotto), Viscott (Gerry Bamman), Culbertson (Sam Anderson), Gidding (J. Patrick McCormack), General Morgan (Marshall Bell), Greenberg (Nicholas Cascone), Barnes (Bruce Jarchow), Higgins (Benjamin Mouton), Vargas (David Pasquesi), Hawthorne (Andrew Robinson), Jeff (Benj Thall), Casey (Bo Sharon), Mike (Nick Browne), Miss Haines (Donna Garrett), Doctor (William Wellman, Jr.), Technicians (Elizabeth Sung, Dinah Lenney), Operator (Tom Dugan), Brande (Dale Dye), Lt. Abbey (John C. Cooke), Infantryman (Fabio Urena), Captain Early (Michael Shamus Wiles), Soldiers (Todd Bryant, Don James, J. Marvin Campbell), Merging Soldier (James Pearson), Danny (Evan C. Morris), Slugged Woman (K.T. Voght), Anchorwoman (Dale Harimoto), Wendy Markham (Alexa Jago), Vince Hayward (Eric Briant Wells), Infected Boy (Scott Armstrong), Newscaster (Marianne Curan), Graves Assistant (Katy Summerland)
Credits: Director: Stuart Orme; Screenplay: Ted Elliott, Terry Rossio, David S. Goyer, based on Robert A. Heinlein's *The Puppet Masters*; Producer:

Appendix 1

Ralph Winter; Photography: Clive Tickner; Production Design: Daniel A. Lomino; Editor: William Goldenberg; Music: Colin Towns.

THE QUILLER MEMORANDUM (1966, 20th Century–Fox, 105 minutes)

Cast: Quiller (George Segal), Pol (Alec Guinness), Oktober (Max von Sydow), Inge (Senta Berger), Gibbs (George Sanders), Weng (Robert Helpmann), Gibb's Associate (Robert Flemyng), Hengel (Peter Carsten), Headmistress (Edith Schneider), Hassler (Gunter Meisner), Jones (Robert Stass), Grauber (Ernst Walder), Oktober's Men (John Rees, Philip Madoc)

Credits: Director: Michael Anderson; Screenplay: Harold Pinter, based on the novel by Adam Hall; Producer: Ivan Foxwell; Photography: Erwin Hillier; Art Director: Maurice Carter; Editor: Frederick Wilson; Music: John Barry.

RED DAWN (1984, United Artists, 114 minutes)

Cast: Jed (Patrick Swayze), Robert (C. Thomas Howell), Erica (Lea Thompson), Matt (Charlie Sheen), Daryl (Darren Dalton), Toni (Jennifer Grey), Danny (Brad Savage), Aardvark (Doug Toby), Mason (Ben Johnson), Eckert (Harry Dean Stanton), Bella (Ron O'Neal), Strelnikov (William Smith), Bratchenko (Vladek Sheybal), Andy (Powers Boothe), Teasdale (Frank McRae), Morris (Roy Jenson), Aardvark's Father (Pepe Serna), Mayor Bates (Lane Smith), Nicaraguan Captain (Judd Omen), Students (Michael D'Agosta, Johelen Carleton), Soldiers (George Ganchev, Waldemar Kalinowski), Yuri (Sam Slovick), Stepan Gorsky (Radames Pera), Mrs. Mason (Lois Kimbrell), Alicia (Elan Oberon), Man on Pole (Harley Christensen), Rat Girl (Tacy Norwood), Tank Survivor (Fred Rexer), Tank Crews (Michael Meisner, Victor Meisner), Rachel (Raquel Provance), Russian Sergeants (Vojo Goric, Ben Schick), KGB Men (Gene Scherer, Tom Ireland), Soldier (Christopher Janczar), Barnes (Phil Mead), Men at Drive-In (Sam Dodge, Ben Zeller, Dan Sparks), KGB Major (George Fisher), Political Officer (Zitto Kazann), Door Gunner (Chuk Besher), Cuban Crew Chief (Jay Dee Ruybal), Firing Squad Officer (Pacho Lane), Latin Soldier (Julius L. Meyer)

Credits: Director: John Milius; Screenplay: Kevin Reynolds, John Milius; Story: Kevin Reynolds; Producers: Buzz Feitshans, Barry Beckerman; Photography: Ric Waite; Production Design: Jackson DeGovia; Editor: Thom Noble; Music: Basil Poledouris.

THE RED MENACE (1949, Republic, 87 minutes)

Cast: Narrator (Lloyd G. Davies), Bill Jones (Robert Rockwell), Nina Petrovka (Hanne Axman), Yvonne Kraus (Betty Lou Gerson), Mollie O'Flaherty (Barbra Fuller), Henry Solomon (Shepard Menken), Earl Partridge (Lester Luther), Jack Tyler (William J. Lally), Inspector O'Toole (Lloyd G. Davies), Reachi (Norman Budd), Father O'Leary (Leo Cleary), Mrs. O'Flaherty (Kay Riehl), Riggs (William Martel), Martin Vejac (James Harrington), Sam Wright (Duke Wiliams), Tom Wright (Napoleon Simpson), Sheriff (Robert Purcell), Benson (Royal Raymond), Schultz (Gregg Martell), Boy (Jimmie Hawkins), Chandler (Marshall Bradford), Riley (John Pimley), Carnival Man (Jim Hayward), Gas Station Owner (George Taylor), Girl in Classroom (Marilyn Criss Kraft), People in Real Estate Office (Bill Free, Gail Bonney), People in Classroom (Theodore T. Sackett, Ralph Loretz, Joe Wallace), Policemen (Arthur Millan, William Hitch), Proprietors (Oscar Weidhaas, Mary DeGolyer), Office Manager (Bernie Marcus), With: Joe Duval, Jean Leighton, Harry Scher, Bill Hudson

Credits: Director: R.G. Springsteen; Screenplay: Albert DeMond, Gerald Geraghty; Story: Albert DeMond; Executive Producer: Herbert J. Yates; Photography: John MacBurnie; Art Director: Frank Arrigo; Editor: Harry Keller.

RED NIGHTMARE (1962, Warner Bros., 29 minutes)

Cast: Jerry Donovan (Jack Kelly), Helen Donovan (Jeanne Cooper), Bill Martin (Peter Brown), Linda Donovan (Pat Woodell), Judge (Andrew Duggan), Russian Officer (Peter Breck), Pete (Robert Conrad), Prosecutor (Mike Road), Narrator (Jack Webb), Major Barnett (Philip Carey), Counter Man (Ashley Cowan), Jimmy Donovan (Ronnie Dapo), Customer (Chad Everett), Sally Donovan (Carol Nicholson), Machinist (Louis Quinn), Ralph (William Reynolds), Sergeant (Van Williams)

Credits: Director: George Waggner; Screenplay: Vincent Fotre; Producers: William L. Hendricks, Jack Webb; Cinematography: Robert Hoffman; Art Director: Carl Macauley; Editor: Folmar Blangsted; Music: Howard Jackson, William Lava.

RENDITION (2007, New Line Cinema, Level 1 Entertainment, 122 minutes)

Cast: Anwar El-Ibrahimi (Omar Metwally), Isabella Fields El-Ibrahimi (Reese Witherspoon), Douglas Freeman (Jake Gyllenhaal), Corrine Whitman (Meryl Streep), Sen. Hawkins (Alan Arkin), Safiya (Hadar Ratzon), Jeremy El-Ibrahimi (Aramis Knight), Nuru El-Ibrahimi (Rosie Malek-Yonan),

Khalid El-Emin (Moa Khouas), Fatima Fawal (Zineb Oukach), Abasi Fawal (Igal Naor), Lina Fawal (Laila Mrabti), William Dixon (David Fabrizio), Bahi (Driss Rouhke), Lee Mayer (J.K. Simmons), Lars Whitman (Bob Gunton), Security Guard (Del Hunter-White), Prison Guard (Boubker Fahmi), Samia Fawal (Nava Ziv), Layla Fawal (Reymond Amsellem), Said Abdel Aziz (Simon Abkarian), Samantha (Wendy Phillips), Alan Smith (Peter Sarsgaard), Sen. Lewis' Aide (Christian Martin), Hamadi (Hassam Ghancy), Omar Adnan (Najib Oudghiri), Rashid Salimi (Omar Salim), Housekeeper (Bunnie Rivera), Student Leader (Noureddine Aberdine), Hamadi's Second in Command (Mohamed El Habib Ahamdane), Khalid's Grandmother (Fatima Reguragui), Sharon Lopez (Anne Betancourt), Al Jazeera Newscaster (Salaheddine Ben Chegra), French Tourist (Natalia Zonova), Hospital Doctor (Hassan Hammouche), Male Security Guard (Thomas Raley), CIA Agents (Skylar Adams, Tim Thomas, Richard Dorton), Tea House Owner (Abdellah Lamsabhi), Hamid (Lasfar Abdelghani), CIA Staffer (Floella Benjamin), Cape Town Businessmen (Akram Allie, Michael Dube, Pope Jerrod, Anthony Watterson), Helpful Woman (Marisia Moreno), Prison Soldier (Tanane Boussif), Taxi Driver (Lotfi Hassan), Donkey Cart Driver (El Oualid Mezouar), Capitol Hill Police (Craig Johnson, Wade Harlan), Reception Guests (Derek Hansen, Steve Tom, Robert Clotworthy), Senate Staffer (Muna Otari), CNN Announcer (Nick Toth), Todd Hamilton (David Randolph), Khalid's Brother (Mustapha Louchou)

Credits: Director: Gavid Hood; Screenplay: Kelley Sane; Producer: Steve Golin, Marcus Viscidi; Photography: Dione Beebe; Production Design: Barry Robison; Editor: Megan Gill; Music: Paul Hepker, Mark Kilian.

RISING SUN (1993, 20th Century–Fox, 129 minutes)

Cast: John Conno (Sean Connery), Web Smith (Wesley Snipes), Tom Graham (Harvey Keitel), Eddie Sakamura (Cary-Hiroyuki Tagawa), Bob Richmond (Kevin Anderson), Yoshida-san (Mako), Sen. John Morton (Ray Wise), Ishihara (Stan Egi), Philips (Stan Shaw), Jingo Asakuma (Tia Carrere), Willy "The Weasel" Wilhelm (Steve Buscemi), Cheryl Lynn Austin (Tatjana Patitz), Greg (Peter Crombie), Rick (Sam Lloyd), Julia (Alexandra Powers), Chief Olson/Interrogator (Daniel Von Bargen), Zelly (Lauren Robinson), Hsieh (Amy Hill), Jim Donaldson (Tom Dahlgren), Tanaka (Clyde Kusatsu), Fred Hoffman (Michael Chapman), Japanese Negotiators (Joey Miyashima, Nelson Mashita), Lauren (Tamara Tunie), Doorman Guard (Tony Ganios), Jeff (James Oliver Bullock), TV Panel (Michael Kinsley, Eleanor Clift, Clarence Page, Pat Choate), Moderator (Steven C. Clemons), Ken Shubik (Dan Butler), Guard (Toshishiro Obata), Redhead (Tylyn John), Blonde (Shelley Michelle), Interviewer (Michele Ruiz), Reporter (Patricia Ayame Thomson), Yakuza Members (Jeff Imada, Max Kirishima), Brothers (Larry O. Williams, Jr., Scot Anthony Robinson, Keith Leon Hickles), Guy at Window (Carl A. McGee), Mean Face (Quincy Adams, Jr.), Big Guy (Cecil Brown), Receptionist (Meagen Fay), Club Manager (Max Grodenchik), Valet (Gunnar Peterson), Morton's Aide (Jessica Tuck), Elevator Guard (Masa Watanabe), Grandma Otis (Minnie Summers Lindsey), Iwabuchi (Paul Fujimoto), Tempura Chef (Kenji), Cop (Michael Leopard), Nakamoto Yakuza (Tak Kubota, Fumio Demura, Tadashi Yamashita, Dennis Ota, Raymond Kitamura), Girl at Eddie's Party (Rita Weibel), Girl in Karaoke Western (Susan Iida), Taiko Drum Master (Seiichi Tanaka)

Credits: Director: Philip Kaufman: Screenplay: Philip Kaufman, Michael Crichton, Michael Backes, based on *Rising Sun* by Crichton; Producer: Peter Kaufman; Photography: Michael Chapman; Production Design: Dean Tavoularis; Editors: Stephen A. Rotter, William S. Scharf; Music: Toru Takemitsu.

ROBIN COOK'S INVASION (1997, NBC, 190 minutes)

Cast: Beau Stark (Luke Perry), Cassy Winslow (Rebecca Gayheart), Dr. Sheila Moran (Kim Cattrall), Pitt (Christopher Orr), Dr. McCoy (Michael Warren), Det. Walt Kemper (Jon Polito), North (Neal McDonough), Nancy Ochoa (Rosana DeSoto), Ochoa (Castulo Guerra), John Ochoa (Louis Crugnali), Andi Vaughn (Maria Celedonio), Dr. Hayden (Stephen Joyce), Mike Landry (Tim DeKay), Leah (Ginny Harman), Denice (Denice Duff), Husband (Ken Kolb), Orderly (Mark deMichele), Medical Examiner (Brian Brophy), Walter Kirkland (Bill Rose), Sgt. Kinsella (M. Richard Greene), Pete (Sam Smiley), Ed Partridge (Dan Danielson), Security Chief (Michael Emanuel), Secretary (Adelina Sindhul), Weller (David Akin), Police Captain (Sanford Gibbons), Sgt. Hoover (John Mack), Paramedic (Larry Jones), Father Nightmare (Terry James), Mechanic (Ken Clark), Girl's Mother (Dawn M. Davis), Cop (George Dobbs), Reporter (Alfred C. Cerullo), Boy (Michael Wayne), with Chuck McCann, Jason Schombing

Credits: Director: Armand Mastroianni; Writer; Rockne S. O'Bannon; Story: Robin Cook; Producers: Jeff Morton, Randy Sutter; Photography: Bryan England; Production Design: Donald Lee Harris; Editor: Scott Vickrey; Music: Don Davis.

ROLLOVER (1981, IPC Films, 115 minutes)
Cast: Lee Winters (Jane Fonda), Hubb Smith (Kris Kristofferson), Maxwell Emory (Hume Cronyn), Roy Lefcourt (Josef Sommer), Sal Naftari (Bob Gunton), Fewster (Macon McCalman), Gil Hovey (Ron Frazier), Betsy Okamoto (Jodi Long), Warner Ackerman (Crocker Nevin), Lipscomb (Marvin A. Chatinover), Whitelaw (Ira B. Wheeler), Khalid (Paul Hecht), Hishan (Norman Snow), Lee's Maid (Nelly Hoyos), Mrs. Emery (Lansdale Chatfield), Mrs. Fewster (Sally Sockwell), Fewster's Daughters (Martha Plimpton, Gaby Glatzer), Dodds (Howard Erskine), Limo Driver (Michael Fiorillo), Newscaster (Marilyn Berger), Mystery Man (Alex Wipf), Older Arab (Ahmed Yacoubi), Faculty Member (Charles Laiken), Nightwatchmen (Stanley Simmonds, E. Brian Dean), Bank Officials (James Sutton, Joel Steadman), Charles Winters (Garrison Lane), Voice (Michael Prince), Secretary (Nina Reeves), Hubb Smith's Secretary (Carolyn Larson), Telex Operator (Rebecca Brooks), Traders (Richard Barbour, Danny Redmon, Eric Bethancourt, Steve Bullard, Neela Eriksen, Lawrence Sellers, Ernie Garrett, Art Hansen, Ira Lewis, Sharon Casey, Bernie Racehelle), Dinner Guests (Keith Eager, Dave Ellsworth), Piano Player (Art Lambert)
Credits: Director: Alan J. Pakula; Screenplay: David Shaber; Story: David Shaber, Howard Kohn, David Weir; Producer: Bruce Gilbert; Photography: Giuseppe Rotunno; Production Design: George Jenkins; Editor: Evan Lottman; Music: Michael Small.

ROSEMARY'S BABY (1968, Paramount, 138 minutes)
Cast: Rosemary Woodhouse (Mia Farrow), Guy Woodhouse (John Cassavetes), Minnie Castevet (Ruth Gordon), Roman Castevet (Sidney Blackmer), Dr. Sapirstein (Ralph Bellamy), Edward Hutchins (Maurice Evans), Terry (Angela Dorian), Laura-Louise (Patsy Kelly), Mr. Nicklas (Elisha Cook, Jr.), Elise Dunstan (Emmaline Henry), Dr. Hill (Charles Grodin), Grace Cardiff (Hanna Landy), Dr. Shand (Philip Leeds), Diego (D'Urville Martin), Mrs. Gilmore (Hope Summers), Rosemary's Girlfriends (Marianne Gordon, Wendy Wagner)
Credits: Screenwriter-Director: Roman Polanski; Based on Ira Levin's novel; Producer: William Castle; Photography: William Fraker; Art Director: Joel Schiller; Production Design: Richard Sylbert; Music: Christopher Komeda; Editor: Sam O'Steen, Bob Wyman.

SABOTEUR (1942, Universal, 108 minutes)
Cast: Barry Kane (Robert Cummings), Pat Martin (Priscilla Lane), Charles Tobin (Otto Kruger), Freeman (Alan Baxter), Mrs. Van Sutton (Alma Kruger), Frank Fry (Norman Lloyd), Miller (Vaughan Glaser), Mrs. Mason (Dorothy Peterson), Robert (Ian Wolfe), Lorelei (Anita Bolster), Siamese Twins (Jeanne and Lynn Roher), Fat Woman (Anita Le Deaux), Bones (Pedro de Cordoba), Young Mother (Kathryn Adams), Truck Driver (Murray Alper), Society Woman (Frances Carson), Midget (Billy Curtis), Foundation Head (Samuel S. Hinds), Sheriff (Charles Halton), Detectives (Hardie Albright, Oliver Blake, Byron Shores, Matt Willis, Jack Cheatham)
Credits: Director: Alfred Hitchcock; Screenplay: Peter Viertel, Joan Harrison, Dorothy Parker; Story: Alfred Hitchcock; Producers: Frank Lloyd, Jack H. Skirball; Photography: Joseph Valentine; Art Director: Jack Otterson; Editor: Otto Ludwig; Music: Charles Previn, Frank Skinner.

SALT (2010, Columbia Tri-Star, 99 minutes)
Cast: Evelyn Salt (Angelina Jolie), Ted Winter (Liev Schreiber), Peabody (Chiwetel Ejiofor), Vassily Orlov (Daniel Olbrychski), Mike Krause (August Diehl), Young Orlov (Daniel Pearce), President Lewis (Hunt Block), Secretary of Defense (Andre Braugher), President Matveyev (Olek Krupa), Young Chenkov (Cassidy Hinkle), Shnaider (Corey Stoll), Chenkov's Parents (Vladislav Koulikov, Olya Zueva), CIA Officers (Kevin O'Donnell, Gaius Charles, Zach Shaffer, Albert Jones, Zoe Lister Jones), Torturer (Paul Juhn), Front Desk Woman (Tika Sumpter), Security Supervisor (David Bishins), Neighbor (Yara Shahidi), Presidential Advisor (Gary Wilmes), National Security Advisor (Jordan Lage), Secret Service Agents (Jeremy Davidson, Kamar De Los Reyes, Frank Harts), Bunker Officer (Michelle Ray Smith), CIA Director Medford (Marion McCorry), Executioner (Vladimir Tevlovski), FBI Agent (Steve Cirbus), Neural Tech (Roslyn Ruff), Bunker Technician (Jeb Brown), Newscaster (Lara Apponyi), New Russian President (Vitali Baganov), Security Officer (Peter Weireter), Interrogator (Ryan Cyrus Shams), Tactical Officer (Colleen Werthmann), Gate Officer (Liam Joynt), Checkpoint Agent (Victoria Cartagena), Martin Crenshaw (Armand Schultz), Basayev (Ivo Velon), General (Victor Slezak), Communications Agent (Dionne Audain), Taxi Driver (Jalil Jay Lynch), CIA Tactical Leader (Mike Colter), Reporters (Bev-

erly Kirk, Barbara Harrison), Bishop (Lynn C. Sanders), Subway Cop (Theresa Caggiano), Russian Agents (Nick Poltoranin, Vladimir Troitsky, Hristo Hristov), Military Aide (James Nuciforo), North Korean MP (Jose L. Rodriguez), Rink Petroleum Security (Avis Boone), Bunker Tech (Scott Dillin, Alexander Martin Jones, Angelo Lopez), Police Captain (Stephen Breach), Washington Reporter (Mike Conneen), News Anchor (Greg Kelly), Reporter (Elizabeth Kaledin), Burly Agent (Angel David), Subway Passenger (Jessica Rich), Reporter (Natalie Gal), Ritual Matchmaker (Cecilia Foss), Fireman (Addison LeMay), Young Shnaider (Luke Trevisan)

Credits: Director: Philip Noyce; Screenplay: Kurt Wimmer; Producers: Lorenzo di Bonaventura; Sunil Perkash; Photography: Robert Elswit; Production Design: Scott Chambliss; Music: James Newton Howard; Editor: Stuart Baird.

SEEDPEOPLE (1992, Full Moon, 81 minutes)

Cast: Tom Baines (Sam Hennings), Heidi Tucker (Andrea Roth), Brad Yates (Dane Witherspoon), Doc Roller (Bernard Kates), Kim Tucker (Holly Fields), Frank Tucker (John Mooney), Mrs. Santiago (Anne Betancourt), Ed Busta (David Dunard), Thurman Rudd (Charles Bouvier), Burt Mosely (Sonny Carl Davis), Deputy Fraser (J. Marvin Campbell), Shooter (Matt Demeritt), Tumbeler (Debbie Carrington)

Credits: Director: Peter Manoogian; Screenplay: Jackson Barr, from an idea by Charles Band; Producer: Anne Kelly; Photography: Adolfo Bartoli; Production Design: R. Clifford Searcy; Editor: Tom Barrett.

SEVEN DAYS IN MAY (1964, Paramount, 118 minutes)

Cast: Col. Martin "Jiggs" Casey (Kirk Douglas), General James Scott (Burt Lancaster), President Jordan Lyman (Fredric March), Eleanor Holbrook (Ava Gardner), Sen. Raymond Clark (Edmond O'Brien), Paul Girard (Martin Balsam), Christopher Todd (George Macready), Sen. Prentice (Whit Bissell), Harold McPherson (Hugh Marlowe), Arthur Corwin (Bart Burns), Col. Murdock (Richard Anderson), Lt. Hough (Jack Mullaney), Col. Henderson (Andrew Duggan), Col. Broderick (John Larkin), Doctor (Malcolm Atterbury), Esther Townsend (Helen Kleeb), Admiral Barnswell (John Houseman), Bar Girl (Colette Jackson), with Fredd Wayne, Rodolfo Hoyos, Clegg Hoyt

Credits: Director: John Frankenheimer; Screenplay: Rod Serling, based on the novel by Fletcher Knebel and Charles W. Bailey II; Producer: Edward Lewis; Photography: Ellsworth Fredricks; Production Design: Cary Odell; Editor: Ferris Webster; Music: Jerry Goldsmith.

THE SIEGE (1998, 20th Century–Fox, 115 minutes)

Cast: Anthony Hubbard (Denzel Washington), Elise Kraft/Sharon Bridger (Annette Bening), Gen. William Devereaux (Bruce Willis), Frank Haddad (Tony Shalhoub), Samir Nazhde (Sami Bouajila), Sheik Ahmed Bin Talal (Ahmed Ben Larby), Meuzzin (Mosleh Mohamed), Tina Osu (Liana Pai), Mike Johnassen (Mark Valley), Fred Darius (Jack Gwaltney), Danny Sussman (David Proval), Floyd Rose (Lance Reddick), INS Official (Jeremy Knaster), INS Uniform (William Hill), Khalil Saleh (Aasif Mandvi), Officer Williams (Frank DiElsi), Officer Henderson (Wood Harris), Anita (Ellen Bethea), Fingerprint Expert (David Costabile), Fiber Expert (Glenn Kessler), Video Agent (Jeffrey Allan Waid), Phone Bank Agent (Tom McDermott), Secretary (Sherry Ham-Bernard), Landlord (Joseph Hodge), Rashad (Joey Naber), Yousuf (Said Faraj), Ali (Alex Dodd), Najiba Haddad (Jacqueline Antaramian), Frank Jr. (Helmi Kassim), Teacher (Ghoulam R. Rasoully), EMT (Joseph Badalucco Jr.), Injured Woman (Diana Naftal), Kaplan (Ben Shenkman), Mayor's Assistant (Barton Tinapp), NYPD Rep (Neal Jones), D.A. (Donna Hanover), Johnson (Peter Schindler), Arab Spokesman (Hany Kamal), Chief of Staff (Chip Zien), Sen. Wright (Dakin Mathews), Congressman Marshall (John Rothman), Speaker of the House (John Henry Cox), Attorney General (E. Katherine Kerr), Army General (Jimmie Ray Weeks), FBI Director (Will Lyman), CIA Director (Ray Godshall), Col. Hardwick (Victor Slezak), Corporal (Chris Messina), Mechanic (Gilbert Rosales), Tariq Hussein (Amro Salama), ACLU Lawyer (Jim Shankman), Journalists (Matt Servitto, Jourdan Fremin), Protest Speaker (Susie Essman), FBI Agents (Jeff Beatty, Graham J. Larson), Pundits (Arianna Huffington, Robert Scheer, Matt Miller), Newscasters (John F. Beard, Sean Hannity, Stan Brooks, Ronald Kuby, Alex Chadwick, Daniel Schorr, Epi Colon, Curtis Sliwa, Judy De Angelis, Susan Stamberg, Luis Jimenez, Mary Alice Williams)

Credits: Director: Edward Zwick; Screenplay: Lawrence Wright, Menno Meyjes, Edward Zwick; Story: Lawrence Wright; Producer: Lynda Obst, Edward Zwick; Photography: Roger Deakins; Production Design: Lilly Kilvert; Editor: Steven Rosenblum; Music: Graeme Revell.

THE SILENCER (1999, Prophecy Pictures, 92 minutes)

Cast: Quinn Simmons (Michael Dudikoff),

Appendix 1

Jason Wells (Brennan Elliott), Neal Donovan (Terence Kelly), Jill Martin (Gabrielle Miller), Holly Sharp (Nicole Oliver), Rodeski (Peter LaCroix), Hale Bryant (Colin Cunningham), Danner (Mike Dopud), McGraw (Doug Abrahams), Senator Cayton (Michael St. John Smith), Det. Keller (William S. Taylor), Det. Hill (Andrew Johnston), Carlos (Lauro Chartrand), Carlson (Geoff Campbell), Ashley (Pamela Fu), Michael (Phillip Batista), Taxi Driver (Ronald Selmour), Robert Wells (George Josef), Williams (Madison Graie), Uniformed Officer (Robert Lee)

Credits: Director: Robert Lee; Screenplay: John Curtis; Producers: John Curtis, Evan Tylor; Photography: Henry Lebo; Production Design: Randy Chodak; Music: Peter Allen; Editor: Gordon Remple.

THE STEPFORD WIVES (1975, Fadsin Cinema Associates/Palomar Pictures International, 115 minutes)

Cast: Joanna Eberhart (Katharine Ross), Walter Eberhart (Peter Masterson), Bobby Markowe (Paula Prentiss), Carol Van Sant (Nanette Newman), Charmaine Wimpiris (Tina Louise), Dr. Fancher (Carol Rossen), Ike Mazzarde (William Prince), Kit Sunderson (Carole Mallory), Marie Axhelm (Toni Reid), Mrs. Cornell (Judith Baldwin), Marie Ann Stravros (Barbara Rucker), Claude Axhelm (George Coe), Ed Wimpiris (Franklin Cover), Raymond Chandler (Robert Fields), Mr. Cornell (Michael Higgins), Ted Van Sant (Josef Sommer), Welcome Wagon Lady (Paula Trueman), Mrs. Kingassa (Martha Greenhouse), Dave Markowe (Simon Deckard), Mr. Atkinson (Remak Ramsay), Kim (Mary Stuart Masterson), Amy (Ronny Sullivan), Cop (John Aprea), Moving Men (Matt Russo, Anthony Crupi), Market Manager (Kenneth McMillan), Nettie (Dee Wallace), Doorman (Tom Spratley), Dale Coba (Patrick O'Neal)

Credits: Director: Bryan Forbes; Screenplay: William Goldman, based on Ira Levin's novel; Producer: Edgar J. Scherick; Photography: Owen Roizman; Production Design; Gene Callahan; Editor: Timothy Gee; Music: Michael Small.

THE STEPFORD WIVES (2004, Paramount, Dreamworks)

Cast: Joanna Eberhart (Nicole Kidman), Walter Kresby (Matthew Broderick), Bobbie Markowitz (Bette Midler), Claire Wellington (Glenn Close), Mike Wellington (Christopher Walken), Roger Bannister (Roger Bart), Jerry Harmon (David Marshall Grant), Dave Markowitz (Jon Lovitz), Pete Kresby (Dylan Hartigan), Kimberly Kresby (Fallon Brooking), Sarah Sunderson (Faith Hill), Herb Sunderson (Matt Malloy), Beth Peters (Kate Shindle), Stan Peters (Tom Riis Farrell), Charmaine Van Sant (Lorri Bagley), Ted Van Sant (Robert Stanton), Carol Wainwright (Lisa Masters), Ed Wainwright (Christopher Evan Welch), Marianne Stevens (Colleen Dunn), Vic Stevens (Jason Kravits), Additional Wife (Emily Wing), Additional Husbands (C.S. Lee, Tony Torn), Helen Devlin (Mary Beth Peil), Heather (Andrea Anders), Hank (Mike White), Barbara (Carrie Preston), "I Can Do Better" Host (Billy Bush), Adam Markowitz (Tyler McGuckin), Ben Markowitz (Nick Reidy), Max Markowitz (Sebastian Rand), Tonkiro (Tanoai Reed), Guards (Blaise Corrigan, George Aguilar), *Balance of Power* Host (Meredith Vieira), Bob (Rick Holmes) Tara (Kadee Strickland), Larry King (Himself), Stepford Guard (Munro M. Bonnell), Nurse (Michelle Durning), Musicians (Kenny Kosek, Will Woodard), Dancers (Elizabeth Austin, Deanna Dys, Joanne DiMauro, Digene Farrar, Bernard Ferstenberg, James Peter Lynch, Shannon McGann, Cristin Mortenson, Elizabeth A. Patek, David Purves, Joseph Ricci, Mark Vaughn)

Credits: Director: Frank Oz; Screenplay: Paul Rudnick, based on Ira Levin's novel; Producers: Scott Rudin, Donald De Line, Edgar J. Scherick, Gabriel Grunfeld; Co-producer Leslie Converse; Photography: Rob Hahn; Production Design: Jackson Degovia; Editor: Jay Rabinowitz; Music: David Arnold.

STRANGE HOLIDAY (1945, Elite Pictures, 55 minutes)

Cast: John Stevenson (Claude Rains), John, Jr. (Bobbie Stebbins), Peggy Lee (Barbara Bates), Woodrow, Jr. (Paul Hilton), Mrs. Stevenson (Gloria Holden), Farmer (Walter White Jr.), Truck Driver (Wally Maher), Newsboy (Tommy Cook), Regan (Griff Barnett), Detectives (Ed Max, Paul Dubov), Secretary (Helen Mack), Examiner (Martin Kosleck), Guard (Charles McAvoy), Betty (Priscilla Loyons), Boy Friend (David Bradford)

Credits: Director-Screenplay: Arch Oboler; Producers: Arch Oboler, Frank R. Donovan, A.W. Hackel, Edward Finney, Max King; Photography: Robert Surtees; Art Director: Bernard Herzbrun; Editor: Fred Feitshans, Jr.; Music: Gordon Jenkins.

STRANGE INVADERS (1983, Orion Pictures, 93 minutes)

Cast: Charles Bigelow (Paul LeMat), Betty Walker (Nancy Allen), Margaret (Diana Scarwid), Willie Collins (Michael Lerner), Mrs. Benjamin (Louise Fletcher), Earl (Wallace Shawn), Waitress/Avon Lady (Fiona Lewis), Arthur Newman (Kenneth Tobey), Mrs. Bigelow (June Lockhart), Prof. Hollister (Charles Lane), Elizabeth (Lulu Sylbert), Tim (Joel Cohen), Teen Boy (Dan Shor), Teen Girl (Dey Young), Gas Station Attendant (Jack Kehler), Detective (Mark Goddard), State Trooper (Thomas Kopache), Editor (Bobby Pickett), Connie (Connie Kellers), Stewardesses (Nancy Johnson, Betsy Pickering), Waiter (Jonathan Ulmer), First Alien (Ron Gillham), Man in Dark Glasses (Al Roberts), Nurse (Edwina Follows), Waitress (Patti Medwid)

Credits: Director: Michael Laughlin; Screenplay: William Condon, Michael Laughlin; Story: William Condon, Michael Laughlin, Walter Davis; Producer: Walter Coblenz; Photography: Louis Horvath; Production Design: Susanna Moore; Editor: John W. Wheeler; Music: John Addison.

TARGET: EARTH (1998, ABC, 95 minutes)

Cast: Detective Sam Adams (Christopher Meloni), Karen Mackaphee (Marcia Cross), Agent Naples (John C. McGinley), Sen. Ben Arnold (Dabney Coleman), Tammy (Courtney Allen Crumpler), Commander Faulk (Chad Lowe), Allison (Melinda Culea), Madeline Chandler (Traci Dinwiddie), Emmett (Jeff Monahan), Carrie (Stephani Victor), Nate (Dilsey Davis), Paul Henke (Jerry Hatmaker), Remo (Jack Moore), Gus Ramus (Alfred Wiggins), Beautician (Jenna Young)

Credits: Director: Peter Markle; Screenplay: Michael Vickerman; Producer: Lee Ratner; Co-Producers: Jake Froelich, Sam Froelich; Photography: Levie Isaacks; Production Design: Vincent J. Cresciman; Editor: Craig Bassett; Music: Peter Bernstein.

TELEFON (1977, MGM, 103 minutes)

Cast: Grigori Borzov (Charles Bronson), Barbara (Lee Remick), Nicolai Dalchimsky (Donald Pleasence), Dorothy Putterman (Tyne Daly), Col. Malchenko (Alan Badel), General Strelsky (Patrick Magee), Marie Wills (Sheree North), Harley Sandburg (Frank Marth), Emma Stark (Helen Page Camp), Doug Stark (Roy Jenson), Mrs. Hassler (Jacqueline Scott), Carl Hassler (Ed Bakey), Harry Bascom (John Mitchum), Father Stuart Diller (Iggie Wolfington), William Enders (Hank Brandt), Stroller (John Carter), Gas Station Attendant (Burton Gilliam), Doctor (Regis J. Cordic), Nurse (Carmen Zapata), Navy Lieutenant (Carl Byrd), Highway Patrolmen (Robert Phillips, Cliff Emmich), Mrs. Maloney (Kathleen O'Malley), Lt. Alexandrov (Ake Lindman), Dalchimsky's Mother (Ansa Konen), TV Newsman (John Hambrick), Reporter (Henry Alfaro), Anchor Woman (Glenda Wina), Salesclerk (Jim Nolan), Receptionist (George Petri), Maitre D' (Jeff David), Petty Officer (Lew Brown), Radar Operator (Peter Weiss), Martin Calender (Alex Sharp), Airport Clerk (Margaret Hall Baron), Hot Rod Kid (Sean Moloney), Russian Steward (Ville Veikko Salminen), Hockey Players (Teppo Heiskanen, Mika Levio), Mrs. Wills' Children (Stephanie Ann Rydall, Derek Rydall)

Credits: Director: Don Siegel; Screenplay: Peter Hyams, Stirling Silliphant; based on the novel by Walter Wager; Producer: James B. Harris; Photography: Michael Butler: Art Director: William F. O'Brien; Editor: Douglas Stewart; Music: Lalo Schifrin.

THEY GOT ME COVERED (1943, RKO, 95 minutes)

Cast: Robert Kittredge (Bob Hope), Christina Hill (Dorothy Lamour), Fauscheim (Otto Preminger), Baldanacco (Eduardo Ciannelli), Mrs. Vanescu (Lenore Aubert), Gloria (Marion Martin), Old Man (Donald Meek), Sally (Phyllis Ruth), Nichimuro (Philip Ahn), Mason (Donald MacBride), Helen (Mary Treen), Mildred (Bettye Avery), Holtz (William Yetter), Faber (Henry Guttman), Gypsy (Florence Bates), Hotel Manager (Walter Catlett), Vanescu (John Abbott), Red (Frank Sully)

Credits: Director: David Butler; Screenplay: Harry Kurnitz; Added Dialogue: Frank Fenton, Lynn Root; Story: Leonard Q. Ross, Leonard Spigelgass; Producer: Samuel Goldwyn; Photography: Rudolph Maté; Art Director: Perry Ferguson; Music: Leigh Harline; Editor: Daniel Mandell.

THEY LIVE (1988, Universal, 97 minutes)

Cast: George Nada (Roddy Piper), Frank Armitage (Keith David), Holly Thompson (Meg Foster), Drifter (George "Buck" Flower), Gilbert (Peter Jason), Street Preacher (Raymond St. Jacques), Family Man (Jason Robards III), Bearded Man (John Lawrenche), Brown-Haired Woman (Susan Barnes), Black Revolutionary (Sy Richardson), Family Man's Daughter (Wendy Brainard), Female Interviewer (Lucille Meredith), Ingénue (Susan Blanchard), Foreman (Norman Alden), Black Junkie (Dana Bratton), Well-Dressed Customer (John F. Goff), Vendor (Norm Wilson), Rich Lady (Thelma Lee), Depressed Human (Stratton Leopold), Arab Clerk (Rezza Shan), Blonde cop (Norman Howell), Neighbor (Larry J. Franco), Biker (Tom Searle), Scruffy Blond Man (Robert Grasmere), Guards (Vince Inneo, Bob Hudson), Manager (Jon Paul Jones), Male News Anchor (Dennis Michael); Female Anchor (Nancy Gee), Young Female Executive (Claudia Stanlee), Woman on Phone (Christine Baur), Pregnant Secretary (Eileen Wesson), Security Guards (Gregory Barnett,

Appendix 1

Jim Nickerson), Second Unit Guard (Kerry Rossall), Naked Lady (Cibby Danyla), Male Ghoul (Jeff Imada), Female Ghoul (Michelle Costello)

Credits: Director: John Carpenter; Screenplay: Frank Armitage, based on the short story *Eight O'-Clock in the Morning* by Ray Nelson; Producer: Larry Franco; Photography: Gary B. Kibbe; Art Director: William J. Durrell, Jr.; Editors: Gib Jaffe, Frank E. Jimenez; Music: John Carpenter, Alan Howarth.

THE THING (1982, Universal, 108 minutes)

Cast: MacReady (Kurt Russell), Blair (Wilford Brimley), Nauls (T.K. Carter), Palmer (David Clennon), Childs (Keith David), Dr. Copper (Richard Dysart), Norris (Charles Hallahan), Bennigns (Peter Maloney), Clark (Richard Masur), Garry (Donald Moffat), Fuchs (Joel Polis), Windows (Thomas Waites), Norwegian (Norbert Weisser), Norwegian Passenger (Larry Franco), Helicopter Pilot (Nate Irwin), Pilot (William Zeman)

Credits: Director: John Carpenter; Screenplay; Bill Lancaster, based on the novella *Who Goes There?* by John W. Campbell.; Producer: David Foster, Lawrence Turman; Photography: Dean Cundey; Production Design: John Lloyd; Editor: Todd Ramsay; Music: Ennio Morricone.

TRAITOR (2008, Overture Films, 113 minutes)

Cast: Samir Horn (Don Cheadle), Roy Clayton (Guy Pearce), Omar (Saïd Taghmaoui), Max Archer (Neal McDonough), Fareed (Ally Khan), Chandra Dawkin (Archie Panjabi), Nathir (Raad Rawi), Bashir (Hassam Ghancy), Leyla (Mozhan Marno), Hamzi (Adeel Akhtar), Carter (Jeff Daniels), Diedre Horn (Lorena Gale), Inspector Gilles (Scali Delpeyrat), Ali (Medhi Ortelsberg), Ahmed (Aizoun Abdelkader), Security Captain (Mohamed Choubi), Wadi (Farid Regragui), Scarecrow (Habib Hamdane), Omar's Crew (Youness Sardi, Joseph Beddelem, Alaa Oumouzoune), Andrew Kelly (Tom Barnett), Ted Blake (Simon Reynolds), Simon (Matt Gordon), Suicide Bomber (P. Rodney Barnes, Shahla Kareen, Ali Momen, Paulino Nunes), Woman (Alex Castillo), Manager (Jeff Kassel), Computer Tech (Mike McPhaden), Munir (Dani Jazzar), Hayes (Jonathan Lloyd Walker), Alvarez (José Heuze), Dupree (Scott Wickware), Iqbal (Elias Zarou), BBC Reporter (Catherine Galloway), Gilles' Deputy (Myriam Blanckaert), Crewman (Nick Alachiotis), FBI Agent (Alex Poch-Goldin), Translator (Natasha Roy), Samir at 10 (Yassine Mamadou), Samir's Father (Omar Mamadou), Fake Cop (Mostafa Hniny), Spanish Patrolman (Michaël Troude), Tour Group Employee (Alfonso Rodriguez Gelos), Bus Driver (Ron Bell)

Credits: Director-Screenwriter: Jeffrey Nachmanoff; Story: Steve Martin, Jeffrey Nachmanoff; Producers: Don Cheadle, David Hoberman, Todd Lieberman, Glynis Murray, Jeffrey Silver; Photography: J. Michael Muro; Production Design: Laurence Bennett; Editor: Billy Fox; Music: Mark Kilian.

TRIBULATION 99: ALIEN ANOMALIES UNDER AMERICA (1992, Other Cinema, 47 minutes)

Credits: Director-Screenwriter-Editor: Craig Baldwin; Photography: Bill Daniel; Music: Dana Hoover.

UNIVERSAL SOLDIER III: UNFINISHED BUSINESS (1998, The Movie Channel, 95 minutes)

Cast: Luc Devereaux (Matt Battaglia), Veronica Roberts (Chandra West), Mentor (Burt Reynolds), Eric Devereaux (Jeff Wincott), Dr. Walker (Richard McMillan), McNally (Roger Periard), Bodyguards (Layton Morrison, Loren Peterson), Charles Clifton (Juan Chioran), Grace (Claudette Roche), Martin Daniels (John Laing), Drunk CEO (Dwayne MacLean), Max (Jovanni Sy), Hugo/GR84 (Lloyd Adams), Lowell/GR85 (Vincent Corazza), Head Chief (David Marsman), Cop (David Blacker), Chief Thorpe (Gerry Mendicino), Freddie Smith (Dan Duran), Busboy (Adrian Churchill), Martinez (Kevin Ruston), Cooper (Desmond Campbell), Jasper (James Kee), Anchorwoman (Carla Collins), John Devereaux (Aron Tager), Danielle Devereaux (Barbara Gordon), Gen. Clancy/GR86 (Thomas Hauff), GR87, age 6 (Nickolas Swan), Med Tech (Matt Birman), Sheriff (John Stoneham Sr.), GR87, age 13 (Brock Clermont), Driver (Ben Brooks), Orderly (Martin Roach), Nurse's Aide (Dana Ishiura), Scully (Philip Williams), Head Nurse (Taren Ash), Dr. Gregor (Jack Duffy), Nurses (Mary Ann Stevens, Leigh E. Brinkman), File Pusher (Danny Lima), Wheelchair Vet (Moris Santia), Passerby (Dan Gallagher), Pilot (John Stoneham Jr.), Air Traffic Controller (Steven Allerick), Sentries (Peter Szkoda, Errol Gee, Bryan Renfro, Robert Racki)

Credits: Director: Jeff Woolnough; Writer: Peter M. Lenkov; Producer: Bob Wertheimer; Photography: Russell Goozee; Production Design: Jasna Stefanovic; Editor: Robert K. Sprogis; Music: John Kastner, Steve Pecile, Ivan Dorochuk, Crunch Recording Group.

VILLAGE OF THE DAMNED (1995, Universal, 98 minutes)

Cast: Alan Chaffee (Christopher Reeve), Dr. Susan Verner (Kirstie Alley), Jill McGowan (Linda Kozlowski), Frank McGowan (Michael Paré), Melanie Roberts (Meredith Salenger), Rev. George (Mark Hamill), Sarah (Pippa Pearthree), Ben Blum (Peter Jason), Callie Blum (Constance Forslund),

Barbara Chafee (Karen Kahn), David (Thomas Dekker), Mara (Lindsey Haun), Robert (Cody Dorkin), Julie (Trishalee Hardy), Dorothy (Jessye Quarry), Isaac (Adam Robbins), Matt (Chelsea DeRidder Simms), Casey (Renée Rene Simms), Lily (Danielle Keaton), Mara at One Year (Hillary Harvey), David at One Year (Bradley Wilhelm), Mara/David at Four Months (Jennifer Wilhelm), Carlton (Buck Flower), Sheriff (Squire Fridell), CHP (Darryl Jones), Deputies (Ed Corbett, Ross Martineau, Skip Richardson), Dr. Bush (Tony Haney), Eye Doctor (Sharon Iwai), Mr. Roberts (Robert L. Bush), Technician (Montgomery Hom), Troopers (Steve Chambers, Ron Kaell), Scientist (Lane Nishikawa), Station Attendant Harold (Michael Halton), Eileen Moore (Julie Eccles), Doctor (Lois Saunders), Labor Room Physician (Sidney Baldwin), Nurses (Wendolyn Lee, Kathleen Turco-Lyon, Abigail Van Alyn), Oliver (Roy Conrad), Young Husband (Dan Belzer), Young Wife (Dena Martinez), Town Hall Woman (Alice Barden), Town Hall Man (John Brebner), Villager (Ralph Miller), Man at Phone (Rip Haight)

Credits: Director: John Carpenter: Screenplay: David Himmelstein, based on the novel *The Midwich Cuckoos* by John Wyndham and the *Village of the Damned* screenplay by Stirling Silliphant, Wolf Rilla, George Barclay; Producers: Michael Preger, Sandy King; Co-Producer, David Chackler; Photography: Gary B. Kibbe; Production Design: Rodger Maus; Editor: Edward A. Warschilka; Music: John Carpenter, Dave Davies.

WALK A CROOKED MILE (1948, Columbia, 91 minutes)

Cast: Daniel F. O'Hara (Dennis O'Keefe), Philip Grayson (Louis Hayward), Dr. Toni Neva (Louise Allbritton), Dr. Ritter von Stolb (Carl Esmond), Igor Braun (Onslow Stevens), Krebs (Raymond Burr)

Credits: Director: Gordon Douglas; Screenplay: George Bruce; Story: Bertram Millhauser; Producer: Grant Whytock; Photography: George Robinson; Art Director: Rudolph Sternad; Editor: James E. Newcomb; Music: Paul Sawtell.

WALK EAST ON BEACON (1952, Columbia, 97 minutes)

Cast: Inspector James Belden (George Murphy), Prof. Kafer (Finlay Currie), Millie (Virginia Gilmore), Lazchenkov (Karel Stepanek), Elaine (Louisa Horton), Danzig (Bruno Wick), Gino (Peter Capell), Dr. Wincott (Robert Dunn), Reynolds (Karl Weber), Mrs. Foss (Vilma Kurer), Vincent Foss (Jack Manning), Torrence (Michael Garrett), Boldany (Robert Carroll), Helmuth (Paul Andor), Robert Martin (Ernest Graves), Mrs. Martin (Rosemary Pettit), Mrs. Kafer (Lotte Palfi), Suspect (Ann Thomas)

Credits: Director: Alfred Werker; Screenplay: Leo Rosten, Emmett Murphy, Leonard Heideman, Virginia Shaler; Producer: Louis De Rochemont; Photography: Joseph Brun; Art Director: Herbert Andrews; Editor: Angelo Ross; Music: Louis Applebaum.

THE WAR WITHIN (2005, Magnolia Pictures, 93 minutes)

Cast: Hassan (Ayad Akhtar), Sayeed Choudhury (Firdous Bamji), Duri Choudhury (Nandana Sen), Fraida S. Choudhury (Sarita Choudhury), Khalid (Charles Daniel Sandoval), Ali Choudhury (Varun Sriram), Rasheeda S. Choudhury (Anjeli Chapman), Gabe (John Ventimiglia), Mike O'Reilly (Mike McGlone), Abdul (Aasif Mandvi), Naved (Ajay Naidu), Imam (Kamal Marayati), Izzy (Wayman Ezell), Saudi Man (James Rana), Steven (Christopher Castelo), News Anchorwoman (Christine Commesso), Carroll (John Zibell), Cops (Joseph Ascolese, Douglas Paretti, Joseph M. Abbott), Agents (Michael Balsley, Robert Carroll, David Bishins), Reporter (Angel Desai), Pakistani Interrogator (Samrat Chakrabarti), Terrorist (Per Melita), CIA Agents (Roy Farfel, Jeff Ward, Glenn Pike), Receptionist (Vanessa Londino), Women (Deepti Gupta, Farah Bala, Deepa Purchit), Passengers (Goli Samii, Troy Hall), Guy in Cab (David Connolly), Ticket Clerk (Dianne Busch)

Credits: Director: Joseph Castelo; Screenplay: Ayad Akhtar, Joseph Castelo, Tom Glynn; Producers: Tom Glynn, Jason Kliot; Joana Vicente; Co-Producers: Gretchen McGowan, Per Melita; Photography: Lisa Rinzler; Production Design: Stephanie Carroll; Editor: Malcolm Jamieson; Music: David Holmes.

WE'VE NEVER BEEN LICKED (1943, Universal, 103 minutes)

Cast: Brad Craig (Richard Quine), Nina Lambert (Anne Gwynne), Deedee Dunham (Martha O'Driscoll), Cyanide Jenkins (Noah Beery Jr.), Salesman (William Frawley), "Pop" Lambert (Harry Davenport), Nishikawa (Edgar Barrier), Col. Jason Craig (Samuel S. Hinds), Commandant (Moroni Olsen), Matsui (Roland Got), Kubo (Allen Jung), Panhandle Mitchell (Robert Mitchum), Fortuno Tavares (Alfredo DeSa), Chip Goodwin (Malcolm McTaggart), Hank James (Gordon Wynne), Adams (Cliff Robertson), Shotgun (Bill Walker), Captains (Kenneth MacDonald, Dean Benton), Willie (Mantan Moreland), Yoshida (Frank Tang), Flight Commander (John Frazer), Conductor (Henry Hall), Soldier (Phil Warren), Students (William

Appendix 1

Blees, Paul Dubov, Dick Chandlee, David Street, Michael Moore, Danny Jackson, Roger Daniel, Dick Morris, Herbert Gunn, Henry Rogers, John Forrest, William Lechner, Bob Lowell, Michael Towne, Bill Nash, Jackie Ray, Jack Edwards Jr., Ward Wood), Soldier (William Ruhl), Deck Officer (Kendall Bryson), Italian Mentor (Franco Corsaro), German Mentor (Walter Bonn), Japanese Mentor (Beal Wong), Seniors (Sammy McKim, John James), Operator (Don McGill), Messenger (Bruce Wong), Sniper (Alex Havier), Naval Officer (Paul Langton). With: Bill Stern, George Putnam

Credits: Director: John Rawlins; Screenplay: Norman Reilly Raine, Nick Grinde; Story: Norman Reilly Raine; Producer: Walter Wanger; Photography: Milton Krasner; Art Directors: Alexander Golitzen, John B. Goodman; Editor: Philip Cahn; Music: Charles Previn.

The Whip Hand (1951, RKO, 82 minutes)

Cast: Matt Corbin (Elliott Reid), Janet Keller (Carla Balenda), Steve Loomis (Raymond Burr), Dr. Wilhelm Bucholtz (Otto Waldis), Dr. Edward Keller (Edgar Barrier), Chick (Michael Steele), Molly Loomis (Lurene Tuttle), Luther Adams (Frank Darien), Garr (Peter Brocco), Peterson (Lewis Martin), Mrs. Turner (Olive Carey), Sheriff (Jameson Shade), Speedboat Pilot (Art Dupuis), Rangers (Brick Sullivan, Bob Thom), Guards (Robert Foulk, William Challee)

Credits: Director–Production Designer: William Cameron Menzies; Screenplay: George Bricker, Frank L. Moss; Story: Roy Hamilton; Producer: Lewis J. Rachmil; Photography: Nicholas Musuraca; Art Directors: Albert S. D'Agostino, Carroll Clark; Editor: Robert Golden; Music: Paul Sawtell.

The Woman on Pier 13 (aka I Married a Communist) (1950, RKO, 73 minutes)

Cast: Nan Collins (Laraine Day), Brad Collins (Robert Ryan), Don Lowry (John Agar), Christine Norman (Janis Carter), Vanning (Thomas Gomez), Jim Travers (Richard Rober), Bailey (William Talman), Arnold (Paul E. Burns), Ralston (Paul Guilfoyle), Charles Dover (G. Pat Collins), Grip Wilson (Fred Graham), Cornwall (Harry Cheshire), Garth (Jack Stoney), Dr. Dixon (Lester Matthews), Evelyn (Marlo Dwyer), Clerk (Erskine Sanford), Secretary (Bess Flowers), Hagen (Charles Cane), Waiter (Dick Ryan), Burke (Barry Brooks), Cahill (William Haade), Bellhop (John Duncan), Waitress (Iris Adrian), Drunk (Don Brodie), Jeb (Al Murphy), Girlfriend (Evelyn Ceder), Stripper (Marie Voe), Tough (George Magrill), Girl (Louise Lane), Policeman (Jim Nolan)

Credits: Director: Robert Stevenson; Screenplay: Charles Grayson, Robert Hardy Andrews; Story: George W. George, George F. Slavin; Producer: Jack J. Gross; Photography: Nicholas Musuraca; Art Directors: Albert S. D'Agostino, Walter E. Keller; Editor: Roland Gross; Music: Leigh Harline.

Zontar, the Thing from Venus (1966, AIP-TV, Azalea Pictures, 80 minutes)

Cast: Dr. Curt Taylor (John Agar), Keith Ritchie (Anthony Houston), Martha Ritchie (Susan Bjurman), Anne Taylor (Patricia De Laney), Gen. Young (Neil Fletcher), Sgt. Magalar (Andrew Traister), Rocket Scientists (Warren Hammack, Jeff Alexander), Gate Guard (Jonathan Ledford), Louise (Colleen Carr), Ledford (George Edgley), Alice (Carol Gilley), Sheriff Brad Crenshaw (Bill Thurman), Townswoman (Bertha Holmes)

Credits: Director-Producer: Larry Buchanan, Screenplay: Hillman Taylor, Larry Buchanan, based on Lou Rusoff's screenplay for *It Conquered the World* (uncredited); Photography: Robert B. Alcott; Art Director: Robert Dracup; Music: Ronald Stein.

Appendix 2

Television Series Credits and Synopses

ALIAS (2001–06, ABC, 105 episodes)
Cast: Sydney Bristow (Jennifer Garner), Jack Bristow (Victor Garber), Arvin Sloane (Ron Rifkin), Michael Vaughn (Michael Vartan), Francine Calfo (Merrin Dungey), Marcus Dixon (Carl Lumbly), Marshall Flinkman (Kevin Weisman), Will Tippin (Bradley Cooper), Irina Derevko (Lena Olin), Sark (David Anders)
A woman discovers that the CIA branch she works for is actually a front for an international criminal cartel.

ANIMORPHS (1998–99, Nickelodeon, 26 episodes)
Cast: Jake Berenson (Shawn Ashmore), Rachel Berenson (Brooke Nevin), Marco (Boris Cabrera), Cassie (Nadia Nascimento), Tobias (Christopher Ralph), Ax (Paulo Costanzo), Principal Chapman (Richard Sali)
Teenagers discover that body-snatching aliens have taken over their home town. A friendly alien shares his shapeshifting abilities with them to give them a chance to fight back.

BEYOND WESTWORLD (1980, CBS, 5 episodes)
Cast: John Moore (Jim McMullan), Simon Quaid (James Wainwright), Pamela Williams (Connie Sellecca), Professor Joseph Oppenheimer (William Jordan), Roberta (Ann McCurry), Foley (Severn Darden)
A criminal scientist uses an army of androids to replace and duplicate people in power, in order to further his own goal of world domination.

DARK SKIES (1996–97, NBC, 20 episodes)
Cast: John Loengard (Eric Close), Kimberly Sayers (Megan Ward), Capt. Frank Bach (J.T. Walsh), Albano (Conor O'Farrell), Dr. Charlie Halligan (Charley Lang), Jim Steele (Tim Kelleher), Juliet (Jeri Lynn Ryan)
Two Kennedy administration workers get caught up in a war between humanity and the alien Hive.

DOLLHOUSE (2009–10, Fox, 26 episodes)
Cast: Echo (Eliza Dushku), Paul Ballard (Tahmoh Penikett), Boyd Langton (Harry Lennix), Topher Brink (Fran Kranz), Adelle DeWitt (Olivia Williams), Dr. Claire Saunders (Amy Acker), Sierra (Dichen Lachman), Victor (Enver Gjokah)
The Dollhouse can program "dolls" to become anyone you wish, from a bodyguard to a girlfriend. Echo, a doll who retains memories of her multiple programs, begins to probe into the mysteries surrounding the Dollhouse's real purpose and the sinister agenda of Rossum, the company that runs it.

FIRST WAVE (1999–2001, USA Network, 66 episodes)
Cast: Cade Foster (Sebastian Spence), Crazy Eddie (Rob LaBelle), Joshua (Roger R. Cross), Jordan Radcliffe (Traci Lords)
A former thief pits his skills against the Gua, aliens infiltrating Earth to lay the groundwork for an invasion.

I LED THREE LIVES (1953–56, Syndicated, 117 episodes)
Cast: Herb Philbrick (Richard Carlson), Eva Philbrick (Virginia Stefan), Special Agent Jerry Dressler (John Zaremba), Special Agent Henderson (Ed Hinton)
Herb Philbrick seems to be an ordinary American, but he's secretly "Comrade Herb," a Communist Party member and Soviet spy—and an FBI counterspy working to thwart the commies' plans to destroy America.

THE INVADERS (1967–68, ABC, 43 episodes)
Cast: David Vincent (Roy Thinnes), Edgar Scoville (Kent Smith)
After discovering that aliens are taking human form in order to conquer our world, architect David Vincent sets out to convince others that the threat is real.

INVASION (2005–06, ABC, 22 episodes)
Cast: Sheriff Tom Underlay (William Fichtner),

Appendix 2

Dr. Mariel Underlay (Kari Matchett), Dave Groves (Tyler Labine), Larkin Groves (Lisa Sheridan), Kira Underlay (Alexis Dziena), Jesse (Evan Peters), Rose Poole (Ariel Gade), Russell Pool (Eddie Cibrian)

Residents of a small Florida town are transformed into "hybrids," part human, part alien.

KINDRED: THE EMBRACED (1996, Fox, 8 episodes)

Cast: Detective Frank Kohanek (C. Thomas Howell), Julian Luna (Mark Frankel), Caitlin Byrne (Kelly Rutherford), Lillie Langtry (Stacy Haiduk), Detective Sonny Touissaint (Erik King), Archon Raine (Patrick Bauchau), Cash (Channon Roe), Daedalus (Jeff Kober), Nino (Peter Rocca), Sasha (Brigid Walsh), Eddie Fiori (Brian Thompson)

An L.A. detective discovers that vampires live among us, masquerading as humans, and finds himself drawn into their shadowy world.

NOWHERE MAN (1995–96, UPN, 25 episodes)

Cast: Thomas Veil (Bruce Greenwood), Alison Veil (Megan Gallagher)

A mysterious conspiracy erases all record of Thomas Veil's existence, forcing the photojournalist to search for the truth about the "Organization."

PREY (1998, ABC, 13 episodes)

Cast: Dr. Sloan Parker (Debra Messing), Tom Daniels (Adam Storke), Dr. Walter Attwoold (Larry Drake), Ray Peterson (Frankie Faison), Dr. Ed Tate (Vincent Ventresca)

A scientist discovers that a super–human race lives among us, passing for human but considering Homo sapiens mere prey for their aggressive impulses.

SLEEPER CELL (2005–06, Showtime, 18 episodes)

Cast: Darwyn Al-Hakim (Michael Ealy), Faris Al-Farik (Oded Fehr), Tommy Allen Emerson (Blake Shields), Christian Aumont (Alex Nesic), Ilija Korjenic (Henri Lubatti), Gayle Bishop (Melissa Sagemiller), Special Agent Ray Fuller (James LeGros)

Darwyn, a federal agent, infiltrates an Islamic terrorist Sleeper cell that passes for regular everyday Americans.

SUPERNATURAL (2005-present, WB/CW)

Cast: Sam Winchester (Jared Padalecki), Dean Winchester (Jensen Ackles)

Two brothers carry on the family tradition of killing supernatural menaces, and discover that among their foes are demons who can possess humans in order to work their evil unsuspected.

THRESHOLD (2005, CBS, 13 episodes)

Cast: Molly Anne Caffrey (Carla Gugino), JT Baylock (Charles S. Dutton), Nigel Fenway (Brent Spiner), Lucas Pegg (Robert Patrick Benedict), Cavennaugh (Brian Van Holt), Arthur Ramsey (Peter Dinklage), Hargrave (Mark Berry), Manning (Scott McDonald)

A crack government team tries to thwart aliens who are "bioforming" humans into duplicates of themselves.

TRAVELER (2007, ABC, 8 episodes)

Cast: Jay Burchell (Matthew Bomer), Tyler Fog (Logan Marshall-Green), Will Traveler (Aaron Stanford), Kimberly Doherty (Pascale Hutton), Carlton Fog (William Sadler), Agent Jan Marlow (Viola Davis), Agent Fred Chambers (Steven Culp), Mystery Man (Neal McDonough).

Two grad students discover that the friend with whom they roomed throughout grad school doesn't seem to exist, is not in any records — and has framed them as terrorists.

24 (2001–2010, Fox)

Cast: Jack Bauer (Kiefer Sutherland), Chloe O'Brian (Mary Lynn Rasjkolb)

A counter–terrorist expert battles various subversive threats in action-filled 24-hour periods.

V (2009-present, ABC)

Cast: Erica Evans (Elizabeth Mitchell), Ryan Nichols (Morris Chestnut), Father Jack Landry (Joel Gretsch), Valerie Stevens (Lourdes Benedicto), Tyler Evans (Logan Huffman), Lisa (Laura Vandervoort), Anna (Morena Baccarin), Chad Decker (Scott Wolf)

Aliens arrive on Earth, promising to renew our society. Secretly, they've been on Earth for decades, working on a conspiracy to undermine us.

WAR OF THE WORLDS (1988–90, Syndicated, 41 episodes)

Cast: Harrison Blackwood (Jared Martin), Suzanne McCullough (Lynda Mason Green), Debi McCullough (Rachel Blanchard), Norton Drake (Philip Akin), Lt. Col. Paul Ironhorse (Richard Chaves), Sylvia Van Buren (Ann Robinson), Sgt. Coleman (Norah Grant), Gen. Wilson (John Vernon), Mrs. Pennyworth (Corinne Conley), John Kincaid (Adrian Paul), Maltzor (Denis Forest), Mahna (Catherine Disher), Adrix (Julian Richings), Bayda (Patricia Phillips), Scoggs (Belinda Metz)

A government task force tackles aliens — survivors of the 1953 Martian invasion — who can take over the bodies of human beings.

THE X-FILES (1993–2002, Fox, 202 episodes)

Cast: Dana Scully (Gillian Anderson), Fox Mulder (David Duchovny), John Doggett (Robert Patrick), Monica Reyes (Annabeth Gish), Assistant Director Walter Skinner (Mitch Pileggi), Cigarette-Smoking Man (William B. Davis), Deep Throat (Jerry Hardin), Mr. X (Steven Williams), Alex Krycek (Nicholas Lea), Well-Manicured Man (John Neville), Bounty Hunter (Brian Thompson), Marita Covarrubias (Laurie Holden), Jeffery Spender (Chris Owens), Diana Fowley (Mimi Rogers), Melvin Frohike (Tom Braidwood), Ringo Langly (Dean Haglund), John Byers (Bruce Harwood)

Two FBI agents discover a conspiracy by highly placed government officials to sell Earth out to alien colonizers.

Individual Episodes

MISSION IMPOSSIBLE: "THE CARRIERS" (11/19/66, CBS, 60 minutes)

Cast: Dan Briggs (Steven Hill), Rollin Hand (Martin Landau), Cinnamon Carter (Barbara Bain), Barney (Greg Morris); Guest Cast: Roger Lee (George Takei), Janos Passik (Arthur Hill), Tigran Portisch (Phil Posner), Guard (Barry Cahill), Instructor (Rick Traeger), Tiso Kastner (Barry Russo)

Credits: Director: Sherman Marks; Teleplay: William Read Woodfield, Allan Balter.

A Soviet training camp is being used to import a deadly plague into the United States.

MISSION IMPOSSIBLE: "THE TOWN" (2/18/68, CBS, 60 minutes)

Cast: Jim Phelps (Peter Graves), Rollin Hand (Martin Landau), Cinnamon Carter (Barbara Bain), Barney (Greg Morris); Guest Cast: Doc (Will Geer), Williams (Eddie Ryder), Jan (Brioni Farrell), Marty (Robert Pickering), Gina (Robyn Millan), Instructor (William O'Connell), Liz (Dee Carroll), Deputy (Gregg Palmer), Mosnyenov (George Perina), Desk Clerk (Glen C. Gordon)

Credits: Director: Michael O'Herlihy; Teleplay: Sy Salkowitz

IMF leader Jim Phelps discovers a small town where every resident is a foreign subversive.

THE OUTER LIMITS: "THE HUNDRED DAYS OF THE DRAGON" (9/23/63, ABC, 60 minutes)

Cast: William Lyons Selby (Sidney Blackmer), Theodore Pearson (Phillip Pine), Carol Selby Conner (Nancy Rennick), Ann Pearson (Joan Camden), Li Chin-Sung (Richard Loo), Dr. Bob Conner (Mark Roberts), Dr. Su-Lin (Aki Akeong), Major Ho Chi-Wong (Clarence Lung), Wen Lee (James Hong), Li Kwan (James Yagi), Frank Summers (Bert Remsen), Carter (Dennis McCarthy), Briggs (Richard Gittings), Bryan (Robert Brubaker), Oriental in Hotel (Eugene Chan), FBI Agent Marshall (Henry Scott), Schumacher's Voice (Vic Perrin), Commentator Voice (Leslie Stevens)

Credits: Director: Byron Haskin; Teleplay: Allan Balter, Robert Mintz.

A Chinese agent is transformed into an exact double of the American president and replaces him.

TWILIGHT ZONE: "A DAY IN BEAUMONT" (4/11/86, CBS, 30 minutes)

Cast: Kevin Carlson (Victor Garber), Faith (Stacy Nelkin), Pops (John Agar), Sheriff (Kenneth Tobey), Major Whitmore (Warren Stevens), Orson (Jeff Morrow), Young Man (Myles O'Brien)

Credits: Director: Philip DeGuere; Screenplay: David Gerrold.

A 1950s couple discovers that everyone around them in the town of Beaumont is an alien infiltrator.

Bibliography

Aaronovitch, David. *Voodoo Histories: The Role of Conspiracy Theory in Shaping Modern History.* New York: Penguin, 2010.

Anchors, William E., Jr. "Beyond *Westworld*." *Epi-Log*, July 1991.

Bell, Tony. "*The Bionic Woman.*" *Epi-Log*, February 1992.

Biskind, Peter. *Seeing Is Believing: How Hollywood Taught Us to Stop Worrying and Love the Fifties.* New York: Pantheon, 1983.

Black, Gregory D., and Clayton R. Koppes. *Hollywood Goes to War: How Politics, Profits and Propaganda Shaped World War II Movies.* Berkley: University of California Press, 1987.

Britton, Wesley A. *Beyond Bond: Spies in Fiction and Films.* Westport, CT: Praeger, 2005.

_____. *Spy Television.* Westport, CT: Praeger, 2004.

Brooks, Tim, and Earle Marsh. *The Complete Directory to Primetime Network and Cable Television Shows: 1946 to Present.* New York: Ballantine Books, 2003.

Dick, Bernard F. *The Star-Spangled Screen: The American World War II Film.* Lexington: University Press of Kentucky, 1985.

Doherty, Thomas. *Projections of War: Hollywood, American Culture and World War II.* New York: Columbia University Press, 1993.

Frentzen, Jeffrey, and David J. Schow. *The Outer Limits: The Official Companion.* New York: Ace, 1986.

Gifford, Denis. *Karloff: The Man, the Monster, the Movies.* Teaneck, NJ: Curtis Books, 1973.

Gorman, Ed, and Kevin McCarthy, editors. *They're Here...: Invasion of the Body Snatchers, A Tribute.* New York: Berkley, 1999.

Grams, Martin, Jr. *I Led Three Lives: The True Story of Herbert A. Philbrick's Television Program.* Albany, GA: Bear Manor Media, 2004.

Hanyok, Robert J. "How the Japanese Did it." *Naval History Magazine*, December 2009.

Harvey, James. *Romantic Comedy in Hollywood: From Lubitsch to Sturges.* New York: Alfred A. Knopf, 1987.

Hickey, Donald R. "The Prager Affair: A Study in Wartime Hysteria." *Journal of the Illinois State Historical Society*, Summer 1969.

Hofstadter, Richard. "The Paranoid Style in American Politics." *Harper's Magazine*, November 1964.

Johnson, Haynes. *The Age of Anxiety: McCarthy to Terrorism.* New York: Harcourt, 2005.

King, Stephen. *Danse Macabre.* New York: Berkley, 1987.

Knappman, Edward W., editor. *American Trials of the 20th Century: From the Scopes Monkey Trial to O.J. Simpson.* Canton, MI: Visible Ink Press, 1995.

Knight, Peter. *Conspiracy Culture: From Kennedy to the X-Files.* New York: Routledge, 2000.

LaValley, Al, editor. *Invasion of the Body Snatchers: Don Siegel, Director.* New Brunswick, NJ: Rutgers University Press, 1989.

Lichtenfeld, Eric. *Action Speaks Louder: Violence, Spectacle and the American Action Movie.* Middletown, CT: Wesleyan University Press, 2007.

MacDonnell, Francis. *Insidious Foes: The Axis Fifth Column and the American Home Front.* Guilford, CT: Lyons Press, 2004.

Maltin, Leonard. *Leonard Maltin's 2008 Movie Guide.* New York: Plume Books, 2007.

Marchis-Mouren, B. "The Myth of Military Necessity for Japanese American Internment." Université de Provence, 1989.

Marill, Alvin H. *Movies Made for Television: The Telefeature and the Miniseries.* New York: Baseline, 1987.

Mavis, Paul. *The Espionage Filmography: United States Releases, 1898 Through 1999.* Jefferson, NC: McFarland, 2001.

Nathan, Debbie, and Snedeker, Michael. *Satan's Silence: Ritual Abuse and the Making of a Modern American Witch Hunt.* New York: Basic Books, 1995.

Navasky, Victor. *Naming Names.* New York: Penguin, 1981.

Nevins, Jess. "Operator 5." *Incognito*, June 2009.

Newitz, Annalee. "The Fembot Mystique." *Popular Science*, August 2006.

Philbrick, Herbert A. *I Led Three Lives: Citizen—"Communist"—Counterspy.* Washington, D.C.: Capitol Hill Press, 1972.

Pizzitola, Louis. *Hearst over Hollywood: Power, Passion and Propaganda in the Movies.* New York: Columbia University Press, 2002.

Press, Andrea L. *Women Watching Television: Gender, Class and Generation in the American Television Experience.* Philadelphia: University of Pennsylvania Press, 1991.

Raleigh, Henry. "In the Wake of the War." *Vanity Fair*, February 1919.

Ross, Steven J. "*Confessions of a Nazi Spy*: Warner Bros., Anti-Fascism, and the Politicization of Hollywood." In *Warners' War: Politics, Pop Culture & Propaganda in Wartime Hollywood*, edited by Johanna Blakley and Martin Kaplan, 48–59. Los Angeles: Norman Lear Center Press, 2004.

Rovner, Matthew. "A Plot Against America: A Jewish Writer's Forgotten 'Future History' of a Future Nazi Takeover." *Jewish Daily Forward*, 2009.

_____. "Whatever Happened to Arch Oboler?" *Parallax View*, 2009.

Schrecker, Ellen. *Many Are the Crimes: McCarthyism in America.* Boston: Little, Brown, 1998.

Seed, David. *Brainwashing: The Fictions of Mind Control—A Study of Novels and Films Since World War II.* Kent, OH: Kent State University Press, 2004.

Shaheen, Jack G. *Reel Bad Arabs: How Hollywood Vilifies a People.* New York: Olive Branch Press, 2001.

Sherman, Fraser A. *Cyborgs, Santa Claus and Satan: Science Fiction, Fantasy and Horror Films Made for Television.* Jefferson, NC: McFarland, 2000.

Sontag, Susan. "The Imagination of Disaster." *Commentary*, October 1965.

Strade, Michael, and Harold Troper. *Friend or Foe: Russians in American Film and Foreign Policy, 1933–1991.* Lanham, MD: Scarecrow Press, 1997.

"War of the Worlds." *Epi-Log*, February 1992.

Warren, Bill. *Keep Watching the Skies! American Science Fiction Movies of the Fifties, the 21st Century Edition.* Jefferson, NC: McFarland, 2009.

White, Patrick J. *The Complete Mission: Impossible Dossier.* New York: Avon, 1991.

Williams, Lucy Chase. *The Complete Films of Vincent Price.* Secaucus, NJ: Citadel Press, 1998.

Index

Numbers in ***bold italics*** indicate pages with illustrations.

Aarniokoski, Doug 187
Aaronovitch, David 4, 18
Abbott, John 197, 205
Abbott, Joseph M. 207
ABC 144, 181, 186, 205, 209, 210, 211
Abdelghani, Lasfar 201
Abdelkader, Aizoun 206
Aberdine, Noureddine 201
Abkarian, Simon 201
Abraham, Falconer 188
Abrahams, Doug 204
Abrahams, John 187
Abroms, Edward 199
Ace 188
Acheson, J. 190
Acker, Amy 209
Ackles, Jensen 162, 210
Ackroyd, Jack 183
Across the Pacific 2, 29, ***31***, 32, 34–35, 181
Acuff, Eddie 39, 188
Adams, Brooke 103, ***105***, 191, ***192***
Adams, Ernie 188
Adams, Joe 196
Adams, Kathryn 202
Adams, Lloyd 206
Adams, Quincy, Jr. 201
Adams, Skylar 201
Adamson, Frank 188
Adamson, James 190
Adamy, Julie 196
Adcox, Thomas 193
Addison, John 205
Adell, Genevieve 191
Adler, Luther 20
Adreon, Franklin 192
Adrian, Iris 208
Agar, John 55, ***56***, 137, 208, 211
Aghdashloo, Shohreh 95
Aguilar, George 204
Ahambane, Mohamed El Habib 201
Ahdout, Jonathan 95
Ahn, Philip 36, 40, 183, 195, 205
Aiello, Danny 188
AIP 118, 146, 184, 186, 188, 193
AIP-TV 208
Akeong, Aki 211
Akhtar, Adeel 93, 206

Akhtar, Ayad 207
Akimoff, Alex 198
Akin, David 201
Akin, Philip 161, 194, 210
Alachiotis, Nick 206
Albright, Hardie 202
Alciatore, Henri 193
Alcott, John 198
Alcott, Robert B. 208
Alden, Norman 205
Alessi, Joseph 196
Alexander, Jeff 208
Alexander, Newell 195
Alexis, Demetrius 198
Alfaro, Henry 205
Alias 180, 209
The Aliens Are Coming 136, 181
All Through the Night 2, 5, 16, 181
Alland, William 192
Allbritton, Louise 207
Allen, Alfred 29
Allen, Harry 197
Allen, Nancy 123, 204
Allen, Peter 204
Allen, Valerie 189
Allen, Woody 78, 187
Allerick, Steven 206
Alley, Kirstie 206
Allie, Akram 201
Allied Artists 189, 191
Allison, Jean 185
Allport, Christopher 190
Aloha Means Goodbye 29, 181
Alper, Murray 202
Alperson, Edward L., Jr. 190
Alter, Eric 187
Alverson, Tim 183
Amazing Stories 127
Amazons 150–1, 181–2
Ambler, Eric 18
American International Pictures *see* AIP
American Legion 45, 54, 64, 66, 76
American Trials of the 20th Century 78
Ames, Jean 181
Ammon, Jack 187
Amram, David 196
Amrer, Alan 134–5
Amsellem, Reymond 201

Anders, Andrea 204
Anders, David 209
Anderson, Axel 197
Anderson, Ernest 189
Anderson, George 23, 182
Anderson, Gillian 138, ***141***, 210
Anderson, Helen 182
Anderson, James 189
Anderson, Jo 193
Anderson, John 186
Anderson, Judith 181
Anderson, Kevin 201
Anderson, Melody 25, 188
Anderson, Michael 200
Anderson, Richard 203
Anderson, Sam 199
Anderson, Stanley 138, 182, 194
Anderson, Sugarfoot 190
Andor, Paul 207
Andrade, Fran 187
Andren, Jean 191
Andrews, Dana 70, ***71***, 187
Andrews, Herbert 207
Andrews, Robert Hardy 208
Andrews, Thea 194
Animorphs 143, 209
Ankrum, Morris 190
Annihilator 136, 182
Antaramian, Jacqueline 203
Antonelli, Laura 186
Anwar, Gabrielle 106, 184, ***184***
Applebaum, Louis 207
Applegate, Katherine 143
Appley, Chris 187
Apponyi, Lara 202
Aprea, John 196, 204
Arabs 4, 89, 90, 93; *see also* Islamic terrorism
Aranas, Raul 193
Archer, Elizabeth 198
Archley, Hooper 188
Arco, Louis 198
Argent, Maurice 191
The Argyle Secrets 23, 182
Aries, Anna 191
Arkin, Alan 200
Arkoff, Samuel Z. 186
Arlen, Richard 189

Arlington Road 2, 3, 4, 177–9, ***179***, 182
Armian, Neda 196
Armitage, Frank 206
Armstrong, Robert 195
Armstrong, Scott 199
Armstrong, Vaughn 189
Arnal, Issa 186
Arness, Jim 49, 67, 183
Arnold, David 204
Arnold, Edward 164, 199
Arnold, Jack 192
Arrants, W. Wayne 183
Arrigo, Frank 200
Artz, Tim 196
Ascolese, Joseph 207
Ash, Taren 206
Ashby, Linden 138, 194
Ashmore, Shawn 209
Askins, Monroe 189
Asner, Edward 170, 193
Astor, Mary 34, 181
The Astronaut's Wife 132, 144, 182–3
The Asylum 132, 192
Atchley, Hooper 188
atheism 51, 57, 65, 67, 76
Attell, Toni 182
Atterbury, Malcolm 203
Aubert, Lenore 205
Aubrey, James T. 188
Audain, Dionne 202
Aurelio, Agnes 193
Austin Powers, International Man of Mystery 146–7
Austin, Elizabeth 204
Avalon, Frankie 146, 147, 186, 197
Avellan, Elizabeth 187
Avery, Bettye 205
Avery, Dylan 166, 195
Aware, Inc. 78
Axelrod, George 196, 196
Axman, Hanne ***49***, 56, 200
Axtell, Kirk 182, 186
Aylward, Rory 208
Azalea Pictures 116–7, 208

Babatunde, Obba 196
Babchack, Jim 189
Baccarin, Morena 210
Bachman, Conrad 182
Back at the Front 41

Index

Bacon, Kevin 193
Badalamenti, Angelo 182
Badalucco, Joseph, Jr. 203
Badel, Alan 205
Baganov, Vitali 202
Bagby, Ross 3
Bagley, Lorri 204
Bahena, Bianca 192
Baikoff, Robert 198
Bailey, Charles 186, 188
Bailey, Charles W., II 203
Bailey, William 190
Bain, Barbara 77, 211
Baird, Stuart 203
Bakaleinikof, (C.) 187, 197
Baker, Frank 197
Bakey, Ed 205
Bakula, Scott 137, 190
Bala, Farah 207
Baldwin, Craig 126, 127, 206
Baldwin, Judith 204
Baldwin, Peter 189
Baldwin, Sidney 207
Balenda, Carla 61, 208
Ballhaus, Michael 189
Balsam, Martin 203
Balsley, Michael 207
Balter, Allan 211
The Bamboo Prison 76
Bamji, Firdous 93, 207
Bamman, Gerry 199
Band, Charles 126, 203
Bank, Ursula 197
Banks, Doug 118, 184
Banks, Howard 188
Banner, John 23, 182
Baptiste, Charles 184
Barbour, Richard 202
Barclay, George 207
Barclay, Joan 35, 184
Barden, Alice 207
Barker, Lex 41, 194
Barker, Tim 199
Barnes, George 185
Barnes, Julian 182
Barnes, P. Rodney 206
Barnes, Susan 205
Barnett, Gregory 205
Barnett, Griff 204
Barnett, Tom 206
Barnitt, Roy 193
Baron, Margaret Hall 205
Barr, Jackson 203
Barrett, Janet 189
Barrett, Tom 203
Barrier, Edgar 61, 207, 208
Barrish, Seth 182
Barry, John 200
Barry, Matthew 198
Barry, P.J. 189
Bart, Roger 151, 204
Bartel, Paul 186
Bartley, Daryl 190
Bartolie, Adolfo 203
Basch, Felix 197

Basehart, Richard 78, 185
Bass, Ron 186
Bassett, Craig 205
Bassett, William 190
Basso, Frank 196
Bataglia, Matt 206
Bates, Alan 82, 199
Bates, Barbara 204
Bates, Florence 205
Batista, Philip 204
Batman (1943) 29, 32
The Battle Cry of Peace 9, 183
Bauchau, Patrick 210
Baur, Christine 205
Bava, Mario 186
Baxter, Alan 202
Baxter, Les 186, 194
Bayer, Michael Bard 189
Bayles, Lee 190
Baylor, Hal 183
Bazelli, Bojan 184
Beach, Laurie 181
Beall, Betty 120, 185
Beard, John F. 203
Beatty, Jeff 203
Beatty, Warren 169, 199
Beaudet, Louise 183
Beaumont, Hugh 189
Beck, Matthew 194
Beckerman, Barry 200
Beddelem, Joseph 206
Beebe, Dione 201
Beecher, Janet 199
Beery, Noah, Jr. 207
Behal, Steve 194
Behind the Rising Sun 32
Beimfohr, Edward 182
Bell, Cliff, Sr. 192
Bell, Marshall 198, 199
Bell, Nancy 188
Bell, Peter 198
Bell, Ron 206
Bella, Rachael 186
Bellamy, Ralph 158, 202
Bellan, Joe 191
Bellini, Nino 198
Belmont, Virginia 183
Beltrami, Marco 187
Beltran, Alma 199
Belzer, Dan 207
Belzer, Richard 190, 199
Ben Chegra, Salaheddine 201
Bender, Russ 193
Benedict, Robert Patrick 144, 210
Benedicto, Lourdes 210
Benefiel, Scott 189
Benesh, Amy 182
Benford, Timothy B. 188
Benge, Wilson 197
Bening, Annette 91, 203
Benjamin, Eric 191
Benjamin, Floella 201
Benjamin, Richard 195
Ben Larby, Ahmed 203
Benn, David 193
Bennett, Laurence 206

Bennett, Marion 194
Bennett, Matt 190
Bennett, Nigel 188
Benoit, Mary 196
Bentley, John 188
Benton, Dean 207
Benzali, Daniel 199
Berenger, Tom 176, 177, 183
Beresford, Evelyn 197
Bergen, Jerry 195
Berger, Anna 189
Berger, Debra 190
Berger, Marilyn 202
Berger, Ralph 183, 187
Berger, Senta 23, 200
Berger, Stephen 183
Bergeron, Loys 194
Berke, William 183
Bernard, Aaron Scott 190
Bernard, Jason 198
Bernard, Sam 195
Bernardi, Herschel 187
Bernstein, Andrew 188
Bernstein, Charles 191
Bernstein, Jacob 188
Bernstein, Peter 205
Bernstein, Walter 78, 188, 189
Berry, Mark 210
Berry, Stephanie 191
Berry, Wesley E. 185
Besher, Chuk 200
Besinger, Mimi 183
Betancourt, Anne 125, 201, 203
Bethancourt, Eric 202
Bethea, Ellen 203
Betrayal from the East (book) 32, 39, 183
Betrayal from the East (film) 2, 4, 39–40, 183
Betrayed 4, 176–7, *177*, 183
Beulah **115**, **116**
Beverly, Helen **21**, 197
Bevis, Leslie 181
Beyond Westworld 155, 209
Biberman, Abner 32, 40, 183, 195
Biberman, Herbert J. 197
Bice, Robert 62, 192
The Big Clock 198
Big Jim McLain 2, 49, 50, 51, 54, 67–8, **67**, 76, 86, 183–4
Billingsley, Barbara 182, 190
Bing, Herman 187
The Bionic Woman 146
Birman, Matt 206
Bishins, David 202, 207
Bissell, Whit 191, 196, 203
Bjurman, Susan 208
Black, Karen 124, 190
Black, Louis 187
Black, William W. 9

Black Dragon Society 1, 32–36
Black Dragons 35–36, **36**, 184
Black Ocean Society 34
Black Tom explosion 7, 8, 28
Blacker, David 194, 206
Blackmer, Sidney 76, 158, 199, 202, 211
Blackton, J. Stuart 9, 183
Blagoi, George 197
Blagol, Nina 198
Blair, Betsy 183
Blair, Gregory 187
Blair, Nicky 196
Blaisdell, Paul 193
Blake, Andre 196
Blake, Arthur 197
Blake, Clement 189, 193
Blake, Oliver 187, 202
Blake, Richard 190, 191
Blakely, Susan 182
Blanchard, Mari 41, 194
Blanchard, Rachel 210
Blanchard, Susan 205
Blanckaert, Myriam 206
Blandick, Clara 199
Blangsted, Folmar 190, 200
Blauvelt, Field 191
Blees, William 208
Bleeth, Yasmine 138, 194
Bleifer, John 188
Bloch, Robert 185
Block, Hunt 87, 202
Blockade 12
Blondell, Joan 185
Blossier, Patrick 183
Blount, Lisa 182
Blue, Monte 181
Blount, Roy, Jr. 196
Blum, Sammy 183, 197
Blythe, Erik 62, 192
Body Snatchers (film) 106–108, **107**, 116, 130, 184, 191
Body Snatchers (novel) 97–99, 184
Boen, Earl 182
Bogart, Humphrey 16, **17**, **31**, 34, 181
Bogert, William 188
bogeymen 3, 22, 43, 55, 86, 88, 89, 166, 169, 178
Boggs, Haskell 189
Bogle, Michael C. 187
Bohn, Merritt 196
Bohnen, Roman 197
Bolender, Bill 194
Bolin, Nick 196
Bolster, Anita 202
Bomer, Matthew 210
Bonar, Ivan 185
Bond, Jackson 108, 191
Bond, Nelson 153
Bond, Renee 191
Bondell, Tony Curtis 194

216

Index

Bondy, Chris 195
Bonn, Walter 208
Bonnell, Munro M. 204
Bonney, Gail 200
Bonomolo, Lyndsey Danielle 182
Boone, Avis 203
Boothe, Powers 200
Bordiggi, Al 191
Borg, Veda Ann 183, 187
Bork, Jessica 192
Borowicz, Dan 189
Borst, Jonathan 196
Bosak, Brian 183
Bottoms, Timothy 124, 190
Bouajila, Sami 91, 203
Bouchet, James 191
Boulton, Matthew 197
Bousman, Tracy 185
Boussif, Tanane 201
Bouvier, Charles 203
Bowden, Joyce Leigh 183
Bowman, Melodee 193
Boyd, Jerry 182
Boyd, Mildred 190
Boylan, John 187
Boyle, Robert 192
Bradbury, Ray 112, 192
Bradford, David 204
Bradford, Johnny 189
Bradford, Lane 192
Bradford, Marshall 200
Bradford, Richard 83, 195
Bradley, Pat 185
Bradley, Paul 190
Braeden, Eric 181
Braham, Lionel 183
Braidwood, Tom 211
The Brain Eaters 5, 115, 117–20, *119*, 128, 184–5
Brainard, Wendy 205
brainchanging 75
The Brainwashed Pilot 76
brainwashing 75–6
Branam, Craig 196
Branch, Houston 188
Brandon, John 194
Brandon, Mark 185
Brandt, Hank 181, 205
Brandt, Janet 187
Brandt, Martin 198
Brascia, John 186
Bratton, Dana 205
Braugher, Andre 202
Breach 5
Breach, Stephen 203
Breaux, Walter 193
Brebner, John 207
Breck, Jonathan 189
Breck, Peter 200
Breen, Joe 11
Brengk, Ernest 197
Brennan, Maureen 187
Brennert, Alan 194
Brent, Eve 187
Brent, Kimberly 184
Brewer, Jameson 194
Brewster, Bonnie 189

Brewster, Jordana 130, 187
Bricker, George 195, 208
Brickman, Greg 186
Brickman, I.D. 193
Bridges, Jeff 177, *179*, 182
Bridges, Krista 194, 195
Bridges, Lloyd 197
Brill, Patti 183
Brimley, Wilford 206
Brinegar, Paul 182
Brink, Johnny 193
Brinkman, Leigh E. 206
Britton, Burt 188
Brocco, Peter 182, 190, 208
Broderick, Matthew 151, 204
Brodie, Don 208
Bronson, Charles 79, *79*, 205
Brooke, Hillary 20, 112, 190, 197
Brooke, Walter 186
Brooking, Fallon 204
Brooks, Barry 208
Brooks, Ben 206
Brooks, Joe 184
Brooks, Rebecca 202
Brooks, Rennie 184
Brooks, Stan 203
Brophy, Brian 201
Brophy, Edward 181
The Brotherhood of the Bell 173–4, 184
Broughton, George 197
Brower, Otto 195
Brown, Blair 182
Brown, Cecil 201
Brown, Jeb 202
Brown, Lew 205
Brown, Lowell 185
Brown, Peter 200
Brown, Timothy P. 184
Brown, Tom 36, 195
Browne, Nick 199
Brubaker, Robert 211
Bruce, Belle 183
Bruce, George 207
Bruhanski, Alex 187
Bruhns, Werner 198
Brummer, Gordon 196
Brun, Joseph 207
Brutsman, Joseph 190
Bryant, Todd 199
Brynner, Yul 188
Bryson, Kendall 208
B'Tiste, I'Lana 193
Buchanan, Larry 208
Buckner, Robert 198
Budd, Norman 57, 200
Buff, Conrad 182
Bukowski, Bobby 182
Bull, Richard 186, 199
Bullard, Benjamin 191
Bullard, Steve 202
Bullock, James Oliver 201
Bullock, Tom 194
Bumstead, Henry 189

Burden, Gary 182
Burgi, Richard 189
Burke, James 181
Burkes, Hunter 182
Burkley, Dennis 198
Burns, Bart 203
Burns, Harry 188
Burns, Paul E. 208
Burr, Raymond 61, 207, 208
Burry, Jennifer 182
Burstyn, Ellen 51, 82, 199
Burton, Bernard 187
Burton, Frederick 185
Burton, Robert 196
Buscemi, Steve 201
Busch, Dianne 207
Bush, Billy 204
Bush, Robert L. 207
Bushelman, John A. 194
Butcher, Andrew 195
Butler, Dan 201
Butler, David 205
Butler, Duana 196
Butler, Tom 188
Byrd, Carl 205
Byrd, Evelyn 196
Byrd, Ralph 23, 182
Byrne, Gabriel 159
Byron, Arthur 163, 199

Cabrera, Boris 209
Caggiano, Theresa 203
Cahill, Barry 211
Cahn, Daniel 190
Cahn, Philip 208
Callahan, Gene 195, 204
Cambas, Jacqueline 195
Camden, Joan 211
Cameron, Kirk 160, 194, 195
Cameron, Rod 37, 188
Camp, Helen Page 205
Campbell, Desmond 206
Campbell, Geoff 204
Campbell, J. Marvin 190, 199
Campbell, John W. 121, 206
Campbell, Shawn 190
Canaan, Christopher 188
Candy, John 193
Cane, Charles 181, 190, 208
Caninenberg, Hans 198
Cannon 190
Cantillo, Jose Pablo 196
Cantrell, Early 183
Capell, Peter 207
Carey, Brian 185
Carey, Leonard 197
Carey, Olive 208
Carey, Philip 189, 200
Carides, Gia 186
Carleton, Johelen 200
Carlisle, Bob 194
Carlson, Les 195
Carlson, Richard 50, 111, *112*, 192, 209

Carnovsky, Morris 197
Carpel, Samantha 182
Carpenter, Fred 183
Carpenter, John 122, 129, 125, 189, 206, 207
Carr, Colleen 208
Carr, Paul 186
Carras, Anthony 186
Carrasco, Jonathan 193
Carreiro, Tony 189
Carrere, Tia 201
Carrington, Debbie 190, 203
Carroll, Dee 211
Carroll, Robert 207
Carroll, Stephanie 207
Carruthers, Bruce 197
Carsetti, Gastone 186
Carson, Frances 202
Carson, Hunter 124, 190
Carson, Jean 189
Carson, Price 194
Carson, Robert 181, 187
Carson, Robert S. 192
Carsten, Peter 200
Cartagena, Victoria 202
Carter, Ellis W. 192
Carter, Gary 193
Carter, Helena 114, 190
Carter, Janis 52, *53*, 55, 208
Carter, John 205
Carter, Maurice 200
Carter, T.K. 206
Cartier, Mike 195
Cartwright, Veronica 25, 103, *105*, 108, 188, 191
Carus, Mickey 191
Cascone, Nicholas 199
Casey, Donna 187
Casey, Sharon 202
Cassavetes, John 157, 202
Cassavetes, Nick 182
Cassidy, Katie 162
Cassidy, Patrick 25, 188
Castelo, Chirstopher 207
Castelo, Joseph 207
Castillo, Alex 206
Castinado, Naya 182
Castle, Irene 28, 199
Castle, Peggie *62*, 192
Castle, Robert 196
Castle, William 202
Castleton, Barbara 45, 185
Catlett, Loyd 182
Catlett, Walter 205
Cattrall, Kim 201
CBS 78, 185, 190, 199, 209, 210, 211
Ceder, Elayne 191
Ceder, Evelyn 208
Celedonio, Maria 201
Cella, Susan 182
Centaur 191
Cerullo, Alfred C. 201
Cervantes, Carlos 182
Chabidon, Ron 187
Chackler, David 207

Index

Chadwick, Alex 203
Chakrabarti, Samrat 207
Challee, William 208
Chambers, Barry 193
Chambers, Mia Arniece 191
Chambers, Steve 207
Chambliss, Scott 203
Chan, Eugene 211
Chan, George B. 181
Chan, Spencer 181, 183
Chandlee, Dick 208
Chandler, Patti 186, 197
Chaney, Jordan 181
Chang, Key 183
Chang, Melle 195
Chang, Paul 197
Chang, Yun Kui 194
Chapin, Tom 196
Chapman, Anjeli 207
Chapman, Mark Lindsay 136, 182
Chapman, Michael 182, 188, 191, 201
Chapman, Thomas C. 182
Charles, Arlene 186
Charles, Gaius 202
Chartrand, Lauro 204
Chase, Alden 45, 187
Chase, Channing 182
Chatfield, Lansdale 202
Chatinover, Marvin A. 202
Chaves, Mykel 194
Chaves, Richard 210
Cheadle, Don 96, 206
Cheatham, Jack 202
Chediak, Enrique 187
Cheng, Mary 197
Cheshire, Harry 208
Chester, Colby 186
Chestnut, Morris 210
Cheung, Margaret 197
China 4, 41, 47, 76–7, 78, 147
Chioran, Juan 206
Chirva, Alex 197
Choate, Pat 201
Chodak, Randy 204
Chong, Peter 183, 198
Choubi, Mohamed 206
Choudhury, Sarita 207
Christensen, Harley 200
Christie, Howard "Red" 187
Christine, Virginia 191
Chudnow, David 182
Churchill, Adrian 206
Ciannelli, Eduardo 205
Cibrian, Eddie 210
Ciccolella, Jude 196
Cirbus, Steve 202
Cistheri, Raymond 184
Civic Duty 87, **94**, 184
civil rights 5, 51–2, 57, 59, 68
Clark, Bobby 191
Clark, Carroll 208
Clark, Dave Allen 182

Clark, Fred 161, 186
Clark, Ken 201
Clark, Martin 182
Clark, Spencer Treat 182
Clark, Wallis 198
Clarke, David 188
Clarke, Robert 184
Clay, Harry 197
Clay, Stanley Bennett 182
Clayton, Don 198
Cleary, Leo 57, 200
Clemons, Steven C. 201
Clennon, David 176, 183, 206
Clermont, Brock 206
Clift, Eleanor 201
Clinker, Nigel 189
Clinton, George S. 183
Close, Eric 142, 209
Close, Glenn 151, 204
Clotworthy, Robert 201
Cloud Ten Pictures 194, 195
Clute, Sidney 186
Clyde, David 197
Coates, Phyllis 192
Cobb, Edmund 188
Cobbler, Jan 188
Coblenz, Walter 205
Coe, George 204
Cohane, Suzanne 199
Cohen, Joel 205
Cohen, Larry 184
Cohen, Michael 184
Cohen, Stuart 182
Coil, Marvin 198
The Coldest Winter 47
Cole, Kimberly L. 184
Cole, Val 185
Coleman, Chuck 190
Coleman, Dabney 184, 205
Colesberry, Robert F. 189
Collective Minds Media 196
Colliers Magazine 98
Collins, Carla 206
Collins, G. Pat 208
Collins, Greg 182
Collis, Jack T. 194
Colman, Henry 185
Colon, Epi 203
Colter, Mike 202
Colton, John 191
Columbia Pictures 187, 192, 195, 198, 207
Columbia Tri-Star 202
Combs, David 208
Combs, Thurman L. 184
Commesso, Christine 207
communism 1, 44–5, 47–8, 53–54, 86
Communist Party of the United States of America 1, 3, 44–5, 47–54, 55–61, 67–70, 76, 102
The Complete Directory to Prime Time Network and Cable TV Shows 70

Condon, Richard 196
Condon, William 205
Confessions of a Nazi Spy 12–15, **13**, 185
Conklin, Chester 183
Conklin, Peggy 199
Conley, Corinne 210
Conneen, Mike 203
Connolly, David 207
Connolly, Myles 198
Connor, James 188
"Conqueror's Isle" 153
Conrad, Robert 200
Conrad, Roy 207
Conrad, William 174, 184
Conried, Hans 183
Conroy, Burt 188
Conspiracy Culture 4, 150
Conspirator 51
Conti, Bill 183
Conti, Sam 191
Contner, James A. 188
Contreras, Luis 190
Converse, Leslie 204
Conway, Dan 183
Conway, Russ 189
Cook, Doria 199
Cook, Elisha, Jr. 202
Cook, Robin 201
Cook, Tommy 204
Cooke, John C. 199
Cooper, Bradley 209
Cooper, Jeanne 200
Cooper, Leslie 187
Cooper, Luray 191
Copelan, Jodie 185
Copland, Ronda 199
Coquillon, John 199
Corazza, Vincent 206
Corbell, Norman 187
Corbett, Ed 207
Corcoran, Bill 195
Cordic, Regis J. 205
Corman, Roger 196
Cornered 20
Cornthwaite, Robert 188
Corrado, Gino 198
Correa, Enrique 196
Corrigan, Blaise 204
Corrigan, Lloyd 196
Corsair, Bill 183
Corsaro, Franco 208
Cort, Bud 190
Corti, David 199
Costa-Gavras 176, 183
Costabile, David 203
Costanzo, Paulo 209
Costello, Michelle 206
Coster, Naum 197
Costner, Kevin 82, 170, 193, 198
Coulouris, George 20, **21**, 197
Covell, James 195
Cover, Franklin 204
Cowan, Ashley 200
Cowan, Jerome 197
Cox, Darryl 182, 193

Cox, Joe Anthony 190
Cox, John Henry 203
Crabe, James 185
Craig, Daniel 108, 191
Craig, Donald 182
Crane, Ed 196
Cravat, Noel 188
Crawford, Jack 183
Crawford, John 189, 192
Crawford, Lana 196
Crawford, Rufus 194
Crawford, Thomas 194
The Creation of the Humanoids 153–4, 185
Credel, Curtis 181
Crehan, Joseph 198
Cresciman, Vincent J. 205
Crichlow, Brenda M. 185
Crichton, Michael 201
Crider, Michael 182
Cristal, Linda 185
Crombie, Peter 201
Cronauer, Gail 193
Crone, Neil 194
Cronyn, Hume 90, 169, 199, 202
Crosby, Wade 62, 188, 192
Cross, David 185
Cross, Marcia 205
Cross, Oliver 198
Cross, Paul 181
Cross, Roger R. 143, 209
Crosse, Clay 194
Crossfire 194
Crosthwaite-Eyre, Caroline 193
Crugnali, Louis 201
Crumpler, Courtney Allen 205
Crunch Recording Group 206
Crupi, Anthony 204
Cudney, Cliff 189
Culea, Melinda 205
Culp, Steven 210
Cummings, Robert 16, 202
Cundey, Dean 182, 206
Cunningham, Colin 204
Curan, Marianne 199
Currie, Finlay 64, 207
Currie, Gordon 160, 194, 195
Curson, Anne 197
Curtis, Billy 202
Curtis, John 204
Curtis, Tony 199
Curtiz, Michael 198
Cusack, Christopher 189
Cusack, Joan 3, 178, 182
Cushing, Bartley 187
Cvetic, Matt 50, 58–61
CW Network 210
Cybulski, Artur 194
Cypher, Jon 190
Czuma, Marek 187

Index

D., Chris 198
D'Agosta, Michael 200
D'Agostino, Albert S. 183, 197, 208
Dahlberg, Chris 191182
Dahlgren, Tom 201
Dale, Virginia 39, 188
Dalley, Ray 196
Dalton, Darren 200
Daly, Joel 183
Daly, Tyne 205
Dampp, Sarah 182
Dangerous Hours 45, 185
Daniel, Bill 206
Daniel, Roger 208
Daniell, Henry 197
Daniels, Jeff 86, 189, 206
Daniels, William 169, 199
Danielson, Dan 201
Danner, Blythe 155, 188
Danse Macabre 98
Danticat, Edwidge 196
Dantine, Helmut 197
Danyla, Cibby 206
Dapo, Ronnie 200
Darby, Jonathan 186
Darden, Severn 209
Darien, Frank 208
Dark Skies 135, 142–3, 209
D'Arno, Albert 198
Darrin, Deanna 186
Darshi, Agam 185
Darst, Danny 196
Darwell, Jane 181
Dauda, Raven 194
Davenport, Harry 39, 188, 207
Davenport, Ned 192
Daviau, Allen 183
David, Adam 195
David, Angel 203
David, Jeff 205
David, Keith 125, 199, 205, 206
Davidovitch, Lolita 193
Davidson, Jack 188
Davidson, Jeremy 202
Davidson, Martin 186
Davidson, Ronald 188, 192
Davies, Brian 189
Davies, Dave 207
Davies, John S. 193
Davies, Joseph P. 18
Davies, Lloyd 56, 57, 200
Davis, Allison Pratt 193
Davis, Dawn M. 201
Davis, Dilsey 205
Davis, Don 194, 202
Davis, Donald 25, 188
Davis, Geena 82
Davis, George 198
Davis, Hope 178, 182
Davis, Jack 197
Davis, Jim 199
Davis, Norman 193
Davis, Peter S. 199
Davis, Robert 185

Davis, Sonny Carl 203
Davis, Viola 210
Davis, Walter 205
Davis, William B. 139, 211
Dawson, Frank 197
Day, Laraine *53*, 55, 208
Day, Richard 195
The Day Mars Invaded Earth 97, 120, 185
Deacon, Richard 190, 191
The Dead Don't Die 159–60, 185
Deakins, Lucy *83*, 195
Dean, E. Brian 202
Dean, Louis 194
DeAngelis, Judy 185, 203
Dearborn, Dalton 193–194
Dearing, Edgar 192
The Death of Me Yet 78, 185
Deckard, Simon 204
De Cordoba, Pedro 202
Deering, John 185
Defenseless 183
deFreitas, Todd 189
DeGolyer, Mary 200
Degovia, Jackson 200, 204
DeGuere, Philip 211
DeKay, Tim 201
Dekker, Thomas 207
Delaney, Kim 186
De Laney, Patricia 208
Delano, Lee 186
Delany, Dana 172, 186
Delerue, George 189
Delevanti, Cyril 197
Delia, Joe 184, 208
De Line, Donald 204
De Linsky, Vic 194
Dell, Charlie 190
Dell, Gabriel 36, 195
Dellahoussaye, Denzel 196
De Los Reyes, Kamar 202
Delpeyrat, Scali 206
Del Val, Jean 198
Demarest, William 181
DeMauro, Nick 182
Demeritt, Matt 203
deMichele, Mark 201
Demme, Jonathan 165, 196
Demme, Josephine 196
Demon Seed 132
DeMond, Albert 200
DeMunn, Jeffrey 183
Demura, Fumio 201
De Niro, Robert 86
Denisof, Alexis 165
Dennis, Fred 182
DeNoble, Jane 196
Depp, Johnny 132, 182
DePrez, Therese 182
de Rochemont, Louis 63, 207
DeSa, Alfredo 207
Desai, Angel 207

De Santis, Tony 194
DeSoto, Rosana 201
DeTolly, Lala 198
Deutsch, Adolph 181
Devane, William 78
The Devil's Child 159, 186
Devine, Andy 187, 199
Devine, Loretta 195
DeWoody, Chrystal 182
Dexter, Alan 189, 192
Dexter, Maury 185
DeZarn, Tim 189
Dhiegh, Khigh 74, 196
Diaquino, John 198
Di Bonaventura, Lorenzo 203
Diehl, August 87, 202
DiElsi, Frank 203
Dietz, Jack 184, 195
Dillard, Mimi 196
Dilley, Leslie 191
Dillin, Scott 203
Dillon, Brendan 185
Dills-Vozoff, Lorine 190
DiMauro, Joanne 204
Dimension Films 187
Di Milo, Tony 189
Dinklage, Peter 210
Dinwiddie, Traci 205
Dirden, Willie 182
Di Reda, Joseph 199
Disher, Catherine 210
Diveny, Mary 189
Divide and Conquer 16
Dixon, Glenn 41, 194
Dixon, McIntyre 188
Dixon, Thomas 187
Dobbs, George 201
Dobson, Tamara 181
Docherty, Mark 185
Dr. Goldfoot and the Bikini Machine 146–7, 186
Dr. Goldfoot and the Girl Bombs 147, 186
Dr. Strangelove 73
Dodd, Alex 203
Dodge, Sam 200
Doherty, Michael 195
Dolan, Robert Emmett 198
Dollhouse 165–6, 209
Donahue, Elinor 190
Donaldson, Patricia 186
Donaldson, Roger 198
Donath, Louis 197
Donato, Christine 194
Donn-Bryne, Brian Oswald 185
Donne, Carole 182
Donno, Eddy 190
D'Onofrio, Vincent 170, 193
Donovan, Frank R. 204
Donovan, King *100*, 101, 191
"Don't Look Now" 125
Doolittle, Don 153 185
Dopud, Mike 204
Dorian, Angela 158, 202

Dorkin, Cody 207
Dorochuk, Ivan 206
Dorr, Lester 195
Dorsey, Sandra 187
Dorton, Richard 201
Dorval, Adrien 187
Dott, James 190
Douglas, Don 32, 195
Douglas, Gordon 190, 207
Douglas, Jerry 159, 185, 193
Douglas, Joan 196
Douglas, Kirk 172, 203
Douglas, Warren 198
Dow, Bill 183
Dow, Lauren 193
Dowd, Ann 196
Downey, Jackie 199
Dowse, Denise 186
Doyle, Kathleen 184
Doyle, Maxine 188
Doyle-Murray, Brian 186, 193
Dracup, Robert 208
Dragon, Carmen 191
Drake, Charles 192
Drake, Chris 183
Drake, Dolores 183
Drake, Larry 210
Dreamworks 204
Dreier, Hans 197
Drew, Roland 181
Drummond, Alice 189
Dube, Michael 201
Du Bois, Michelle 182
DuBose, Columbia 193
Dubov, Paul 204, 208
DuBrey, Claire 45, 185
Duchovny, David 138, 140, *141*, 211
Duchowny, Roger 193
Duckey, Paul 199
Ducommun, Rick 187
Dudikoff, Michael 171, 203
Duff, Denice 201
Duff, Howard 198
Duff-Griffin, William 189
Duffy, Jack 206
Duffy, William 190
Dugan, Tom 199
Dugan, Tommy 199
Duggan, Andrew 172, 200, 203
Duke, Deborah 187
Dumke, Ralph 191
Dunard, David 203
Dunard, David S. 194
Duncan, Alan 185
Duncan, John 208
Dungey, Merrin 209
Dunlap, Paul 184
Dunn, Carolyn 25, 188
Dunn, Colleen 204
Dunn, Robert 207
Dunn, Roger 195
Dunn, Teddy 196
Dunne, Steve 185

INDEX

DuPar, Edwin 190
Dupont, Danielle 191
Duprez, June 33, 34, 195
Dupuis, Art 208
Duquesne spy ring 16, 48, 63
Duran, Dan 206
Durant, Ted 189
Durbin, John 182
Durning, Michele 204
Durrell, William J., Jr. 206
Duryea, Dan 197
Dushku, Eliza 165, 209
Dutton, Charles S. 210
Duval, Joe 200
DuVall, Clea 130, 187
Duvall, Robert 191
Dwyer, Marlo 208
Dye, Dale 190, 193, 199
Dyne, Aminta 197
Dys, Deanna 204
Dysart, Richard 206
Dziena, Alexis 210
Dzundza, George 197, 198

Eager, Keith 202
Ealy, Michael 93, 210
Earle, Marilee 70, *71*, 187
East Side Kids 36–37
Eaton, Shirley 147, 197
Eccles, Julie 207
economic warfare: Arab 90; Japanese 29, 41–3, 90
Ede, George 189
Edelman Randy 186
Edeson, Arthur 181
Edgley, George 208
Edward, Monique 194
Edwards, Bruce 183
Edwards, Jack, Jr. 208
Edwards, James 196
Edwards, Sam 185
Edwards, Tony 187
Eggar, Samantha 182
Eggenton, Joseph 184
Eggert, Nicole 182
Egi, Stan 201
Ehrenfreund, Heinz 198
Eight O'Clock in the Morning 206
Eirik, Sten 194
Eisen, Lorn 195
Eisen, Robert S. 191
Eisler, Gerhardt 58–9
Ejiofor, Chiwetel 87, 202
Elcar, Dana 185
Eldredge, George 117, 192
Eldredge, John 189
Elise, Christine 184
Elise, Kimberly 196
Elite Pictures 204
Elliot, Fran 194
Elliott, Brennan 171, 204
Elliott, Erica 153, 185
Elliott, R. Bruce 193
Elliott, Ted 199

Ellis, Edward 163, 199
Ellsworth, Dave 202
Elrod, Josh 196
Elswit, Robert 203
Emanuel, Michael 201
Emmich, Cliff 191, 205
End of Days 159
Endfield, Cyril 182
Enemies Within 10–11
The Enemy Within 172, 186
Engel, Roy 189
England, Bryan 202
English, Richard 184
Erickson, Leif 112, 190
Eriksen, Neela 202
Ermey, R. Lee 108, 184
Eronel Productions 182
Erskine, Howard 202
Escape 153
Esmond, Carl 20, 197, 207
Essex, Harry 112, 192
Essman, Susie 203
Eszterhas, Joe 183
Eurist, Clarence 182
Evans, Douglas 189, 198
Evans, Maurice 158, 184, 202
Everest, Barbara 197
Everett, Chad 200
Everhart, Jim 188
Executive Action 166–8, *167*, 186
The Experts 84–86, *85*, 123, 186–7
Exterre, Estelle 196
Eye of the Needle 5
Ezell, Leo 194
Ezell, Wayman 207

Fab 5 Freddy 196
Fabian 186
Fabrizio, David 201
The Faculty 110, 112, 130–2, *131*, 187
Fadden, Tom 191
Fadsin Cinema Associates 204
Fagan, Ronald J. 185
Fahmi, Boubker 201
Fahnbulleh, Laha 182
Fair, Jody 184
Fair Pretender 8
Faison, Frankie 210
Faith, Dolores 121, *122*, 189
Faithfull, Todd 195
Falkenhain, Patricia 189
The Fall of a Nation 9–10, *10*, 187
Farabee, Carol 194
Faraj, Said 203
Farber, Jodi 193
Farfel, Roy 207
Farkas, Jo 194
Farley, James 195
Farmer, Frank 190
Farmiga, Vera 196

Farrar, Digene 204
Farrell, Brioni 211
Farrell, Charles 46, *46*, 187
Farrell, Tom Riis 204
Farrow, Mia 157, *158*, 202
Faulk, John Henry 78
Fay, Meagen 201
Faye, Joey 188
Faylen, Frank 198
FBI 12, 13, 48, 50, 58, 59, 60, 63, 64, 68–9, 91, 138–9, 171, 176–7
Feagin, Hugh 193
Fear on Trial 78
Fearing, Kenneth 198
The Fearmakers (film) 54, 58, 70–2, *71*, 76, 187
The Fearmakers (novel) 187
Fee, Melinda 181
Fehr, Oded 93, 210
Fehr, Rudi 181
Feigelson, J.D. 194
Feitshans, Buzz 200
Feitshans, Fred 186
Feitshans, Fred, Jr. 204
Feld, Rudi 182
Feldary, Eric 197
Fellows, Robert 184
Fenjves, Pablo F. 186
Fenner, Walter 188
Fenton, Frank 205
Ferguson, Jessie Lawrence 181
Ferguson, Perry 205
Ferguson, William J. 183
Fernandez, Jorge 193
Fernandez, Margarite 190
Ferrara, Abel 107, 184
Ferrer, Miguel 196
Ferry, David 195
Ferstenberg, Bernard 204
Fichtner, William 145, 209
Field, Logan 173, 184
Field, Mary 197
Fielding, Edward 197
Fields, Christopher John 186
Fields, Darlene 189
Fields, Holly 125, 203
Fields, Robert 204
fifth column: definition 1; German 15–16; Japanese 30, 35, 41
Fighting Youth 45–7, *46*, 187
Finch, Howard 90, 188
Finn, Mickey 196
Finnegan, John 193
Finney, Edward 204
Finney, Jack 97, 98, 99, 102, 107, 110, 118, 184, 191
Finta, Brady 189
Fiorillo, Michael 202
First Wave 143–4, 209
Fischer, David 187

Fischer, Robert C. 198
Fish, Steven B., II 192
Fisher, David 191
Fisher, George 200
Fisher, Lola 182
Fisk, Jack 191
Fiske, Robert 184
Fitts, Rick 190
Flanagan, Michael 189
Flannery, William 198
Flemyng, Robert 200
Fletcher, Louise 123, 124, 190, 204
Fletcher, Neil 208
Flippin, Lucy Lee 188
Flower, Buck 207
Flower, George "Buck" 205
Flowers, Bess 196, 208
Floyd, Susan 191
Flynn, Colleen 186
Follows, Edwina 205
Folse, Gabriel 182
Fonda, Jane 90, 202
Fonda, Peter 154, 188
Fondacaro, Salvatore 190
Fong, Harold 183
Fong, John 197
Fontelieu, Stocker 187
Foo, Lee Tung 181, 196
Foody, Ralph 183
Foran, Dick 70, *71*, 187
Forbes, Bryan 204
Forbidden Area 74, 76, 78, 86
Forbstein, Leo 181, 185
Ford, Anitra 148, 191
Ford, Glenn 52, 173, 184
Ford, Henry 1, 9
Ford, Ross 198
Ford, Wallace 181
Foreign Correspondent 12
Foreman, Deborah 84, 186
Forest, Denis 210
Forrest, John 208
Forrest, Michael Stone 191
Forrest, William 190, 195
Forslund, Constance 206
Forsyth, Rosemary 184, 185
Forsythe, Fredrick 198
Fortell, Albert 195
Foss, Cecilia 203
Foster, David 206
Foster, Meg 185, 198, 205
Foster, Preston 33, *33*, 195
Fotre, Vincent 200
Foulger, Byron 197
Foulk, Robert 208
Fowler, Gene, Jr. 189
Fox 209, 210
Fox, Billy 206
Fox, Colin 160, 194
Fox, Edward Lyell 28
Fox, Stacie 194
Fox, Wallace 195
Foxwell, Ivan 200

Index

Foy, Bryan 190, 195
Frain, James 145
Fraker, William 202
Francen, Victor 197
Frances, Doug 182
Franchi, Franco 186
Francis, John 196
Franco, Larry J. 205, 206
Frank, Jerry 194
Frank, Pat 74
Franke, Christopher 186
Frankel, Mark 160, 210
Franken, Al 196
Frankenheimer, John 196, 203
Frankenstein 156, 187
Frankfather, William 190
Franklin, Irene 199
Franz, Arthur 114, 190
Franz, Eduard 173, 184
Fraser, Alex 182
Fraser, Phyliss 187
Fraser, Sally 193
Frawley, William 207
Frazer, John 207
Frazer, Robert 184
Frazier, Ron 202
Fredricks, Ellsworth 191, 203
Free, Bill 200
Freed, Bert 190
Freed, Donald 186
Frei, Sally 186
Fremin, Jourdan 203
French, Charles K. 199
Fridell, Squire 207
Friedkin, Jay 187
Friedman, Rabbi Morris S. 189
Friend or Foe? 80
Fritch, Hanson 199
Frnka, Roxie M. 193
Froelich, Jake 205
Froelich, Sam 205
Froelick, Anne 197
The Front 78, 86, 187-8
Frost, Alan 118, 184
Fruichantie, Teri Hunter 192
Frye, Gil 185
Fu, Pamela 204
Fudimura, Kunio 194
Fuentes, Derren 191
Fujimoto, Paul 201
Fujimoto, Tak 196
Fujioka, John 188
Fukunaza, Akiru 184
Full Moon 126, 203
Fuller, Barbra 57, 200
Funck, Hans 191
Fung, Gabriela 196
Fung, Paul 183
Futureworld 154-5, 188

G-Men vs. the Black Dragon 37, **38**, 188
Gaba, Marianne 186
Gade, Ariel 144, 210
Gail, Max 181

Gal, Natalie 203
Gale, Lorena 206
Gallagher, Dan 206
Gallagher, Megan 174, 210
Galloway, Catherine 206
Gallup, Ralph 199
Galt, John William 193
Gambina, Ralph 196
Gamble, Mason 178, 182
The Game 2
Gamet, Kenneth 183
Gan, Chester 181
Ganchev, George 200
Ganios, Tony 201
Ganis, Glenda 186
Ganz, Bruno 196
Garber, Victor 137, 180, 209, 211
Gardner, Ava 172, 203
Gardner, Jack 188
Garfield, Julie 188
Gargan, William 23, 182
Garland, Beverly 115, **116**, 193
Garland, Robert 198
Garner, Jennifer 180, 209
Garner, Josh 189
Garr, Teri 82, 199
Garrett, Donna 199
Garrett, Ernie 202
Garrett, Michael 207
Garrett, Patsy 199
Garrison, Gil 194
Garrison, Grant 182
Garrison, Jim 171, 193, 194
Garson, Robert 29
Garwood, Tara 191
Gaskins, Yolanda 186
Gastrock, Phillip 187
Gates, Harvey 184, 194, 195
Gates, Larry 101, 191
Gates, Nancy 197
Gayheart, Rebecca 201
Gee, Errol 206
Gee, Nancy 205
Gee, Timothy 204
Geer, Will 77, 166, 184, 186, 211
Gehring, Ted 199
Geisreiter, Eric 183
Gelb, Bruce 193
Geldard, Ed 154, 188
Gelikhovsky, Nikolai 198
Gelos, Alfonso Rodriguez 206
Genie Productions 185
Gennaro, Gino 188
Georgaris, Dean 196
George, George W. 208
Geraghty, Gerald 200
Gerrold, David 211
Gershenson, Joseph 192
Gerson, Betty Lou 57, 200

Gerstle, Frank 190
Gertz, Irving 187
Geter, Leo 198
Ghancy, Hassam 201, 206
Giardino, Mark 190
Gibbons, Sanford 201
Gibson, Thomas 186
Gifford, Alec 193
Gilbert, Bobby 190
Gilbert, Bruce 202
Gilbert, Edwin 181
Giler, David 199
Giles, Jerry 193
Gilgreen, John 181
Gill, Megan 201
Gillett, Chris 194
Gillette, Penelope 199
Gilley, Carol 208
Gillham, Ron 205
Gilliam, Burton 205
Gilmore, Art 198
Gilmore, Barry 188
Gilmore, Virginia 184, 207
Gilyard, Clarence 194, 195
Ginter, Lindsey 190
Gish, Annabeth 140, 211
Gittes, Harry 195
Gittings, Richard 211
Gjokah, Enver 209
Glaser, Paul Michael 182
Glaser, Vaughan 202
Glasgow, Gil 194
Glass, Everett 191
Glasser, Albert 192
Glasser, Isabel 186
Glatzer, Gaby 202
Glave, Karen 195
Glazer, Marat 192
Gleason, Jackie 181
Gleason, Stephen 189
Gleboff, George 198
Glennon, Bert 198
Glick, Mark S. 186
Glickman, Mort 188
Globus, Yoram 191
Glover, Edmund 183
Glynn, Tom 207
Goddard, Charles 199
Goddard, Mark 205
Godshall, Ray 203
Goff, John F. 205
Golan, Menahem 191
Goldberg, Adam 156, 187
Goldblum, Jeff 103, **105**, 191
Golden, Robert 195, 197, 208
Goldenberg, Sam 198
Goldenberg, William 200
Goldfinger 41 77
Goldman, Bo 195
Goldman, William 204
Goldoni, Lelia 191
Goldsmith, Jerry 184, 203
Goldsmith, Paul 182
Goldstein, William 181
Goldwyn, Samuel 205
Golin, Steve 201

Golitzen, Alexander 208
Golland, Joseph 187
Golling, Alexander 198
Golm, Ernest 198
Golm, Lisa 198
Gomes, Marc 194
Gomez, Cindy 195
Gomez, Thomas 55, 208
Gonzalez, Jimmy 189
Goodman, Joe 194
Goodman, John B. 208
Goodrow, Gary 191
Goozee, Russell 206
Gorai, Tom 182
Gorcey, Bernard 184
Gorcey, David 195
Gorcey, Leo 36, 195
Gordon, Barbara 206
Gordon, Dick 190
Gordon, Glen C. 211
Gordon, Julia Swayne 183
Gordon, Marianne 202
Gordon, Matt 206
Gordon, Roy 70, 187
Gordon, Ruth 158, 202
Gordon, Stuart 107, 184
Goric, Vojo 195, 200
Gossett, Robert 178, 182
Got, Roland 37, 181, 188, 207
Gottlieb, Andrew 194
Gough, Jim 193
Gough, Lloyd 186, 188
Gould, Graydon 186
Goyer, David S. 199
Graham, Fred 208
Graham, Scott 184
Graie, Madison 204
Grant, David Marshall 204
Grant, Helena 197
Grant, James Edward 184
Grant, Norah 210
Grant, Winston E. 184
Grapewin, Charles 199
Grasmere, Robert 205
Graver, Gary 191
Graves, Ernest 63, 207
Graves, Peter 77, 115, 193, 211
Gray, Lisa 197
Gray, Sherman 188
Grayson, Charles 208
Green, Alfred E. 192
Green, Gilbert 186
Green, Lynda Mason 210
Green, Mary Ashleigh 182
Greene, Angela 188
Greene, Graham 197
Greene, Harrison 188
Greene, Hiram Moe 28
Greene, M. Richard 201
Greene, Steven 187
Greenhouse, Martha 204
Greenstreet, Sidney 34, 181
Greenwald, Kenneth 182
Greenwood, Bruce 174, **175**, 210

Index

Greer, Dabbs 191
Gregory, James 74, 196
Gremillion, Barry 188
Grenville, George 186
Gretsch, Joel 210
Grey, Duane 193
Grey, Jennifer 200
Grieves, Russ 185
Griffin, Sean 181
Griffith, Charles B. 193
Grigoriev, Andrei 187
Grimaldi, Hugo 189
Grinde, Nick 208
Grodenchik, Max 201
Grodin, Charles 202
Gross, Andrew 194
Gross, Arye 84, *85*, 186
Gross, Charles 193
Gross, Jack J. 208
Gross, James 181
Gross, Roland 208
Grubbs, Gary 182, 193
Grunfeld, Gabriel 204
Grusin, Dave 188
Guerra, Castulo 201
Gugino, Carla 145, 210
Guilfoyle, Paul 20, 197, 208
Guilty by Suspicion 86
Guinness, Alec 23, 200
Gunn, Herbert 208
Gunton, Bob 193, 201, 202
Gupta, Deepti 207
Gurievsky, Michael 193
Guttman, Henry 198, 205
Guttman, Ronald 195
Gwaltney, Jack 203
Gwynne, Anne 207
Gyllenhaal, Jake 200

H&R Travis Editorial Services 191
Ha, Benita 185
Haade, William 208
Haas, Robert 181
Hackel, A.W. 204
Hackman, Gene 82, 198
Haddon, Laurence 181
Hagerthy, Ron 59, 189
Hagi, James 196
Haglund, Dean 211
Hagon, Rex 188
Hahn, Rob 204
Haiduk, Stacy 210
Haight, Rip 207
Hain, Judy 190
Hake, Jeremiah 191
Halberstam, David 47
Hale, Karen 189
Hall, Adam 200
Hall, Albert 183
Hall, Don 191
Hall, Henry 207
Hall, Huntz 36, 195
Hall, Misty 182
Hall, Sherry 183
Hall, Tony 189
Hall, Troy 207

Hallahan, Charles 206
Haller, Daniel 186
Halmi, Robert 199
Halsey, Mary 183
Halston, Thirl 187
Halton, Charles 181, 202
Halton, Michael 207
Ham-Bernard, Sherry 203
Hambrick, John 205
Hamdane, Habib 206
Hamill, Lucille 183
Hamill, Mark 206
Hamilton, George 159, 185
Hamilton, J. Frank 39, 181, 188
Hamilton, Jill 197
Hamilton, John 181
Hamilton, Linda 82
Hamilton, Roy 208
Hamilton, Sue 186
Hamlisch, Marvin 187, 195
Hammack, Warren 208
Hammer, Alvin 182
Hammer, Ben 191
Hammond, Rod 185
Hammouche, Hassan 201
Hampton, Grayce 197
Hancock, Lou 195
Haney, Tony 207
Hannibal, Marc 184
Hannity, Sean 203
Hanover, Donna 203
Hansen, Art 202
Hansen, Derek 201
Hanson, Erick 183
Hardacre, Richard 194
Hardin, Jerry 139, 195, 211
Hardin, Ty 189
Harding, Ann 18, 197
Hardy, Trishalee 207
Hare, Kristina 194
Hare, Lumsden 198
Harimoto, Dale 199
Harker, Ruston 183
Harlan, Kenneth 184
Harlan, Wade 201
Harline, Leigh 205, 208
Harman, Ginny 201
Harmon, Frank 183
Harrell, James N. 193
Harriman, Fawne 181
Harrington, Curtis 185
Harrington, James 200
Harris, Baxter 193
Harris, Donald Lee 202
Harris, Ed 181
Harris, JoAnne 199
Harris, Julie 182
Harris, Laura 187
Harris, Theresa 190
Harris, Tom 196
Harris, Tymberly Canale 196
Harris, Wood 203
Harrison, Barbara 203

Harrison, Joan 202
Harrison, Robert 181
Harrison, Toshi 189
Hart, David 189
Hart, Dorothy 60, 189
Hart, Harvey 181
Hart, Susan 146, 186
Hartell, Glenn 196
Harter, Leslie 189
Hartigan, Dylan 204
Hartnett, Josh 130, 187
Harts, Frank 202
Harvey, Hillary 207
Harvey, John Joseph 194
Harvey, Laurence 74, 196
Harvey, Nigel 187
Harvey, Paul 199
Harwood, Bruce 211
Haskin, Byron 211
Hassan, Lotfi 201
Hathaway, Maggie 196
Hatmaker, Jerry 205
Hatosy, Shawn 130, 187
Hauer, Rutger 80, 198
Hauff, Thomas 194, 206
Haupt, Whitey 192
Hauser, Robert B. 184
Hausserman, Ernst 198
Havier, Alex 208
Hawkins, Jimmie 200
Haworth, Edward 191
Hayek, Salma 187
Hayes, Donald 182
Hayes, Helen 64, *65*, 198
Hayes, W. Donn 192
Haynes, Victoria 196
Hays Office 11–12
Hayward, Jim 200
Hayward, Louis 207
Haze, Jonathan 193
Headin' for God's Country 39, 188
Healy, Caroline 187
Heard, John 176, 183
Hearn, Fred G. 10, 194
Hearst, William Randolph 9–10, 28, 199
Hearst Over Hollywood 28
Hebert, Chris 190
Hecht, Paul 202
Heffron, Richard T. 188
Heflin, Van 65, 198
Heideman, Leonard 207
Heinlein, Robert A. 117, 118, 127, 199
Heiskanen, Mika Levio 205
Hellman, Bonnie 193
Hellman, Lillian 49
Helm, Brigitte 146
Helpmann, Robert 200
Henderson, Douglas 196
Henderson, Maye 196
Hendricks, William L. 200
Hennings, Sam 125–6, 203
Henry, Emmaline 202

Hepker, Paul 201
Hepler, Heather 182
Her Country First 8, 9
Herbert, Henry 199
Herman, Leonard W. 185
Herriott, Arthur W. 195
Herron, Bob 183
Herthum, Harold 193
Hertzog, Lawrence 175
Herzberg, Ilona 196
Herzbrun, Bernard 192, 204
Hess, Jayne 186
Heuze, José 206
Heydt, Louis Jean 39, 183
Heyward, Louis M. 186
Hickles, Keith Leon 201
Hickman, Dwayne 146, 186
Hickock, Molly 196
Hickox, Sid 181
Hicks, Chuck 186
The Hidden World 127
Higgins, Craig 190
Higgins, Jean 182
Higgins, Michael 204
The Highest Trump 9
Hightower, Sally 190
Hill, Amy 201
Hill, Arthur 77, 154, 188, 211
Hill, Dean 190
Hill, Faith 204
Hill, Jack 118, 184
Hill, John 195
Hill, Steven 211
Hill, William 203
Hilliard, Sherry 194
Hillier, Erwin 200
Hillman, Sid 182
Hilton, Cathy 191
Hilton, Paul 204
Himmelstein, David 207
Hindiman, Earl 199
Hindle, Art 191
Hinds, Samuel S. 202, 207
Hines, Ronald 199
Hinkle, Cassidy 202
Hinsburger, Laura 186
Hinton, Annie 189
Hinton, Ed 209
Hiona, Sam 191
Hired Gun 86, 88
Hirsch, James G. 190
Hirschbiegel, Oliver 191
Hiss, Alger 47
Hitch, Wiliam 200
Hitchcock, Alfred 16, 202
Hitchcock, Robyn 196
Hitler's Daughter (film) 25–26, 188–9
Hitler's Daughter (novel) 188
Hivilo, Alar 190
Hix, Kim 194
Hniny, Mostafa 206
Ho, A. Kitman 194
Hoberman, David 206

Index

Hodge, Joseph 203
Hoffman, David 198
Hoffman, Max, Jr. 35, 184
Hoffman, Robert 200
Hofstadter, Richard 2, 4
Hogan, Sam 196
Hokanson, Mary Alan 190
Holbrook, Brad 196
Holcomb, Harry 196
Holden, Gloria 204
Holden, Larry 186
Holden, Laurie 211
Holden, Richard 195
Holland, Ray 188
Hollywood Goes to War 32
Hollywood Pictures 199
Holmes, Bertha 208
Holmes, David 207
Holmes, Jim 190
Holmes, Luree 186
Holmes, Rick 204
Holmes, William J. 199
Hom, Cindy 182
Hom, Montgomery 207
Homans, Robert 188
Homolka, Oscar 197
Honda, Ralph 184
Hong, James 211
Hoo, Edward Soo 195
Hoo, Hugh 183
Hood, Gavid 201
Hooper, Tobe 190
Hoover, Dana 206
Hoover, J. Edgar 12, 13, 63, 170
Hope, Bob 18, 205
Hopf, Hans 197
Hopper, Dennis 198
Hopton, Russ 197
Hopton, Russell 183
Horn, Leroy R. 183
Horsley, David S. 192
Horton, Louisa 207
Horvath, Charles 189
Horvath, Louis 205
Hotton, Donald 190
The House on Carroll Street 86, 189
The House on 92nd Street 48, 63
House Un-American Activities Committee (HUAC) 14, 48, 49, 50, 60, 67, 68, 78, 86
Houseman, John 172, 203
Houston, Anthony 208
Howard, Art 199
Howard, James Beattie 196
Howard, James Newton 203
Howard, Tom 193
Howarth, Alan 206
Howarth, Roger 155
Howell, C. Thomas 160, 200, 210
Howell, Norman 205

Hoyos, Nelly 202
Hoyos, Rodolfo 203
Hoyt, Clegg 203
Hristov, Hristo 203
HUAC *see* House Un-American Activities Committee
Huang, Essie 197
Hubbard, John 183
Huber, Harold 32, 183, 195
Hudson, Bill 200
Hudson, Bob 205
Huffington, Arianna 203
Huffman, John-Kenneth 189
Huffman, Logan 210
Hughes, David 184
Hughes, Howard 61
Hughes, Kathleen 192
Hughes, Lloyd 45, 185
Hughes, Mary 186
Hughes, Peter 199
Huling, Lorraine 9, 187
The Human Duplicators 120–1, *122*, 189
Hunt, Jimmy 112, 190
Hunter, Edward 75
Hunter, William 185
Hunter-White, Del 201
Hurst, Paul 67, 183
Hurst, Richard 186
Hurt, John 80, 198
Hush, Lisabeth 184
Hussey, John 182
Huston, John 34, 181
Huston, Walter 18, 197
Hutshing, Joe 194
Hutton, Pascale 210
Hyams, Peter 206
Hyde-White, Wilfrid 197
Hynd, Alan 32, 39, 183
Hyndman, Eldridge 195
Hytten, Olaf 197

I Led Three Lives (book) 68–9
I Led Three Lives (1953–56) 3, 50, 51, 68–70, 73, 209; "Civil Defense" 69; "Newsreel" 49–50, 69–70
I Married a Communist see The Woman on Pier 13
I Married a Monster 189
I Married a Monster from Outer Space 117, 189
I Was a Communist for the FBI (film) 3, 50, 54, 58–61, *59*, 189–90
I Was a Communist for the FBI (radio) 61
Idiot's Delight 12
Iida, Susan 201
Ikuma, Bishop Kinai 184
I'm Scared 99
Imada, Jeff 201, 206
Iman 198

Ince, Thomas H. 185
Indrisano, John 189, 196
Inescort, Frieda 197
Ingrassia, Ciccio 186
Ingvarsson, Nanna 191
Inneo, Vince 205
"Into Your Tent I'll Creep" 125
The Invaders (1967) 134–6, ***135***
The Invaders (1995) 137, 190, 209
Invaders from Mars (1953) 112–5, ***113***, 190
Invaders from Mars (1986) 143, 190–1
Invasion 135, 144–5, 209–10
The Invasion 108–110, 191
Invasion of the Bee Girls 5, 147–8, ***149***, 191
Invasion of the Body Snatchers (1956) 2, 5, 66, 100–103, ***100***, ***101***, 106, 116, 191
Invasion of the Body Snatchers (1978) 103–6, ***104***, ***105***, 191–2, ***192***
Invasion of the Body Snatchers (novel) *see Body Snatchers*
Invasion of the Pod People 132–3, 192
Invasion USA (1952) 61–3, ***62***, 74, 81, 192
Invasion USA (1985) 82
The Invisible Monster 179–80, 192–3
IPC Film 202
Ireland, Marin 196
Ireland, Tom 200
Irwin, Bill 196
Irwin, Boyd 197
Irwin, Nate 206
Isaacks, Levie 205
Ishiura, Dana 206
Ishmael, Marvin 194
Islamic terrorism 2, 86, 87, 88, 89, 91, 93, 95, 96
It Came from Outer Space 97, 111–2, ***112***, 137, 192
It Came from Outer Space II 112, 192
It Can't Happen Here 11–12
It Conquered the World 115–7, ***115***, ***116***, 193, 208
It's a Bird ... It's a Plane ... It's Superman 4
It's Alive 132
Ivanek, Zeljko 196
Ivers, Robert 189
Iwai, Sharon 207

Jaccard, Jacques 199
Jackson, Brad 192
Jackson, Colette 203

Jackson, Danny 208
Jackson, David S. 194
Jackson, Doug 193
Jackson, Howard 200
Jackson, Ron 193
Jackson, William 182
Jacobi, Derek 198
Jacobs, Judith C. 183
Jaeckel, Richard 64, 198
Jaffe, Allen 185
Jaffe, Gib 206
Jaffe, Michael 184
Jaffrey, Sakina 196
Jagger, Dean 51, 64, ***65***, 173, 184, 198
Jago, Alexa 199
Jakes, Bishop T.D. 194
Jakoby, Don 190
Jakubowicz, Alan 191
James, Brion 182
James, Don 199
James, John 208
James, Terry 201
James Bond films 73, 121
Jameson, Nick 190
Jamieson, Malcolm 207
Jamison, Peter 184
Jamrog, Joe 188
Janczar, Christopher 200
Janssen, Famke 130, 187
Janssen, Pete 187
Japan 11, 27, Russo-Japanese War 27–8, 34
Japanese Americans: 89; college students 34; internment 2, 27, 30, 32, 34, 37; loyalty 30, 32, 35
Jarchow, Bruce 199
Jarre, Maurice 198
Jason, Peter 125, 205, 206
Jay, Helen 189
Jazzar, Dani 206
Jbara, Gregory 189
Jefferies, Amanda 191
Jeffrey, Peter 198
Jenkins, George 199
Jenkins, Gordon 202, 204
Jenkins, Jerry 194
Jenkins, Richard 195
Jennings, DeWitt 199
Jensen, David 187
Jenson, Roy 200, 205
Jerome, Howard 195
Jerome, Timothy 183
Jerrod, Pope 201
Jet Pilot 3, 84
JFK 5, 9, 164, 169–71, 193–4
JFK assassination 4, 5, 69, 87, 126, 127, 142, 166–71
Jimenez, Frank E. 206
Jimenez, Luis 203
Jimenez, Roberto 195
Jingu, Miyoshi 196
Johansen, Virgil 197
John, Terry 199
John, Tylyn 201

Index

Johnson, Ben 200
Johnson, Brad 194, 195
Johnson, Brett 190
Johnson, Brian 182
Johnson, Craig 201
Johnson, Ed 183
Johnson, Georgann 188
Johnson, Henry 187
Johnson, Howard 183
Johnson, Nancy 205
Johnson, P. Lynn 185
Johnson, Paul 196
Johnson, Russell 192
Johnson, Shelly 186
Johnson, Tefft 183
Johnson, Tom 184
Johnson, Wes 191
Johnston, Andrew 204
Johnston, Jim 187
Johnston, J.J. 193
Joiner, Andrew 185
Jolie, Angelina 87, 202
Jolley, I. Stanford 184
Jones, Albert 202
Jones, Alexander Martin 203
Jones, Carolyn 191
Jones, Darryl 207
Jones, Gordon 183
Jones, Gorilla 190
Jones, Jason 195
Jones, John Randolph 189
Jones, Jon Paul 205
Jones, Justin 192
Jones, Larry 201
Jones, Mickey 193
Jones, Neal 203
Jones, Tommy Lee 128, 170, 193
Jones, Zoe Lister 202
Jordan, Bobby 195
Jordan, Jimmy 197
Jordan, William 199, 209
Josef, George 204
Joyce, Bill 199
Joyce, Brenda 33, 195
Joyce, Stephen 201
Joynt, Liam 202
Juhn, Paul 202
Jung, Allen 37, 188, 207
Jungle Heat 41, *42*, 194
Jungmann, Eric 187

Ka, Shing 196
Kadar, Ann Mahoney 187
Kadler, Karen 193
Kaell, Ron 207
Kahn, Karen 128, 207
Kaiser, Erwin 198
Kaiser, Sid 191
The Kaiser's Finish 10, 194
Kajganich, David 191
Kaledin, Elizabeth 203
Kalinowski, Waldemar 200
Kamal, Hany 203
Kangrga, Rick 184
Kareen, Shahla 206
Karen, James 190

Karlin, Fred 188
Karnes, Robert 186
Karns, Todd 198
Karp, David 184
Kassel, Jeff 206
Kassim, Helmi 203
Kastner, John 206
Katch, Kurt 197
Katcher, Aram 192
Kates, Bernard 125, 203
Katzman, Sam 184, 195
Kaufman, Peter 201
Kaufman, Philip 104–5, 109, 191, 201
Kaufman, Robert 186
Kaufman, Rose 191
Kaufman, Willy 185
Kaulback, Brian 195
Kava, Caroline 195
Kavanagh, Kevin 197
Kay, Edward J. 185
Kazann, Zitto 200
Keach, James 186, 187
Keach, Stacy, Sr. 199
Keating, Fred 183
Keaton, Danielle 207
Kee, James 206
Keehne, Virginia 190
Keeley, David 196
Keep 'Em Flying 5
Keep Watching the Skies! 112, 113, 114, 117
Kehler, Jack 190, 205
Keitel, Harvey 201
Kellard, Robert 182
Kelleher, Tim 142, 209
Keller, Harry 200
Keller, Walter E. 208
Keller, William 191
Kellers, Connie 205
Kelly, Anne 203
Kelly, Colin 197
Kelly, George 193
Kelly, Greg 203
Kelly, Jack 73, 200
Kelly, Michael A. 191
Kelly, Nancy 40, 183
Kelly, Patsy 202
Kelly, Paul 199
Kelly, Terence 171, 204
Kelly-Young, Leonard 186
Kemplen, Ralph 198
Kempster, Victor 193
Kenaston, Rita 196
Kenji 201
Kennedy, Arthur 52
Kennedy, Douglas 190
Kennedy, Madge 8
Kennedy, Patrick 182
Kennedy, T.J. 193
Kennedy, Tom 192
Kennedy, Tufford 194
Kennedy assassination *see* JFK assassination
Kenny, Shannon 190
Kent, Charles 183
Kent, Suzanne 181
Kerr, E. Katherine 203

Kerr, Edward 183
Kerwin, Brian 193
Kessler, Glenn 203
Keys, Robert 183
Khan, Ally 206
Khouas, Moa 201
Kibbe, Gary B. 206, 207
Kidman, Nicole 108, 151, 191, 204
Kiel, Richard 121, *122*, 189
Kilgour, Joseph 183
Kilian, Mark 201, 206
Kilman, Buzz 196
Kilvert, Lilly 203
Kimball, Ann 189
Kimball, Russell 188
Kimbrell, Lois 200
Kimbrough, Charles 188
Kimmel, Bruce 187
Kimmins, Kenneth 190
Kindred: The Embraced 160, 210
King, Emmett 199
King, Eric 190
King, Erik 210
King, Gayle 196
King, Larry 204
King, Max 204
King, Sandy 207
King, Wright 191
Kingsford, Walter 199
Kinney, Terry 106, *107*, 184
Kinoshita, Robert 185
Kinsley, Michael 201
Kinski, Klaus 147, 197
Kippen, Manart 18, 197
Kirishima, Max 201
Kirk, Beverly 203
Kirke, Donald 188
Kirkland, Sally 193
Kissel, Audrey 194
Kitamura, Raymond 201
Kiwe, Til 198
Klausmann, Rainer 191
Kleb, Helen 196, 203
Klein, I.W. 188
Klein-Rogge, Rudolf 146
Kleiner, Towje 198
Kliot, Jason 207
Kludjian, Christine 189
Knaggs, Skelton 188
Knaster, Jeremy 203
Knebel, Fletcher 186, 203
Knight, Aramis 200
Knight, Peter 4, 150, 142
Knight, Wayne 193
Knowles, Harry 187
Knox, Frank 30
Knox, Terence 190
Kober, Jeff 210
Kobliansky, Nick 198
Kobrin, Ron 189
Koch, Howard W. 194, 198
Koftinoff, Gary 195
Kohn, Howard 202
Kolb, Ken 201

Komeda, Christopher 202
Konen, Ansa 205
Konrad, Dorothy 188
Koontz, Dean 156
Kopache, Thomas 205
Korean War 49, 60, 64, 67, 68, 70, 74, 76
Korukoryai *see* Black Dragons
Kosek, Kenny 204
Kosiciuk, Christopher 194
Kosleck, Martin 181, 204
Kotto, Yaphet 199
Koulikov, Vladislav 202
Kovacs, Laszlo 195
Kozlowski, Linda 206
Kraft, Marilyn Criss 200
Kramer, Hope 189
Kranz, Fran 209
Krasner, Milton 208
Kratzberg, Eli 185
Krause, Peter **94**, 184
Kraushaar, Raoul 190
Kravits, Jason 204
Kretschmann, Thomas 156, 187
Krims, Milton 185
Kristofferson, Kris 90, 202
Krizman, Serge 187
Kroga, John 185
Krohn, Charles 188
Krueger, Scott 193
Kruger, Alma 16, 202
Kruger, Ehren 182
Kruger, Otto 16, 202
Kruger, Paul 197
Krugg, Lou 196
Krupa, Olek 202
Kubasik, Chris 183
Kubota, Tak 201
Kuby, Ronald 203
Kurer, Vilma 207
Kurnitz, Harry 205
Kurusu, Saburo 30, 35, 39
Kusatsu, Clyde 201
Kuter, Leo K. 190
Kuttner, Henry 125
Kuznetzoff, Adia 198

LaBelle, Rob 143, 209
Labine, Tyler 144, 210
labor movement 5, 9, 45, 52, 57, 60
Laborteaux, Matthew 181
Lachman, Dichen 209
Lacksye, James 183
Lackteen, Frank 188
LaCroix, Peter 204
Laemmle, Carl 187
Lage, Jordan 202
Lagerfelt, Caroline 194
LaHaye, Tim 161, 194
Laiken, Charles 202
Laing, John 206
The Lake 138, 194
Lakeshore Entertainment 182

Index

Lally, William J. 56, 200
Lalonde, Paul 194
Lalonde, Peter 194
La Mal, Isabelle 183
Lambert, Art 202
Lambert, Steve 190
Lamour, Dorothy 18, 205
Lamsabhi, Abdellah 201
Lancaster, Bill 206
Lancaster, Burt 80, 168, 171, 186, 198, 203
Lancaster, Ellen 182
Lancer, Martin H. 187
Landau, Martin 77, 211
Landslide Pictures 185
Landy, Hanna 202
Lane, Charles 205
Lane, Garrison 202
Lane, Lenita 189
Lane, Louise 208
Lane, Mark 186
Lane, Pacho 200
Lane, Priscilla 16, 202
Lang, Archie 186
Lang, Charley 209
Lang, Fritz 197
Langan, Glenn 41, 194
Lange, Arthur 184
Lange & Porter 184
Langedijk, Dirk 160, 194
Langford, Odin K. 193
Langton, Paul 208
Lansbury, Angela 74, 196
Lanter, Andrew 185
Lanyer, Charles 182
La Planche, Rosemary 183
LaPore, Richard 196
Larkin, John 203
LaRocco, Carl 181
La Rose, Melba 189
Larroquette, John 193
Larsen, William 193
Larson, Carolyn 202
Larson, Darrell 188, 196
Larson, Graham J. 203
LaRue, Roger 182
La Salle, Richard 185
Latell, Lyle 187, 190
Laughlin, Michael 205
Laura, Ernesto 103
Laurence, John 196
Laurie, Miracle 165
Laurie, Piper 130, 187
Lauter, Ed 186
Lava, William 190, 200
Lawrenche, John 205
Lawson, Wayne 183
Lawton, Thais 183
Lazar, Andrew 183
Lazar, Paul 196
Lazarus, Paul N., III 188
Lea, Homer 28
Lea, Nicholas 211
Leading Comics 29
Leadley, Ernie 197
Leavitt, Sam 186, 187
Lebo, Henry 204
Lechner, William 208
Le Deaux, Anita 202

Lederer, Francis 13, 185
Ledford, Jonathan 208
Lee, China 186
Lee, C.S. 204
Lee, Daisy 195
Lee, Dana 188
Lee, Eddie 188
Lee, Eugene 190
Lee, George 183, 188
Lee, Joanna 120, 184
Lee, Louise 197
Lee, Robert 204
Lee, Thelma 205
Lee, Wendolyn 207
Leeds, Philip 202
LeFevre, Adam 191, 196
Lefkowitz, Steve 191
Left Behind (film) 160–1, 194–5
Left Behind (novel) 160, 161, 194
Left Behind II: Tribulation Force 161–2, 195
Legneur, Charles 197
LeGros, James 210
Leicester, Margot 199
Leigh, Frank 197
Leigh, Janet 75, 96
Leigh, Rowland 197
Leighton, Jean 200
Lem, Grace 183
LeMat, Paul 123, 204
LeMay, Addison 203
Lemmo, Joan 199
Lemmon, Jack 170, 193
Lenard, Grace 189
Lenet, Ava 191
Lenkov, Peter M. 206
Lenney, Dinah 199
Lennix, Harry 209
Lenski, Robert W. 181
Lenz, Kay 25, 188
Leon, Connie 197
Leonetti, Tommy 189
Leong, James B. 188
Leonoff, Gabriel 197, 198
Leopard, Michael 201
Leopold, Stratton 205
LePere, Ray 193
Lerner, Fred 194
Lerner, Michael 123, 204
Leskin, Boris 189
Lessey, George 198
Lester, Bill 189
Lethal Weapon 2 3
Let's Get Tough! 36–37, 195
Leung, Jacqueline 195
Leva, Scott 190
Levay, Sylvester 182
Level 1 Entertainment 200
Leven, Boris 190
Levin, Ira 159, 202, 204
Levin, Sidney 188
Levine, Robert 194
Levine, Ted 183, 196
Levinson, Art 195
Levitt, Steve 187

Levy, Weaver 183
Levykh, Ella 187
Levykh, Michael 187
Lewarne, Prue 196
Lewis, Ed 199
Lewis, Edward 186, 203
Lewis, Fiona 204
Lewis, Geoffrey 182
Lewis, George J. 188
Lewis, Ira 202
Lewis, Lillian 194
Libertini, Richard 183
Lichterman, Marvin 188
Lieb, Robert 199
Lieberman, Todd 206
Lieving, Sarah 192
Lillard, Matthew 186
Lima, Danny 206
Lin, Lucy 182
Lindau, Rolf 198
Linder, Cec 25, 188
Linder, Max 197
Lindman, Ake 205
Lindon, Lionel 196
Lindsey, Minnie Summers 201
Lister, Chez 195
Little Nikita 83–4, **83**, 195
Little Tokyo, USA 2, 32–34, **33**, 195–6
Littleton, Carol 197
Litvak, Anatole 185
Liu, Chief 183
Lively, William 188
Livingston, Benjamin 194
Lloyd, Doris 197
Lloyd, Frank 202
Lloyd, John 206
Lloyd, John Bedford 196
Lloyd, Norman 16, 202
Lloyd, Sam 201
Lo, Ming 189
Lobban, Deborah 188
Lockhart, Craig 184
Lockhart, Gene 197
Lockhart, June 205
Lockhart, Kathleen 197
Lockmiller, Richard 181
Lodato, Carlo 184
Lofting, Morgan 181
Logue, Spain 193
Lok, Christine 197
Lomino, Daniel A. 200
Londino, Vanessa 207
London, Steve 189
Long, Amy 193
Long, Geovonne 196
Long, Jodi 202
Longman, Mike 193
Lontoc, Leon 184
Loo, Richard 33, 39, 76, 181, 183, 195, 211
Loose Change 9, 164
Loose Change 9/11: An American Coup 166, 195
Lopez, Angelo 203
Lopez, Manuel 183
Lord, Marjorie 23, 182

Lords, Traci 144, 209
Loretz, Ralph 200
Lorre, Peter 16, 181
Lottman, Evan 202
Louchou, Mustapha 201
Louden, Thomas 197
Louise, Tina 148, 204
Loung, Peter 194
Louviere, Billy 187
Lovejoy, Arthur 189
Lovejoy, Frank 58, **59**, 89
Lovejoy, Ray 189
Lovitz, Jon 204
Low, Lonny 190
Lowe, Chad 205
Lowell, Bob 208
Lowell, Tom 181, 196
Lowitch, Klaus 198
loyalty oaths 60, 65
Loyons, Priscilla 204
Lubatti, Henri 93, 210
Luceri, Michael 183
Lucisano, Fulvio 186
Ludden, Allen 188
Luddy, Tom 191
Ludlum, Robert 80, 199
Ludwig, Edward 184
Ludwig, Otto 202
Lugosi, Bela 35, **36**, 184
Lukas, Paul 13, 185
Lukats, Nick 187
Luke, Keye 181
Lumbly, Carl 209
Lumet, Sidney 196
Lund, Deanna 186
Lund, Marie 197
Lundigan, William 39, 188
Lung, Charlie 188
Lung, Clarence 211
Luther, Lester 57, 200
Lyman, Will 203
Lynch, Barry 186
Lynch, Jalil Jay 202
Lynch, James Peter 204
Lynch, Ken 117, 189
Lynch, Richard 83, 195
Lyons, Marty 184
Lys, Lya 185
Lytton, L. Rogers 9, 183

Maadsen, Michael 156
Macauley, Carl 200
Macauley, Richard 181
MacBride, Donald 205
MacBurnie, John 200
Mac Coll, James 168, 186
MacDonald, Flora 187
MacDonald, J. Farrell 187, 195
MacDonald, Kenneth 207
MacDonald, Ryan 186, 193
MacDonnell, Frances 7, 15, 16, 30
MacFadden, Hamilton 187
MacFadyen, Christine 194, 195

Index

MacGregor, Scott 197
MacGregor, Warren 192
Mack, Eric 197
Mack, Helen 204
Mack, John 201
Mackenzie, Harris 182
Mackie, Anthony 196
MacLane, Barton 181
MacLean, Dwayne 206
MacLeod, Dylan 185
MacMillan, Kenneth 199
MacNiven, David 194
Macready, George 121, 189, 203
Mad Chance Productions 182
Madigan, Sharon 191
Madoc, Philip 200
Madrid, Robb 195
Madsen, Michael 187
Magee, Frank 181
Magee, Patrick 205
Magid, Ron 192
Magnolia Pictures 207
Magnuson, Nat 192
Magrill, George 190, 208
Maher, Wally 204
Mahin, John Lee 198
Mahoney, John 183
Mainprize, James 188
Mainwaring, Daniel 191
Majoros, Ashley 189
Mako 201
Malbandian, Albert 191
Malek-Yonan, Rosie 200
Mallory, Carole 148, 204
Malloy, Matt 204
Malone, Dudley Field 197
Malone, Nancy 189
Maloney, Denis 194
Maloney, Peter 193, 206
Malyon, Ely 185
Mamadou, Omar 206
Mamadou, Yassine 206
The Man from U.N.C.L.E. 73
The Man He Found 61
Manchester, Jack 194
The Manchurian Candidate (film 1962) 5, 41, 74–6, 161, 196
The Manchurian Candidate (film 2004) 86 164–5, 196–7
The Manchurian Candidate (novel) 75, 196
Mandell, Daniel 205
Mandvi, Aasif 203, 207
Manelis, Ken 182
Manlove, Dudley 185
Mann, Chris 188
Manning, Jack 207
Manning, Knox 192
Manoogian, Peter 203
Mansano, Roy 190
Mansfield, Alma 189
Mansfield, Duncan 183
Many Are the Crimes 58
Manza, Paul 189

Marayati, Kamal 207
March, Fredric 171, 203
Marcovicci, Andrea 187
Marcus, Bernie 200
Margolin, Stuart 155, 188
Margot, Rosa 198
Margulies, David 188
Margulies, William 194
Marischka, George 198
Markle, Peter 205
Marks, Jay 192
Marks, Owen 185, 198
Marks, Sherman 211
Markstein, George 198
Marlowe, Frank 189
Marlowe, Hugh 203
Marno, Mozhan 206
Marquette, Jacques R. 181
Marrs, Jim 171, 194
Mars, Kenneth 199
Marsh, Wally 183
Marshall-Green, Logan 210
Marshek, Archie 197
Marsman, David 206
Marston, Joel 187
Martel, June 46, *46*, 187
Martel, William 200
Martell, Gregg 200
Marth, Frank 205
Martin, Barney 189
Martin, Christian 201
Martin, Duane 187
Martin, D'Urville 202
Martin, Jared 210
Martin, John C. 193
Martin, Lewis 208
Martin, Lock 190
Martin, Marion 205
Martin, Steve 206
Martin, William 197
Martineau, Ross 207
Martinelli, Tony 188
Martinez, Dena 207
Martinez, Jacquin 186
Masak, Ron 181
Mashita, Nelson 201
Mason, Gaylord C. 189
Mason, Maria 193
Mason, Tom 181, 199
Massen, Osa 197
Masset, Andrew 188
The Master Race 20, *21*, 197
Masters, Lisa 204
Masters, Mike 196
Masterson, Danny 187
Masterson, Mary Stuart 204
Masterson, Peter 148, 204
Masterson, Whit 185
Mastroianni, Armand 201
Masur, Richard 206
Matchett, Kari 95, 144, 184, 210
Maté, Rudolph 205
Mathews, Dakin 203
Mathews, Delane 190
Matt, Hank 189

Matthau, Walter 170, 193
Matthews, Dakin 186
Matthews, Hillary 190
Matthews, Lester 181, 197, 208
Maude, Beatrice 191
Maurice, Mary 183
Maus, Rodger 190, 207
Max, Ed 204
Maxim, Hudson 183
Maxwell, John 198
Maynard, Mimi 186
Mayo, Frank 197
Mayo, Martha 199
Mazzola, Frank 182
McAvoy, Charles 204
McBride, Stephanie 196
McBurney, Simon 196
McCain, John 87
McCain, Robert Stacy 52
McCalman, Macon 202
McCann, Chuck 201
McCann, Frances 153, 185
McCarey, Leo 5, 66, 67, 198
McCarthy, Dennis 211
McCarthy, Sen. Joseph 4, 48
McCarthy, Kevin 100, *100*, *101*, *104*, 191
McCaughan, Charles 189
McCauley, James 196
McClenny, Catherine 188
McClure, Doug 78, 185
McCormack, J. Patrick 199
McCorry, Marion 202
McCullough, Carolina 193
McCullough, Lisa 195
McCurry, Ann 209
McDaniel, Sam 181
McDermott, Tom 203
McDonald, Chris 187
McDonald, Scott 210
McDonough, Neal 201, 206, 210
McDowell, Lilly 196
McEachin, James 184, 185
McElduff, Ellen 193
McElroy, Alan 194
McGann, Shannon 204
McGavin, Darren 78, 185
McGee, Carl A. 201
McGibbon, Clayton Ed 188
McGill, Barney 199
McGill, Don 208
McGillis, Kelly 86, 189
McGinley, John C. 205
McGinn, Walter 199
McGiver, John 75, 196
McGlone, Mike 207
McGowan, Gretchen 207
McGrady, Michael 190
McGuckin, Tyler 204
McGuire, Maeve 189
McGuire, Paul 189
McHugh, Frank 181, 198

McKay, Craig 197
McKay, Scott 188
McKenna, Robert 195
McKim, Sammy 208
McKinney, Bill 193, 199
McLendon, Errol 193
McLinn, Lloyd 191
McMahon, David 190
McMillan, Kenneth 204
McMillan, Richard 206
McMullan, Jim 209
McMurray, Sam 188
McMurtry, Jonathan 195
McNamara, Patrick 188
McNeely, Joel 189
McPeak, Sandy 198
McPhaden, Mike 206
McQueen, Red 183
McRae, Frank 200
McRaney, Gerald 181
McTaggart, Malcolm 207
McVeigh, Lee 191
McVeigh, Timothy 4, 177, 178
McWade, Robert 199
McWilliams, Caroline 181
Mead, Phil 200
Meakin, Charles 199
Means, Randy 193
Medina, Julio 195
Medwid, Patti 205
Meehan, Elizabeth 188
Meek, Donald 205
Meeker, George 192
Meeker, Ralph 185
Meester, Leighton 95
Meet Boston Blackie 12
Megowan, Don 153, 185
Meisel, Kurt 198
Meisle, William 196
Meisner, Gunter 198, 200
Meisner, Michael 200
Meisner, Victor 200
Melita, Per 207
Mell, Randle 189
Meloni, Christopher 138, 205
Melton, Frank 184
Melton, Larry 194
Melton, Troy 185
Men in Black 128
Mendicino, Gerry 206
Menken, Shepard 57, 200
Menslage, Frederick 190
Menzies, William Cameron 114, 124, 190, 208
Meredith, Lucille 205
Merlin, Joanna 191
Merrill, Todd 190
Merrithew, Lindsay 25, 188
Messemer, Hannes 198
Messina, Chris 203
Messing, Debra 210
Metcalf, Laurie 193
Metropolis 146
Metty, Russell 183, 197
Metwally, Omar 95, 200

Index

Metz, Belinda 210
Mexico 11, 28
Meyer, Julius L. 200
Meyer, Nicholas 191
Meyer, Stan 187
Mezouar, El Oualid 201
MGM 189, 191, 198
Michael, Dennis 205
Michael, Peter 198
Michaels, Kay 186
Michelle, Shelley 201
Michonne, Danielle 182
Midler, Bette 151, 204
The Midwich Cuckoos 129, 132, 207
Milan, George 185
Milavich, Ivana 186
Milford, John 181
Milian, Tomas 193
Milicevic, Ivana 187
Milius, John 200
Millan, Arthur 200
Millan, Robyn 211
Milland, Ray 18, 160, 185, 197
Miller, Arlin L. 195
Miller, Charles 188
Miller, David 186
Miller, Dick 193
Miller, Gabrielle 204
Miller, Helen 193
Miller, Ivan 188
Miller, Jean H. 191
Miller, Matt 203
Miller, Michael 188
Miller, Michael Ray 193
Miller, Ralph 207
Miller, Seton I. 197
Miller, Stephen E. 183
Millhauser, Bertram 207
Millican, James 50, 58, 189
The Million Eyes of Sumuru 147, 197
Mills, Daniel 189
Mills, Zeke 193
Milton, David 184, 195
Mims, William 185
Mines, Lee 191
Ming, Moy 36, 195
Ministry of Fear 18–19, 197
Minkoff, Laurence 186
Minor, Willie 194
Mintz, Robert 211
Mirkovich, Steve 183
Missick, Dorian 196
Mission: Impossible: 211; "The Carriers" 77, 211; "The Town" 77, 211
Mission to Moscow 18, *19*, 47, 197–8
Mission to Moscow (book) 18
Mr. Moto's Last Warning 12
Mitchell, Elizabeth 210
Mitchell, Irving 184
Mitchell, James 188

Mitchell, Millard 195
Mitchell, Red 193
Mitchum, John 205
Mitchum, Robert 207
Mitzner, Dean 182
Miyashima, Joey 201
Miyazaki spy case 39
Moffat, Donald 206
Mohamed, Mosleh 203
Mohr, Gerald 62, *62*, 192
Mohr, Hal 185
Mokuaki, Sam 184
Molin, Bud 187
Molina, Roland 190
Moll, Mariquita 196
Moller, Gunnar 198
Moloney, Sean 205
Momen, Ali 206
Monaghan, Greg 181
Monahan, Jeff 205
Monoghan, James P. 184
Monogram 184, 195
Mooney, John 203
Moor, Bill 189
Moore, Anthony 194
Moore, Clayton 35, 184
Moore, Dennis 187
Moore, Henrietta 185
Moore, Jack 205
Moore, Maureen 189
Moore, Michael 208
Moore, Regan 194
Moore, Susanna 205
Moorhouse, Bert 190, 197
Moosekian, Duke 190
Moreland, Mantan 207
Moreno, Marisia 201
Morgan, Clive 197
Morgan, Garfield 198
Morgan, William 188
Mormino, Carmen 194
Morricone, Ennio 206
Morris, Dick 208
Morris, E.J. 193
Morris, Evan C. 199
Morris, Greg 211
Morris, Howard 193
Morris, Oswald 198
Morrison, Ann 189
Morrison, Alan 197
Morrison, Bruce 199
Morrison, James 183
Morrison, Layton 206
Morrison, Lew 185
Morrison, Sunshine Sammy 195
Morrow, Jeff 137, 211
Mortenson, Cristin 204
Mortimer, Ed 199
Morton, Jeff 202
Morton, Joe 132, 182
Mosley, Walter 196
Moss, Frank L. 208
Mostel, Zero 78, 187
Moston, Murray 188
Mouton, Benjamin 199
The Movie Channel 206
Moxey, John Llewellyn 185

Moy, Wood 191
Mrabti, Laila 201
Mues, Joachim Dietmar 198
Muir, Florabel 187
Muir, Gavin 197
Mule, Francesco 186
Mullaney, Jack 146, 186, 203
Mullen, Gordon 185
Mullen, Virginia 192
Mulligan, Terry David 183
Mullins, Larry "Moon" 187
Murdoch, Laurie 185
Muro, J. Michael 206
Murphy, Al 208
Murphy, Dick 191
Murphy, Donna 182
Murphy, Emmett 207
Murphy, George 63, 207
Murphy, Michael 188
Murphy, Reilly 106, 184
Murray, Forbes 188
Murray, Glynis 206
Murray, Jack 184
Murray, Tom 195
Musca, Tom 195
Musuraca, Nicholas 208
My Son John 5, 49, 50, 51, 52, 58, 64–67, 198
Myers, Stanley 199
Myktiuk, Lubomir 195
Mylong, John 197

Naber, Joey 203
Nachmanoff, Jeffrey 206
Nadell, Joseph 193
Nader, George 120, 147, 189, 197
Naftal, Diana 203
Naga, Khaled Abol 95, 185
Nahera, Rick L. 195
Naidu, Ajay 207
Nalder, Reggie 185, 196
Naming Names 48
Naor, Igal 201
Napier, Alan 20, 183, 197
Napier, Charles 196
Nascimento, Nadia 209
Nash, Bill 208
Nason, Danae 192
National Films 187
Navsky, Victor 48
Nazi Spies in America 12
Nazis 1, 3, 11–26, 61, 86
The Nazis Strike 15–16, 18
NBC 181, 182, 186, 194, 201, 209
Neal, Edwin 193
Nealy, Frances 196
Neame, Ronald 198
Negin, Louis 195
Negley, Howard 190
Negron, Joel 191
Neill, Noel 192
Neilsen, Eric 189
Neiwert, David 28

Nelkin, Stacy 137, 211
Nell, Krista 197
Nelson, Craig T. 198
Nelson, Ed 118
Nelson, Edward 184
Nelson, John 191
Nelson, Phil 184
Nelson, Ray 206
Nemoy, Leonard 184
Nesic, Alex 93, 210
Nesmith, Ottola 197
Network 90
Neumann, David 196
Neumann-Viertel, Elisabeth 198
Neuwirth, Bebe 130, 187
Neville, John 211
Nevin, Brooke 209
Nevin, Crocker 202
New, Robert C. 193
New Line Cinema 200
Newberry, Norman R. 181
Newcomb, James E. 207
Newcombe, Jessica 197
Newitz, Annalee 146
Newman, Emil 184, 195
Newman, Laraine 124, 190
Newman, Nanette 148, 204
Niblo, Fred 185
Nichols, Barbara 121, 189
Nicholson, Carol 200
Nicholson, James H. 186
Nicholson, Laura 186
Nickelodeon 143, 209
Nickerson, Jim 206
Nickolaus, John, Jr. 185
Nigaia, Anjul 194
Nigh, William 184
Nilsson, Anna Q. 188
Nimoy, Leonard 103, *105*, 118, 120, 184, 191
9/11 87, 91, 166
Nishikawa, Lane 207
Nispel Marcus 187
Niven, Barbara 189
No Way Out 82–3, 198
Noble, Chelsea 194, 195
Noble, Thom 200
Nogulich, Natalija 155
Nolan, Jim 205, 208
Noonan, Tom 182
Norris, Dean 193
Norris, Edward 189
Norris, Eric 190
Norris, Karen 196
Norris, Richard 196
North, Wilfred 183
North, Sheree 205
North Star 47
Northam, Jeremy 108, 191
Northrup, Harry S. 183
Northup, Harry 196
Norwood, Tacy 200
Norwood, Willie, Jr. 186
Not of This Earth 5
Nowhere Man 174–5, *175*, 210

Index

Nowicki, Tom 187
Noyce, Philip 203
Nuciforo, James 203
Nugent, Edward 46–7, 187
Nugent, Richard 197
Nunes, Paulino 206
Nupuf, Mason 190
Nystuen, Sally 193

O'Bannon, Dan 190
O'Bannon, Rockne S. 201
Obata, Toshishiro 201
Oberon, Elan 200
Oboler, Arch 22, 204
O'Brien, Chris 181
O'Brien, Edmond 172, 203
O'Brien, Myles 211
O'Brien, Tom 182
O'Brien, William F. 205
Ocko, Daniel 198
O'Connell, Ruary 194
O'Connell, William 185, 211
Odell, Cary 203
The Odessa File (film) 24, *24*, 198
The Odessa File (novel) 198
O'Donnell, Joseph 188
O'Donnell, Kevin 202
O'Driscoll, Martha 207
Of Missing Persons 99
O'Farrell, Conor 209
O'Gatty, Jimmy 189
O'Herlihy, Dan 62, 192
O'Herlihy, Michael 211
Okazaki, Bob 194
O'Keefe, Dennis 207
Okey, Jack 29, 197
Oland, Warner 29, 199
Olbrychski, Daniel 87, 202
Oldman, Gary 193
O'Leary, William 186
Olin, Lena 209
Oliver, Nicole 204
Olmstead, Dan 196
Olsen, Erik 186
Olsen, Moroni 197, 207
Olson, Nancy 183
Olthof, Dirk 181
Oltmans, Willem 193
O'Malley, Kathleen 205
O'Malley, Pat 191, 198
O'Malley, Polly 189
The Omen 159
Omen, Judd 200
On the Trail of the Assassins 194
Once Upon a Honeymoon 15
O'Neal, Patrick 204
O'Neal, Ron 81, 200
O'Neill, Henry 185
Orchard, Imbert 187
Orion Pictures 204
Orme, Stuart 199

Orr, Christopher 201
Orrison, Jack 189
Orsini, Candy 184
Ortelsberg, Medhi 206
Orth, Frank 195
Orwig, Bob 194
Orzazekski, Kasia 189
Osborne, Holmes 194
Osment, Haley Joel 194
Osmond, Cliff 191
O'Steen, Sam 202
The Osterman Weekend (film) 80–1, 198–9
The Osterman Weekend (novel) 80, 199
O'Sullivan, William J. 188
Ota, Dennis 201
Otari, Muna 201
Other Cinema 206
Ottenheimer, Albert M. 188
Otterson, Jack 202
Ottesen, Steve 182
Ottman, John 191
Oudghiri, Najib 201
Oukach, Zineb 201
Oumouzoune, Alaa 206
The Outer Limits: "The Hundred Days of the Dragon" 76–7, 211
Overby, Rhonda 191
Overton, Evart 183
Overture Films 206
Owens, Chris 211
Oz, Frank 204
Ozag, Michael 193

Pacek, Michael 195
Pack of Lies (film) 51, 82, 177, 199
Pack of Lies (play) 199
Padalecki, Jared 162, 210
Padden, Sara 184
Page, Anthony 199
Page, Clarence 201
Pai, Liana 203
Pakula, Alan J. 199, 202
Palfi, Lotte 207
Palmer, Gregg 211
Palmer, Maria 197
Palmer, Max 190
Palomar Pictures International 204
Panjabi, Archie 206
Panzer, William N. 199
Paoli, Dennis 184
Papazian, Robert A. 186, 190
The Parallax View 168, 199
Paramount 185, 186, 189, 196, 197, 198, 199, 202, 203, 204
The Paranoid Style in American Politics 2
Paré, Michael 206
Paretti, Douglas 207
Paris, Manuel 183

Paris, Renée 188
Parker, Dorothy 202
Parker, Eleanor 197
Parker, Max 181
Parks, James 182
Parnell, Brian Augustus 191
Parnell, Emory 195, 198
Parr, Charles T. 194
Parriott, James D. 190
Parrish, Leslie 74, 196
Parrott, Jim 195
Parsons, Milton 185
Parsons, Rodger 183
Partlow, Richard 182
Pasquesi, David 199
Patek, Elizabeth A. 204
Pathé International 199
Patinkin, Mandy 86, 189
Patitz, Tatjana 201
Patria 10, 28–29, 199
Patrick, Robert 130, 140, 187, 211
Patriot Games 89
Pattee, Rachel 162
Patterson, Kenneth 191
Patton, Frank 189
Patton, Will 82, 198, 199
Patus, John 195
Paul, Adrian 210
Paulsen, Albert 196
Payne, Julie 196
Payne, Suzie 183
Paynter, David M. 195
Pearce, Daniel 202
Pearce, Guy 206
Pearl, Barry 182
Pearl, Daniel 187, 191
Pearl Harbor 29–30, 32, 35, 37–8, 41, 68
Pearson, Drew 39–40, 183
Pearson, James 199
Pearthree, Pippa 206
Pecile, Steve 206
Peck, Anthony 186
Peckinpah, Sam 191, 199
Pederson, Alan C. 182
Pehme, Tina 185
Peil, Mary Beth 204
Pellington, Mark 182
Pellow, Clifford A. 183
Pembroke, George 35, 184
Peña, Elizabeth 190, 193
Pender, Paul 182
Penikett, Tahmoh 165, 209
Penland, Cheryl 193
Pennebaker, Ted 194
Penner, Josh 194
Penner, Marty 194
Penner, Toby 194
Pera, Radames 200
Perada, Allen 184
Pereira, Hal 189, 197, 198
Perella, Marco 193
Perez, Vincent 156, 187

Perez-Campbell, Joaquin 196
Periard, Roger 206
Perillo, Joey 196
Perina, George 211
Perkash, Sunil 203
Perkins, David 188
Perkins, Jack 191
Perkins, Osgood 199
Perkins, Pat 193
Perreau, Gigi 114, 197
Perreau, Janine 190
Perrin, Vic 211
Perry, Al Kealoha 184
Perry, Brien 189
Perry, Luke 201
Persky, Marilyn 188
Personal History 12
Pesci, Joe 193
Peters, Evan 210
Peterson, Diane 182
Peterson, Dorothy 202
Peterson, Gunnar 201
Peterson, Loren 206
Petri, George 205
Pettit, Rosemary 207
Phelps, Lee 183
Philbrick, Herb 50, 51, 52, 54, 56, 68–70, 76, 209
Phillippe, Andre 191
Phillips, G. Elvis 184
Phillips, Greigh 184
Phillips, Patricia 210
Phillips, Robert 205
Phillips, Sandra 189
Phillips, Wendy 201
Phipps, Bill 190
Phoenix, River 83, *83*, 195
Phoenix, Summer 187
Pi 2
Picerni, Paul 189
Pickering, Betsy 205
Pickering, Robert 211
Pickett, Bobby 205
Pickle, Bill 194
Piel, Edward 184
Pierce, Arthur C. 189
Pierce, Michael C. 196
Pierpoint, Eric 190
Pierson, Carl 184
Pike, Glenn 207
Pileggi, Mitch 139, 211
Pilon, Daniel 194
Pimley, John 200
Pine, Phillip 77, 211
Pine, Robert 173, 184
Pinner, Dick 192
Pinter, Harold 200
Piper, Roddy 124, 125, 205
Pipitone, Nino 37, 38, 188, 195
Pittman, Tom 181, 191
Player, Susie 191
Pleasance, Donald 78, 205
Plimpton, Martha 202

Index

Plowright, Hilda 197
Poch-Goldin, Alex 206
Podhora, Roman 187
Poe, Laura 178, 182
Poindexter, Lawrence 190
Poitier, Sidney *83*, 195
Poland, Joseph 188
Polanski, Roman 159, 202
Poledouris, Basil 182, 200
Polis, Joel 206
Polito, Gene 188
Polito, Jon 201
Polito, Sol 185
Pollard, Snub 190
Poltoranin, Nick 203
Ponicsan, Darryl 186
Poole, Duane 189
Porter, Joan 188
Portman, Rachel 197
Posey, Parker 156, 187
Posner, Alan H. 182
Posner, Phil 211
Potter, Luce 190
Powell, Dick 20
Powell, Linda 182
Powers, Alexandra 201
Powers, Beverly 191
Pozniak, Beata 193
Prager, Richard 8
Pratt, Judson 188
Precious Freedom 22
Preger, Michael 207
Preminger, Otto 205
Prentiss, Paula 148, 169, 199, 204
The President Vanishes 9, 163–4, 199
Pressman, Lawrence 186
Preston, Carrie 204
Preston, Kelly 84, 186
Previn, Charles 202, 208
Prey 155–6, 210
Price, Brandon J. 191
Price, Stanley 179, 192
Price, Steve F., Jr. 194
Price, Vincent 146, 186
Priddy, Nancy 181
The Pride of Palomar 29
Prince, Michael 202
Prince, Robert 182, 185
Prince, Ron 182
Prince, William 204
A Prodigal in Utopia 185
Production Code Administration 11
Prophecy Pictures 203
Prosky, Robert 194
Proval, David 203
Provance, Raquel 200
The Prussian Cur 9
Pryor, Nicholas 181
Public Deb. No. 1 45
Puglia, Frank 197
Pugliesse, Al 182
Pugsley, Don 190
Pulford, Lee 199
Pullen, William 192
The Puppet Masters (film) 120, 127–8, 199–200

The Puppet Masters (novel) 97, 117–8, 130, 199
Purcell, Robert 200
Purchit, Deepa 207
Purves, David 204
Purvis, Jim 187
Putnam, George 208
Pyne, Daniel 165, 196

Quarry, Jessye 207
The Quiller Memorandum (film) 23, 200
The Quiller Memorandum (novel) 200
Quine, Richard 37, 207
Quinn, Arthur T. 183
Quinn, Louis 200
Quintrall, Kristen 192

Raben, Alexis 191
Rabinowitz, Jay 204
Racehelle, Bernie 202
Rachmil, Lewis J. 208
The Rack 76
Racki, Robert 206
Ragin, John S. 199
Raimond, Larry 184
Raine, Norman Reilly 208
Rainey, Ford 199
Rains, Claude 20, 204
Raley, Thomas 201
Ralph, Christopher 209
Rambo (cartoon) 3, 34
Ramirez, Anthony 193
Ramsay, Remak 188, 189, 204
Ramsay, Todd 206
Rana, James 207
Rand, Sebastian 204
Randolph, David 201
Randolph, Henry 184
Ransford, Maurice 195
Rasjkolb, Mary Lynn 210
Rasoully, Ghoulam R. 203
Ratner, Lee 205
Ratzon, Hadar 200
Ravich, Rand 183
Rawi, Raad 206
Rawlins, David 199
Rawlins, John 208
Rawlinson, Herbert 182
Ray, Jackie 208
Raymond, Royal 200
Raymond, Usher 187
Reagan, Barry 190
Reagan, Ronald 80, 81
Reason, Rhodes 194
Rebhorn, James 189
Red Dawn 81–82, 200
The Red Menace *49*, 50, 56–7, 73, 84, 200
Red Nightmare 22, 51, 58, 73–4, 200
Redd, Ray 193
Reddick, Lance 203
Redman, Anthony 184
Redmon, Danny 202

Reed, Arthur 195
Reed, Rondi 182
Reed, Steve 193
Reed, Tanoai 204
Reel Bad Arabs 89
Rees, John 200
Rees, Roger 108, 191
Reeve, Christopher 129, 206
Reeves, Nina 202
Regan, Charles 192
Regragui, Farid 206
Reguragui, Fatima 201
Reid, Elliott 61, 208
Reid, Marc 187
Reid, Toni 204
Reidy, Nick 204
Reilly, Elizabeth A. 189
Reineke, Gary 26, 188
Reitzen, Jack 182
Remick, Lee 79, *79*, 205
Remple, Gordon 204
Remsen, Bert 211
Renaldo, Alyson 196
Renaldo, Duncan 198
Renavent, Georges 197
Rendezvous 11
Rendition 87, 95–6, 200–1
Reneau, John 194
Renfro, Bryan 206
Renfroe, Jeff 185
Renna, Chris 193
Rennick, Nancy 211
Rennie, Guy 191
Reno 196
Renwick, Alan 199
Republic 179, 188, 200
Reticker, Hugh 181
Revell, Graeme 203
Revenge of the Stepford Wives 150
Rexer, Fred 200
Reynolds, Burt 180, 206
Reynolds, Harry 195
Reynolds, Kevin 200
Reynolds, Marjorie 20, 197
Reynolds, Simon 206
Reynolds, William 200
Rhoads, Ingrid 195
Ricci, Joseph 204
Rice, Brett 187
Rice, Florence 36, 195
Rich, Jessica 203
Rich, Katie 194
Rich, Ted 185
Richards, Addison 183, 188
Richardson, Jack 45, 185
Richardson, Robert 194
Richardson, Skip 207
Richardson, Stephen 196
Richardson, Sy 205
Richings, Julia 210
Richman, Charles 9, 183, 199
Richter, W.D. 191
Ridenour, Craig 194

Ridges, Stanley 20, 197
Ridgle, Elston 182
Ridgway, Josh 182
Riehl, Kay 200
Rifkin, Ron 180, 193, 209
Riley, George 185
Rilla, Wolf 207
Rinaldi, Antonio 186
Rinzler, Lisa 207
Riordan, Robert 196
Rising Sun (film) 41–3, 90, 201
Rising Sun (novel) 41–2, 201
Ritchie, Stan 191
Ritt, Martin 78, 188
Ritter, Fred A. 192
Rivas, Geoffrey 194
Rivera, Bunnie 201
RKO 61, 183, 197, 205, 208
Roach, Martin 206
Road, Mike 200
Robards, Jason 172, 186
Robards, Jason, III 205
Robbins, Adam 207
Robbins, Herb 191
Robbins, Tim 3, 178, 179, 182
Robeling, Albin 197
Rober, Richard 54, 55, 208
Roberds, Michael 185
Roberts, Al 205
Roberts, Arthur 188, 190
Roberts, Kim 185
Roberts, Mark 211
Roberts, Roy 189
Robertson, Cliff 207
Robertson, George 193
Robertson, George R. 25, 188
Robin Cook's Invasion 109, 137–8, 201–2
Robinson, Andrew 199
Robinson, Ann 210
Robinson, Bob 197
Robinson, Chris 193
Robinson, Darla Mason 191
Robinson, Edward G. 14, 185
Robinson, Edward G, Jr. 192
Robinson, George 207
Robinson, Lauren 201
Robison, Barry 201
Robles, Rudy 181
Roby, Erica 133, 192
Rocca, Peter 210
Rocha, Winston 194
Roche, Claudette 206
Roche, Jim 196
Rockwell, Robert *49*, 56, 200
Rode, Christopher 189
Rodensky, Schmuel 24, 198
Rodgers, Pam 186

229

Index

Rodin, Merrill 197
Rodine, Alex 188
Rodine, Alex Rodzi 193
Rodrigo, Al 190
Rodriguez, Christina 187
Rodriguez, Jose L. 203
Rodriguez, Robert 187
Roe, Channon 190, 210
Roelfs, Jan 183
Rogers, Ginger 15
Rogers, Henry 208
Rogers, Mimi 211
Roher, Jeanne 202
Roher, Lynn 202
Rohm, Maria 197
Rohmer, Sax 27, 147, 197
Roizman, Owen 204
Rolf, Frederick 189
Rollover 90, 202
Rook, Roger 190
Rooker, Michael 193
Root, Lynn 205
Rosales, Gilbert 203
Rose, Bill 201
Rose, Norman 188
Rose, Skip 189
Roselli, Lauren 196
Rosemary's Baby (film) 2, 132, 157-9, **158**, 202
Rosemary's Baby (novel) 202
Rosen, Charles 192
Rosenbloom, Maxie 189
Rosenblum, Steve 203
Rosener, George 185
Rosenthal, Alan 194
Rosing, Bodil 185
Ross, Angelo 207
Ross, Katharine 2, 148, 204
Ross, Kenneth 198
Ross, Leonard Q. 181, 205
Ross, Marion 138, 194
Ross, Mike 189
Ross, Sandi 195
Rossall, Kerry 206
Rossen, Carol 204
Rossio, Terry 199
Rosten, Leo 207
Roth, Andrea 125, 203
Roth, Bobby 186
Roth, Nick 186
Rothman, Eli 185
Rothman, John 203
Rothschild, Richard Luke 188
Rotter, Stephen A. 201
Rotunno, Giuseppe 202
Rouhke, Driss 201
Rowe, Hansford 181
Rowe, Korey 195
Roy, Natasha 206
Royce, Lionel 185
Rubes, Jan 186
Rucker, Barbara 204
Rudin, Scott 196, 204
Rudley, Herbert 197
Rudnick, Paul 204
Rudolph, Maya 186

Ruff, Roslyn 202
Ruge, George Marshall 186
Ruge, Steven 186
Rugolo, Pete 185
Ruhl, William 208
Ruick, Mel 195
Ruiz, Michele 201
Rumann, Sig 185
Rumrich, Guenther 12
Runyon, Marie 196
Rupp, Debra Jo 190
Rush, Barbara 111, 192
Rusoff, Lou 208
Russell, A.J. 185
Russell, Edmond 197
Russell, Eric Frank 125
Russell, John L., Jr. 192
Russell, Kurt 122, 206
Russell, Paula 181
Russell, Rosalind 199
The Russians Are Coming, the Russians Are Coming 73
Russo, Barry 211
Russo, Christopher M. 196
Russo, Matt 204
Russo, Perry R. 193
Russom, Leon 198
Ruston, Kevin 206
Ruth, Phyliss 205
Rutherford, Kelly 210
Rutowski, Richard 194
Ruybal, Jay Dee 200
Ryan, Dick 208
Ryan, Jeri Lynn 209
Ryan, John 188
Ryan, Robert **53**, 55, **56**, 186, 208
Ryan, Tim 189
Rydall, Derek 205
Rydall, Stephanie Ann 205
Ryder, Eddie 211
Ryen, Richard 198

Saboteur 16, 202
Sachse, Salli 186, 197
Sackett, Theodore T. 200
Sadler, William 210
Sagemiller, Melissa 93, 210
St. Jacques, Raymond 205
St. James, David 190
St. James, Rebecca 194
St. John, Nicholas 184
St. Paul, John 193
Salama, Amro 203
Salenger, Meredith 206
Sali, Richard 143, 209
Salim, Omar 201
Salkowitz, Sy 211
Salminen, Ville Veikko 205
Salt 87-8, 202-3
Salter, Charles T., Jr. 195
Salter, Elliot 192

Saltzman, Philip 181
Samii, Goli 207
Samuels, Terry 194
Samuelson, Marc 182
Samuelson, Peter 182
Sande, Walter 190
Sanders, Charles 182
Sanders, Denis 191
Sanders, George 185, 200
Sanders, Henry 186
Sanders, Hugh 189
Sanders, Jay O. 193
Sanders, Lynn C. 203
Sandoval, Charles Daniel 207
Sane, Kelley 201
Sanford, Erskine 197, 208
Santia, Moris 206
Santiago, Stacey Newsome 196
Santori, Gina 182
Saper, Jack 181
Sarandon, Chris 198
Sardi, Youness 206
Sarin, Vic 194
Sarsgaard, Peter 201
Sasaki, Miyoko 194
Sasser, Reid 191
Satan's Silence **157**
Sattin, Lonnie 189
Saunders, Lois 207
Savage, Brad 200
Savitsky, Sam 198
Sawtell, Paul 207, 208
Sawyer, Connie 192
Sawyer, Forrest 194
Sawyer, Joe 13, 185, 193
Sax, Carroll 184
Sayles, Francis 197
Saylor, Katie 191
Scalia, Jack 181
Scalia, Pietro 194
Scanlin, Tim 191
Scardon, Paul 183
Scarwid, Diana 123, 204
Schaaf, Geoff 189
Schallert, William 150, 181
Scharf, William S. 201
Scheer, Robert 203
Schell, Maria 198
Schell, Maximilian 24, 198
Schenck, Aubrey 194
Schenck, Earl 10, 194
Schenck, George 188
Schepps, Shawn 183
Scher, Harry 200
Scherer, Gene 200
Scherick, Edgar J. 204
Schertler, Jean B 191
Schick, Ben 200
Schierhorn, Will 187
Schiff, Richard 184-185
Schifrin, Lalo 199
Schiller, Joel 202
Schindler, Peter 203
Schlom, Herman 183
Schneider, Edith 200

Schofield, Peter 199
Scholl, Hirsh 188
Schombing, Jason 201
Schorr, Daniel 203
Schrecker, Ellen 58
Schreiber, Liev 87, 164, 196, 202
Schreiber, Pablo 196
Schroder, Ernst 198
Schultz, Armand 202
Schumann-Heink, Ferdinand 198
Schumm, Hans 181, 198
Schwartz, Howard 188
Schwartz, Maurice 197
Schwartz, Terry 195
Schwarzenegger, Arnold 159
Schwegler, Paul 187
Sci-Fi Channel 193
Scoenfeld, Aaron 196
Scolari, Peter 151, 181
Scott, Ben R. 194
Scott, Carey 194
Scott, George C. 78
Scott, Henry 211
Scott, Jacqueline 205
Scott, Johnny 197
Scott, Leigh 192
Scott, Mike 188
Scott, Morton 188
Scott, Nathan 193
Scott, Shaley 192
Scowley, Stacey 165
Screen Gems 182
Searcy, R. Clifford 203
Searle, Tom 205
Searles, Baird 104
Secret Agent of Japan 29
Secrets of the Red Bedroom 82
Seedpeople 125, 203
Segal, George 23, 200
Segall, Stu 189
Seibert, Reid 183
Seid, Art 185
Seidner, Irene 181
Seitz, John 190, 193
Selk, George 192
Sella, Robert 182
Selland, Marie 191
Sellecca, Connie 209
Sellers, Lawrence 202
Selmour, Ronald 204
Semple, Lorenzo, Jr. 199
Sen, Nandana 93, 207
The Sentinel 5
Sepia Films 185
Sergey, Filonov 187
Serling, Rod 186, 203
Serna, Pepe 200
Serrano, Nestor 95
Servitto, Matt 203
Seven Days in May (film) 5, 171-2, 186, 203
Seven Days in May (novel) 186, 203
Sexton, Merlyn 194
Shaber, David 202

230

Index

Shade, Jameson 208
Shadow Conspiracy 5
Shadow on the Land 22
Shaffer, Zach 202
Shaheen, Jack 89
Shahidi, Yara 202
Shaler, Virginia 207
Shalhoub, Tony 91, 203
Shams, Ryan Cyrus 202
Shan, Rezza 205
Shank, Gregg 120, 185
Shankman, Jim 203
Shanks, Priscilla 182
Shannon, Harry 39, 188
Shapiro, Paul 190
Shaps, Cyril 198
Sharmat, Mary 183
Sharon, Bo 199
Sharp, Alan 199
Sharp, Alex 205
Sharp, Henry 197
Shaughnessy, Kristen 196
Shaver, Helen 198
Shaver, Richard 127
Shaw, C. Montague 188
Shaw, Robert 190
Shaw, Stan 201
Shawn, Wallace 204
Shayne, Konstantin 58, 189, 197
Shayne, Robert 190
Sheen, Charlie 200
Shehata, Michael 196
Shellen, Stephen 181
Shelley, Joshua 188
Shenkman, Ben 203
Sheridan, Ann 45, 187
Sheridan, Jamey 189
Sheridan, Lisa 210
Sheriff, Paul 185
Sherlock, Charles 190
Sherman, Howard 189
Sherman, Orville 118, 184
Sherman, Vincent 181
Sherrod, Edgar 199
Sheybal, Vladek 200
Shiban, John 187
Shields, Blake 93, 210
Shilio, Michael 198
Shin, Anna 196
Shindle, Kate 204
Shire, David 189
Shirley, Arthur 9, 187
Shonberg, Burt 184
Shonteff, Lindsay 197
Shoop, Clarence A. 192
Shor, Dan 205
Shores, Byron 202
Showtime 210
Shuck, Peter 181
Sia, Beau 196
Sibelius, Celia 185
Sidley, Robert 187
The Siege 91, **92**, 203
Siegel, Don 102–3, 191
Siegel, Howard 183
The Silencer 171, 203–4
Silk Stockings 3, 84, 86
Silliphant, Stirling 207

Silva, Henry 74, 196
Silver, Jeffrey 206
Silver, Joel 191
Silver, Michael Buchman 186
Silvers, Phil 181
Simmonds, Stanley 202
Simmons, Gene 91
Simmons, J.K. 201
Simms, Chelsea DeRidder 207
Simms, Jay 185
Simms, Renée Rene 207
Simon, Mayo 188
Simons, Robyn 187
Simpson, Douglas 190
Simpson, Eliza 196
Simpson, Malcolm 196
Simpson, Mickey 182
Simpson, Napoleon 58, 200
Simpson, Robin 182
Simunovich, Zinko 184
Sinatra, Frank 74, 196
Sinatra, Tina 196
Sinclair, Ronald 186
Sindhul, Adelina 201
Singh, Narda 187
Skinner, Frank 202
Skipper, Michael 193
Skirball, Jack H. 202
Sklar, Zachary 194
Slade, Suzanne 189
Slater, John J. 188
Slavin, George F. 208
Sleep No More 103
sleeper agents 79, 83, 87, 93, 165, 180
Sleeper Cell 93, 210
Slezak, Victor 202, 203
Slezak, Walter 15
Sliwa, Curtis 203
Slovick, Sam 200
Small, Michael 199, 202, 204
Small, Stanley 184
Small, Sylvia 184
Smiley, Sam 201
Smillie, Bill 185
Smith, Anna Deavere 196
Smith, Charles Martin 84, 186
Smith, Jason D. 189
Smith, Johnny L. 184
Smith, Joseph 189
Smith, Keith 136, 184
Smith, Kent 209
Smith, Lane 200
Smith, Leonard 183
Smith, Lorraine 192
Smith, Malcolm 185
Smith, Michael St. John 171, 185, 204
Smith, Michelle Ray 202
Smith, Robert 192
Smith, Scott 189
Smith, Will 128
Smith, William 147, 191, 200

Smith, William Craig 184
Smith Act 48, 60, 70
Smithers, William 173, 184
Snider, Gary 187
Snipes, Wesley 201
Snow, Norman 202
Snyder, Edward J. 187
Soak the Rich 45
Sockwell, Sally 202
Soderling, Walter 197
Sokol, Marilyn 188
Sokoloff, Vladimir 197
Solo, Robert H. 107, 191
Solomon, David 182
Somers, Fred 197
Sommer, Josef 108, 186, 188, 191, 202, 204
Somova, Tanya 198
Sondreal, Leona E. 196
Song, Alfred 183
Song of Russia 47
Sontag, Susan 3
Southcott, Tim 185
Sowl, Paula 189
Spacek, Sissy 170, 193
Spafford, John 195
Spalding, Harry 185
Sparer, Paul 189
Sparks, Adrian 193
Sparks, Dan 200
Spelling, Aaron 185
Spence, Sebastian 143, 209
Spencer, Franz 192
Spicuzza, Alvin 193
Spies 11
Spigelgass, Leonard 181, 205
Spikers, Ray 196
Spiner, Brent 144, 210
Spivy, Madame 196
Spratley, Tom 204
Springsteen, R.G. 200
Sprogis, Robert K. 206
Sprouse, Cole Mitchell 183
Sprouse, Dylan Thomas 183
The Spy Who Came In from the Cold 73
Sriram, Varun 207
Stafford, Grace 185
Staiger, Scherry 189
Stalin, Josef 18
Stamberg, Susan 203
Standing, Percy 187
Stanford, Aaron 210
Stanlee, Claudia 205
Stanley, Forrest 29
Stanton, Harry Dean 200
Stanton, Paul 181
Stanton, Robert 189, 204
Stanton, Todd 190
Starr, Christopher 198
Starr, Sam 192
Stass, Robert 200
Stay, Richard 193
Steadman, Joel 202

Steadman, Robert 186
Stebbins, Bobbie 204
Stechschulte, Tom 196
Steele, Michael 208
Stefan, Virginia 209
Stefanovic, Jasna 206
Steffen-Fluhr, Nancy 103
Stein, Jacob 182
Stein, Ronald 208
Steinbeck, Rudolf 198
Steinberg, Irving 196
Steiner, Max 198
Stengler, Mack 182
Stepanek, Karel 63, 207
The Stepford Children 150
The Stepford Husbands 150
The Stepford Wives (film 1975) 2, 5, 204
The Stepford Wives (film 2004) 150, 151–2, 204
The Stepford Wives (novel) 148, 150, 204
Stephens, Janaya 160, 194, 195
Stephenson, James 185
Sterler, Hermine 183
Stern, Bill 208
Sternad, Rudolph 207
Stevens, Eileen 191
Stevens, George 183
Stevens, Leslie 211
Stevens, Mary Ann 206
Stevens, Onslow 207
Stevens, Stella 181
Stevens, Warren 211
Stevenson, Bill 195
Stevenson, Bob 197
Stevenson, Charles C., Jr. 189
Stevenson, Robert 208
Stevenson, Tom 181
Stewart, Catherine Mary 182
Stewart, Douglas 192
Stewart, Jon 187
Stewart, Margie 183
Stewart, Tasha 195
Stewart, Tonea 184
Steyermark, Alex 187
Stine, Clifford 192
Stock-Poynton, Amy 194
Stockwell, Dean 196
Stokes, Murray 193
Stoll, Corey 202
Stolzenberger, Leslie 183
Stone, Bobby 195
Stone, George E. 32, 195
Stone, Milburn 190
Stone, Oliver 194
Stone, Sean 193
Stoneburner, Sam 193
Stoneham, John, Jr. 188, 206
Stoneham, John, Sr. 206
Stoney, Jack 208
Stopover Tokyo 41
Storey, Howard 183
Storey, Michael 195
Storke, Adam 155, 210

Index

Stossel, Ludwig 181
Stout, Archie 184
Stout, Rex 164
Stowe, Madeline 151, 181
Stract, Günter 198
Stradling, Harry 198
Strange, Glenn 198
Strange, Kim 195
Strange Holiday 3, 20–22, 73, 74, 204
Strange Invaders 123, 137, 204–5
The Stranger 22
The Stranger Within 132
Streep, Meryl 96, 164, 196, 200
Street, David 208
Strickland, Kadee 204
Stringer, Lee 182
Stroble, Hans 182
Strong, Leonard 195
Strong, Mark 198
Strub, Ann 193
Sullivan, Brick 189, 208
Sullivan, C. Gardner 185
Sullivan, James 192
Sullivan, Ronny 204
Sully, Frank 181, 187, 205
Summer, Leslie 186
Summerland, Katy 199
Summerour, Lisa 186
Summers, Hope 202
Sumpter, Tika 202
Sunderland, John 194
Sung, Elizabeth 199
Sunjata, Daniel 195
Supernatural 162, 210
Surtees, Robert 204
Susman, Todd 190
Sutchy, Susanne 195
Sutherland, Donald 103, *105*, 127, 170, 191, 193, 199
Sutherland, Kiefer 93, 210
Sutter, Randy 202
Sutton, James 202
Swan, Nickolas 206
Swan, Robert 183
Swan, William 199
Swanson, Deborah 182
Swayze, Patrick 81, 200
Sweeney, Fred 198
Sweeney, Mary 191
Swinney, Lauren 187
Sy, Jovanni 206
Sylbert, Lulu 123, 205
Sylbert, Richard 196, 202
Sylos, Paul 189
Symington, Donald 188
Szabo, Sandor 198
Szkoda, Peter 206

Tabarrok, Michals 195
Tabarrok, Nicholas D. 195
Taber, Alton 185
Tachibana spy case 39
Tagawa, Cary-Hiroyuki 201
Tager, Aron 206
Taggart, Gary 193
Taghmaoui, Saïd 206
Tahi, Moana 186
Takei, George 211
Takemitsu, Toru 201
Talbiri, R.L. 194
Talbott, Gloria 117, 189
Tales of Tomorrow: "Conqueror's Isle" (1953) 153
Tallas, Gregg 182
Talmadge, Norma 183
Talman, William 55, 208
Tamm, Mary 198
Tanaka, Seiichi 201
Tandy, Jessica 86, 189
Tang, Frank 207
Tannen, Charles 32, 195
Tarcai, Mary 182
Target: Earth 138, 205
Taurog, Norman 186
Tavoularis, Dean 201
Taylor, Antoine 196
Taylor, Cloie Wyatt 191
Taylor, Darien 184
Taylor, Eric 184
Taylor, George 200
Taylor, Hillman 208
Taylor, Kent 120, 185
Taylor, Robert 51
Taylor, Ronnie 187
Taylor, William S. 204
Teilhet, Darwin 187
Telefon (1977) 78–80, *79*, 205
Telefon (novel) 205
Tellegan, Mike 198
Terry, Todd 182
Terry, Valya 198
Tevlovski, Vladimir 202
Tew, James 189
Tewes, Lauren 193
Thackery, Bud 188
Thal, Eric 127, 199
Thall, Benj 199
Thayer, Lorna 181
Theiss, Brooke 195
Theron, Charlize 132, 182
They Got Me Covered 18, 205
They Live 124–5, *124*, 205–6
They're Here... 107
Thiel, Nick 187
Thimig, Helene 197
The Thing 2, 121–3, 206
The Thing from Another World 121
Thinnes, Roy 134, *135*, 137, 190, 209
The Third Level 99
Thom, Bob 208
Thomas, Ann 207
Thomas, Dave 187
Thomas, Ray Anthony 196
Thomas, Richard 190
Thomas, Tim 201
Thompson, Brian 210, 211
Thompson, Fred Dalton 198
Thompson, Lea 200
Thompson, Susanna 194
Thompson, Wesley 181
Thomson, Patricia Ayame 201
Thordsen, Kelly 169, 187, 199
Thorn, Bob 208
Thornton, Auden 182
Thorpe, Jim 187
Thourlby, William 196
Thrasher, Harold 195
Threshold 129, 135, 144, 210
Thurman, Bill 208
Tickner, Clive 200
Tidy, Frank 188
Tilly, Meg 106, *107*, 184
Time and Again 99
Tinapp, Barton 203
Tippit, Wayne 193
Tirl, Gerigi Jiri 194
Tobey, Kenneth 123, 137, 205, 211
Tobias, George 197
Tobin, Matthew 188
Toby, Doug 200
Todd, Edward 188
Tokyo File 412 41
Tom, Lauren 186
Tom, Steve 201
Tomasini, George 189
Tomasino, Vanesa 185
Tong, Kaity 196
Tong, Kam 181
Tooley, Jennie 182
Toomey, Regis 40, 183
Torme, Mel *71*, 187
Torn, Tony 204
Torre-Lopez, Roma 196
Toth, Nick 201
Tourneur, Jacques 187
Toward the Unknown 76
Tower, Michael 192
Towers, Harry Alan 197
Towne, Aline 180, 192
Towne, Michael 208
Towns, Colin 200
Townsend, Barbara 182
Tracey, Ian 185
Tracy, Blumes 194
Tracy, Lee 40, 183
Traeger, Rick 211
Traister, Andrew 208
Traitor 96, 206
Trapido, Joel 184
Traveler 175–6, 210
Travis, Neil 198
Travis, Richard 197
Travolta, John 84, *85*, 186
Tree, Dorothy 185
Treen, Mary 189, 205
Tremblay, Anthony 193
Trevisan, Luke 203
Trial 52
Tribulation 99: Alien
Anomalies Under America 126–7, 206
Tribulation Force 195
Triesault, Ivan 198
Troitsky, Vladimir 203
Troude, Michaël 206
Trowbridge, Charles 197
Trowell, Katherine 194
Trueblood, Guerdon 182
Trueman, Paula 204
Trujillo, Raoul 190
Trumbo, Dalton 186
Tryon, Tom 117, 189
Tsukamato, Raynum 196
Tuck, Jessica 201
Tucker, Sandy 187
Tucker, Tommy 195
Tull, Henry, III 193
Tully, Phil 190
Tunie, Tamara 201
Turco-Lyon, Kathleen 207
Turman, Lawrence 206
Turner, Frank C. 187
Turrou, Leon G. 12–13, 185
Tuttle, Lurene 208
20th Century-Fox 185, 190, 198, 200, 201
24 2, 87, 88, 93–95, 210
Twilight Zone: "A Day in Beaumont" 136–7 211
Tyler, Deneen 187
Tylor, Evan 204
Tyrell, Frank 183

Ullman, Elwood 186
Ulman, Sidney M. 199
Ulmer, Jonathan 205
United Artists 183, 187, 194, 196, 200
Universal 187, 193, 205, 206, 207
Universal Soldier III: Unfinished Business 180, 206
Unveragh, Adrian 184
Uphill, Cheryl 185
UPN 175, 189, 210
Urena, Fabio 199
Urquhart, Gordon 184
USA network 187, 188, 209
USSR 3, 18, 44–5, 47, 48, 61, 74, 77–80, 81–86, 128
Utt, Kenny 196

V 145, 210
Valdez, Maria 183
Valentine, Joseph 202
Valk, Kate 196
Valley, Mark 203
Valor of Ignorance 28
Vampire: The Masquerade 160
Van, Jason 189
Van Alyn, Abigail 207
Van Bergen, Ben 183

232

Index

Vance, Louis Joseph 199
Van Cleef, Lee 115, 193
Vandervoort, Laura 210
Van Eeghen, Henk 186
Van Effenterre, Joele 183
Van Hart, Matt 195
Van Heerden, Ava 194
Van Holt, Brian 144, 210
Van Oostrum, Kees 186
Van Sickel, Dale 187, 192
Van Sloan, Edward 198
Van Stralen, Anton 196
Vareux, Denise 197
Vargas, Jacob 195
Varno, Roland 183
Vartan, Michael 180, 209
Vath, Richard 185
Vaughn, Jean 196
Vaughn, Mark 204
Vaughn, William 185
Veidt, Conrad 16, 181
Velon, Ivo 202
Ventimiglia, John 207
Ventresca, Vincent 210
Vera, Julia 190
Verdoni, Bruno 185
Verne, Kaaren 16, 181
Vernon, Glen 182
Vernon, John 210
VeSota, Bruno 184
Vetri, Victoria 147, 191
Vicente, Joana 207
Vicini, Eric A. 193
Vickerman, Michael 205
Vickers, Yvette 185
Vickrey, Scott 202
Victor, Henry 183, 185, 198
Victor, Stephani 205
Vieira, Meredith 204
Viertel, Peter 202
Village of the Damned (1960) 129, 207
Village of the Damned (1995) 128, 144, 206–7
Villari, Libby 187
Vince, Pruitt Taylor 193
Visaroff, Michael 198
Viscidi, Marcus 201
Vitagraph 9, 183
Vitarelli, Joseph 190
Viteychuk, Chris 187
Vittes, Louis 189
Vives, Vivianne 182
Voe, Marie 208
Vogan, Emmett 195
Vogeding, Frederick 185
Voght, K.T. 199
Vogt, Vic 183
Voight, John 185
Voight, Jon 24, 164, 196, 198
Von Bargen, Daniel 187, 201
Von Brandenstein, Patrizia 183
Von Klaussen, Ronald 193
Von Kotze, John 197
Von Leer, Hunter 186

Von Sydow, Max 23, 200
Von Twardowsky, Hans 185
Voodoo Histories 4, 18, 164
Voosloo, Arnold 95

Wachsman, Jessica 185
Wade, Linda Flores 193
Waggner, George 200
Wagner, Billie 194
Wagner, Jefferson 183
Wagner, Max 190
Wagner, Wendy 202
Waid, Jeffrey Allan 203
Wainwright, James 155, 209
Waite, Ric 200
Waites, Thomas 206
Wald, Jerry 181
Wald, John 195
Walder, Ernst 200
Waldis, Otto 61, 208
Walk a Crooked Mile 48, 207
Walk East on Beacon 63–4, 207
Walken, Christopher 151, 204
Walker, Bill 207
Walker, Jonathan Lloyd 206
Walker, Lewis "Jiggs" 196
Walker, Ray 198
Walker, Robert 51, 64, 198
Walker, Shirley 193
Wall, Fay 183
Wallace, Dee 204
Wallace, Joe 200
Waller, Eddy 188
Wallis, Hal 181
Walsh, Brigid 210
Walsh, John 182
Walsh, J.T. 142, 209
Walter, Jerry 191
Walter, Tracey 186, 196
Walters, Susan 189
Wanger, Walter 12, 102, 191, 199, 208
Wanted: Dead or Alive 91
War of the Worlds 135, 138, 210
The War Within 31, 207
Waram, Percy 197
Ward, Alan 183, 197
Ward, Amanda 192
Ward, Elaine 189
Ward, Jeff 207
Ward, Megan 142, 209
Ward, Sandy 186
Ware, Susan 190
Warner, Jack 18
Warner, Julie 127, 199
Warner Brothers 12, 15, 181, 184, 185, 189, 191, 193, 194, 197, 200
Warren, Bill 112, 113, 117
Warren, Jennifer 151, 181
Warren, Michael 201

Warren, Phil 207
Warschilka, Edward A. 207
Washburn, Bryant 183, 197
Washington, Billy D. 182
Washington, Dennis 198
Washington, Denzel 91, *92*, 164, 196, 203
Washington, Ukee 196
Wassill, Chuck 189
Watanabe, Masa 201
Watch on the Rhine 15, 49
Waters, Chuck 199
Waterston, Sam 172, 197
Watkin, Pierre 198
Watson, Jan 186
Watson, John 187
Watson, Minor 64, 197, 198
Watson, William 186
Watterson, Anthony 201
Way, Guy 191
Wayne, Fredd 203
Wayne, John 67, *67*, 183
Wayne, Michael 201
WB Network 210
Weatherwax, Paul 192
Webb, Charlie 182
Webb, Jack 73, 200
Webb, Parker 191
Webb, Richard 59, 179, 189, 192
Webb, Roy 183
Webb, Rudy 195
Webber, Andrew Lloyd 198
Weber, Dewey 194
Weber, Karl 207
Webster, Ferris 196, 203
Webster, Tony 198
Wechter, David 187
Weddle, Vernon 199
Weeks, Jimmie Ray 203
Weibel, Rita 201
Weidhaas, Oscar 200
Weir, David 202
Weireter, Peter 202
Weisman, Jessica 182
Weisman, Kevin 209
Weiss, Peter 205
Weisser, Norbert 206
Welbeck, Peter 197
Welch, Christopher Evan 204
Welch, Robert 48
Welden, Ben 181
Welles, Orson 22
Wellman, William A. 199
Wellman, William, Jr. 199
Wells, Eric Briant 199
Welsh, Ken 189
Wendkos, Paul 184
Wendt, George 86
Werker, Alfred 207
Wertheimer, Bob 206
Werthmann, Colleen 202
Wesson, Eileen 205

West, Chandra 180, 206
West, Elliott 187
West, Tegan 190
Westerfield, James 41, 194
Westfall, Mischa 198
Weston, Celia 108, 191
Westworld 154
We've Never Been Licked 37–8, 207–8
Wexley, John 185
Weyl, Carl Jules 185, 198
Whaley, Frank 193
Wharton, Leopold 199
What Is Communism? 51, 70, 76
Wheat, Jim 193
Wheat, Ken 193
Wheeler, Big Jim 196
Wheeler, Ira B. 202
Wheeler, John W. 199, 205
The Whip Hand 3, 61, 208
Whipper, Leigh 197
Whipple, Shonda 190
Whitaker, Forest 106, 172, 184, 186
White, Cary 187
White, Gregory 191
White, Kevin C. 183
White, Mike 204
White, Stanley 194
White, Walter, Jr. 204
Whitemore, Hugh 199
Whitman, Gayne 183
Whitman, Walt 185
Whitney, Claire 194
Whittredge, J.R. 187
"Who Goes There?" 97, 121, 206
Why We Fight 15, 16, 18, 32
Whytock, Grant 207
Wick, Bruno 207
Wicker, Timothy 182
Wickware, Scott 206
Wiff, Biff 195
Wiggins, Alfred 205
Wiggins, Wiley 187
Wilbur, Crane 190
Wilcox, Frank 181, 190
Wilder, Alan 183
Wiles, Michael Shamus 199
Wilhelm, Bradley 207
Wilhelm, Jennifer 207
Wilkinson, Cassius 196
Willes, Jean 191
Williams, Denver 182
Williams, Duke 58, 200
Williams, John 194
Williams, Mary Alice 203
Williams, Olivia 165, 209
Williams, Philip 206
Williams, Steven 211
Williams, Van 200
Williamson, Kevin 131, 132, 187
Willis, Bruce 91, 203

INDEX

Willis, Gordon 199
Willis, Katherine 187
Willis, Matt 202
Willis, Paul 187
Willis, Susan 187
Willman, Noel 198
Willock, Dave 192
Willoughby, Rick 185
Wilmes, Gary 202
Wilrich, Rudolph 188
Wilson, Carey 199
Wilson, F. Stewart 191
Wilson, Frederick 200
Wilson, Norm 205
Wilson, Stanley 192
Wilson, Trey 189
Wilson, President Woodrow 8, 28, 29
Wilton, Eric 197
Wiltshire, Miles 189
Wimble, Chris 199
Wimmer, Kurt 203
Wina, Glenda 205
Winans, Be Be 196
Wincott, Jeff 191, 206
Windsor, Marie 185
Wing, Emily 204
Winger, Debra 176, 177, 183
Winkler, Irwin 183
Winston, Steve 183
Winter, Ralph 194, 200
Winter Kills 168, 171
Winters, Michael 194
Wipf, Alex 202
Wirth, Billy 184
Wisberg, Aubrey 183
Wise, Ray 201
Witherspoon, Dane 203

Witherspoon, Reese 95, 200
Witney, William 188
Wittig, Joshua 195
Wodetzky, Christine 198
Wolf, Scott 210
Wolfe, Donald 189
Wolfe, Ian 202
Wolfe, John Leslie 191
Wolfington, Iggie 205
The Woman on Pier 13 50, 52, *53*, 54, 55–6, *56*, 102, 208
Wong, Beal 195, 208
Wong, Bruce 208
Wong, Daniel 194
Wong, Jean 183
Wong, R. 191
Wong, Victor 183
Wood, Douglas 199
Wood, Elijah 130, 187
Wood, Ward 208
Woodard, Will 204
Woodell, Pat 200
Woodfield, William Read 211
Woodley, Becky 191
Woods, Harry 199
Woolf, John 198
Woolner Brothers Pictures 189
Woolnough, Jeff 206
World War I 1, 7–11
World War II 1, 15–22, 29–41
World War III 82
Worth, Cedric 199
Worth, Constance 37, 188
Worth, Nicholas 198

Worthington, William 199
Wright, Alona 189
Wright, Carolyn T. 193
Wright, Jeffrey 109, 191, 196
Wright, Lawrence 203
Wright, Richard S. 182
Wulff, Scott 190
Wurtzel, Stuart 189
Wyatt, Eustace 197
Wyman, Bob 202
Wyndham, John 129, 207
Wynne, Gordon 207
Wynter, Dana 100, *100*, *101*, 191
Wyprachtiger, Hans 198

The X-Files 135, 137, 138–142, *141*, 210–11

Yacoubi, Ahmed 202
Yagi, James 211
Yamashita, Tadashi 201
Yates, Cassie 198
Yates, Herbert J. 200
Yates, Peter 189
Ybarra Al 184
Yeager, Biff 182
Yedidia, Mario 190
yellow peril 27–28, 38
Yetter, William 205
Yong, Madame Soo 183
You Only Live Twice 77
Young, Christopher 191
Young, Dey 205
Young, Homer Jon 182
Young, Jack 198
Young, James 64, 198

Young, Jenna 205
Young, Sean 82, 198
Young, Victor 197
Yulin, Alexis 189
Yung, Sen *see* Victor Sen Yung
Yung, Victor Sen 34, 183, 181, 195
Yusim, Marat 189

Zabriskie, Grace 186
Zahler, Gordon 189
Zahrn, Will 183
Zak, Tom 195
Zale, Dan 187
Zanett, Guy 183
Zapata, Carmen 205
Zaremba, John 209
Zarou, Elias 195, 206
Zea, Kristi 197
Zeek, Dawn 193
Zehetbauer, Rolf 198
Zeisler, Alfred 198
Zeitlin, Denny 192
Zeitlin, Esther 198
Zeller, Ben 200
Zeman, William 206
Zibell, John 207
Zien, Chip 203
Zinner, Peter 186
Ziskin, Laura 198
Ziv, Nava 201
Zonova, Natalia 201
Zontar, the Thing from Venus 116, 208
Zueva, Olya 202
Zugsmith, Albert 192

www.ingramcontent.com/pod-product-compliance
Lightning Source LLC
Chambersburg PA
CBHW081552300426
44116CB00015B/2849